CONTENTS

FIGURES

IN THE LOBBY

From its opening shots, David Fincher's *Alien3* (US 1992) is resolutely concerned with ending, with the death of its heroine, the destruction of its monsters, and the termination of the *Alien* film series, of which it is now the third part.[1] Already the sequel of a sequel – which was itself an elaborate reprise of Ridley Scott's *Alien* (UK/US 1979) – Fincher's episode attempted to bar the way for any subsequent films by killing off the one character on whom the films had come to depend. About midway through *Alien3*, its protagonist, Ellen Ripley (Sigourney Weaver), knowing that she will soon die, goes in search of the alien creature, hoping that it will kill her before she is killed by its sibling that is growing inside her. It is one of the film's little jokes. At nearly all other times in the *Alien* films, as generally in horror movies, characters who find themselves alone in poorly lit places are surprised by monsters and despatched. But when Ripley goes looking for the monster, it is not lurking, but hiding, refusing to do what it normally does. 'Don't be afraid', Ripley coaxes, 'I'm part of the family. You've been so long in my life, I can't remember anything else.' In the course of writing this book I have come to know what she means. I have been living with the aliens of Fincher's film – not to mention several other monsters – since at least 1996, when Alex Wright first laid the idea of this book in my mind. The book itself has become a kind of alien.

When I told people I was writing a book on theology and film they would often ask two questions I found difficult to answer: what films did I discuss and what was the book about. It was not easy to answer the first of these questions because I realized that my choice of films was the result of accident rather than method. They are films I have seen and enjoyed, and deemed appropriate for the ideas I wanted to explore, but most are not obviously 'religious' or overly concerned with the body and desire.

Gilbert Perez notes that we 'respond to the movies of our youth with something like the feelings of first love',[2] and this may explain why some films receive more attention than others, and the films of Stanley Kubrick and Nicolas Roeg in particular. Their films may have impressed because I saw them when I was at my most impressionable, and many of the other films that appear in the book – especially those by David Fincher and Lars von Trier – reawakened the same impressionability.[3] They had the force of reminding me that cinema could still shock, surprise and delight.

The 1970s, and then the 1980s, constitute a period when I began to go to the cinema as an independent viewer, when I could 'own' my viewing, when cinema not only enthralled and entertained, but began to claim a serious consideration. It was then that I developed a double vision – learned from the study of literary texts – in which one is both distanced and immersed in the film, cutting and connecting between different kinds of attention, discernment and discourse. The trick, as Steven Shaviro argues, is to maintain a naïve stance within critical film viewing, a critical moment within the pleasure of watching movies, which is often more than pleasure: 'a rising scale of seduction, delirium, fascination, and utter absorption in the image'.[4]

As to the difficulty of explaining what the book is about, that follows from writing the kind of book that finds its subject in and through its writing. Like the reader, I have had to await its arrival.

The Cut that Connects

The idea of connecting the apparently unconnectable, of aliens with the desiring body, and of both with theology, predated my fateful conversation with Alex, since earlier in the same year I had presented a public lecture in which I explored some of the connections that now inform the fourth chapter of this book. These connections are between the human body and the figure of the alien, between what we think is most our own and most foreign to it. They are the intimate connections of what we think most unconnected. *Alien Sex* is concerned with connection, or rather dis/connection; with the necessity of disjunction for union, of distance for proximity. The alien is necessary for its opposite, the self-same, which is thereby never really opposite, never really its own, self-possessed reality, just as the alien is never wholly other. For the alien is just the other side of our skin; the inside of our outside. While it appears most distant, it is most close, our most inward but unacceptable being. It is thus all too often abjected, disavowed and destroyed.[5] Yet its unutterable proximity holds open the possibility of its embrace, of connecting across the divide, without denying the difference of one side and the other. This is the possibility of the membrane, of the tissue that separates and connects; the communion of skin. It is the possibility of a desire that flows between bodies; between two shots of a film, two lovers in a bed, between creatures and their creator. It is the difference that unites; the cut that connects.

Cinema is the product of many endeavours, the result of strange complicities between art and science, the poetic and the technical. Yet it is in the conjunction of opposites that we find what best characterizes the cinema. It is a copulative art, which unites by disjoining. It is in the cutting (montage) of shots that cinema produces its peculiar power to establish the relationships of a world – the looks between characters, the feelings between words – and thus to excite and move its viewers. Cinematic space – the relationship of objects and characters and their interactions – is largely constructed through editing. When we see a shot of a character looking out of the picture frame followed by one of something else, a thing or person, it is natural to suppose that the character is looking at that something else; we see what she sees, following her gaze. Toward the end of Alfred Hitchcock's *Saboteur* (USA 1942), the fifth columnist Frank Fry (Norman Lloyd) is pictured in a taxi. He looks to his right, out of its window. In the next shot we see what he sees: a large ocean liner, capsized by its pier. It is the *SS Alaska* that Fry had sabotaged in a preceding scene. The ship has clearly been photographed from a moving car, and when the next shot cuts back to Fry in the taxi, we know that he – and we – have witnessed the results of his sabotage. He turns away from the window with a vague smile of satisfaction on his face. But the actor Norman Lloyd never saw the ship through the window of his taxi. He was photographed at the Universal film studios in California, seated in a stage taxi, while the ship was several thousand miles away in New York, being the *SS Normandie* that had capsized at its berth. But when the shot of the ship is spliced between those of Fry looking out of the film frame, the *Normandie/Alaska* finds itself in the same narrative space as its saboteur; or rather we, the viewers, find it there, directed to see by the look of the character.[6]

In the cinema it is the looking of characters, and the gaze of camera and audience that crosses the cut between the frames of a film, the shots and characters of a scene, the distance between viewer and viewed. The cinematic effect would have little power if it were not for the craving of its viewers to find relationships, to see connections. Cinema is powered by the parodic imagination. With bodies, the cinematic gaze becomes the touch of desire, a yearning that is itself a kind of gazing, just as gazing is a kind of yearning, a reaching out to touch and handle. 'She hadn't realized the day before that eyes are miraculous hands, had never enjoyed the delicate tact of the cornea, the eyelashes, the most powerful hands, these hands that touch imponderably near and far-off heres. She had not realized that eyes are lips on the lips of God.'[7]

Hélène Cixous' delight on losing her myopia and regaining her sight of far-off objects – crossing the distance between them and herself with the touch of her eyes – calls for the language of divinity, since the caress of vision comes to her as a donation that gives. 'Violent gentleness, brusque apparition, lifting eyelids and: the world is given to her in the hands of her eyes. And what was given to her that first day was the gift itself, giving.'[8] Thus sight, coming to Cixous as a donating gift, names a yet more fundamental desire than that of bodies and their gazing. More than a connection across the cut of cinematic shots or sexed bodies, the gift of sight names the desire that traverses the cut between creature and creator, the distance that harbours all bodies.

Each body comes into the world from another body, and only becomes other to that body when cut from it, severed from the maternal womb. Yet it is the cut of child from mother that allows each to connect with the other, just as the child is the fruit of cut (sexed) bodies. Thus the magic of the cinematic cut that connects is already the paradox of sexed bodies that must be cut in order to connect, separated for the possibility of union. The topic around and within which this book wanders – wonderingly – is the cut and connection of bodies, treated as analogy for the viewing of cinema and the seeing of God, with sight the analogy for desire, for the traversal of the distance between. Perhaps because this is a wandering, errant theology, it knows no way of stopping such analogies from reversing, from becoming indeterminately ordered parodies of one another, and so the book ventures that they might be/come one another, or more nearly one another than some may care to suppose. Seeing in church and cinema may be different from one another, but perhaps not so different; and likewise divine communing and bodily coupling – different, but not completely different.

Parodic Parables

This book is set in what Karl Barth described as the 'world of mixed and relative secularism', a world that has known Christianity, but where Christianity is now forgotten or only half-remembered. It is a world in which the church's speaking of Christ still echoes, but only as background noise to the cries of other gospels, other sirens of salvation.[9] For Barth this is the world of 'Christian culture', which we might now describe as post-Christian. The early Barth would have spoken of God's judgement on such a world, but the later Barth, nearing the end of his *Church Dogmatics*, could begin to hear God's invitation in the 'godlessness' of such a culture. For no matter how far we might wander from God, God never leaves our side, or ceases to speak to us in the words of others.

Jesus spoke of God and of God's household in stories about mundane life, as if they were 'photographs of everyday happenings'. Yet these stories were transformed in the telling of Jesus. '[E]veryday happenings become what they were not before, and what they cannot be in and of themselves.' Told by Jesus, these stories of 'labourers, householders, kings, fathers, sons', are made to speak of other things, of God's presence on earth. From Jesus' telling of parables, Barth learns that 'there can be other true words alongside the one Word of God'.[10] There can be 'parables of the Kingdom' to be heard in the clamour of the secular world, signs of God's presence among the God forsaking.[11] 'The more seriously and joyfully we believe in [Jesus Christ], the more we shall see such signs in the worldly sphere, and the more we shall be able to receive true words from it.'[12]

Moreover, the worldly sphere may better speak true words, show truer signs, than the world of the church; better attest to Christ in the things that are not Christ, than those who confess Christ to the world. Christ appears in alien forms, in the humanity of those who find a 'simple solidarity' with others, who are ready to 'understand and forgive'.[13] Barth insists that the world's speaking has to be tested; it has to agree with scripture, with the 'dogmas and confessions' of the church, and it must bear good fruit.[14] But these tests are themselves tested, since if the alien speaks the truth, it will lead us more 'deeply' into scripture, challenging superficial readings,[15] and we may find that the church's 'traditional norms' need to be revised.[16] The alien can call the church to repentance.[17]

Hearing Christ in the alien, in secular speaking, will always be doubted by some, even by most in the church. 'As a rule there will be only a more or less feeble vanguard of hearers which is persecuted by a large majority of non-believers, and an apparently not inconsiderable rearguard of those who never seem to hear aright in this respect.'[18] Consequently, the stranger's voice must be heard with circumspection, and can never be made definitive for the whole community. Rather it should be made to bear fruit. Those who hear Christ's word in the alien should not keep it to themselves. 'They should hold it up as an invitation and summons to others, to the whole community, to share it with them.'

> They should show themselves to be such as have heard a true word and been radically smitten by it. They should bring forth the appropriate fruits. And then, with a readiness to be corrected, they should leave it to the power of the true word, by the ministry (and not the assertive claim) of its confession, to cause its truth to shine to others and to awaken its recognition and confession in them too. If it is a true word, the time will inevitably come sooner or later when it can make its way and do its work in and to the whole community.[19]

It is in the light of Barth's reflections on worldly parables, alien speaking, on the strange lights that shine in the *theatrum gloriae Dei*, that we can venture to look upon the alien visions of the cinema, the sex and violence of Hollywood, its luminary bodies. In contemporary cinema we often hear the echoes of Christian voices, the remnants of an ancient faith. Many films offer parodic reversals of Christian parables; stories of sacrifice and redemption, exemplary of Christ's travails. But beyond these we may also find Barth's 'parables of the Kingdom', stories and images which – for the attentive listener and viewer – speak words and show signs that resonate with the depths of scripture and the devotion of the saints, and yet challenge their familiar appropriations. And when we begin to attend to such parodic parables, we may discover that all our comforts and satisfactions are turned upside-down, and we are challenged to look again, to see the world remade, a theatre shining with the light of God, in places that we thought unlit.[20]

Bedroom Deities

What has Christ to do with Aphrodite? The question is as old as Christianity itself. Tatian, in the second century, was quite clear that Aphrodite and Christ had nothing whatsoever in common.[21] In order to be united with Christ one had to forgo all other unions. Sexual relations, even with husband or wife, destroyed communion with Christ. Paul was being sarcastic or misread when he appeared to allow sexual relations between Christian spouses.[22] For Tatian's Paul, all sexual intercourse is satanic, a union of 'corruption', and Paul permits it for married Christians only because they are enslaved to devilish fornication.[23] Paul's acceptance of marital sex is 'so grudging that he is really saying No to it altogether.'

> He agreed to their [husband and wife] coming together again because of Satan and because of weakness of will, but he showed that anyone who is

> inclined to succumb is going to be serving two masters, God when there is agreement [to abstain from sex], and weakness of will, sexual immorality, and the devil when there is not.[24]

According to Tatian, Paul does not really permit sexual intercourse at all, since all sex is fornication, and fornication satanic. Adam and Eve were banished from paradise for having sex.

Tatian's strict encraty was too much for most of the Church Fathers, several of whom were moved to contest Tatian's total renunciation of sexual congress. 'He is playing intellectual tricks with the truth', Clement of Alexandria asserted against Tatian.[25] For Clement, the difference between 'fornication and marriage' is as great as that which 'separates the devil from God'.[26] Celibacy is not opposed to marriage, but a pious and rational option alongside marriage, to be enjoyed in its own way. Both the 'person who takes his food gratefully, and the one who equally gratefully abstains with an enjoyment marked by self-discipline must follow the Logos in their lives.'[27] It is the same when the food is the body.[28]

> In general, all the Apostle's letters teach responsible self-control. They embrace thousands of instructions about marriage, the production of children, and domestic life. Nowhere do they blackball marriage, provided that it is responsible. They preserve the connection between the Law and the gospel. They welcome the man who embarks responsibly on marriage with gratitude to God, and the man who takes celibacy as his life companion in accordance with the Lord's will, each, as has been called, making his choice in maturity and firmness.[29]

Nevertheless, Clement shared Tatian's distrust of the libidinal body, even if not to the same degree. For Clement, Adam and Eve sinned not because they had sex, but because they had it *too soon*, not having waited for 'the right moment of rational will'.[30] Healthy sex was disciplined sex; rational and dispassionate, responsible. And Clement shared Tatian's belief in the demonic powers that could so easily overcome the unwary soul in moments of bodily lust, the fear of which appears to have motivated Tatian's celibacy.[31] No less than his pagan neighbours, Tatian believed that human interests were subject to those of the Greek pantheon, to the likes of Artemis and Apollo, Poseidon and Kronos, and above them all, Zeus.[32] But while these figures were immortal deities for pious pagans, for Tatian they were demons, fallen angels; and Zeus, the first born and most subtle, was their leader.[33] The identification of the serpent in Genesis with the chief of the Greek gods was Tatian's particular take on the popular story of the fallen angels, who had slept with the daughters of men in Genesis, and obsessed Enoch in his dreams.[34] They are the 'elemental spirits of the world' who, as Paul noted, enslaved humanity until the coming of Christ.[35]

Among the demon-gods was Aphrodite, who as every Greek knew, ruled the passions of men and women. She gave her name to the intimacies of sexual coupling, to the *aphrodisia* or arts of sexual congress, that together with the pleasures and desires they produced, constituted a close compact of bodily interests.[36] Desire (*epithumia*) flows from between bodies, since it is want of that which gives pleasure and makes happy. It is attracted by the beautiful and the good; by the beauty of the body and the good of carnal caresses. For the ancient world, as for the modern, the want, satisfaction and agitation of bodies formed an integrated subject of moral concern. 'It was this dynamic relationship that constituted what might be called the texture of the ethical experience of the *aphrodisia*.'[37] For ancient (male) pagans, the moral anxieties occasioned by such experience concerned the latter's frequency and social propriety. The *aphrodisia* were to be enjoyed moderately and properly, the man taking the active part and the woman or boy taking the passive role. 'For a man, excess and passivity were the two main forms of immorality in the practice of the *aphrodisia*.'[38] But for Tatian, the experience was always deathly, since the demon Aphrodite was the lust of all copulating bodies, no matter how moderate and seemly their embraces. Aphrodite was present in their members, delighting in their 'conjugal embraces'.[39]

Sex was dangerous because it was idolatrous, incurring the wrath of the Lord and the penalty of death. Even if it is your own wife who 'secretly entices' you to the worship of other gods, you must show her no 'pity or compassion', but kill her, and others like her. 'Stone them to death for trying to turn you away from the Lord your God.'[40] And one such enticement is the caress of the flesh, even though it is that of your wife, since it is the touch of Aphrodite. The ancient Hebraic connection between fornication and idolatry, and their horrific punishments, were repeated by Paul,[41] and together these linkages fed Tatian's paranoia.[42] Only by spurning the flesh could one be sure of spurning alien gods, and so escape God's wrath.[43]

As we have seen, Tatian's strong reading of Paul was not endorsed by other exponents of Christian life, such as Clement of Alexandria. Their more obvious reading of Paul allowed for licit sexual relations in Christ. However, they did recognize with Tatian the possibility of alien contacts, idolatrous couplings. Both parties agreed that divinity is present in sexual congress, and their difference concerned the identity of the god: Aphrodite or Christ.[44] Which god had power in the bedroom? The tension between the two divinities constitutes the space of *Alien Sex*. While the greater part of the Christian church has sided with Clement against Tatian, the fear that all sex is alien sex has shadowed the tradition. However, the tradition has been equally troubled by the refutation of Tatian, since it also divinizes sex. If fornication is to chastity (proper and moderate sexual relations) as idolatry is to true worship, then the latter is a matter of proper sexual intercourse (appropriate *aphrodisia*), and Christ becomes an amorous deity, the third party in responsible Christian coupling. For Clement, 'responsible marriage' is eating from the 'Tree of Life' – the flesh of Christ.[45] '"A tree of life," says the prophet, "grows in the soil of a healthy desire," teaching that desires held in the living Lord are good and pure.'[46]

There are those for whom Clement's account of desire is incompatible with a properly Christian idea of love. Thus for Anders Nygren, Clement's depiction of Christian agape bears the stamp of Platonic eros.[47] Nygren's Lutheran account of Christian love insists upon a sharp distinction between a possessive eros and a dispossessive agape, the one motivated by want of the beautiful, while the other is utterly unmotivated, being purely plenitudinous and unseeking. We are not loved by God because we are lovely; but we are lovely because loved by God.[48] The contrast is excessive, but if forced to accept Nygren's dichotomy, then we must choose that which he labels as 'Catholic',[49] and go with Clement in asserting that all love is of the beautiful, and that God loves us because we are lovely.[50] We must go with the Pseudo-Dionysius, for whom yearning and love, eros and agape, have one and the same meaning. For the One who makes the world 'is, as it were, beguiled by goodness, by love, and by yearning and is enticed away from his transcendent dwelling place and comes to abide within all things, and he does so by virtue of his supernatural and ecstatic capacity to remain, nevertheless, within himself'.[51]

We are created through and out of love, and God's creation is not other than good and beautiful and so lovely. 'Ah, you are beautiful, my beloved, truly lovely.'[52] We are lovely because loved into being, born out of God's ecstatic transcendence. Moreover, God sees the loveliness we cannot, and in learning to love as God sees, we learn that love of the lovely is precisely not motivated (acquisitive) because attracted, because participating in a movement, a flow, a becoming. Nygren contrasts the 'ceaseless ascent' of human eros with the downward 'stream' of God's agape.[53] But the teaching of the Fathers is that there are not two movements but one; that we participate in the circulation of God's love, ascending in God's descending. We are as two lovers who can no longer tell in whose body they feel their pleasure, each ecstatic in the other. We are lost in the trinitarian dance.[54]

Cinematic Body Theology

One difficulty in writing about film is that it is writing and not showing, the audience must read rather than watch and if images are to be seen, they are seen in the mind's eye, in the cinema of the imagination. In one sense, of course, all cinema takes place in the imagination of the viewer. David Hume (1711–76) suggested that the 'mind is a kind of theatre, where several perceptions successively make their appearance; pass, re-pass, glide away, and mingle in an infinite variety of postures and situations'.[55] One can easily suppose that had there been an eighteenth-century cinema, Hume would have found it a more apt likeness for his picture of the mind as an infinitely variable stream of perceptions, flowing with an 'inconceivable rapidity', in a 'perpetual flux and movement'.[56]

Already, Hume's theatre is like a half-imagined, but unnamed cinema, its glides and minglings like the fades and dissolves of film imagery, celluloid perceptions. Even more, Hume's mind-theatre captures the experience of losing oneself in the film, that moment when, in the darkness and warmth of the cinema, one forgets the uncomfortable seat, the strangers around one, coughing and munching popcorn, and becomes the motion of the film, the flow of the music: besotted with the moving picture. For Hume's theatre is nothing but the 'successive perceptions', the passings and repassings, the glides and minglings of experience, that alone 'constitute the mind'.[57] There is nothing else, the mind is the theatrical performance, the moving picture. 'For my part, when I enter most intimately into what I call *myself*, I always stumble on some particular perception or other, of heat or cold, light or shade, love or hatred, pain or pleasure. I never can catch *myself* at any time without a perception, and never can observe any thing but the perception'.[58]

The likeness of moving pictures to the perceiving mind is enough to remind us that though the former are shown upon a screen they are seen by the latter, in the intimate cinema of the eye, the picture house of the imagination. This last, the imagination, does not wait upon eye and screen, but from the first attends their seeing. Even before our eyes become accustomed to the dark, we see by the light of the imagination, and its light allows us to go on seeing even when the film has finished and the house lights turned up. Thus films have an existence not only for the duration of their showing, but in the memory of the imagination, and that is how they can appear in books, in the writing and reading of texts. But in the latter they take on a different form; at once impoverished, because lacking sensation – the saturated colours of Technicolor or the vibrancy of stereo sound – but also enriched, because mingled with memories and fancies, with other words and tunes. In recollection, films can be re-edited and reshot, and informed by other films, by other images and other texts. Many of the films discussed in this book are based upon preceding novels, and where appropriate novel and film are considered together, not to mention with other films and books, so that in a sense they have been refilmed and rewritten. On occasion it has also been found useful to draw in other images, so as to produce a mingling of perceptions, that while it cannot reproduce the sensation of cinema, may promote a reimagining of the film, and the production of new vision.

The theology imagined in this book might best be described as 'body theology'. While Mary Timothy Prokes claims Pope John Paul II as the 'leading advocate' of body theology, having begun to lay its foundations in 1978 at his weekly audiences, many will more readily associate the term with the work of James B. Nelson.[59] Body or sexual theology, according to Nelson, is more than just theology of the body or sex, a theological interrogation of bodily desires. 'It is a way of taking sexual/bodily experience seriously in conversation with and in the reshaping of our theological perceptions and categories.'

> It invites us to listen to the body's own speech, to think theologically with and through our bodies. It is convinced that the sexuality that has such power in our lives – the source of such anxiety, such joy, such yearning, such shame, such woundedness, such curiosity, such fulfilment – must be very close to the centre of things. It involves embracing our embodiment not as curse or affliction, nor as incidental to our search for meaning, but as opportunity to learn the poetry of mortal dwelling and, understanding more of that poetry, to live differently.[60]

Nelson's appeal to the body, to the poetry of mortal flesh, is not an appeal to something that is simply given, separable from the social sinews and cultural skin that informs our bodily experience. Rather it is to attend to the way in which our culturally mediated body – what one might call our body-culture – always already informs our theological attentions.[61] For when we think, it is our sexed body that thinks, with all its relationships, wounds, anxieties and desires. While it is readily accepted that 'feminist theology' written by women, or 'queer theology' written by gays and lesbians, is informed by the bodily experience of their authors, this is less well accepted, if not denied, when it comes to theology written by socially dominant, 'heterosexual' men. But their theology is also informed by the desires of their flesh, the social locations of their embodiment. Some of the most interesting explorations in the fields of philosophy and theology have been concerned with the appearance of the author's body in work from which it was thought to be absent, work that was supposed to be the product of discarnate, unlocated intelligences.[62] Body theology attends to the body of theology, to the fleshly moment in thinking 'God', and as such is not so much defined by a particular subject – the sexed body – as by its attention to that which is present in all theology: the body of desire. This is a multi-membraned body, layered with many meanings and types of flesh, being the body of the theologian, the body of the church that informs his or her ecclesio-cultural experience, and the body of Christ, whose body is the church, in all its diverse embodiments.

There is thus a sense in which body theology, like narrative theology, is ubiquitous to all theology.[63] But the theology of *Alien Sex* is also more circumscribed than this suggests, since it may also be described as 'cinematic theology'. In the same way as Nelson's 'sexual theology' is not simply a theology *of* sex, so cinematic theology is not simply a theology *of* cinema, a theological critique of film, its plots and characterizations. Rather cinematic theology attends to the practices of cinema and the languages of film in order to think theologically with and through cinema.[64] It is theology in the mode of cinema, and as such acknowledges the possibility of doing theology in and through film, and through writing on film. In much the same way as Stephen Mulhall argues for 'film as philosophy',[65] *Alien Sex* supposes the possibility of film as theology, and cinema as the socio-technical apparatus by which such theology is produced and consumed. This means, of course, that *Alien Sex* is at best a proto-cinematic theology, a book wanting to be a film. As a book, *Alien Sex* is cinematic body theology: theology thinking the desiring body (of theology) through cinema. And as such, the focus of the book is quite limited. All discourses constitute their subjects through looking and not looking, by not seeing all the possible connections. The desiring body at which this book looks is abstracted from the multitude of circumstances that go to make up bodily life. It is focused on the yearning body, longing for the caress of another.

Epitome

Alien Sex is divided into four parts, the first part containing an introductory chapter on the subject of the body's desire. This opening chapter is concerned with the amorous 'look' that motivates the crossing of the cut, the distance between film shots, coupled bodies and the soul and her lover. 'Let him kiss me with the kisses of his mouth!'[66] The chapter sketches an account of dispossessive desire as movement towards the other, as becoming-other; and as participation in a yet more fundamental movement toward the Other from whence comes our be/com/ing. Desire of the other's body images (analogizes/parodies) the desire of the body's Other. Reading the Song of Songs with Gregory of Nyssa shows us that our desire is always-already the Other's desire of our desiring.

The next three parts of the book – Cavities, Copulations and Consolations – are not directly related to the three topoi of cinema, body and theology, since these thematics are to be found in each of the book's parts, indeed in each of its chapters. Yet perhaps one topic dominates in each part. Thus the two chapters of part 2 (Cavities) are concerned with cinema as social apparatus, as both technical mechanism and public institution, as a set of practices for the production and consumption of films. While the book does not support any one film theory, the notion of the 'cinematic apparatus', as famously expounded by Christian Metz, is given a certain privilege.[67] However, it is only a very small part of Metz's theory that is assumed, indeed hardly more than that already stated. It is not so much Metz's (Lacanian) psychoanalysis of cinematic experience that is of interest, as his account of how a socio-technological apparatus – the conjunction of viewers and text within a social practice that is also a technology – produces cinematic experience. The second part of the book explores certain parallels between the cinema and the church, viewing them as institutions for the production of vision, spaces for the projecting of dreams, caves for the inciting of desire. 'Upon my bed at night I sought him whom my soul loves'.[68] The third chapter, in particular, develops a cinematic ecclesiology that understands the church as the space in which the Spirit shines on the bodies of its participant viewers, who are also projector and screen as well as audience: a carnal cinema of desiring bodies.

Having established a theological setting for writing about film – or a cinematic setting for the writing of theology – the third part of the book (Copulations) turns from the production of vision to the visions produced, as they relate to the desiring body. The third part offers four interrelated essays on spiritual and bodily desire, with particular reference to films by David Fincher, Ken Russell, Lars von Trier and Neil Jordan. The chapters are written neither from wholly within the movie house nor the church, but from a space between, the border-crossing that separates and connects, beset by demons but promising bodily transfiguration. This space is not an easy habitation, though it is one that many of us now endure and, on occasion, enjoy. In turn, the four chapters consider the sexual cut that exists within as well as between bodies – the distance that alienates us from our own flesh (chapter 4); the parody or analogy of spiritual yearning with bodily lust, both in the Christian conception of God as Trinity (chapter 5) and in the bodies of Christian saints (chapter 6); and, finally, desire for the familial body of the heavenly household (chapter 7). Together, these chapters develop an image of dispossessive desire. 'My beloved thrust his hand into the opening, and my inmost being yearned for him. I arose to open to my beloved, and my hands dripped with myrrh, my fingers with liquid myrrh, upon the handles of the bolt. I opened to my beloved . . .'[69]

The fourth part of the book (Consolations) offers a christological reflection on bodily desire as not merely parodying, but producing a spiritual community that betokens on earth what is consummated in heaven. Developing themes already broached in the book's introductory chapter on desire, and through asking the impossible question of Jesus' sexuality, the last part of the book offers an answer to the question posed here, in the lobby. With Gregory of Nyssa, once more, the last chapter of the book enters the paradisal space of the garden. There – with Mary Magdalene – we learn how to touch the risen Christ, because touched by him, and so how to touch one another without fear of demonic possession or divine retribution.

If readers of the last two chapters sense something of the melancholy that infuses the two films they discuss – Nicolas Roeg's *The Man Who Fell to Earth* (US 1976) and Derek Jarman's *The Garden* (UK 1990) – that is not entirely inappropriate. For these last chapters attempt to show a film, a vision, that is not yet playing on the main screens of the ecclesiacinema, though on occasion one may see truncated versions. The 'director's cut' can be seen only in more local picture houses of the imagination, in more domestic, household settings, where perhaps two or three have gathered together for a meal, for angelic conversation and intercourse. 'Eat, friends, drink, and be drunk with love.'[70] These are people who, unlike Mary Magdalene in the garden of the tomb,[71] have been permitted to touch and embrace the risen Christ. For they have heeded what Mary was sent to teach them. It is among such friends that the film may be seen, flickering across their bodies like light caught in a breeze, and as gentle as an eyelash brushing a lover's cheek.

Credits

For those with an archaeological interest, and out of gratitude to the relevant editors and publishers, I must note that earlier versions – 'rough cuts' –

of chapters or parts of chapters in this book appeared as 'Seeing in the Dark', *Studies in Christian Ethics*, 13/1 (2000): 33–48, and as 'Looking: The Ethics of Seeing in Church and Cinema' in *Faithfulness and Fortitude*, edited by Mark Thiessen Nation and Samuel Wells (Edinburgh: T. & T. Clark, 2000), pp. 257–85; 'Ending Sex' in *Sex These Days: Essays on Theology, Sexuality and Society*, edited by Jon Davies and Gerard Loughlin (Sheffield: Sheffield Academic Press, 1997), pp. 205–18; 'God's Sex', *New Blackfriars*, 79 (1998): 18–25, and in *Radical Orthodoxy: A New Theology*, edited by John Milbank, Catherine Pickstock and Graham Ward (London: Routledge, 1999), pp. 143–62; 'Sex Slaves: Rethinking "Complementarity" After I Corinthians 7.3–4' in *Is There a Future for Feminist Theology?*, edited by Deborah F. Sawyer and Diane M. Collier (Sheffield: Sheffield Academic Press, 1999), pp. 173–92; 'The Want of Family' in *The Family in Theological Perspective*, edited by Stephen Barton (Edinburgh: T. & T. Clark, 1996), pp. 307–27; and 'The Man Who Fell to Earth', *Theology and Sexuality*, 13 (2000): 92–118, and in *The Blackwell Companion to Postmodern Theology*, edited by Graham Ward (Oxford: Blackwell, 2000), pp. 24–47.

Much of this book was written while I was the Head of Department of Religious Studies at the University of Newcastle upon Tyne (1996–2001), and I must thank my colleagues for their support throughout that period, as also the University for granting me a sabbatical semester in 1999–2000. I must also thank my editors at Blackwell, Alex Wright and Rebecca Harkin. Alex commissioned *Alien Sex*, and Rebecca has seen it through to completion, and both have been exceptional in their sustained encouragement and enthusiasm for the project.

Over the years many people have contributed to my thinking on theology, cinema and sexuality, either through their writing or in response to something I have written, or by a simple stray remark or emailed note that has stayed with me, informing my theological intuition. There will be some I have failed to remember, and of those I do recall, some may have little recollection of their influence, and be surprised at their inclusion. Nevertheless, I hope that those remembered will accept my gratitude, and those forgotten excuse my faulty memory. Of those I do remember, my grateful thanks to Pamela Sue Anderson, Bettina Bergo, Sarah Boss, Sarah Coakley, Jon Davies, Malcolm Edwards, Paul Fletcher, David Ford, Stanley Hauerwas, Eibhlin Inglesby, Grace Jantzen, Ursula King, Ann Loades, Alison Milbank and John Milbank, David Moss, Susan Parsons, Michael Purcell, Ben Quash, Esther Reed, Eugene Rogers, Deborah Sawyer, Paul Julian Smith, Janet Martin Soskice, Elizabeth Stuart, Graham Ward, Sam Wells, Scott Wilson, Rowan Williams, Linda Woodhead and Alex Wright.

There are three people I must thank in particular: Gavin D'Costa for continuing, with much fortitude and generosity, to challenge my more wayward thoughts; Tina Beattie for writing the one really searching review (thankfully unpublished) of my previous book, and to which this book is in part a most inadequate response, as well as for her continuing inspiration and encouragement; and finally to Andrew Ballantyne for sitting through more alien films than he would have done by himself (none at all) and for listening patiently to my cinematic enthusiasms, to which he responded with just the right balance of interest and incredulity.

Gerard Loughlin
Vézelay, Epiphany 2003

All biblical quotations are from the New Revised Standard Version of the Bible (Oxford University Press 1991), unless otherwise stated.

Notes

1 See Stephen Mulhall, *On Film* (London: Routledge, 2001).
2 Gilbert Perez, *The Material Ghost: Films and their Medium* (Baltimore: The Johns Hopkins University Press, 1998), p. 3.
3 David Lynch is another director who made film new for me, but unfortunately it has not been possible to include a discussion of his films in the present book.
4 Steven Shaviro, *The Cinematic Body* (Minneapolis: University of Minnesota Press, 1993), p. 10. Shaviro is arguing against those psychoanalytic film theorists – Christian Metz and Laura Mulvey are cited – for whom the 'love of cinema' is pathological, a pleasure that must be abolished in favour of 'scientific' film theory. On overcoming the love of cinema see Christian Metz, *The Imaginary Signifier: Psychoanalysis and the Cinema*, translated by Celia Britton, Annwyl Williams, Ben Brewster and Alfred Guzzetti (Bloomington and Indianapolis: Indiana University Press, [1977] 1982), pp. 14–16; and for a general introduction to the pleasures of film watching see Thomas Sutcliffe, *Watching* (London: Faber & Faber, 2000).
5 On the alien within and without, the foreigner who contests and maintains our identity, see Julia Kristeva, *Strangers to Ourselves*, translated by Leon S. Roudiez (London: Harvester Wheatsheaf, 1991).
6 On how the looking of characters stitches together the shots of a film, and stitches – 'sutures' – the viewer into the film, see Stephen Heath, 'Narrative Space' in *Questions of Cinema* (London: Macmillan, 1981), pp. 19–75. 'The

spectator will be bound to the film as spectacle as the world of the film is itself revealed as spectacle on the basis of narrative organization of look and point of view that moves space into place through the image-flow; the character, figure of the look, is a kind of perspective within the perspective system, regulating the world, orientating space, providing directions – and for the spectator' (p. 44). On filmic or televisual space and its relation to geographic or architectural space see Andrew Ballantyne, 'Architectonics of "The Box": Television's Spatiality' in *Television: Aesthetic Reflections*, edited by Ruth Lorand (New York: Peter Lang, 2002), pp. 127–38.

7 Hélène Cixous, 'Savoir', in Hélène Cixous and Jacques Derrida, *Veils*, translated by Geoffrey Bennington (Stanford, CA: Stanford University Press, [1998] 2001), pp. 1–16 (p. 9). Cixous' complex image reminds us that though 'sight' has been the privileged – and denigrated – metaphor for pure, unembodied cognition, it remains an utterly bodily sensation. René Descartes appealed to the sense of touch in order to explain how light impressed itself in the cave of the eye. Just as the blind 'see with their hands', or with the help of a stick, so the eye senses the touch of light, as transmitted through the 'medium of air'. René Descartes, *Optics*, first discourse: of light, in *Discourse on Method, Optics, Geometry and Meteorology*, translated by Paul J. Olscamp (Indianapolis: Bobbs-Merril, [1637] 1965), pp. 67–8. See also Emmanuel Levinas, 'Language and Proximity' in *Collected Philosophical Papers*, translated by Alphonso Lingis (Dordrecht: Kluwer Academic Publications, 1993), pp. 109–26. 'The visible caresses the eye. One sees and one hears like one touches' (p. 118). Prior to Levinas and Cixous, prior to Descartes, Aristotle had established sight as a kind of touching, since what is seen affects the organ of sight through the medium of light in air, which is the 'presence of fire or something like it in the transparent'. Aristotle, *De Anima*, translated by Hugh Lawson-Tancred (Harmondsworth: Penguin Books, 1986), 418b–419b (pp. 173–6).

8 Cixous, 'Savoir', p. 9.

9 Karl Barth, *Church Dogmatics*, IV/3: *The Doctrine of Reconciliation*, translated by G.W. Bromiley, edited by G.W. Bromiley and T.F. Torrance (Edinburgh: T. & T. Clark, 1961), p. 120.

10 Barth, *Church Dogmatics*, IV/3, p. 113.

11 Barth, *Church Dogmatics*, IV/3, p. 117.

12 Barth, *Church Dogmatics*, IV/3, p. 122.

13 Barth, *Church Dogmatics*, IV/3, p. 125.

14 Barth, *Church Dogmatics*, IV/3, pp. 126–7.

15 Barth, *Church Dogmatics*, IV/3, p. 126. This is to draw out an unstated implication of Barth's analysis. He insists on scripture as the final and absolute norm (pp. 130–1), but its 'investigation, exposition and application' (p. 131) has to be pursued; we have to labour for its meaning in the Spirit. The scripture may be the 'regular way' to Christ, but as such it is an undertaking, a journey, an adventure.

16 Barth, *Church Dogmatics*, IV/3, p. 127.
17 Barth, *Church Dogmatics*, IV/3, p. 129.
18 Barth, *Church Dogmatics*, IV/3, p. 132.
19 Barth, *Church Dogmatics*, IV/3, pp. 134–5.
20 I return to the parodic in chapter 5 (God's Sex) below, unsettling the comforts of theological analogy.
21 The following reading of Tatian is indebted to Kathy L. Gaca, 'Driving Aphrodite from the World: Tatian's Encratite Principles of Sexual Renunciation', *Journal of Theological Studies*, 53 (2002): 28–52. For Aphrodite – as she appears in Homer, Hesiod and Sappho – see Paul Friedrich, *The Meaning of Aphrodite* (Chicago: University of Chicago Press, 1978).
22 1 Corinthians 7.1–5.
23 See Tatian, *On Perfection*, fragment 1 in *The Ante-Nicene Fathers*, vol. 2: *Fathers of the Second Century*, edited by Alexander Roberts, James Donaldson and A. Cleveland Coxe (Edinburgh: T. & T. Clark, 1994), p. 82; fragment 5 in Tatian, *Oratio ad Graecos and Fragments*, edited and translated by Molly Whittaker (Oxford: Clarendon Press, 1982), pp. 79–81; quoted in Gaca, 'Driving Aphrodite from the World', p. 33.
24 Tatian quoted in Clement of Alexandria, *Stromateis: Books 1–3*, translated by John Ferguson (Fathers of the Church, 85; Washington DC: Catholic University of America Press, 1991), 3.81.1–2 (p. 306). The 'licentious tenets' of the gnostics refuted in the third book of Clement's *Stromateis* were considered so shocking by the editors of the standard English translation, that they gave the book in Latin, for 'scholars only'. See *The Ante-Nicene Fathers*, vol. 2, p. 381 n.1.
25 Clement of Alexandria, *Stromateis*, 3.81.3 (p. 306).
26 Clement of Alexandria, *Stromateis*, 3.84.4 (p. 309).
27 Clement of Alexandria, *Stromateis*, 3.85.2 (pp. 309–10).
28 The alimentary and the libidinal – the hunger of and for flesh – are repeatedly conjoined in ancient writers, both pagan and patristic, with one hunger following from the satisfaction of the other. Thus Clement reports that the Carpocratian Christians, having 'stuffed themselves' at their love-feasts, 'knock over the lamps' so as not to 'expose their fornicating "righteousness", and couple as they will with any woman they fancy.' *Stromateis*, 3.10.1 (p. 262). Clement more positively links sex with eating when he likens Christian marriage to eating from the Tree of Life. See *Stromateis*, 3.104.2 (p. 322).
29 Clement of Alexandria, *Stromateis*, 3.86.1 (p. 310). Against Tatian and other teachers who wrote against marriage, Clement likes to point out that for the Apostle (Paul) the ideal bishop is one who has already learned how to rule his household, which is constituted through marriage (1 Timothy 3.2–4; Titus 1.6). See, for example, *Stromateis*, 3.79.6, 3.108.2 (pp. 305, 325).
30 Clement of Alexandria, *Stromateis*, 3.94.3 (p. 315); see also 3.103.1 (p. 321).
31 See Clement's *Exhortation to the Heathen* in *The Ante-Nicene Fathers*, vol. 2, pp. 171–206. It is not entirely clear to what extent Clement deploys the notion

of the demonic metaphorically, since for the most part he offers naturalistic explanations for the invention of the gods, and derides the manufacture of their images. It is the power of these images and their accompanying stories over their devotees that constitutes their demonic force, like the feelings of anger and covetousness which can lead people to slay others, and which passions are called 'demons' alongside the likes of Artemis and Zeus. See *Exhortation*, ch. 3 (p. 183). It is because the gods are dead men and women, that they are at best 'shades and demons . . . being in reality unclean and impure spirits, acknowledged by all to be of an earthly and watery nature, sinking downwards by their own weight, and flitting about graves and tombs, about which they appear dimly, being but shadowy phantasms' (*Exhortation*, ch. 4, p. 189). Clement's demonic gods are akin to those of Athenagoras, for whom the demons are the giants of Genesis 6.1–4, the powers that attract people to the otherwise insensible images of the gods. See Athenagoras, *A Plea for Christians* in *The Ante-Nicene Fathers*, vol. 2, chs. 24 and 25 (pp. 142–3). See further chapter 2 (Seeing in the Dark) below.

32 See Tatian, *Address to the Greeks*, ch. 8, in *The Ante-Nicene Fathers*, vol. 2, pp. 65–82 (p. 68).

33 Genesis 3.1; Tatian, *Address to the Greeks*, ch. 7, in *The Ante-Nicene Fathers*, vol. 2, pp. 65–82 (pp. 67–8).

34 Gaca, 'Driving Aphrodite from the World', p. 37; *The Book of Enoch*, translated by R.H. Charles (London: SPCK, [1917] 1997), ch. 8 (p. 35). On these angels see further chapter 8 (*The Man Who Fell to Earth*) below.

35 Galatians 4.3; Colossians 2.8. For this reading see Gaca, 'Driving Aphrodite from the World', p. 42.

36 On the ancient *aphrodisia* see Michel Foucault, *The Use of Pleasure* (vol. 2 of *The History of Sexuality*), translated by Robert Hurley (Harmondsworth: Penguin Books, [1984] 1992), pp. 38–52.

37 Foucault, *Use of Pleasure*, p. 43.

38 Foucault, *Use of Pleasure*, p. 47. See also Peter Brown, *The Body and Society: Men, Women and Sexual Renunciation in Early Christianity* (London: Faber & Faber, [1988] 1989), ch. 1 (pp. 5–32).

39 Tatian, *Address to the Greeks*, ch. 8 (p. 68). It was Aphrodite who led on Clement's licentious Carpocratians: '"The Cyprian goddess is there when you are full," they say.' Clement of Alexandria, *Stromateis*, 3.10.1 (p. 262).

40 Deuteronomy 13.6–11. On the terrible consequences of making eyes at other gods see also Deuteronomy 4.25–31, 29.10–28.

41 Romans 1.22–7.

42 See Numbers 25.1–13; 1 Corinthians 10.7–8 and 1 Thessalonians 4.3–6.

43 Gaca, 'Driving Aphrodite from the World', p. 45. Gaca argues that Tatian's encratism represents a greater gulf between Christian and pagan sexual morality than that envisaged by Michel Foucault and Dale B. Martin, both of whom trace a Stoic continuity between Christian and pagan interests. 'Prior to the rise of Christianity, no Greeks thought it possible or desirable to eliminate

the powers and effects of Aphrodite. Though pre-Christian Greeks had their own reasons for being sexually inhibited, the Greeks never aspired to eliminate sexual activity altogether, let alone eradicate the gods responsible for human erotic behaviour.' (p. 47) For Martin see *The Corinthian Body* (New Haven: Yale University Press, 1995). Rather than choose between these approaches, a less tidy, more variegated account will allow for both the continuities and discontinuities suggested by Martin and Gaca.

44 Gaca, 'Driving Aphrodite from the World', p. 49.

45 '[T]he revealed knowledge of the truth is also an eating from the Tree of Life. So it is possible for responsible marriage to take from that tree.' Clement of Alexandria, *Stromateis*, 3.104.2 (p. 322).

46 Clement of Alexandria, *Stromateis*, 3.103.4 (p. 322). The prophetic verse is Proverbs 13.12.

47 Anders Nygren, *Agape and Eros*, translated by Philip S. Watson (London: SPCK, [1953] 1982), pp. 359–68.

48 Nygren, *Agape and Eros*, pp. 722–25.

49 Nygren, *Agape and Eros*, p. 739.

50 Clement of Alexandria, *The Paedagogus* (The Instructor), bk 1, ch. 3; in *The Ante-Nicene Fathers*, vol. 2, pp. 209–98 (pp. 210–11).

51 Pseudo-Dionysius, *The Divine Names*, 712B, in *Pseudo Dionysius: The Complete Works*, translated by Colm Luibheid and Paul Rorem (New York: Paulist Press, 1987), p. 82.

52 Song of Songs 1.16.

53 Nygren, *Agape and Eros*, pp. 740–1.

54 On joining the dance see further below chapter 5 (God's Sex).

55 David Hume, *A Treatise of Human Nature*, edited by Ernest C. Mossner (Harmondsworth: Penguin Books, [1739–40] 1969/1985), bk 1, section 6, p. 301.

56 Hume, *Treatise*, p. 300. This is not to endorse the view that our knowledge of the world is knowledge of certain mental entities that appear on a screen *between* the world and us. For Hume there is nothing between, since the 'self', if it is anything, is the screen.

57 Hume, *Treatise*, p. 301.

58 Hume, *Treatise*, p. 300.

59 See Mary Timothy Prokes FSE, *Toward a Theology of the Body* (Edinburgh: T. & T. Clark, 1996), p. x. For Pope John Paul II's body theology see *Original Unity of Man and Woman: Catechesis on the Book of Genesis* (Boston: St Paul Books, 1981); *The Theology of Marriage and Celibacy* (Boston: St Paul Books, 1986).

60 James B. Nelson, 'On Doing Body Theology', *Theology and Sexuality*, 2 (1995): 38–60 (p. 46). This article was the keynote speech at the launch conference for *Theology and Sexuality*, held at the University of Newcastle upon Tyne in September 1994.

61 See James B. Nelson, *Body Theology* (Louisville, KY: Westminster/John Knox Press, 1992), pp. 42–50. It is because culture goes all the way down that the distinction between sex and gender – sex as a natural given and gender as a social construct – while sometimes useful, collapses under pressure. It is not maintained in this book. Sex, as much as gender, is the effect of what Judith Butler calls 'performativity', constantly repeated patterns of discourse and behaviour that establish both what appears to view and what is beneath or behind the view. The prediscursive is an effect of discourse; or better, the *venture* of a social imagination, the process of what Butler calls 'materialization', by which bodies are brought to matter. It does not follow from this that what is seen and unseen is unreal or only ideal, but that it is never stable, because always mobile, always in formation and so (open to) reformation. See further Judith Butler, *Bodies that Matter: On the Discursive Limits of 'Sex'* (London: Routledge, 1993), ch. 1 (pp. 1–23).

62 For example see Pamela Sue Anderson, *A Feminist Philosophy of Religion* (Oxford: Blackwell, 1998), pp. 3–27; Grace Jantzen, *Becoming Divine: Towards a Feminist Philosophy of Religion* (Manchester: Manchester University Press, 1998), ch. 1; and Sarah Coakley, *Powers and Submissions: Spirituality, Philosophy and Gender* (Oxford: Blackwell, 2002), chs. 5 and 6 (pp. 89–105), and her unpublished Riddell Memorial Lectures, 'Knowing Otherwise' (Newcastle upon Tyne, 1999).

63 On the 'ubiquity' of narrative theology see Gerard Loughlin, *Telling God's Story: Bible, Church and Narrative Theology* (Cambridge: Cambridge University Press, [1996] 1999), pp. ix–x.

64 For a different theological approach see *Explorations in Theology and Film: Movies and Meaning*, edited by Clive Marsh and Gaye Ortiz (Oxford: Blackwell, 1997). Marsh and Ortiz argue for a dialogue between theology and film in pursuit of human truth. Cinematic theology is not a dialogue, but a 'becoming-other'. For yet another approach see Margaret R. Miles, *Seeing and Believing: Religions and Values in the Movies* (Boston: Beacon Press, 1996), who offers an ethical ('cultural studies') critique of some of the social values in mainstream Hollywood films; a prophylactic against cinematic seduction.

65 Mulhall, *On Film*, p. 6. There are of course many philosophers who have written on film, but few regard film as itself a form of thinking. Among those who do, the most prominent must be Gilles Deleuze, for whom the 'great directors' are not merely comparable with 'painters, architects and musicians', but with thinkers. 'They think with movement-images and time-images instead of concepts . . . [T]he cinema . . . forms part of art and part of thought, in the irreplaceable, autonomous forms which these directors were able to invent and get screened, in spite of everything.' See Gilles Deleuze, *Cinema 1: The Movement Image*, translated by Hugh Tomlinson and Barbara Habberjam (London: Athlone Press, [1983] 1992), p. xiii; see also *Cinema 2: The Time-Image*, translated by Hugh Tomlinson and Robert Galeta (London: Athlone Press, [1985] 1989), ch. 7.

66 Song of Songs 1.2.

67 See Metz, *The Imaginary Signifier*, pp. 42–87. For critical discussion of Metz's apparatus theory see *The Cinematic Apparatus*, edited by Teresa de Lauretis and Stephen Heath (New York: St Martin's Press, 1980).

68 Song of Songs 3.1.

69 Song of Songs 5.4–6.

70 Song of Songs 5.1.

71 John 20.11–18.

Part I

INTRODUCTION

Let him kiss me with the kisses of his mouth! (Song of Songs 1.2)

Figure 1 Reading the Body

Leonard (Guy Pearce) and Natalie (Carrie-Anne Moss) in *Memento* (Christopher Nolan, USA 2000). Photo: British Film Institute.

Chapter 1

DESIRING BODIES

The scene opens with a close-up of Leonard's face, Guy Pearce's face: stubbled, sharply boned, handsome, with bleached hair and two scratches on his left cheek. He is lying on his back, in bed, looking up at the ceiling; bathed in a soft, pale yellow morning light.[1] We hear his thoughts as he pulls them together, out of sleep. 'Awake.' An observation and a question, as if he had to name the experience of awakening in order to imagine and remember it as his own experience. And indeed, forgetting and imagining is Leonard's constant condition in Christopher Nolan's film noir, *Memento* (USA 2000). Following the rape and murder of his wife, Leonard has lost the ability to make new memories, and apart from his life before that traumatic event – that his anterograde amnesia allows him to remember partly (selectively) – his world begins anew every 15 minutes. By means of notes on the reverse of Polaroid photographs, and messages tattooed on his body, on arms, legs and chest – one laterally reversed so that he can read it in the mirror – Leonard reconstitutes his world, repeatedly. He tells anyone who will listen of his search for the murderer of his wife, his need to avenge the world he has lost.[2]

'Oh, where am I?' Leonard wonders as he looks around the room: a cage with two birds, a gold-framed picture by the door, a drawing of a young girl. 'Somebody's bedroom.' Perhaps it is his room? Then he realizes that he is not alone in the bed. He has raised himself on his right arm and seen a sleeping woman – Natalie (Carrie-Anne Moss) – lying close beside him. 'Oh, must be her room.' Leonard has taught himself not to show surprise at what might be the everyday, as it keeps befalling him anew. 'Oh, who is she?' With his moving she begins to awaken, and her left hand falls against his shoulder. With a start Natalie opens her eyes, and she too is a little surprised to find him there, for she only met him yesterday. 'It's only me,' he reassures. He has remembered who he is, the man who cannot remember, and who must now, again, piece together where he is and why he is there, and with whom he has been sleeping. His own body will prove to be the clue he needs, a living memento of his dismembered life.

The Other Between

Many will have been there, like Leonard, like Natalie. Upon waking you find yourself in bed with a stranger. Who is he? How did he get there? Or, finding the bed unfamiliar, how did you get here? And then you remember. But in the moment before you recall how his body came to be lying beside your own, perhaps still sleeping, you are disconcerted by his presence, by the warmth of his flesh. Even as you seek to name him, your own identity is disturbed, dislocated, for a moment undone, rendered indeterminate. The space between your bodies becomes a distance within yourself, opening between 'consciousness' and 'identity'. Then he rolls over, moves closer, and still sleeping extends his arm in a half-intended embrace, and the touch of skins covers the distance within, and you remember who you are: yourself and the stranger.

Between the intimacy of sheets, between one body pressed against another, each following the other's posture and curves – the convex nestling in the concave, as one spoon lies against another – there is still a space, a distance, a hair's breadth. The stranger with whom you awaken may have been long known to you, a long-time companion, a dear friend, a spouse. Yet even in moments of intimacy, when your beloved gives himself to you and you to him, he is still beyond your grasp, a stranger to the caress of your flesh. This is what the phenomenologist Emmanuel Levinas – here a phenomenologist of sexual desire – calls the 'pathos of voluptuosity'.[3] No matter how close the embrace, the 'coinciding of the lover and the beloved, is charged by their duality: it is simultaneously fusion and distinction'.[4] In 'the other's proximity, distance is integrally maintained',[5] even as proximity calls forth the desire for union with the other.

Eros is not so much the destruction of self or other, as their transformation, by making one present to the other, so that the other is not encompassed by the self, or the self submerged in the other, for that would be the destruction of their relationship. Rather the self – the 'I' – goes beyond itself, becoming the self of the other, for 'the amorous subjectivity is transubstantiation itself'.[6] The presence of one to the other – of one *in* the other – is made possible through the distance of proximity, through the 'absence' that opens in the nearness of the other's body. 'What one presents as the failure of communication in love precisely constitutes the positivity of the relationship; this absence of the other is precisely its presence *as* other.'[7]

To encounter the other in this way, as absent even when most close, *because* most close, is to encounter the other as 'feminine' – so Levinas avers. In the erotic embrace there is no overcoming of the other as other, no denial of the fundamental duality and alterity announced in the other's body, pressed against your own. 'The other as other is not here an object that becomes ours or becomes us; to the contrary, it withdraws into its mystery.'[8] This withdrawal – which is the mystery of the 'feminine' – is not that of the 'mysterious, unknown or misunderstood woman', but is that 'mode of being that consists in slipping away from the light'.[9] It is the appearing of that mysterious alterity that hides in being, in the body that encompasses your own, that holds you, not with the strength of enfolding arms, but with a tender otherness, an essential alienness to yourself. 'The transcendence of the feminine', Levinas tells us, 'consists in withdrawing elsewhere, which is a movement opposed to the movement of consciousness. But this does not make it unconscious or subconscious, and I see no other possibility than to call it mystery.'[10]

The 'feminine' is the mystery of the other, and as such is not your projection. It is not something you can possess or own, even as you hold his body most dearly. The erotic embrace, the sexual relationship, is 'neither a struggle, nor a fusion, nor a knowledge . . . It is a relationship with alterity, with mystery – that is to say, with the future, with what (in a world where there is everything) is never there, with what cannot be there when everything is there – not with a being that is not there, but with the very dimension of alterity.'[11] The erotic is the lure and embrace of the truly alien, the flesh that is other.

Needless to say, Levinas's feminization of alterity, his understanding of the 'feminine' as 'the *of itself other*, as the origin of the very concept of alterity',[12] has given rise to much criticism, most famously, and caustically, by Simone de Beauvoir in *Le Deuxième Sexe* (1949).

> I suppose that Levinas does not forget that woman, too, is aware of her own consciousness, or ego. But it is striking that he deliberately takes a man's point of view, disregarding the reciprocity of subject and object. When he writes that woman is mystery, he implies that she is mystery for man. Thus his description, which is intended to be objective, is in fact an assertion of masculine privilege.[13]

Levinas's response to this criticism is reluctant and less than pellucid. 'All these allusions to the ontological differences between the masculine and the feminine would appear less archaic if, instead of dividing humanity into two species (or into two genders), they would signify that the participation in the masculine and in the feminine were the attribute of every human being.'[14] It would appear that Levinas, in admitting his 'archaic' use of terms, would not want to deny that woman is also a subject, and that in the man she too can discover the feminine other. Thus for Levinas, 'masculine' and 'feminine' are not biological but ontological distinctions, modalities of being that might be ascribed to either sex.[15] No doubt Levinas is betrayed by a certain cultural context, but his 'feminine' is figural, culturally motivated but biologically arbitrary.[16] 'Masculine' and 'feminine' are attributes of every human being, and Levinas wonders if this might not be the meaning of Genesis 1.27: 'male and female created he them.'[17]

If, biologically speaking, Levinas's use of 'masculine' and 'feminine' is gender neutral, why does he not employ non-gendered terms, thus avoiding the cultural figurations of man and woman as 'virile' and 'modest', 'active' and 'passive'? It is in part because he wants to avoid any abstraction of eros, which, after all, is an intimacy of gendered bodies. Furthermore, he wants to avoid any suggestion that the erotic relation is simply symmetrical, a relationship of two subjects, for both of whom the other is an object, as in de Beauvoir's correction of Levinas. From the outside the relationship may appear symmetrical; but viewed from inside the relationship is a doubled, reciprocal asymmetry, for it is in the erotic relationship that we discover otherness itself: the Other in the other. Thus Levinas takes (hetero)sexual difference – which he holds to be fundamental – as a figure for the yet more fundamental difference of the same from the other, of *ipseity* from *alterity*. It is then not so much the 'feminine' that is the 'of itself other', as the difference of the 'feminine' from the 'masculine', that again should not be understood as a biological difference, as between the sexes, but as a carnal distance, between bodies.

What is at issue here is the discovery and preservation of *difference*, of a radical otherness that cannot be collapsed into the same; denied in favour of an undifferentiated totality, a single flesh. Thus Levinas refuses Aristophanes' myth of humanity's ancient tripartite nature, which is said to have consisted of the male, female and androgyne, with each gender a whole couple, with four arms, four legs, a single head with two faces, that runs by turning somersaults.[18] It was only with their cleaving that erotic desire was born in these comical beings, as each half yearned for his or her other part, for that which they now lacked. The fulfilment of desire then consists in the (re)union of two complementary bodies – the male with the male, the female with the female, and the androgyne with his or her other half, once more forming an originary whole. Levinas rejects this myth of sexual union as the fusion of complements, for that which complements yourself, that which fills up your lack of self and returns you to yourself, is not other than yourself. There is no going outside of yourself, no meeting with another, but only more of yourself: an engorged solipsism. Thus the idea of complementary bodies – so pervasive in Christian marital theology – betrays a ('masculine') desire to possess the other, as that which will satisfy your want of self.[19] Those who seek for their complement – always heterosexual (androgynous) in the prevailing Christian rendition, but also homosexual (male and female) in the original Platonic joke – seek for that which they can grasp and hold, but which they can never really receive as different from themselves, as the appearing of the Other in flesh. They can never caress the alien.

One should not suppose that each embrace, each and every coupling, opens onto alterity, onto the mystery that withdraws even as one seeks to encircle, hold and possess the other. Often, if not always, the meeting of bodies is but an intercourse of pleasure, a satisfaction of want, a temporary satiety that quickly passes so that we can want again. This is the repeated longing and satisfaction of those seeking to fuse with their other half. In such relationships the other remains within the projection of the self, so that even though mutually agreed, contracted – either through the laws of church and state, or through hurried arrangements ('Your place or mine?') – it is always the hired use of the other's flesh, the negotiated pleasure of their body. But even if much sex is like this, Levinas points to the possibility of something more, to a transcendence or intensity of yearning that is other than want, a passing from need to a different, deeper desiring. When we caress the skin of the other, we do not always know what it is that we seek to touch. 'It is like a game with something slipping away, a game absolutely without project or plan, not with what can become ours or us, but with something other, always other, always inaccessible, and always still to come [à venir].'[20]

Desiring Distance

> To expend oneself, to bestir oneself for an impenetrable object is pure religion. To make the other into an insoluble riddle on which my life depends is to consecrate the other as a god; I shall never manage to solve

> the question the other asks me, the lover is not Oedipus. Then all that is left for me to do is to reverse my ignorance into truth. It is not true that the more you love, the better you understand; all that the action of love obtains from me is merely this wisdom: that the other is not to be known; his opacity is not the screen around a secret, but, instead, a kind of evidence in which the game of reality and appearance is done away with. I am then seized with that exaltation of loving *someone unknown*, someone who will remain so forever: a mystic impulse: I know what I do not know.[21]

In the above quotation, Roland Barthes (1915–80) – a phenomenologist of sorts, here a phenomenologist of amorous yearning – finds, like Levinas, that to embrace the beloved is to embrace the unknown. Perhaps, as Barthes suggests, this is a perversity of the lover, who makes the beloved opaque, turning him into an unsolvable riddle, a consecrated divinity. Yet if the 'action of love' is not something that I initiate but by which I am initiated – a 'constant *initiation* into a mystery rather than *initiative*'[22] – then Barthes' account is similar to that which Levinas names as an encounter with the 'feminine', a meeting with the mystery of the other, who withdraws, but does not leave. Barthes, however, wastes no time in telling us that this withdrawal is also the advent of the god, so that what Levinas names the 'feminine' can also be named the 'religious' or 'mystical'. Levinas may be more circumspect, more philosophically tentative, than Barthes, but he is also less solipsistic, since on his account the transcendent movement of desire is not so much the action of the lover as the effect of a preceding passion. Levinas ventures that transcendent desire is not an apophatic idolatry, but the disclosure of the Other in the other's flesh, so that the lover's desiring is already the disclosing, the giving of the Other's infinite difference. That which withdraws in the erotic embrace is also that which approaches, and approaches by withdrawing. It is the approach of the Other, that, in a further venture, is also the approach of God – there being no other route by which God can come to us.[23] God does not abandon the face of the beloved, but is so fully present, that there is nothing to be seen except the beloved's face.

On this reading, Levinas and Barthes open for us the analogous or parodic[24] relationship between desire of the flesh and desire of that which is beyond all flesh, but on which all flesh depends. Levinas's concern to delineate a union without the dissolution or fusion of its terms repeats the 'mystical' concern of both Jewish and Christian traditions to think the relationship of creature to Creator without the destruction of one by the other. Indeed Levinas makes the two relationships homologous, so that eros names both sexual and mystical union, in which the 'absence of the other is precisely its presence as other'.[25] Moreover, the homologous terms do not appear successively, as if one led to the other, but intensively, inside one another. These intensive, interpenetrating relationships appear as the fundamental unknowability in that most intimate of knowledge, the caress and embrace of the other's body. This is one way in which sex is always alien sex; the cut and difference between bodies that brings them together and keeps them apart, even when – particularly when – they are most amorously conjoined. There is always an alien dimension in the most passionate of conjunctions, a dimension that discloses a yet deeper strangeness. It is this alien depth or intensity that has always already initiated the desire to know the otherness of and beyond the body. This is the theological venture upon alien sex that Levinas and Barthes here open for us. But it was, of course, opened much earlier in the Christian tradition, from its beginning.

Renunciation and Return

Ancient pagans, such as Galen, the second-century physician, were amazed by the early Christians' renunciation of sexual congress. 'Their contempt for death is patent to us every day, and likewise their restraint from intercourse. For they include not only men but also women who refrain from intercourse all through their lives.'[26] This text may be a later Christian interpolation, but second-century Christians, such as Clement of Alexandria (c. 150–c. 215), certainly boasted of their renunciation of sex, and indeed of sexual desire itself.[27] Yet, paradoxically, even as Christians put aside their sexual wants in pursuit of spiritual gratification, their bodies remained as the measure and, later, the figure of their mystical devotion. The ascetics of the fourth and fifth centuries who went into the desert to find their God, also found the deep sexuality of their bodies, that could always return to ground their spiritual ascents. Sexual craving became an inverse measure of their relationship to Christ, an 'ideogram', as Peter Brown puts it, of their 'unopened heart'.[28]

> [Sexuality] became the privileged window through which the monk could peer into the most private reaches of the soul. In the tradition of Evagrius,[29] sexual imaginings were scrutinized minutely in and of themselves. They were held to reveal concretely (if shamefully) the presence in the soul of yet more deadly, because more faceless drives: the cold cramp of anger, pride, and avarice. Hence the abatement of sexual imaginings, even the modification

> of night emissions, was closely observed as an index for the monk of the extent to which he had won through to a state of single-hearted translucence to the love of God and of his neighbours.[30]

Later medieval ascetics, who also sought to climb heaven's ladder, found in their bodily desires, not the measure of their failure, but a means for their ascent, the body becoming the locus for their union with Christ. These are most famously the women mystics of the thirteenth and fourteenth centuries, such as Hadewijch of Antwerp, Mechtild of Magdeburg (c. 1207–82) and Julian of Norwich (1342–1416). They did not need to renounce their own bodies in order to find Christ, since their flesh, like his, was already womanly, Christ having taken his humanity from his mother.[31] Male ascetics often imagined themselves in womanly terms, as they also imagined Jesus, from whose breasts they fed, and from whose maternity they were to receive and learn charity. 'Christ our Lord . . . stretches out his hands to embrace us, bows down his head to kiss us, and opens his side to give us suck; and though it is blood he offers us to suck we believe that it is health-giving and *sweeter than honey and the honey-comb* (Psalms 18.11).'[32] These men demonstrated their renunciation of the world by symbolically condescending to take on the socially inferior role of the woman, of the mother and nurse; but women were already that role, and so could only identify more intensely with what they already were. And they were the maternal humanity of Christ.

> The human mother will suckle her child with her own milk, but our beloved Mother, Jesus, feeds us with himself, and, with the most tender courtesy, does it by means of the Blessed Sacrament, the precious food of all true life . . . The human mother may put her child tenderly to her breast, but our tender Mother Jesus simply leads us into his blessed breast through his open side, and there gives us a glimpse of the Godhead and heavenly joy – the inner certainty of eternal bliss . . . A kind, loving mother who understands and knows the needs of her child will look after it tenderly just because it is the nature of a mother to do so. As the child grows older she changes her methods – but not her love.[33]

Moreover, for medieval women – as women – there was no pretence, no metaphor in their becoming brides of Christ. The nuns at Rupertsberg, where Hildegard of Bingen (1098–1179) was abbess, wore bridal gowns when receiving communion.[34] When they took Christ into their mouths, they were eating not only true flesh, but also the flesh of their bridegroom, their eternal lover. Thus eucharistic devotions could became ecstatic, passionate consummations of desire.

> Thus [Christ] gave himself to me in the shape of the sacrament, in its outward form, as the custom is; and then he gave me to drink from the chalice . . . After that he came himself to me, took me entirely in his arms, and pressed me to him; and all my members felt his in full felicity, in accordance with the desire of my heart and my humanity. So I was outwardly satisfied and fully transported. And then, for a short while, I had the strength to bear this; but soon, after a short time, I lost that manly beauty outwardly in the sight of his form. I saw him completely come to naught and so fade and all at once dissolve that I could no longer recognize or perceive him outside me, and I could no longer distinguish him within me. Then it was to me as if we were one without difference.[35]

In such oral copulation – when 'eating God', as Mechtild of Magdeburg put it[36] – the sexuality of these celibate women was not so much sublimated, as 'simply set free'.[37] The distinction between sexuality and sacramentality became indeterminate, and the body's desire participated in the desire of God. It was not only women, such as the thirteenth-century Hadewijch, who desired Christ's body, but men also. One day, in the twelfth century, Rupert of Deutz (c. 1075–1129/30) found the wooden figure of the crucified Christ – that he was wont to embrace – coming alive and returning his caress, and then, later, kissing him deeply with an open mouth, tongue to tongue.[38] The fourteenth-century hermit-theologian, Richard Rolle (d. 1349), warned against the snares of female flesh, the deadly delights of carnal desire, even within marriage.[39] But his longing for Christ is that of the lover for his beloved, and while alluding to the Song of Songs, and thus to the feminine soul,[40] Richard's 'lover' is undoubtedly male, a man who has escaped the love of women for a better, truer love.[41]

> I ask you, Lord Jesus
> To develop in me, your lover,
> An immeasurable urge towards you,
> An affection that is unbounded,
> A longing that is unrestrained,
> A fervour that throws discretion to the winds!
> The more worthwhile our love for you,
> All the more pressing does it become.
> Reason cannot hold it in check, fear does not make it tremble,
> Wise judgement does not temper it.[42]
>
> Jesus, when I am in you, and on fire with joy,
> And when the heat of love is surging in,
> I want to embrace you, the most loving, with my whole being.[43]

For a modern sensibility, Rolle's passionate treatise on the fire of divine love is intensely homoerotic, and the more so the more it denigrates the carnal and the sensual. For as with all this literature of divine love-making, Rolle must evoke the very thing he disparages in order to express a spiritual felicity that exceeds the embraces of interpenetrating bodies. The flesh he would shun provides the metaphoric body with which he embraces his heavenly lover. In drag, as the soul-bride of the Song of Songs, Rolle writes:

> [W]hen I feel the embrace and caress of my Sweetheart I swoon with unspeakable delight, for it is he – he whom true lovers put before all else, for love of him alone, and because of his unbounded goodness! And when he comes, may he come into me, suffusing me with his perfect love . . . Love is making me bold to summon my Beloved that he might comfort me, come unto me, and *kiss me with the kiss of his mouth.*[44] For the more I am raised above earthly thoughts the more fully do I enjoy the pleasure I long for; the more carnal longings are banished, so much the more truly do the eternal ones flare up. Let him kiss me and refresh me with his sweet love; let him hold me tight and kiss me on the mouth, else I die; let him pour his grace into me, that I grow in love.[45]

The sensual body is given up so that it can return, but now more bodily, more intensely, for 'the delights of loving Christ are sweeter than all the tasty pleasures of the world and the flesh'.[46] In Rolle, as in other medieval mystics, theology becomes an *ars erotica*. It is concerned with evoking the ecstatic union of the soul with Christ, that, even as it surpasses the pleasures of the flesh, always returns to the body; to the meeting, biting, engulfing of lips and tongues, to that fateful opening verse from the Song of Songs that resounds throughout medieval theological erotica: 'Let him kiss me with the kisses of his mouth!'[47]

In the Flesh

Ever since men and women began to tell the story of Jesus Christ, their relationship to God has been a relationship of the flesh, since God only comes to them in the body of the other.[48] The gospel has always been a story of carnal desire and erotic encounter, and only the gnostic who fears and hates the material world would deny this. It is supposed by many that Christians are called to renounce desire in favour of pious *apatheia*, but such a view misses the paradoxes of Christian thought. Paul – and certainly

Augustine after him – may have found desire the gateway for death, but in Christ death becomes the gateway to eternal life.[49] Paul may have urged the lustful to marry as a way of curbing their libido,[50] but at the same time they were to become the brides of Christ, impatient for the consummation of their wedding night.[51] Thus when the cultural critic, Jonathan Dollimore, tells us that for 'the early Christian ascetics', mutability had become the 'savage' agent of death, 'located firmly *inside* desire', he is only partly, patchily right; not really right at all.[52] His short account of saints Paul, Gregory of Nyssa, John Chrysostom and Augustine, attends only to the first part of the story, to the advent of death for want of an apple.[53] Dollimore entirely neglects the second part of the story, which for the saints is the more primordial: the advent of Christ out of desire of our desiring, of wanting only that we want his life, which is that of infinite eros. Dollimore rightly notes the connection of death with desire in Christian thought. But he misses their transfiguration in Christ: the turning of death into life, of mutability (entropy) and (sexual) want into the infinite becoming and boundless desire of the trinitarian charity, which as such is the source of their creaturely parodies (instability and sexual craving). Indeed, for Gregory of Nyssa (c. 330–c. 395), it is the ability to change toward the good, 'from glory to glory',[54] that is the mark of human perfection. 'For that perfection consists in our never stopping in our growth in good, never circumscribing our perfection by any limitation.'[55]

Desire is deathly for Gregory of Nyssa, but it is also the way of life, that which enraptures the soul and moves it toward the good, infinitely. This is not a matter of two different kinds of desire, as between two different kinds of love, eros and agape. The latter distinction, as famously advanced by Anders Nygren, is overwrought, overly concerned to delimit pagan passions from Christian charity, human from divine love.[56] In someone like Gregory of Nyssa, we find a much more fluid conception of the desiring body, and not least because the body is produced by desire. The body is drawn by the desirable, a movement occasioned by the attractive and beautiful, and so a motive participation in that which attracts, as a shining light catches the eye and makes us look. After Freud, it is too easy to assume that desire is only, or most fundamentally, hunger; and that this is how it was understood from the first, as when Socrates argues that Eros is the love of what is lacking, the child – as Diotima explains – of Poros and Penia, want and resourcefulness.[57] But Diotima's Eros does not want just anything, but that which is good, and it is the good by which Eros is enlivened, Eros being the love of the good.[58] Thus we are not so far from Plato's pagan eros when we come to the ascetic-theologians of the fourth century; but this is not because they were being pagan. They were being Christian. Gregory reads Plato through Exodus, not Exodus through Plato.

Gregory's Moses is an exemplar of the erotic man, who, replete with God's gifts, still yearns for that by which he is already filled, requesting as if he had never received, 'beseeching God to appear to him, not according to his capacity to partake, but according to God's true being'. Moses is the 'ardent lover of beauty' who yearns 'to be filled with the very stamp of the archetype'.[59] This erotic impulse can never be satiated, since God is infinitely other, and so always withdrawing and always arriving, filling the soul with the desire to follow after.[60] Just as Moses, placed in the cleft of the rock, was permitted to see God pass by, from behind, so God's arrival and appearing is at the same time a withdrawal, since God is always going on ahead, infinitely.[61] One can never get in front of God, and so never see his face. To see God is to follow God.[62] To ascend the mountain and see God is to see God's unseeability, an ever further distance.[63] It is to want to see God all the more. 'This truly is the vision of God: never to be satisfied in the desire to see him.'[64]

Desire of God is not simply opposed to the want of more earthly pleasures, since sensual desire is also of the good, and so a primer in desire for that which is alone truly good, for that which gives life. In his dialogue *On the Soul and the Resurrection*, Gregory's sister, Macrina – who plays Diotima to his Socrates[65] – tells us that the impulses of the soul can 'become instruments of virtue or wickedness', just as steel can be made into swords or ploughshares. Thus desire, when virtuously directed, can 'mediate to us the divine and immortal pleasure'.[66] Desire only becomes deathly when it mistakes a sign for that which is signified, an earthly for a heavenly good, turning us away from being itself, from the divine becoming that is excessive of all signs, the source of their coming to be and passing away.[67]

But more importantly, the desire for God is God;[68] it is God's attractiveness (beauty) in the world.[69] To desire God is already to participate in God, to be produced by God's desiring, and so to 'see' God, as Gregory teaches. Those who desire God do so because they are first desired by God, caught up into the dynamic of God's desiring, God's eternal, primordial movement. The priority of God's desire is figured in the arrow shot by the divine archer, wounding the soul with faith and love. Then the soul becomes the arrow, held firm in the arms of the archer,[70] shot forth and yet still embraced. 'All at once I am launched through space, and at the same time I rest in the hands of the Lord.'[71]

The becoming of the creature – that many contrast with the supposed stasis of the divine being – is, for Gregory, a reflection, an analogous movement, of the Creator's always prior becoming. The creature, who comes into being out of nothing, parodies the becoming of God out of God, the infinite source of becoming-being. The fountain in the garden of the Song of Songs provides Gregory with a profoundly paradoxical image for the eternal becoming of God, as of an ever-moving stillness.[72] Constantly flowing, never changing but always new, this water fills the soul with its life, so that the soul's love is the love of the ever-flowing waters, and these she receives when she kisses Christ, a divine gift of bodily fluids.

> This is truly the summit of paradox. For while all other wells contain their water in tranquil quiet, only the Bride possesses it flowing within herself, so that it has both a well's depth and a river's perpetual movement . . . In her minute way, she imitates the Fountain in becoming a fountain, Life in becoming life, Water in becoming water . . . And this Water flows from God (for the Fountain itself says: 'I emanate from God and I am coming'), and the soul welcomes it as it enters her basin, and the soul thus becomes a reservoir of living Water . . . The fountain is none other than the mouth of the Bridegroom, from which the words of eternal life gush forth . . . Since, then, he who wishes to drink ought to bring his mouth to the fountain, and since the Lord is himself this fountain . . . the soul that wishes to put her lips to this mouth from which Life springs forth says the following words: 'May he kiss me with a kiss from his mouth.'[73]

'I am going away, and I am coming to you'[74] (Trinitarian *Excursus*)

The Levinasian account of the erotic relationship, of the 'feminine' other or depth that, in the body of the other, withdraws as one draws near – drawing near by withdrawing – strangely parallels the triune structure of God's approach in Christ. For that also has the dynamic of drawing one into a mystery that withdraws even as it attracts, that attracts by withdrawing. But in the gospel, this depth or distance is not named the 'feminine', but the 'Father'. This is the name that Jesus gives to the mystery from which he comes and to which he goes, the absolute alterity that shines in his face, that draws people to him. The Father is the vertiginous depth of Christ's body, the dark density of his flesh, the distance that opens and draws on in his touch. When Philip asks to see the Father, Jesus is almost bewildered. 'Have I been with you all this time, Philip, and you still do not know me?'[75] For to be with Jesus is to see the Father. Has Philip not heard the paternal resonance in Jesus' voice? 'The words that I say to you I do not speak on my own; but the Father who dwells in me does his works.'[76] To see Jesus is to see the Father; and Jesus is all there is to see. It is the very movement of the Father's withdrawal that draws the disciple on. The Father is always arriving because always departing, as also Christ, who departs in order to return. 'I am going away, and I am coming to you.'[77]

This profoundly mystical, carnal theology was undone when it was supposed possible to see the Father other than by seeing Christ. The retreating, divine darkness of the flesh was lost once it became possible to image the Father other than by imaging Christ, to picture the Father as leaning over, watching, holding, or simply standing or sitting alongside the Son, to imagine the Father as one of three men.[78] This was to forget – perhaps never to have learned – the ascent of Moses toward the dark light of God's desire.[79] For, as Gregory of Nyssa taught, the more one sees in the light of God, the more one sees what is not seen, the uncontemplated in the contemplated.[80] 'This is the true knowledge of what is sought; this is the seeing that consists in not seeing, because that which is sought transcends all knowledge, being separated on all sides by incomprehensibility as by a kind of darkness.'[81] And this is to 'apprehend reality', as Gregory teaches, and catch there, in the light, the mystery that slips away from the light, the 'luminous darkness' that appears in the face of Christ, and then in the fellowship of the body.

That the Father appears only in the appearing of the Son was forgotten more in the West than in the East, but in the East also. The seventh ecumenical council (Nicea II, 787) reaffirmed the teaching of Pope Gregory II (669–731) that the Father cannot be represented apart from the Son, because no one knows what the Father is. '[I]f we had seen and known Him as we have seen and known His Son, we would have tried to describe Him and to represent Him in art.'[82] The only image fitting for the unseen Father is either no image at all, or the image of the Son in whom the unseen is seen. Picturing the Father alone is not merely an aesthetic failing, but a spiritual error, a fall into idolatry. The practice is widespread in the West and also in the East since the seventeenth century, and this despite the condemnation of such images by the Great Council of Moscow in 1666–67.[83] The Council was responding to existing images, to proliferating traditions of iconic representation that it could lament, but not halt. 'At a time when the Orthodox tradition was betrayed, as much in the image itself and in its conception as in thought, the decision of the Great Council of Moscow categorically to prohibit any representation of the Deity is an authentically Orthodox echo of the patristic theology of the icon.'[84]

Depicting the Father destroys the dynamic unity of the three-fold mystery. The doctrine of the Trinity ceases to be a primer in looking, a grammar for the seeing of Christ's body, and instead is reduced to a descriptive, tri-theistic speculation; a mythological fancy.[85] The triune movement can be seen – pictured – only intensively, as the darkness that appears in the light, as the depth of the surface that leads forward as it withdraws. By the light of the Spirit – the pentecostal flame – we can see the Father in the face of the Son, and the Son in the bodies of others.

Dispossessive Desire

Jesus said to the crowds who insisted on following him: 'Whoever comes to me and does not hate father and mother, wife and children, brothers and sisters, yes, and even life itself, cannot be my disciple'.[86] It would seem that those who would love and follow Jesus must hate everyone else, including those to whom they are most attached by blood and affection. Jesus is a jealous lover, who demands to be the sole object of their craving. He will not play the paramour, the 'bit on the side', the casual fling. Many have taken Jesus at his word and refused the amorous attention of others, denying themselves homely affection and sexual gratification, and fleeing their spouses and offspring for the quietude of the desert (the monastic abode). Thus, in the fourteenth century, Margery Kempe fled her husband's bed for the arms of Christ, who appeared to her, sitting on her bedside, as 'the most seemly, most beauteous, and most amiable' of men.[87] Before the Bishop of Lincoln, Margery and her husband, John, took a vow of chastity,[88] which was also, in effect, her marriage vow to Christ, with a ring on which – by Christ's command – she had engraved, 'Jesus est amor meus' (Jesus is my love).[89] Later she was to have a vision of Christ lying beside her, his face turned toward her, the 'handsomest man that ever might be seen or imagined'.[90] Christ had earlier explained to her that it 'is appropriate for the wife to be on homely terms with her husband. Be he ever so great a lord and she ever so poor a woman when he weds her, yet they must lie together and rest together in joy and peace. Just so must it be between you and me.'

> Therefore I must be intimate with you, and lie in your bed with you. Daughter, you greatly desire to see me, and you may boldly, when you are in bed, take me to you as your wedded husband, as your darling, and as your sweet son, for I want to be loved as a son should be loved by the mother, and

> I want you to love me, daughter, as a good wife ought to love her husband. Therefore you can boldly take me in the arms of your soul and kiss my mouth, my head, and my feet as sweetly as you want.[91]

Though, on her own account, Margery Kempe was considered crazed by many of her contemporaries, there is a touching domesticity about her devotion to Christ, even though he leads her to spurn more immediate, though mundane, affections. She is but one of many who have renounced the flesh in order to become one of Christ's 'exclusive' lovers, following his command to abandon all others for love of him, and this despite his obvious promiscuity (polygamy). For many today the demands of this singular devotion to Christ will seem too strange, too wayward, to offer a productive ascesis of desire, a truly charitable ascesis; but there is another way of taking Jesus at his word.

The implied injunction to abandon family and even life for the sake of Christ is followed in Luke by a more extended, but equally extravagant claim upon our credulity. Just as someone who would build a tower must first count the cost, or the king who would wage war must first estimate his chances of success, so the would-be disciples of Jesus must be equally prudent and give away all of their possessions.[92] Dispossession is necessary for discipleship; without it, those who would follow will go astray. To love Jesus alone, as he wants, one must be free of all possessive relationships, free of the illusion that other people belong to you, are yours, extensions of yourself. One cannot love Jesus possessively, since we are to be his, not he ours. Learning to love Jesus is learning to let him go. If we did not, we could not abide it that he loves others as much as he loves us, and loves them indiscriminately. The pain is not that Christ loves someone else, but anyone else, everyone else, even the person you most despise.

It would then be that to love Jesus exclusively is to be free to love others as well, but dispossessively. The gospels narrate the story of the disciples' training in such dispossessive love. They tell a love story about men and women who fall for Jesus, head over heels, blindly, as their families and friends must have thought, abandoning, as they did, everyone and everything in order to follow him. Each disciple chooses to follow Jesus freely, yet none can give a reason for doing so. As they fish, just off the edge of the sea, a stranger approaches and invites them to leave their nets, their livelihoods, and go with him. And they do.

The love story of Jesus and his disciples traces the turning of their possessive desire into a dispossessive love, so that at the last they no longer need to touch and hold on to him. They can let him go, and in that leaving find him returning. In this way they regain paradise. It would be wrong to think that the first disciples who spurned marriage, making themselves as if eunuchs for the kingdom of heaven,[93] or the later disciples who went into the desert, were simply fleeing the body and its wants. Rather they were pursuing a paradisal desire, that was not craving but charity, not the satisfaction of hunger but the pleasure of participating in the movement of the beautiful. In the garden, Adam and Eve coupled not out of want of being – of needing to be needed – but out of that abundant joy that comes from the beauty of the good, from the pleasure of being made for the making of love.[94] In a fallen world this is not something that is naturally given. It has to be learned, practised, and practised not just through renunciation but also in dispossessive forms of sexual relationship. This is a venture for the living flesh, the desiring body of Christ, the carnal community that, held in the embrace of the Lord, is shot forth as the arrow from the bow, wounded with the flight of desire.

*

Guy Pearce's body, Leonard's body, is repeatedly undressed in Nolan's *Memento*, as Leonard seeks for the clues to his past life that he thinks are written on his skin. But his body is unable to tell him the truth, since the significance of each terse message changes with each rereading of his flesh. Indeed, Leonard's body becomes increasingly lethal for those whom he encounters, a carnal mnemonic of their impending demise. Like them, he does not know how to read his own flesh, or reads it too late. The viewer of *Memento* has similar trouble in learning how to read Leonard's skin, and it is only at the end of the film that the beginning of the story becomes clear; only after one has left the cinema that the story preceding the film's narration becomes visible, in memory.

The meaning of *Memento* is sought in its back-story, in what has happened prior to the start of the film, the 'incident' that has traumatized Leonard's life. But in order to grasp this past, we, like Leonard with his notes and polaroids, have to recollect the film's diverse scenes, seeking their connections, in order to produce an orderly summary that will, perhaps, disclose the truth. There is a curious and pleasing parallel between this labour and the medieval monastic tradition of memory-work (*memoria*), which sought to contemplate divine truth through recollecting the words and images of scripture. The monk's first task was to divide the text into memorable sections, which the meditating monk could later recollect. As Hugh of

St Victor advised, we should 'from every study or lesson gather up things brief and secure, which we hide away in the little chest of our memory, from which later they may be drawn when any subject has need.'[95] For from these scriptural seeds, stored in our memory chests, will grow a 'great tree of knowledge', that will 'break into flame in our heart', as Peter Chrysologus put it in the fifth century.[96] The words of scripture begin to glow with meaning when recollected in memory.[97]

For the medieval tradition, memory is meditation, since the latter requires that we bring to mind those texts and images we have collected in our minds, and there allow them to burn with the intensity of their inexhaustible meaning.[98] Moreover, in recalling scripture we are remembering the future, since scripture shows us what is to come as well as what is past. Memory is never simply melancholic but always also anticipatory, a motive for action. Leonard moves forward by looking back, his scriptural seeds being the collection of notes, photographs and tattoos that he keeps on and about his person, which on each rereading and reordering impel him to new actions. His is an exterior memory, stored on his flesh and extended body.

The medieval tradition also developed an exterior memory, a mnemonic extension of the mind. In some instances this was the decorated cell, on the walls of which were painted images that were to be used for meditation, as in the monastery of San Marco in Florence, painted by Fra Angelico (Giovanni da Fiesole) in the 1440s. The retreat of the monk to his cell recalls the Roman tradition of withdrawing into a small room or closet (*exedra* or *cubiculum*), an 'invention chamber',[99] as Mary Carruthers calls it. There one could remember, meditate and compose one's thoughts, speeches and writings. In Cicero's dialogues 'On Oratory', Lucius Crassus retires to his closet, where he reclines on a couch (*lectulus*) while meditating on his debates with Marcus Antonius.[100] Such a room was likely to have been painted, not so much with subjects for reflection, as with pastoral scenes in which Crassus could wander meditatively, a matrix for the mind.[101] 'Such murals can be used to map out one's topics during invention, somewhat as a mandala-picture does in traditions of Buddhist contemplation. They provide "where" to catch hold of the process of thinking something through.'[102]

Like Crassus, the monk finds his cell the proper place for memory-work, and like the monk, Leonard retires to his motel room in order to remember and meditate upon his notes and other mementos. On his wall he pins up his map, around which he places his collection of polaroids. They form something like a medieval *pictura*, an arrangement of images in a church that, like the thinker's painted cubicle, provides a framework for meditation. The Venerable Bede tells us that the pictures Benedict Biscop brought back from Italy to Wearmouth, were so arranged in the church that all who entered, 'should either look on the gracious face of Christ and his saints, although in an image; or might recollect in their minds more feelingly the grace of the Lord's incarnation; or having the perils of the Last Judgement as it were before their eyes, might remember to examine their consciences more exactly'.[103] The images together formed a picture of the soul's place in Christ's story, of what has been and is to come, and which, when remembered, prompts the soul to action. So similarly Leonard, through the arrangement of his pictures and notes, seeks to find a meaningful world in which he can have an identity, a motive for moving forward.

Amorous Memory

In one scene of *Memento*, Leonard creates for himself another living memento in addition to his own body, hiring a hooker to play the part of his dead wife. As on the night when Leonard's wife was murdered, the hooker must get out of bed and go to the bathroom. Closing the door, she wakens Leonard, who reaches out to the now empty side of the bed, wondering where he is, but also, perhaps, recalling the body that once used to lie beside his own.

The monk's cell was also a site for remembered affections, since it was likened to the bridal chamber in the Song of Songs, a place for divine intimacies.[104] Bernard of Clairvaux likened the several senses of scripture – plain, moral and divine – to three spaces: the garden, the storehouse, in which the fruits of the garden are kept, and the bedroom in which the monk contemplates the garden's divine mystery, the soul's bridegroom.[105] But unlike Leonard's paid bed-companion – who is both a ghostly memento of his dead wife, and, when he finds her snorting coke in the bathroom, utterly mundane – the monk's lover is altogether more passionate. When the bride waits upon the bridegroom, the monk upon the Word in the words of scripture, it is best to be lying down, reclining on one's bed, as is Crassus in his cubiculum or Boethius in his cell, at the start of the *Consolation of Philosophy*, or, indeed, Augustine – lying on the ground – when he hears the words 'tolle, lege', take, read.[106] For then the bridegroom can 'wondrously and yet pleasurably' wear out the bride, as Bernard of Clairvaux remarks.[107]

The monk not only made love to the text, he also devoured it, since the most basic hunger for food could also provide a bodily trope for union with Christ. Texts were consumed in the refectory, along with the food, and later, when the monk was alone in his cell, those texts could – through *memoria* – give rise to visions, as food to dreams. From 'eating the book' came sight, and from sight new understanding and writing, a proliferation of texts.[108]

The monk on his bed was to read and recollect the words of scripture with desire, casting his lustful gaze upon the body of the text, finding consummation in the words written upon its skin.[109] Poor reading, inattentive and disordered, is a form of wantonness or fornication (*fornicatio*), a straying of thoughts (*peruagatio cogitationum*), a lack of faithful focus.[110] 'Our minds think of some passage of a psalm', John Cassian wrote. 'But it is taken away from us without our noticing it, and, stupidly, unknowingly, the spirit slips on to some other text of Scripture.'

> [T]he spirit rolls along from psalm to psalm, leaps from the gospel to St Paul, from Paul to the prophets, from there it is carried off to holy stories. Ever on the move, forever wandering, it is tossed along through all the body of Scripture, unable to settle on anything, unable to reject anything or hold on to anything, powerless to arrive at any full and judicious study.[111]

This is forever Leonard's plight, the difficulty of keeping focused, as he repeatedly reorders his memories, his notes and photographs. As long as he concentrates on a particular topic or task he can remember what he has just done, what he is doing and what he is going to do. But a sudden distraction – the slam of a car door – or a moment of tiredness, and his concentration is broken, the immediate past gone, and once more, like Sisyphus, he must begin his memorial labours.

Leonard strangely repeats the medieval practice of *memoria*, the memory-work by which texts and images are made to disclose their meanings. As with the monk who sought his identity in union with the body of Christ, so Leonard seeks in his own body for the identity he once had with his wife, whose absence from his bed is made present through repeated scenes of his awakening in motel beds or in the beds of others. And strangely, Leonard's memory-work figures that of *Alien Sex*, which is to read the flesh for signs of that other body in which our desires find their source and fulfilment. Like Leonard we have our own body texts – which include Leonard's body – and around which we have ordered a series of images. Our reading may be more wanton than John Cassian would have approved, but it is no less focused on the body's grace than is the monk's desire for the *visio Dei*. Texts and images form a *pictura* that, as at Wearmouth, will lead us to 'look on the gracious face of Christ and his saints, although in an image', and to recollect 'more feelingly the grace of the Lord's incarnation', the embodiment of the divine Eros.

Notes

1 Everything in the film is caressingly lit and crisply photographed by Wally Pfister. On the film and its making see James Mottram, *The Making of Memento* (London: Faber & Faber, 2002).

2 The film itself is a kind of mirror image, telling its tale in reverse order, so that the last scene of the story is the first in the film's narrative. Thus the viewer experiences something of Leonard's bewilderment, having to reinterpret each scene as the film retraces the course of events. The film can be understood only when remembered, when its scenes are reordered and differently connected.

3 Emmanuel Levinas, *Time and the Other*, translated by Richard A. Cohen (Pittsburgh, PA: Duquesne University Press, [1979] 1987), p. 86. For brief introductions to Levinas's thought see Richard Kearney, *Dialogues with Contemporary Continental Thinkers: The Phenomenological Heritage* (Manchester: Manchester University Press, 1984), pp. 47–70; Gerard Loughlin, 'Other Discourses', *New Blackfriars*, 75 (1994): 18–31. Levinas writes from within the tradition of phenomenology as most immediately determined by Edmund Husserl and Martin Heidegger, and inaugurated by René Descartes (see John Milbank, 'The Soul of Reciprocity Part One: Reciprocity Refused', *Modern Theology*, 17 (2001): 335–91). Though Levinas's reflections start out from the singular consciousness, they do not – *pace* Milbank – succumb to the dualism of self and body inaugurated in Cartesian thought. For Levinas, consciousness is always bodily, always the sensibility of corporeality. No less than Milbank, Levinas holds intersubjectivity to be at the same time interobjectivity. Milbank too closely follows Phillip Blond's wayward reading of Levinas's texts, which fails to attend to the 'erotic' in Levinas. See Phillip Blond, 'Emmanuel Levinas: God and Phenomenology', in *Post-Secular Philosophy: Between Philosophy and Theology*, edited by Phillip Blond (London: Routledge, 1998), pp. 195–228. For a more sensitive reading of Levinas that attends to the key notions of transcendent desire and 'proximity' see Brian Schroeder, 'The (Non)Logic of Desire and War: Hegel and Levinas' in *Philosophy and Desire*, edited by Hugh J. Silverman (New York: Routledge, 2000), pp. 45–62.

4 Emmanuel Levinas, *Totality and Infinity: An Essay on Exteriority*, translated by Alphonso Lingis (Pittsburgh: Duquesne University Press, [1961] 1969) p. 270.

5 Levinas, *Time and the Other*, p. 94.
6 Levinas, *Totality and Infinity*, p. 271.
7 Levinas, *Time and the Other*, p. 94; emphasis added. For an earlier statement of this view see *Existence and Existents*, translated by Alphonso Lingis (Pittsburgh, PA: Duquesne University Press, [1988] 1978/2001), pp. 98–9.
8 Levinas, *Time and the Other*, p. 86.
9 Levinas, *Time and the Other*, p. 87.
10 Levinas, *Time and the Other*, p. 88.
11 Levinas, *Time and the Other*, p. 88.
12 Emmanuel Levinas, *Ethics and Infinity: Conversations with Philippe Nemo*, translated by Richard A. Cohen (Pittsburgh, PA: Duquesne University Press, [1982] 1985), p. 66.
13 Simone de Beauvoir, *The Second Sex*, translated and edited by H.M. Parshley (London: Everyman's Library, [1949] 1993), p. xlv.
14 Levinas, *Ethics and Infinity*, p. 68.
15 See Richard A. Cohen, *Elevations: The Height of the Good in Rosenzweig and Levinas* (Chicago: University of Chicago Press, 1994), ch. 9. It would seem that Luce Irigaray mistakes Levinas's deployment of these terms, as does Tina Chanter. See Luce Irigaray, 'The Fecundity of the Caress', in *An Ethics of Sexual Difference*, translated by Carolyn Burke and Gillian C. Gill (London: Athlone Press, [1984] 1993), pp. 185–217; and Tina Chanter, *Ethics of Eros: Irigaray's Rewriting of the Philosophers* (London: Routledge, 1995), ch. 5. But see also Tina Chanter's more nuanced, searching and 'charitable' critique of Levinas in *Time, Death, and the Feminine: Levinas with Heidegger* (Stanford, CA: Stanford University Press, 2001), ch. 1 and conclusion (pp. 37–74, 241–60).
16 The same would hold for Levinas's use of 'maternity' in *Otherwise than Being*, where it names the ethical relationship of responsibility for the other. 'Maternity, which is bearing par excellence, bears even responsibility for the persecuting by the persecutor.' But this does not mean that men are outside the ethical relationship. See Emmanuel Levinas, *Otherwise than Being, or, Beyond Essence*, translated by Alphonso Lingis (Pittsburgh, PA: Duquesne University Press, [1974] 1998), p. 75.
17 Levinas, *Ethics and Infinity*, pp. 68–9.
18 Plato, *The Symposium*, 189c–193c; in *The Dialogues of Plato*, vol. 2, translated by R.E. Allen (New Haven: Yale University Press, 1991), pp. 130–4. See Levinas, *Totality and Infinity*, p. 254; and *Time and the Other*, p. 86.
19 For a discussion of 'complementarity' see Gareth Moore, *The Body in Context: Sex and Catholicism* (London: SCM Press, 1992), ch. 7. Moore shows how much theology inscribes a set of differing cultural stereotypes upon the bodies of men and women. Thus Henry Peschke tells us that the 'male is more active and outgoing; he possesses greater courage to assail. The female is more receptive and protective; she shows greater fortitude to endure . . . The logic of facts and keen penetration are characteristic of the man; the

woman is more led by emotion, sensitivity and intuition. He is ruled by principles, she by love.' (C.H. Peschke, *Christian Ethics* [Dublin: Goodliffe Neale, 1978], vol. 2, p. 377; quoted in Moore, *Body in Context*, p. 121.) Such a differentiation of the sexes is a solipsistic return to the same, since the womanly traits are the disavowed projection of a masculine paranoia. See further Daphne Hampson, *After Christianity* (London: SCM Press, 1996), pp. 192–3, and chapter 6 (Sex Slaves) below.

20 Levinas, *Time and the Other*, p. 89.

21 Roland Barthes, *A Lover's Discourse: Fragments*, translated by Richard Howard (London: Jonathan Cape, [1977] 1979), p. 135.

22 Levinas, *Totality and Infinity*, p. 270.

23 Christian theology finds the coming of God in the 'going towards God' that, for Levinas, is the 'going towards the other person'. 'I can only go towards God by being ethically concerned by and for the other person.' Levinas in Kearney, *Dialogues with Contemporary Continental Thinkers*, p. 59.

24 See further below, chapter 5 (God's Sex).

25 Levinas, *Time and the Other*, p. 94.

26 Galen quoted in Peter Brown, *The Body and Society: Men, Women and Sexual Renunciation in Early Christianity* (London: Faber & Faber, 1988), p. 33.

27 Brown, *Body and Society*, p. 31.

28 Brown, *Body and Society*, p. 230.

29 Evagrius Ponticus (346–99) departed Constantinople for the Nitrian desert, between Alexandria and Cairo. His writings, particularly his treatise on prayer, influenced later ascetic theologians, such as John Cassian (c. 360–c. 430) and Maximus the Confessor (c. 580–662).

30 Peter Brown, 'Late Antiquity' in *A History of Private Life*, vol. 1: *From Pagan Rome to Byzantium*, edited by Paul Veyne (Cambridge, MA: Harvard University Press, 1987), pp. 235–311 (p. 300).

31 Here I am following the argument of Caroline Walker Bynum, as developed in her wonderful collection of essays, *Fragmentation and Redemption: Essays on Gender and the Human Body in Medieval Religion* (New York: Zone Books, 1992). For a contrary judgement on a slightly earlier, twelfth-century tradition of 'affective mysticism' see Grace M. Jantzen, *Power, Gender and Christian Mysticism* (Cambridge: Cambridge University Press, 1995), pp. 123–33. '[F]or a man to become spiritual he must increasingly become what he is; but for a woman to become spiritual, she must become what she is not' (p. 130). But this plays down the extent to which someone like Bernard of Clairvaux (1090–1153) – whom Jantzen discusses at this point – played the 'bride' in relation to Christ his bridegroom, and 'mother' to his monks – a maternity that was not merely sentimental but practical, required for the well-being of the monastic family. See further Caroline Walker Bynum, *Jesus as Mother: Studies in the Spirituality of the High Middle Ages* (Berkeley: University of California Press, 1982), ch. 4.

32 *The Monk of Farne: The Meditations of a Fourteenth-Century Monk*, translated by a Benedictine nun of Stanbrook (Baltimore: Helicon Press, 1961), p. 64; quoted in Bynum, *Fragmentation and Redemption*, p. 159. See further Bynum, *Jesus as Mother*, ch. 4. While attending to those medieval men who availed themselves of a womanly persona, it should be noted that in the later medieval period the attribution of feminine qualities was increasingly confined to women. See Hildegard Elisabeth Keller, *My Secret Is Mine: Studies on Religion and Eros in the German Middle Ages* (Leuven: Peeters, 2000), ch. 1. Keller describes the solidifying of earlier (Origenist) gender fluidities as a process of 'sexualization', since it tied both genders to their nominal sexes (p. 32). She follows John Bugge in identifying Bernard of Clairvaux's bridal mysticism as the paradoxical 'apotheosis of the woman's marriage to Christ' (John Bugge, *Virginitas: An Essay in the History of a Medieval Ideal* (The Hague: Martinus Nijhoff, 1975), p. 92). After Bernard, it became increasingly difficult for men to play the bride. Instead, they were confined to playing the brothers of the bridegroom, his representatives or panders, guiding women to his marriage bed. In modernity it is still just possible for men to play the bride, but in Catholicism women are definitively excluded from the role of the bridegroom, unlike men. It is part of the burden of *Alien Sex* to advocate a 'return' to a more fluid body. For premodern mutability see further Caroline Walker Bynum, *Metamorphosis and Identity* (New York: Zone Books, 2001). Bynum crosses narrative with Judith Butler's 'performativity' to produce a sense of 'self' as a *changing* storied 'shape'. '[M]y self is my story, known only in my shape, in the marks and visible behaviors I manifest – whether generic or personal. I am my skin and scars, my gender and pigment, my height and bearing, *all forever changing* – not just a performance, as some contemporary theory would have it, but a story.' (Bynum, *Metamorphosis and Identity*, p. 181; emphasis added.)

33 Julian of Norwich, *Revelations of Divine Love*, translated by Clifton Wolters (Harmondsworth: Penguin Books, 1966), ch. 60 (p. 170); cited also in Bynum, *Fragmentation and Redemption*, p. 164.

34 Bynum, *Fragmentation and Redemption*, p. 61.

35 Hadewijch, vision 7, in *Hadewijch: The Complete Works*, translated by Columba Hart (New York: Paulist Press, 1980), pp. 280–1; quoted in Bynum, *Fragmentation and Redemption*, p. 120.

36 Mechtild quoted in Bynum, *Fragmentation and Redemption*, p. 130.

37 Bynum, *Fragmentation and Redemption*, p. 134.

38 See John H. Van Engwen, *Rupert of Deutz* (Berkeley: University of California Press, 1983), pp. 51–2; cited in Bynum, *Fragmentation and Redemption*, p. 86.

39 '[T]here are men so perverse that they are consumed by uncontrollable lust for their own wives for the sake of their beauty, and the more quickly the body is reduced by their strength, the more they give themselves to satisfy their carnal lusts. But even while they are enjoying their delights they are beginning to fail; while they flourish they perish.' Richard Rolle, *The Fire*

of Love, translated by Clifton Walters (Harmondsworth: Penguin Books, 1972), ch. 24 (p. 117). For Rolle, as for St Paul long before him, marriage is the antidote to lust. On this view of marriage see further below, chapter 6 (Sex Slaves).

40 Rolle, *Fire of Love*, ch. 26 (p. 122).

41 '[A] man who honestly wants to love Christ must not let his imagination toy with the love of women.' Rolle, *Fire of Love*, ch. 29 (p. 136). Rolle does admit that there are pleasures in female companionship – 'as for example in mutual conversation, or seemly contact, or a happy marriage' – but men and women must not 'indulge the voluptuous pleasure of carnal love, and come together in their vile passion', as would seem to have been happening all around him. Rolle, *Fire of Love*, ch. 39 (p. 176), ch. 41 (p. 188).

42 Rolle, *Fire of Love*, ch. 17 (pp. 98–9).

43 Rolle, *Fire of Love*, ch. 35 (p. 154).

44 Song of Songs 1.2.

45 Rolle, *Fire of Love*, ch. 26 (pp. 123–5).

46 Rolle, *Fire of Love*, ch. 26 (p. 126).

47 See Denys Turner, *Eros and Allegory: Medieval Exegesis of the Song of Songs* (Kalamazoo: Cistercian Publications, 1995) and E. Ann Matter, *The Voice of my Beloved: The Song of Songs in Western Medieval Christianity* (Pennsylvania: University of Pennsylvania Press, 1990). The Song of Songs was to exert its influence beyond the medieval period into that of the early modern, informing the mystical writings of two of its most notable exponents, the Spanish Carmelites, St John of the Cross (1542–91) and St Teresa of Ávila (1515–82). Both saints wrote in what Richard Rambuss identifies as a tradition of 'sacred eroticism', stemming from the Song of Songs, and which continued, for example, in the less obviously 'mystical' writings of seventeenth-century English poets like Richard Crashaw (1612/13–49), John Donne (1572–1631) and George Herbert (1593–1633). See Richard Rambuss, *Closet Devotions* (Durham, NC: Duke University Press, 1998). Other Renaissance poets who might be placed in this tradition, from across Europe, are Miguel de Guevara (c. 1585–c. 1646), Jean de La Ceppède (1548–1623) and the Polish poet Zbigniew Morsztyn (c. 1620–90). See Peggy Rosenthal, *The Poets' Jesus: Representations at the End of a Millennium* (New York: Oxford University Press, 2000), pp. 14–17. For the Song of Songs in the Protestant Reformation see George L. Scheper, 'Reformation Attitudes Toward Allegory and the Song of Songs', *PMLA (Proceedings of the Modern Language Association of America)*, 89 (1974): 551–62.

48 Matthew 25.45.

49 Romans 5.12–21.

50 1 Corinthians 7.2. See further below chapter 6 (Sex Slaves).

51 See 2 Corinthians 11.2 and Ephesians 5.27, and behind them – in the tradition of mystical interpretation – the Song of Songs. As noted by John A.T. Robinson, sexual union with Christ is also used by Paul in 1 Corinthians

6.17 and Romans 7.4. See *The Body: A Study in Pauline Theology* (London: SCM Press, 1952), p. 64.

52 Jonathan Dollimore, *Death, Desire and Loss in Western Culture* (London: Allen Lane The Penguin Press, 1998), p. 43.

53 The identification of the tree of knowledge of good and evil (Genesis 2.16–17) as an apple tree derives from the Song of Songs 2.5 and 7.8. But the tree has also been identified as a figtree.

54 2 Corinthians 3.18. King James version.

55 Gregory of Nyssa, *On Perfection*, PG 46.285A-D, quoted in *From Glory to Glory: Texts from Gregory of Nyssa's Mystical Writings*, translated by Herbert Musurillo SJ (Crestwood, NY: St Vladimir's Seminary Press, [1961] 1979), p. 84. See also in the same book Jean Daniélou's introduction, pp. 46–56; and Rowan Williams, *The Wound of Knowledge: Christian Spirituality from the New Testament to St John of the Cross* (London: Darton, Longman & Todd, 1979), pp. 62–4.

56 Anders Nygren, *Agape and Eros*, translated by Philip S. Watson (London: SPCK, [1932–9] 1953). Nygren distinguishes vulgar from heavenly eros, the love of the sensible from the supersensible, and insists that between vulgar eros and Christian agape 'there is no relation at all', whereas between Christian agape and heavenly eros there is a born rivalry, the one 'entering the lists' against the other. 'Agape stands alongside, not above, the heavenly Eros; the difference between them is not one of degree but of kind. There is no way, not even that of sublimation, which leads over from Eros to Agape' (pp. 51–2). Though not mentioning Nygren, Francis Watson – in *Agape, Eros, Gender: Towards a Pauline Sexual Ethic* (Cambridge: Cambridge University Press, 2000) – similarly divorces agape from eros, placing the latter outside the domain of the former, excluded from the *ekklesia* (p. 208), the *koinonia* of agape (p. 211) which permits only a sanctified eros, when it is kept behind the veil (p. 259), its beauty hidden from view.

57 Plato, *Symposium*, 200e, 203a–e (pp. 143, 146–7). Freud did not write so much about desire (*Begehren*) as about the wish (*Wunsch*) and the libido. But he explicitly identified libido with hunger, and his extended notion of sexuality with the 'Eros of the divine Plato.' See Sigmund Freud, 'Three Essays on the Theory of Sexuality' (1905) in *The Penguin Freud Library*, vol. 7: *On Sexuality*, edited by James Strachey and Angela Richards (Harmondsworth: Penguin Books, 1991), pp. 43 and 45.

58 Plato, *Symposium*, 206a (p. 150).

59 Gregory of Nyssa, *Life of Moses*, translated by Abraham J. Malherbe and Everett Ferguson (New York: Paulist Press, 1978), paragraphs 230 and 231 (p. 114). As Enobarbus says of Cleopatra, God 'makes hungry where most she satisfies'. (William Shakespeare, *Antony and Cleopatra*, Act III, Scene 2, ll. 237–8.) I am grateful to Brian Horne for reminding me of this line. For much of the following exposition I am indebted to Hans Urs von Balthasar,

Presence and Thought: An Essay on the Religious Philosophy of Gregory of Nyssa, translated by Mark Sebanc (San Francisco: Ignatius Press, [1988] 1995).

60 John 14.28.

61 Exodus 33.21–23.

62 Gregory of Nyssa, *Life of Moses*, paragraphs 251–253 (pp. 119–20); quoted in Balthasar, *Presence and Thought*, p. 102. For a homoerotic reading of Gregory's reading of Moses' encounter with God, the pleasure of which I forgo, see Virginia Burrus, *'Begotten, Not Made': Conceiving Manhood in Late Antiquity* (Stanford, CA: Stanford University Press, 2000), pp. 127–9.

63 Gregory of Nyssa, *Life of Moses*, paragraphs 232 and 233 (pp. 114–15).

64 Gregory of Nyssa, *Life of Moses*, paragraph 239 (p. 116).

65 Gregory's dialogue is complexly related to Plato's *Symposium*, *Phaedrus* and *Phaedo*. For discussion of Gregory's 'Macrina', arguing that she is both Diotima and Socrates, the means by which Gregory can be both feminized 'man' and masculinized 'woman', see Burrus, *'Begotten, Not Made'*, pp. 112–22.

66 Gregory of Nyssa, *On the Soul and the Resurrection*, translated by Catherine P. Roth (Crestwood, NY: St Vladimir's Seminary Press, 1993), ch. 3 (p. 57). See Balthasar, *Presence and Thought*, p. 160 n. 25.

67 Gregory of Nyssa, *Life of Moses*, paragraph 234 (p. 115).

68 'God is love, and those who abide in love abide in God, and God abides in them' (1 John 4.16).

69 'And I, when I am lifted up from the earth, will draw all people to myself.' (John 12.32.) Christ's death on the cross is paradigmatic of God's dispossessive love, the divine eros that is not want, but love of the good; the beauty of the trinitarian charity.

70 Song of Songs 2.6.

71 Gregory of Nyssa, *Commentary on the Song of Songs*, 852A–853A; quoted in Balthasar, *Presence and Thought*, p. 160. In late medieval German interpretations of the Song of Songs, the soul-bride herself becomes an archer, who, when she ravishes the bridegroom's heart with the glance of her eyes (Song of Songs 4.9), shoots Christ with her arrow, or pierces him with her spear. '[T]he soul forces God to do what she wants. This is called wounding because the soul acquires power over God, she draws her bow and shoots him in the heart. The bow which she draws is her heart. She draws it and shoots in heated desire for God and hits the true mark. In this way she attains the highest point of perfection.' (*Das Buch der geistlichen Armuth*, 64.13–19; quoted in Keller, *My Secret Is Mine*, p. 253.) On this and other remarkable gender reversals, in which a feminine/phallic soul penetrates Christ, see Keller, *My Secret Is Mine*, ch.5, especially pp. 248–60. However, Christ's wounding by the bride's love is not unique to this German tradition, and can be found in the early modern period. See, for example, Fray de los Angeles (1532–1609), *The Loving Struggle between God and the Soul*, translated by Eladia Gómez-Posthill (London: Saint Austin Press, [1600] 2000). 'The more

pliable the bow is, the more it curves, and the farther the arrow will go . . . Similarly, the greater our humility and trust in God, the higher the soul will soar, and the more we shall wound him [God] in love' (p. 76).

72 Song of Songs 4.12–15.

73 Gregory of Nyssa, *Commentary on the Song of Songs*, 780A; quoted in Balthasar, *Presence and Thought*, pp. 157–8.

74 John 14.28.

75 John 14.9.

76 John 14.10.

77 John 14.28.

78 The tradition developed various images of the Father, such as in the Old Testament Trinity of the three 'angels' who visited Abraham and Sarah (Genesis 18.1), now most famously painted by Andrei Rublev (c. 1411). But this was not a direct imaging of the Trinity, since the divine persons 'appear' as the three androgynous guests seated at Rublev's table. More direct imagining of the Father appears in the Divine Paternity, with the Son on the lap of the Father, and the Spirit in the form of a dove (also known as the Seat of Mercy – *Gnudenstuhl* – when the Father displays the crucified body of the Son); or in the New Testament Trinity that seats Father and Son on thrones, again with the dove of the Spirit. But the Father truly came into his own when he began to be represented as the Ancient of Days from Daniel 7.9. For many in the West this old man, with his hair like 'pure wool', is God the Father; the deity of bourgeois patriarchy (as pictured by William Blake).

79 Exodus 20.21.

80 Gregory of Nyssa, *Life of Moses*, paragraph 162 (p. 95).

81 Gregory of Nyssa, *Life of Moses*, paragraph 163 (p. 95).

82 Pope Gregory II to the iconoclast emperor Leo III; quoted in Leonid Ouspensky, *The Theology of the Icon* (Crestwood, NY: St Vladimir's Press, 1992), vol. 1, p. 154. This statement was produced in the midst of the iconclast crisis, with its inception in 726, when the Christ icon above the golden gateway of the imperial palace in Constantinople was destroyed, and its conclusion in 843, with the Council of Constantinople that declared the Triumph of Orthodoxy. These exact dates are, of course, imprecise measures of eighth to ninth-century iconoclasm.

83 Ouspensky, *Theology of the Icon*, vol. 1, p. 154; vol. 2, ch. 16 (pp. 371–409).

84 Ouspensky, *Theology of the Icon*, vol. 2, p. 409.

85 The point is not that depictions of the Father are 'faulty intellectual exercises', as David Brown supposes, but that they are faulty visions, failures of the imagination. See David Brown, 'The Trinity in Art', in *The Trinity: An Interdisciplinary Symposium on the Trinity*, edited by Stephen T. Davis, Daniel Kendall SJ and Gerald O'Collins SJ (Oxford: Oxford University Press, 1999), pp. 329–56 (p. 352). It is even more wide of the mark to suppose that the objection to imaging the Father stems 'from residual notions of the Father

as in some sense superior to the other two persons in virtue of being their *arche* or source' (pp. 344–5). On the contrary, it is the image of the divine paternity that promotes the subordination of the Son to the Father. On the doctrine of the Trinity as grammar see Gerard Loughlin, *Telling God's Story: Bible Church and Narrative Theology* (Cambridge: Cambridge University Press, [1996] 1999), pp. 190–7.

86 Luke 14.26.

87 *The Book of Margery Kempe*, translated by B.A. Windeatt (Harmondsworth: Penguin Books, 1985), bk I, ch. 1 (p. 42).

88 *Book of Margery Kempe*, bk I, ch. 15 (p. 69). On the practice of chaste marriage see Dyan Elliot, *Spiritual Marriage: Sexual Abstinence in Medieval Wedlock* (Princeton: Princeton University Press, 1993).

89 *Book of Margery Kempe*, bk I, ch. 31 (p. 114).

90 *Book of Margery Kempe*, bk I, ch. 85 (p. 249).

91 *Book of Margery Kempe*, bk I, ch. 36 (p. 126).

92 Luke 14.28–33.

93 Matthew 19.12.

94 Genesis 1.28–31. Here I am imagining, *pace* Augustine and others, that Adam and Eve enjoyed prelapsarian sex before their expulsion from paradise. On the garden see further below, chapter 9 (*The Garden*).

95 Hugh of St Victor, 'De modo dicendi et meditandi', *Patrologia latina* 176.878; quoted in Mary Carruthers, *The Craft of Thought: Meditation, Rhetoric, and the Making of Images, 400–1200* (Cambridge: Cambridge University Press, 1998), p. 64. I am indebted to Carruthers' marvellous book for the medieval tradition of memory-work utilized in this section of the chapter. On medieval memory see also Mary Carruthers' early work *The Book of Memory: A Study of Memory in Medieval Culture* (Cambridge: Cambridge University Press, 1990) and Janet Coleman, *Ancient Medieval Memories: Studies in the Reconstruction of the Past* (Cambridge: Cambridge University Press, 1992).

96 Peter Chrysologus, *Sermo* 98, ll. 28.33 (Corpus christianorum, series latina 24A.603); quoted in Carruthers, *Craft of Thought*, p. 64.

97 Peter Chrysologus, *Sermo* 96, ll. 6–10 (Corpus christianorum, series latina 24A.592); quoted in Carruthers, *Craft of Thought*, p. 45.

98 In meditation we remember not the past, but present tokens of the past. See Augustine, *Confessions*, translated by Henry Chadwick (Oxford: Oxford University Press, 1992), X.8 (12); and on Augustine's memory see Coleman, *Ancient and Medieval Memories*, ch. 6. 'In so far as any past experience has meaning, its meaning is in the present grasped by the mind's gaze. Whatever the pastness of the past is, it *is* only in the present and the meaning itself has no temporal modes despite the ambiguities of grammar. There is a sense, then, in which Augustine the Roman orator has destroyed the past as meaningfully distinct from the now, and made all Christians paradoxically memoryless' (p. 100). Leonard's present is Augustine's memoryless memory.

99 Carruthers, *Craft of Thought*, p. 177.

100 Cicero, *De Oratore*, III.v.17 in the Loeb Classical Library; quoted in Carruthers, *Craft of Thought*, p. 177. On Cicero see further Coleman, *Ancient and Medieval Memories*, ch. 3.

101 Carruthers points us to the cubiculum from the Pompeian villa of Fannius Synestor at Boscoreale (40–30 BC), which can now be seen in the Metropolitan Museum of Art, New York. See Carruthers, *Craft of Thought*, pl. 15.

102 Carruthers, *Craft of Thought*, p. 178.

103 Bede, *Vita sanctorum abbatum monasterii in Uyramutha et Gyruum*, 6 (Loeb Classical Library); quoted in her own translation in Carruthers, *Craft of Thought*, p. 204.

104 Carruthers, *Craft of Thought*, p. 171.

105 Bernard of Clairvaux, *Sermones super Cantica*, 23.II.3; quoted in Carruthers, p. 240.

106 'I threw myself down somehow under a certain figtree, and let my tears flow freely.' Augustine, *Confessions*, VIII.12 (28), p. 152. '[T]he scene as a whole, from start to finish, is a paradigmatic instance of the inventive orthopraxis of reading described by others among [Augustine's] contemporaries. Its steps include the thinker's initial anguish expressed and maintained by his continual weeping, his cognitive use of mental imaging, his repetition of Psalm *formulae*, his prone posture to resolve the crisis in his thinking.' Carruthers, *Craft of Thought*, p. 176.

107 Bernard of Clairvaux, *Sermons super Cantica*, 23.IV.11; quoted in Carruthers, *Craft of Thought*, p. 176.

108 Revelation 10.9–10; Ezekiel 2.8–3.3. See Loughlin, *Telling God's Story*, pp. 102–3, 244–5.

109 Carruthers, *Craft of Thought*, p. 111.

110 See John Cassian, *Conference* XIV.11 in *The Nicene and Post-Nicene Fathers*, edited by Philip Schaff and Henry Wace (Edinburgh: T. & T. Clark, 1998), vol. XI (Sulpitus Severus, Vincent of Lerins, John Cassian), p. 441; quoted in Carruthers, *Craft of Thought*, p. 82.

111 John Cassian, *Conference* X.13 in *Nicene and Post-Nicene Fathers*, vol. XI, p. 409; translated in Carruthers, *Craft of Thought*, p. 83.

Part II

CAVITIES

Upon my bed at night I sought him whom my soul loves.
(Song of Songs 3.1).

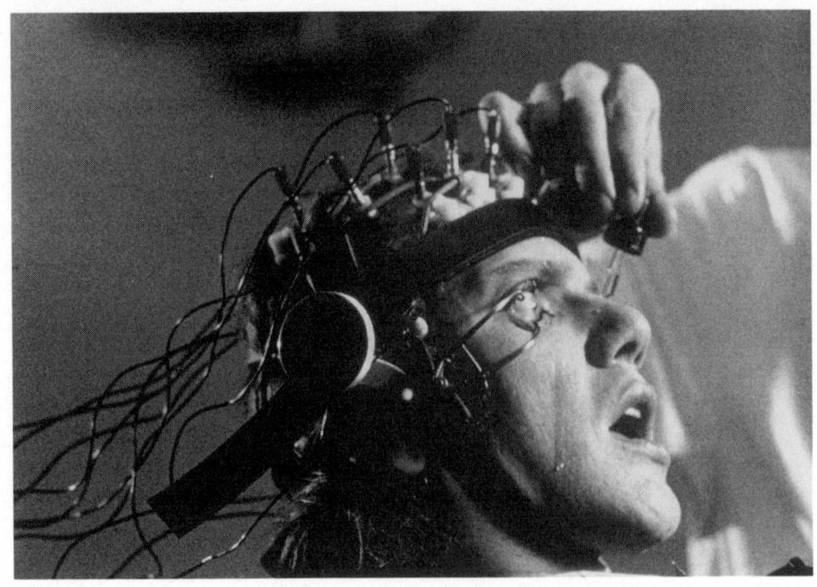

Figure 2 Looking in the Cave

Alex (Malcolm McDowell) in *A Clockwork Orange* (Stanley Kubrick, UK 1972).
Photo: British Film Institute.

Chapter 2

SEEING IN THE DARK

If at first we walked in a garden, of grasses, herbs and fruit trees,[1] and rested beneath their boughs, we later sought darker refuge in the safety of the cave. We were become like the apes, the early hominids, who, at the beginning of Stanley Kubrick's *2001: A Space Odyssey* (1968), shelter beneath rock, fearful of the night and its savageries. While Kubrick's film tells the story of our ascent from the cave, from the earth on which we walk to the stars above our heads, it is still told in the cavern of the cinema, a technological marvel that mimics the ancient practice of telling stories in the shelter of the night, when the sun has set and it can no longer dazzle our eyes, blinding us to other imagined worlds, other ways of being human.

Plato's parable of the cave locates the truth of the world outside and above the cave, among the stars.[2] Yet it would seem that the cave is the womb of our imagination, the place in which we can see the truth of the real. Rather than escaping the cave, we must go within in order to see what is without. This trope is the burden of this chapter, a reversal of Plato – and thus in some sense still Platonic – that is repeated in thinking about church and cinema. I shall suggest that in both cinematic and ecclesial caverns, the real is suspended, bracketed, and that this is not its destruction but its mobilization. This suspension of the real is necessary for faithful living, for being able to see and live by the light that burns in the dark.

This necessity is not without its dangers, however, and it is with the fear of images, of shadows and illusions, that I begin. In the first instance, these are the images of ancient religion, and in the second, those of modern cinema. To look upon either is to participate in phantom, alien dreams, the imaginings of others. Entering the darkened chamber of temple or cinema permits a reciprocal entry, through the eye, of alien spectres. The danger is one of demon possession.

Demons

From the earliest days of cinema, the perceived power of film to possess its viewers, impelled the desire to control the content and distribution of films. While those concerned to resist censorship asserted film's ineffectuality or neutrality, propagandists of all persuasions saw in cinema a tool for social transformation. For in writing its images on the silver screen, the cinema writes them on the retina of the eye, and thus on the mind of the viewer. The light of the image strikes from screen to screen, from the cinematic to the retinal, the first reflecting, the second altogether more permeable, allowing the image to penetrate to that final screen which is the play of consciousness itself. As Freud mused, the mind is like a 'photographic apparatus, or something of the kind', forming conscious images at an ideal, intangible point within the apparatus.[3] If today scientists are proposing a prosthetic cinema, a machine that writes moving images directly on the retina of the eye,[4] they are only intensifying what has long been feared from before the birth of the cinema: that to look upon an image is to be looked at, and thus possessed, the image taking up residence within the mind and body of the viewer.

Such was the fear of the second-century Christian apologists who sought immunity from the hostility of neighbours and local authorities. They wrote their apologies in order to gain freedom for themselves and their co-religionists to profess the name of Christian without persecution.[5] For the most part, their texts flatter and entreat their addressees, defend the author and his fellow Christians and revile their enemies. To the latter are ascribed all manner of foolishness, including the worship of images. In their attack on Greek religious art, the Christian apologists sought to show the congruence of Hebrew prophecy with Greek philosophy, indeed drawing upon an older tradition of Hellenistic-Jewish apology, and like it, asserting the dependency of the philosophers on the prophets. The ancient wisdom of both Greek and Hebrew supported the Christians' denunciation of contemporary religious art, and in this they flattered their addressees' contempt for popular and superstitious forms of religiosity.

Christians did not participate in the worship of the temples, nor publicize their own cultic practices. This led to the charge of atheism, to which the apologists responded with a Stoic disdain for cult objects and rituals. The temples, divine images and sacrifices were at best allegories of where the invisible God is to be truly found and worshipped: in the human person and in a virtuous life. The truly spiritual, God-filled person has no need of imagery. Moreover, in rejecting religious imagery, the Christians were seeking to repeat that earlier, more primitive time, when, as many pagans believed, society was simpler and purer, and people worshipped without images.[6]

Clement of Alexandria alone among the apologists used the Platonic topography of two worlds, upper and lower, noetic and phenomenal, to denounce religious art as illusion and deceit. Mimetic artistry produces only shadows of the things it would portray, and this is especially so in seeking to picture the divine, since what are reproduced – human and animal forms – are themselves merely shadows, phenomenal objects of which we have opinion but no true knowledge. The dangers inherent in the making and use of such objects are evident in the story of Pygmalion, whose love for the simulacrum of his own making can never be returned. The realism and beauty of the statue is deathly. Thus Christians, in refusing the allure of the mimetic arts, refuse the enthralment of shadows and are able to worship the invisible God.[7]

The deceit and impropriety of representing the invisible God was further supported by appeal to the ancient Greek tradition of anti-anthropomorphism in religion, which mocked the idea that in a human form one can see the God who is like no one.[8] Clement's pagan contemporary, Celsus, could press this even further, in claiming against Genesis, that man was not made in the image of God because God has no form whatsoever.[9] The apologists, in addition to accusing the pagan Greeks of anthropomorphism, chided them for being hylotheists, worshippers of matter (*hyle*). Ignoring the symbolic interpretation of cult figures, the apologists mocked those who worshipped sticks and stones, mistaking them for the non-material divine.[10]

Notwithstanding their scorn for those who imbued insensible matter with divinity, the apologists contended that demonic powers had taken up residence in cult statues. They made this accusation in defending Christians against the charge of superstition, turning the accusation against their accusers, while insisting upon the calm, rational and inward nature of Christian piety. The apologists attributed the foolishness of pagan idol worship to the power of the demons who, in animating the otherwise senseless cult images, took possession of their acolytes. These demons were in a sense material, having bodies that needed to be fed on the blood and scraps of the cult sacrifices. 'It is these demons [*daimones*]', Athenagoras tells us, 'who drag men to images', and 'give birth to illusions which bring with them a mad passion for idols'.

> When the soul is weak and docile, ignorant and unacquainted with sound teachings, unable to contemplate the truth . . . the demons associated with

> matter, because they are greedy for the savour of fat and the blood of sacrifices, and because their business is to delude humans, take hold of these deceitful movements in the soul of many, and by invading their thoughts flood them with illusory images which seem to come from the idols and statues.[11]

For Athenagoras and other apologists, idol worship is ethically debilitating, leading to moral and mental collapse. The degeneration attendant upon cult worship is nowhere more evident than in the sexual licence sanctioned by stories of divine debauchery, the sexual misdemeanours of the gods, whose material images were foolishly, dangerously worshipped in the temples. In this way the apologists again turned an accusation – that of sexual immorality – against their accusers. It was not Christians, but pagans who flouted common decency through their worship of immoral divinities. The behaviour of Christians was altogether seemly, and their complaint against pagan perversity was one already made of Homer and Hesiod by Greek moralists, such as Plato.

There are of course instabilities in the apologists' ridicule of their opponents. On the one hand they mocked the idea that senseless matter could be imbued with spiritual presence through consecration, yet on the other hand, they allowed in some cases the effectiveness of such invocations, albeit to conjure malign forces. More generally, they practised their own Christian cult, which involved the use of material objects, and which was premised on the belief that God had taken human form in Christ and took form again in the eucharistic elements. Thus the attack on Greek religious art has to be understood as a particular polemic, responding in kind to specific accusations. Pagans and not Christians, fail to worship true divinity, mistaking matter for spirit; pagans and not Christians are given to superstition and sexual licence, and the focus and (imbued) agent of these failings is the cult image; a mere shadow of a shadow, flickering in the fire-light of the temple, wreathed in the smoke and stench of slaughtered animals.

The second-century apologists are not therefore anomalous with regard to the later development of Christian art, as it came to adorn the underground burial chambers of third-century Christians. Nor anomalous with regard to the possible use by Christians, already in the second century, of generic figures, such as shepherds and fishermen, for pietistic purposes.[12] Neither do the apologetic texts rule out the later use, from the fourth century onwards, of images in the Christian cult; pictures and effigies of Christ, his mother and the other saints. Later Christians could always avoid the gross errors that the apologists attributed to pagan imagery, by deploying a symbolist theory, a distinction between signifier and signified – the very move advanced by astute pagans, but tactically ignored by the apologists. Nevertheless, the second-century apologists exemplify a recurring distrust of representation in general, and of religious imagery in particular, especially where it encroaches upon divine invisibility. Moreover, they ethicized the making and use of images, as leading to vicious rather than virtuous behaviour. Though often dormant, this concern has never died in Greco-Western and Christian traditions, and has attended the cinema throughout its life.

At the end of 1973, just after Christmas, William Friedkin's film of William Peter Blatty's *The Exorcist* was released in North America. The effect that the film and its publicity had on audiences in America and elsewhere, make it a perfect metaphor for the power of film. Its story of demon possession so possessed audiences that many thought the film itself possessed. The Christian evangelist, Billy Graham, reputedly asserted that there was an evil 'embodied' or 'buried' within 'the celluloid of the film itself'.[13]

Set in the suburbs of Washington DC, the film tells the story of the young Regan McNeil's (Linda Blair) possession by an ancient, pre-Christian force, the demon Pazuzu, and its eventual exorcism by Father Damien Karras SJ (Jason Miller). In the interests of 'verisimilitude', Friedkin insisted that the special effects should, for the most part, be produced on set, mechanically, rather than optically,[14] and any creakiness in the stage machinery was disguised through skilful editing and pacing of the material, and the manipulative use of sound effects. The publicity for the film prepared audiences to expect something more than mere trickery, something that was perhaps truly demonic.

Thus the film's production was believed to have been cursed, with a number of deaths attributed to its malignancy. The actor Jack MacGowran died shortly after completing his scenes in the film. Linda Blair's grandfather died, as did the brother of Max von Sydow, who was playing the part of Father Merrin SJ. There were various injuries and mishaps during filming, and eventually the studio set burnt down, and on a Sunday. Friedkin was not averse to spreading these stories, blaming delays in the production of the film on the interference of devils.[15] He also suggested that there was something fiendish about the special effects, inventing bogus explanations, such as the use of electro-magnetism for the levitation of Linda Blair, and asserting of her head's bone-breaking 360 degree turn, that 'any way you think I did it is not the way we did it'.[16]

While the combination of skilful acting, inventive effects and cinematic craft, with astute publicity, produced a commercial success, it also produced devilish effects in its audiences. Reportedly, people vomited and fainted, had heart attacks and miscarriages, all of which furthered interest in the film, for as one woman said, 'I want to see what everybody is throwing up about'.[17] Four women in Toronto were in need of psychiatric care after seeing the film. In Europe there were reports of people so possessed by the film, that they were led to criminal and suicidal behaviour. There were calls for the film to be banned in West Germany when a teenager shot himself after seeing the film, and in England people made the obvious connection when a 16-year-old boy died from an epileptic attack, a day after seeing *The Exorcist*. In 1974, the murderer of a 19-year-old girl pleaded that he had felt something take possession of him when seeing the film. 'It was not really me that did it. There was something inside me'.[18] It is little wonder then that the Christian 'Festival of Light' in Britain picketed showings of the film, warning against demonic powers; though in 1975 the film was banned in Tunisia for being Christian propaganda.[19]

William Friedkin's film is exemplary of cinema's power to affect an audience, because at least in popular folklore, its audiences, or some members of them, became possessed in the way that its central character is possessed. Like her, they underwent physical changes, fainting and vomiting, and in more extreme cases, causing harm to themselves and others. The film itself became the possessing agent, the demon; its celluloid became demonic. Moreover, within the film, the demon is itself metaphoric of cinema, since it possesses the girl in order to be seen and cause terror in those who witness her possession. As Mark Kermode notes in his analysis of the film, various characters – Regan's mother, the doctors and priests – on hearing the demonic noises within Regan's bedroom, rush toward it and the camera rushes with them and enters the room with them.[20] But before we are shown what is within, we are shown the revulsion and terror on their faces, as they stand in the doorway, looking in, spectators of the film's horror. We see in them what is about to happen to us, as we too are caught in the gaze of the cinematic demon.

As in the second century so in the twentieth, people fear possession by the images on which they like to look. They fear that they or others, usually others, will be corrupted by showings in the dark, by powers that at the same time they know to be illusions: senseless matter and shadows on the wall. And as in the second century so in the twentieth, Plato's parable of the cave proves to be an enduring picture of our relationship to images, as much in the picture palace as in the temple. For uncannily, at the dawn of philosophy, Plato imagined the cinema: the projection of moving pictures in the dark, a trick of light and shade taken for reality.

Plato's Cinema

> Imagine the condition of men living in a sort of cavernous chamber underground, with an entrance open to the light and a long passage all down the cave. Here they have been from childhood, chained by the leg and also by the neck, so that they cannot move and can see only what is in front of them, because the chains will not let them turn their heads. At some distance higher up is the light of a fire burning behind them; and between the prisoners and the fire is a track with a parapet along it, like the screen at a puppet show, which hides the performers while they show their puppets over the top . . . Now behind this parapet imagine persons carrying along various artificial objects, including figures of men and animals in wood or stone or other materials, which project above the parapet. Naturally, some of these persons will be talking, others silent . . . prisoners so confined would have seen nothing of themselves or one another, except the shadows thrown by the fire-light on the wall of the Cave facing them . . . And they would have seen as little of the objects carried past . . . Now, if they could talk to one another, would they not suppose that their words referred only to those passing shadows which they saw? . . . And suppose their prison had an echo from the wall facing them? When one of the people crossing behind them spoke, they could only suppose that the sound came from the shadow passing before their eyes . . . In every way, then, such prisoners would recognize as reality nothing but the shadows of those artificial objects.[21]

Since the invention of cinema, its affinity with Plato's cave has often been remarked. F. M. Cornford, in his 1941 translation and commentary on *The Republic*, noted that a 'modern Plato would compare his cave to an underground cinema, where the audience watch the play of shadows thrown by the film passing before a light at their backs.'

> The film itself is only an image of the 'real' things and events in the world outside the cinema. For the film Plato has to substitute the clumsier apparatus of a procession of artificial objects carried on their heads by persons who are merely part of the machinery, providing for the movement of the objects and the sounds whose echo the prisoners hear.[22]

The puppeteers or mechanicals, who are merely part of the cave's machinery, answer to that other chamber which precedes the projector and the screen, namely the mechanical eye, the *camera obscura* that produces the celluloid image, the puppet or effigy whose shadow is cast on the wall of the cave. Like cinematic screen images, Plato's shadows are double simulations, the ghosts of ghosts.

Plato, and the Christian apologists after him, would have us shun these phantoms, especially when the product of the poetic imagination, since as such they are insubstantial deceits; doubly deceitful not only in the structure of their production, being twice removed from source, but also in their deceiving. They not only pass themselves off as realities, but offer corrupted images of the Good, presenting the degenerate as edifying. They are treacherous, both ontologically and ethically (epistemologically).[23] Thus Socrates objects to 'Homer and Hesiod and the poets' for telling stories about gods who commit horrible crimes, punish fathers unmercifully and make war among themselves. The children of the state should not be told such tales, but rather stories 'designed to produce the best possible effect' in them, by showing only excellent characters.[24] In the modern world it is not only Homer and Hesiod we must shun, but the fictions that play in our contemporary cave, the cinema, which is also one of our cherished temples, where the screen deities enthral and excite our devotions.

When in May 1967, Michael Cooper and Terry Southern submitted a screenplay of Anthony Burgess' novel *A Clockwork Orange* (1962) to the British Board of Film Censors, they were told that it was unacceptable, that it would not get even an X certificate. While Audrey Field, in her censor's report, noted that the script contained a moral message indicting a 'world in which violence is the only law and human beings are programmed like computers', she felt that the Board could not countenance the showing of 'vicious violence and hooliganism by teenagers' to teenagers.[25] Nothing came of the Cooper–Southern script, which the producer Sandy Lieberson wanted to film with Mick Jagger and the other Rolling Stones, nor of Ken Russell's interest in the novel.[26] Instead it was filmed by Stanley Kubrick, with Malcolm McDowell in the lead role, the film being released at the end of 1971 in North America, and at the beginning of 1972 in Britain, with an X certificate.

Kubrick's film answers to the problematic of Plato's cave, not only because it is illusory like all films, a play of shadows, and not only because it seemed – in the eyes of some – to laud the deplorable, inviting the audience to exult with its protagonists in scenes of brutality and rape, but because it thematizes the seductive power and social effects of cinema.[27] The narrator of both book and film, whose narration beguiles reader and viewer, is Alex DeLarge,[28] a mere youth of 15 in the book, though significantly older in the film – Malcolm McDowell being nearly 28 when he played the character. Alex still lives with his parents and nominally attends school, but spends most of his time with his droogs (friends), speaking their Russian-cockney slang or nadsat, drinking at the Korova milkbar, where the milkshakes are laced with more than fruit-flavours, real 'horrorshow' (good), and indulging in acts of violence: beating up tramps, fighting other gangs, and making surprise visits on such as the author of *A Clockwork Orange*, 'making his litso [face] all purple and dripping away like some very special sort of juicy fruit', and gang-raping his wife.[29] Alex and his droogs also go to the 'sinny' (cinema), though 'only for a yell or a razrez [cut, rip, tear] or a bit of in-and-out in the dark'. But that is the 'filthy old Filmdrome, peeling and dropping to bits'.[30] Later in the story Alex enters a somewhat different cinema, a modern version of Plato's cave.

Plato's picturegoers are held in their seats and made to look at the screen, at the flickering shadows on the back wall of the cave, and listen to the reflected sounds of the puppeteers, which they take to be made by the shadows. The inhabitants of the cave are like those people who sit in the front row of the cinema, so as to avoid all distractions and lose themselves in the world of the film; like the philosopher Wittgenstein, who would sit 'as far to the front as he could get', leaning forward in his seat so as to be 'utterly absorbed by the film'.[31] But Plato's movie-watchers have no choice in the matter, they are more like Alex in Kubrick's film, as he undergoes the Ludovico technique, a 'very simple but very drastic' behavioural therapy.[32] The technique is intended to cure Alex of his desire for 'ultra-violence', and at first seems to involve nothing more than going to the pictures and watching some films. But Alex is strapped into his seat, his head clamped and his eyes held open, so that he cannot shut his 'glazzies' but must watch the film, which turns out to be not so much 'horrorshow', as 'a real show of horrors'.[33]

Alex is shown scenes of extreme violence – a man being beaten, a woman being raped – as well as war footage of Nazi troops and aerial bombardments. Alex is impressed.

> So far the first film was a very good professional piece of sinny, like it was made in Hollywood. The sounds were real horrorshow. You could slooshy the screams and moans, very realistic, and you could even get the heavy breathing and panting of the tolchocking malchicks, at the same time. And then what do you know. Soon our dear old friend the red red vino on tap, the same in all places like it is put out by the same big firm, began to flow. It was beautiful. It's funny how the colours of the real world only seem really real when you viddy them on the screen.[34]

However, as Alex continues to watch, unable to take his gaze from the screen, he begins to realise that he is 'not feeling all that well'.[35] The scenes that would once have excited him, now take on new associations as the drug with which he has been dosed begins to take effect, causing violent nausea. After nearly two weeks of this treatment the drug is no longer needed, the mere thought, let alone sight, of aggressive behaviour induces sickness. Even in sleep, in dreams – which Alex thinks are 'really only like a film inside your gulliver [head]'[36] – the treatment has its effect, and he awakes retching. In this way Alex is cured, and he is returned to the community.

Alex is not affected by the horror films in themselves, but by the drug that attends them, administered by the cinema's technicians. To have an effect, the film images must first be augmented by the drug, the *pharmakon* that saves by making ill. It is not the images as such, but the context of their viewing that affects Alex. The peaceable Alex is produced by infusing the images with the power to promote fear and distress, rather than incite emulation. Dr Brodsky and his assistants are like the puppeteers in Plato's cave. In the novel, Alex first sees them as 'shadows' moving behind a wall of 'frosted glass' beneath the 'projection holes' in the back wall of the cinema.[37] Like Plato's mechanicals, they produce the images on the screen, but they also produce associated feelings in Alex. In this, they are less like the mechanicals and more like the demons in the temples, who 'drag men to images', and 'by invading their thoughts flood them with illusory images which seem to come from the idols and statues'. It is not the images, but the demons by which people are possessed, and in Alex's case the demons are Dr Brodsky and his assistants.

For Anthony Burgess, the central burden of his story is that Alex is perhaps more sinned against than sinning in having his free will destroyed through the Ludovico technique, making him a moral automaton, a clockwork orange. In the novel this concern is expressed by the prison 'charlie' [chaplain], who protests that Alex has ceased to be both a wrongdoer and a 'creature capable of moral choice'.[38] At the end of the novel, Alex regains his moral freedom, and in the last chapter begins to abandon his former life, becoming increasingly interested in settling down and fathering a child. He freely becomes what 'society' would wish him to be. However, this last chapter was omitted from the American edition of the book, and it was this edition that Kubrick filmed, so that in the movie Alex's regained 'freedom' still leads him to choose self-indulgence and violence. As a consequence, the film can seem more concerned with the good of choosing than with that which is chosen. Yet the film's undoubted irony may be more subtle than Burgess's own reworking of this theme in his musical-play version of *A Clockwork Orange*, which ends with a chorus in which the value of 'free choice' is lauded as the meaning of 'human freedom'.[39]

The chorus was written in protest against the ending of Kubrick's film, being immediately preceded by the stage direction: 'A man bearded like Stanley Kubrick comes on playing, in exquisite counterpoint, "Singin' in the Rain" on a trumpet. He is kicked off the stage.'[40] Unfortunately, the chorus so emphasizes choice for choice's sake, that one forgets that Alex's change of interests is not simply a matter of choice but of the company he keeps and the passage of time – he has just turned 18 at the end of the novel. Ethics is not just a matter of 'will', but of bodies and their social contexts, of their schooling in moral imagination. New images have come to dominate Alex's life.

> Walking the dark chill bastards of winter streets . . . I kept viddying like visions, like these cartoons in gazettas. There was Your Humble Narrator Alex coming home from work to a good hot plate of dinner, and there was this ptitsa all welcoming and greeting like loving . . . I had this sudden very strong idea that if I walked into the room next to this room where the fire was burning away and my hot dinner laid on the table, there I should find what I really wanted . . . for in that other room in a cot was laying gurgling goo goo goo my son. Yes yes yes, brothers, my son. And now I felt this bolshy big hollow inside my plott, feeling very surprised too at myself. I knew what was happening, O my brothers. I was like growing up.[41]

Neither the book nor the film excuses Alex's behaviour, but in both moral depravity is shown to afflict all sections of society. This is especially evident in the film, where victims as well as assailants inhabit a pornographic culture that relentlessly codes women as sexual objects, ever ready to comply with heterosexual male fantasies. Most famously, the Korova milk-bar, in which the film opens, is furnished with naked female mannequins, legs apart and breasts thrust forward.[42] As well as Alex and his droogs, the Korova also attracts 'sophistos from the TV studios around the corner'. Later in the film, one of the droogs' bourgeois victims is killed with a 'very important work of art', a large ceramic phallus.[43] The demons are everywhere, as are the images they inhabit.

Yet both Plato and the apologists imagined that it is possible to escape the illusory and deceitful and find a way out of the cave, to the real, the true and the good. The apologists in particular invoked a Christian worship free from the dangers in the temples. But in Plato matters are not so certain, and we must now explore the paradox of Plato's parable, before turning to consider why the church can no more escape the cave than it can the cinema, but must ceaselessly venture the difference between shadows, between demon and Spirit.

Socrates' Magic

Plato's parable of the cave supposes that we can see the distinction between shadow and reality, interior and exterior. Plato's Socrates adopts an omniscient perspective that can see both sides of the parapet wall, both the puppets and the shadows they cast. Yet at the same time, Socrates insists that both he and his interlocutor, Glaucon, are inside the cave, on the inner side of the parapet wall. For 'the prison dwelling corresponds to the region revealed to us through the sense of sight, and the fire-light within it to the power of the Sun'.[44] It is a moment of Platonic irony. For if the parable of the cave is true, if we and Socrates mistake shadows for reality, then Socrates' parable is itself but an appearance, a flickering shadow on the wall of the cave, an illusion; and more generally, what we take to be real, is really shadow.

This paradox often goes unremarked, or if noted then disarmed. Thus Desmond Lee cautions against taking Plato 'too solemnly'. Plato only means that 'the ordinary man is often very uncritical in his beliefs', and we are to suppose that neither Socrates nor Glaucon, or ourselves, are ordinary men.[45] But Plato's analogy in this regard is quite specific: the sun is the fire, and we are the prisoners, and as such see only shadows. This is why Glaucon has already been warned that Socrates' account might be a forgery. The three related similes of sun, line and cave are all meant to suggest what the Good is like, but they are only shadows, children (copies) rather than parents (originals), interest on a loan but not the loan itself. 'You must see to it', Socrates warns, that 'I do not inadvertently cheat you with false coin'.[46] Thus while Socrates is 'caught in his own game',[47] as Luce Irigaray puts it, and forgetful of the screen upon which the Good is projected, this necessary subterfuge is yet slyly remarked by Socrates. Philosophers are magicians also.

To live in Plato's cave, not as one of the prisoners, but as Socrates or Glaucon, would be to live like John Murdoch in Alex Proyas's *Dark City* (1997). In the time before the story of the film opens, Murdoch (Rufus Sewell) is like most of the city's other inhabitants, prisoners who do not know they are prisoners in a city that is the projection of the 'strangers', aliens who come among them as animated corpses, demons in dead matter.

Each night, at midnight, the city stops. Its machinery halts, and everyone sleeps. It is then that the strangers transform the city through their collective and mechanically augmented will power, raising and lowering city blocks, rearranging roads and rail tracks, and changing the memories of the city's inhabitants. No one has knowledge of these nocturnal transformations, which occur both within and without their minds; no one knows that they – and not the aliens – are really strangers to themselves, their bodies occupied by multiple characters. No one realizes that it is always night in the city, and that no one has been outside its limits, which anyway can never be found, because the roads are never quite as remembered. Anyone searching for the exit loses the way. The story of the film is the escape of the 'prisoner' Murdoch from the cave of the city.

Murdoch's escape is at first accidental, in that the drugs administered to change his memories don't take, and he awakens as the city sleeps, having gained some of the strangers' telekinetic powers. Later, his journey out of the city-cave is assisted by Dr Schreber (Kiefer Sutherland), who is reluctantly working for the strangers, producing the memory cocktails that are nightly administered to the city's sleeping inhabitants. Schreber inducts Murdoch into the mechanism of the dream-city. Like Socrates to Glaucon, Schreber carefully explains to Murdoch the means by which the shadows are cast. In order to learn the secret of the city, Murdoch does not ascend above it, but is led beneath it, into its bowels. Nor is he simply the prisoner become Glaucon, he is a Glaucon who comes to realize that Socrates' tale of an upper, more real world, is itself a shadow, a forgery.

Throughout the film, Murdoch is searching for the city's exterior, impelled by childhood memories of a visit to a seaside resort, Shell Beach, of which he has a memorial postcard. They are memories of golden sand, blue sea and bright sunlight, and they are all the product of one of Dr Schreber's cocktails. By insisting on the veracity of this memory, Murdoch is led to a door through which both he and we the audience, momentarily catch a glimpse of sea and sky, before realizing that it is only an electrically lit hoarding, advertising the pleasures of Shell Beach. Refusing to admit that his memory is but an illusion, and convinced that he has reached the edge of the city, Murdoch tears down the poster, and begins to smash the wall behind it, until he breaks through, revealing that outside the city there is nothing, save the limitless depths of outer-space. The city is a machine between worlds, producing its reality out of the dreams and memories of its human inhabitants, as these are cut and pasted by the strangers. The view of the city in the void is an impossible one, seen with dead eyes, apparently those of Inspector Bumstead (William Hurt), as he is swept through the hole in the wall, and out, not into an upper world of dazzling light, but into the darkness of the void, punctured only by distant stars.

Proyas's interpretation of Plato's parable takes seriously Socrates' warning to Glaucon as to its veracity, the fact that Socrates tells his tale from within the cave, imagining an exterior that can be only a shadowy projection. At the end of Proyas's film, Murdoch defeats the strangers, and takes control of the city's cinematic apparatus, remaking the world after his own desires and memories. He surrounds the city with a sea, and makes the sun to rise, before walking off with his beloved, toward Shell Beach. In this way the film has a conventional 'happy ending', that is nevertheless disturbing, since John Murdoch's newly enlightened world exists only as he wills it, based on childhood memories that are themselves illusions, without originals within the city-cave. Plato offers no reason for the apparatus of his cave-world, for why the mechanicals run it as they do.[48] Proyas's puppeteers – the strangers – are aliens who have perhaps abducted their prisoners from the earth, in order to study the nature of humanity, but the original of the city is off-stage, unknown and unknowable. Its reality is suspended or bracketed.

Reality is equally suspended in Plato, since it is located outside that which can be known. Plato ventures that the story of the cave is a shadow of this outside, but it is only a venture, a flickering of fire-light. Can we trust the mechanical, the philosopher-magician who shows us the shadow? In Proyas's retelling of the story, Murdoch takes control of the cave, and from then on he will conjure the shadows, and the inhabitants of the once dark city must trust his judgement. Murdoch answers to a certain contemporary nihilism, since unlike Plato, he is disabused of any hope of an outside. For him, there is now only the cave, and he is its Demiurge. Might the same not be said of those who inhabit the church, since they also are a kind of dreamer, and the church a kind of cave, a kind of cinema?

Contesting Cinema

When Camille Paglia first saw Walt Disney's *Snow White and the Seven Dwarfs* (1937), she was transfixed by the Wicked Queen, a 'temperamental diva bitch', who didn't have to be charitable and didn't have to be nice. The Wicked Queen was totally unlike the Virgin Mary, the ideal of womanhood that Catholicism presented to the young Camille. 'OK? Mary, this silent mother; and here was the witch queen who has this weird dialogue in the mirror and it didn't have to be charitable and it didn't have to be nice. I thought she was fabulous'.[49] There was simply no competition. The contest between the Wicked Queen and the Queen of Heaven may seem frivolous, but Paglia contends that cinema is 'the single biggest cultural threat to the Christian church since Islam in the medieval period'.[50]

In the Wicked Queen, Paglia sees not only the projection of negativity toward the real mother, but also the return of a 'pre-Christian form of the malevolent nature mother', a 'persona lying utterly outside the moral universe of Christianity'.[51] This answers to Paglia's more general contention, that in cinema – and especially the cinema of Hollywood – we see the return of repressed but never finally vanquished pagan powers. 'The twentieth century is not the Age of Anxiety but the Age of Hollywood. The pagan cult of personality has reawakened and dominates all art, all thought. It is morally empty but ritually profound. We worship it by the power of the western eye. Movie screen and television screen are its sacred precincts'.[52] Once more the demons drag people to images and intoxicate their minds with illusions.

Camille Paglia is not the first to have suggested a fundamental contest between church and cinema. As early as 1913, Edward Rees noted that the poor and destitute of England had learned to escape the 'squalid monochrome' of their lives and gratify the 'lust of the eye' at 'the pictures'. For 'twopence' they could sit for two hours in a 'pleasant torpor', revelling in the 'exploits of Jim and Cracksman and Moose Jaw's scalping raid'. The passivity of their viewing produced a 'febrile type of character, feeble in self-direction, hungry for pleasure, and expectant of it without the preliminary tax which makes pleasure healthful'. The poor squandered their money on such a doubtful pleasure because the pictures offered them a sight of paradise with which neither the music hall, public house or 'Primitive Methodist chapel' could compete. Rees warned that the pictures threatened 'the churches and friendly societies, certain theatres and goose clubs with unheeding impartiality'.[53]

A more recent staging of the conflict between church and cinema, and the moral enervation of the latter, was offered by David Lodge in his first novel *The Picturegoers* (1960). The novel describes the impact of the local cinema on the Catholic community of 'Brickley', and the fruitless attempts of Father Kipling to win back his flock from the temptations of what Alex and his droogs will come to know as the 'sinny'. Father Kipling is convinced that the Saturday night flicks are an occasion of sin, and in a desperate bid to offer a rival attraction, moves the Thursday Benediction to Saturday evening, which results in empty pews.[54]

As the character Mark Underwood notes, Father Kipling is 'fighting a losing battle'.[55] Cinema has already become a substitute for religion, and Mark fears that it will become a substitute for life. But as a substitute for religion, cinema parodies the church, so that the church in its worship becomes a less interesting, less seductive parody of the cinema. Mark muses that 'going to church was like going to the cinema: you sat in rows, the notices were like trailers, the supporting sermon was changed weekly. And people went because they always went. You paid at the plate instead of at the box-office, and sometimes they played the organ. There was only one big difference: the main feature was always the same'.[56] Yet this recurring 'feature' is not without its effect, offering an education in 'looking' that by the end of the novel, has led Mark to lose his atheistic faith and resolve on life as a Dominican.

Christ's Cave

Cinema can be viewed as a quasi-religious practice. It is this not only in its use of religious symbols and themes, but in and through its social practice, which congregates people in the dark for visions of desire. Like church, cinema creates social bonds through the projection of other forms of life that exceed the mundane, through the production of visions or dreams that can be sustained only through their repeated attendance. Of course, one might want to say that cinema as religion is an impoverished substitution for what the church offers, even if it is as close as many people now come to the latter. One might also want to question the longevity of such a socio-religious practice much beyond the twentieth century, for it is possible that we are now living in the last days of cinema. Technological developments promise new media, which will intensify what is increasingly for many their only social bond, the consumption of infinitely commodified pleasures. Nevertheless, movie going has enjoyed a rebirth in recent years, with the advent of video, DVD and pay-TV enhancing rather than diminishing the communal viewing of film.[57] It is as if the video of the film, usually only available sometime after the release of the picture in the movie house, has become part of household devotion, not supplanting but supplementing communal worship. It is like the candle blessed in the church, taken home and used for apotropaic effect, which in the case of the video is to avert tedium and constitute a socio-sacral memory of the film through repetitious viewing of it in whole or in part, alone or with partners and friends.

One might want to say that the church is more akin to theatre than cinema, since its visions are not merely presented in word and image, but dramatically enacted, both liturgically and charitably, in the services and sacrifices of common life. Indeed, insofar as modern Western theatre has its roots in the liturgies of the medieval church, we may properly think the church's worship theatrical: the staging of a story for the edification of an audience.[58] The religious play-cycles of late fourteenth and fifteenth-century Europe, dramatized and supplemented the biblical story, and were performed in the civic spaces of town and city. They had been developed from early, more obviously ecclesial performances. The most influential of these were the Palm Sunday and then the Corpus Christi processions, that were staged with enthusiasm throughout fourteenth-century Europe.[59] The progress of the consecrated host, the Blessed Sacrament, out of the church and into the marketplace, or around the bounds of the parish, came to be accompanied by increasingly elaborate *tableau vivants*, mimes of the Christian mysteries (*mystères mimés*) that were performed on wagons and drawn through the streets. Such mobile theatrical scenes largely predated the later and more sophisticated mystery and miracle plays, such as those performed at the end of the fourteenth century in York (England), and that used elaborate props and scenery, requiring stationary staging.[60] The civic performance of these divine dramas became the pride and joy of the craft-gilds and fraternities that financed and sustained them, and in England they lasted until the Reformation. The York Corpus Christi cycle was last performed in 1569.[61] Such plays have been revived in the twentieth century, but more for entertainment than edification, celebrating 'heritage' rather than corporate salvation. At York, in 2000, the mystery plays were staged within the Minster, and though this location was unhistorical, it reminds us that even before the development of such dramas in the fourteenth century, the church had already come to understand its liturgy as a dramatic enactment of the one true drama of God (re)making the world in Christ.

In the ninth century, Amalarius of Metz (c. 780–850/1), in his *Liber officialis* had produced an account of the Mass as liturgical drama, with its various parts representing moments in the passion and resurrection of Christ. 'He understands the Mass as a real repetition of the Passion, but also as an imaginative dramatisation of the Passion narrative. What happens on the altar is real; what the celebrants and the people are instructed to do around that reality is a play-pretend game.'[62] The plan of Byzantine and Romanesque churches, with apse, chancel and nave, provided a stage and auditorium, and the decoration of the grander basilicas, showing the saints and Christ in majesty, constituted scenery for the drama, accentuating its cosmic significance. In the eleventh and twelfth centuries, the developing use of music in the liturgy led to the Mass becoming a stylized music-drama, with some passages of plainsong explaining or expanding upon others, the sense of which might otherwise be lost through their enhancement with contrapuntal melodies. In time, the more prosaic recitatives were themselves elaborated as dialogical exchanges. But the attraction of these explanatory tropes was their emotional power, permitted by the use of a single note for each syllable. The music and the singer could imitate and evoke the intensity of the drama. In the twelfth century, Aelred of Rievaulx (1109–67) would complain of monks who too passionately mimicked their characters, with groans and sighs, and overtly theatrical gestures.[63] From the tenth century came one of the most popular tropes, the 'Quem quaeritis?' ('Whom do you seek?'), which expanded on the story of the three Marys and their meeting with the angel at the tomb of Christ, and which was first developed as an introit for the Easter Mass and then later used at the end of Matins. In St Ethelwold's tenth-century directions for its proper performance, one monk was to sit with palm in hand by the sepulchre-altar, imitating the angel at the tomb, while three others, with their thuribles, were to approach delicately, being the three women with their spices, arriving to anoint Christ's body. The angel-monk was to sing with a dulcet tone.[64] All delighted in the acting out of this story, because it announced the resurrection of Christ, the culmination of the Easter week liturgy, which was and remains the most theatricalized part of the ecclesial calendar.

Insofar as the cinema repeats the theatre as drama, the comparison of church and cinema merely locates a more populist analogue for the church as acting-space, as the *locus* of a social practice in which God's truth is dramatized. It is a nice fact that just as the medieval church provided the story for later, more secular dramatics, so some of the earliest films presented scenes from the Bible, and in much the same way as in the Corpus Christi processions and later play cycles. As early as 1897, a five minute *Passion of Christ* was filmed in Paris, while two Americans, Walter Freeman and Charles Webster, filmed *The Horitz Passion Play* in Bohemia. In the following year, Henry Vincent and William Paley filmed *The Mystery of the Passion Play of Oberammergau* on the roof of the Central Palace Hotel in New York. The revelation that the film was home produced had no effect on its popularity in the USA, and it was welcomed enthusiastically by both Catholics and Protestants.[65]

Like the development of medieval religious drama, from silent mimes to elaborate performances with special stage effects, so the cinematic Bible developed from short, silent scenes, into extended dramas, eventually presented in colour, stereophonic sound and cinemascope. Just as the medieval play cycles could vary in length, from sometimes only one to many scenes from the biblical story, so the early films could be shortened or lengthened, depending on theatrical schedules and audience interests. Sidney Olsott's *From the Manger to the Cross* (1912) came with optional scenes for Catholic audiences, picturing Jesus meeting his mother and then Veronica on his way to Calvary.[66] And just as the medieval plays expanded on certain moments in the biblical story, so films would elaborate on various scriptural scenes.

The early films of Christ's life partook of the liturgical in a manner akin to the relationship between the medieval plays and the church's ritual pieties. This is perhaps nowhere better seen than in Cecil B. DeMille's religious staging of the production of his 1927 *King of Kings*. DeMille not only hired a Jesuit, Father Daniel A. Lord, as an advisor on the film, but also arranged for the celebration of Mass every morning on the set, as well as daily prayers for other religious groups.[67]

The potential rivalry of church and cinema is suggested by the fact that both can be understood as parodies of one another, both being places where dreams are projected; 'inside' places where images of an 'outside', other than that from which the viewers have come, are shown. When the lights go down, one can see other imagined worlds, other ways of being human. This is to repeat the identity and distinction already drawn between Christian and pagan in the ancient world. In all three places, temple, church and cinema, we can detect the shadow of the cave, which establishes the distinction between the illusory and the real. And, as the discussion of Proyas's *Dark City* suggests, that distinction is itself shadowy, suspending the real and revealing its identification to be a venture of the imagination.

At the same time, what makes any particular image compelling, inviting trust, is not the image alone, but the power with which it is invested by others. By demons, the apologists claim of pagan statuary; by medical technicians, Burgess and Kubrick claim of Alex's 'show of horrors'; by society, we might say, of the films that at any one time grip the public imagination; and by the Holy Spirit in the community, we might further say, of the images proffered in the church, as when Lodge's Mark Underwood comes to see the 'real presence' through the eucharistic practice of the 'drab, smug, self-righteous people' of Brickley, 'who coolly lined up to snap their dentures on the living Christ'.[68] It is thus a matter of discerning the context in which an image can nourish its viewers, feeding their imaginations and ethos.[69]

Desiring Dreams

Like cinema, the church is a place for the projection of dreams, for the showing and seeing of other ways of being human; for seeing what it is to be social, for showing what it is to be a creature.[70] Like Plato's cinema-cave, the church marshals its inhabitants for the participative viewing of images, scenes of dispossessive charity and fellowship. A distinction between reality and representation is maintained, yet overcome, because invisible. The church acts in memory of its Lord, yet the past that is remembered, and the future that is invoked, as if they were absent, are really present, in the tokens and actions of the memorial. What appears as deconstructive irony in Plato, is positively embraced in the Christian cave, where it is held that knowledge of the exterior can be gained only inside the enclosure. The dazzling light of the real is to be seen by firelight.

The church is Plato's cave turned inside-out, since what he refuses to acknowledge for the sake of the game, is openly avowed in the church, or at least avowed in certain of its symbolics and practices. Which is to say that the church reflects itself as *herself*, as the cave in which life is made and formed. From the first, Christian theology has thought the cave the womb of life, human and divine, the space for the imagining of a different reality, or rather for imagining reality differently. Sigmund Freud was only repeating a series of theological symbolic displacements when he related the womb with the dream symbols of 'pits, cavities and hollows', 'churches and chapels'.[71] In the Freudian context, an appropriate example would be Leonardo da Vinci's *Virgin of the Rocks* (c. 1508), in which the mother of the child is pictured in a kind of grotto, perhaps viewed from the deeper interior of the cave, looking toward the entrance.[72] We are again reminded that unlike Plato's story, the Christian tale locates the Good not beyond but within the cave.

Christ is traditionally pictured as born in a cave and in the resurrection reborn from one. Thus the new life offered by Christ, individual and communal, comes forth not only from the actual womb of the Virgin, but also from the cave-womb of the tomb, that ancient underground cinema in which the dream of another life, another way of living this life – in the face of death – is projected. Freud's equation of womb, cave and chapel repeats a set of substitutory identifications already at play in the Christian imaginary and issuing in the complex symbolics of Leonardo's painting, or, indeed, in the more humble Christmas crib that uses crumpled brown paper to represent the rocky enclosure of the divine nativity.[73]

Freud's theory of dreams is not incidental to the present discussion, for he famously defined dreams as wish-fulfilments, as he also claimed of religious beliefs, making the latter a form of dreaming. No doubt attracted by the simplicity of his theory, Freud claimed that *every* dream was the fulfilment of a wish. '"What", asks the proverb, "do geese dream of?" And it replies: "Of maize." The whole theory that dreams are wish-fulfilments is contained in these two phrases.'[74] In *The Interpretation of Dreams* (1900) Freud laboured to show us how this could be true of every dream, even the most unpleasant, as when a father dreams of his burning child.[75] In the case of the dream that is religion, Freud finds it the fulfilment of humanity's 'oldest, strongest and most urgent wishes', in particular the wish for paternal protection, for security in an otherwise indifferent world.

> Thus the benevolent rule of a divine Providence allays our fear of the dangers of life; the establishment of a moral world-order ensures the fulfilment of the demands of justice, which have so often remained unfulfilled in human civilization; and the prolongation of earthly existence in a future life provides the local and temporal framework in which these wish-fulfilments shall take place.[76]

As 'illusions', religious beliefs are not (necessarily) erroneous, in the sense of contradicting reality. Indeed, they may be true. They are only illusions in being born of desire, motivated by wishes. Their relationship to reality is not impugned by naming them as illusions. Naming them as 'delusions', however, is another matter, and Freud was under no illusion (or so he thought) that religious beliefs were not other than delusions; not only born of wishful thinking, but contradicted by 'everything we have laboriously discerned about the reality of the world'.[77] That we can hope to know anything of reality except through the hard labour of science is itself an illusion, a wish for cheap knowledge, as offered by the 'easy' answers of religious doctrine. Freud will not refute, but only mock religious belief, since it is only of the 'highest and most sacred things' that a 'sensible person will behave so irresponsibly or rest content with such feeble grounds for his opinions and for the line he takes'.[78] While Freud's analysis of religious dreams at best answers to those of a 'paternal' nature, and hardly recognizes the ambiguous and often tragic elements in Christian dreaming, it yet discloses the desire that constitutes the Christian life, the yearning for a 'return' from the future.

Freud allowed that his own ruminations might be illusory, but insisted that if so they were capable of correction. 'If experience should show –

not to me, but to others after me, who think as I do – that we have been mistaken, we will give up our expectations . . . Since we are prepared to renounce a good part of our infantile wishes, we can bear it if a few of our expectations turn out to be illusions.'[79] Freud feverishly wished to be taken seriously as a scientist, repeatedly insisting on the scientific nature of psychoanalysis, which would imply its openness to confirmation and correction through repeated testing. However, like many powerful myths, it is the beauty of psychoanalysis to be experimentally unfalsifiable, and so less than scientific in the modern sense. Thus even if a patient's dream appears to frustrate rather than to fulfil a wish, the latter's frustration fulfils the patient's secret wish to falsify Freud's theory of dreams. 'These dreams appear regularly in the course of my treatments when a patient is in a state of resistance to me; and I can count almost certainly on provoking one of them after I have explained to a patient for the first time my theory that dreams are fulfilments of wishes.'[80] However, the religious person has no reason to mock Freud's theories of dreaming or of religion, for while Freud's 'discovery' of the origin of religion in desire is belated, that origin is well named. The birth of belief in desire is obscured in the many theological discourses that forget that theology is finally rooted in *prayer*. Freud's analysis of religion will not surprise anyone who daily prays for their bread, for the forgiveness of their sins, and for the coming of God's peace.

Freud's too easy contrast of the ease of religious doctrine with the labour of scientific theory, is perhaps due to his ignorance of the arduous, patient and always tested nature of religious faith. It certainly has something to do with his unwillingness to admit the imaginative element in science, particularly in his own 'scientific' endeavours. Freud's claim that religion tells us more about ourselves than it does about the world, is just as true of his own writings, the delusional aspects of which are offset by the fecundity of his story telling.[81] It is thus that his erroneous reading of religion yet reveals a profound truth. Just as Freud was able to find in dreams the very opposite of what they appear to portend, so we find in his account of religion a belated discernment of religious belief as social dreaming, as the fulfilment of a wish, a desire, for the remaking (redemption) of reality as it is, for seeing it truly. However, there is one important theological correction or clarification to be made to this appropriation of Freud's theory.

Belief is not born of a wish for comfort or compensation – which Christian faith offers only in the most ambiguous of fashions – but of a desire that is itself born in us, the fruit of an always prior union to our desiring, our yearning for a union that exceeds all known unions. It is not that the wish for God's embrace – the embrace of creation in the body of Christ – gives rise to belief in God, but that *that in which we believe* gives birth to the wish, to the desire for our embrace. To wish for God is to participate in God's own desiring, which, as perpetual abundance and donation, means that our desiring is not to want that which we lack, but to become that which we are given to be: dispossessive lovers, denizens of the Kingdom, embracing because embraced by God.[82]

*

No less than Freud's dreaming, cinema also deals in wishes, in the secret desires of its audience. And no less than the cinema, the church proffers the fulfilment of wishes, that are themselves formed and tutored through the sacramental realization of what is yet anticipated, hoped for and desired. Fundamentally, the Christian cave projects that which is alone truly desirable, the projected image enticing the gaze of the congregation by whom it is projected, caught up in the power of the Spirit, the trinitarian 'apparatus'. As with *The Exorcist*, to see is to be seen and possessed, and indeed to see the crucified Christ might be to react with an equal horror and terror; but to see the crucified become the risen Christ, is to have terror give way to wonder; and to see Christ present in the Eucharist, in the bread and the wine and the gathered community, is to have wonder transfused with joy and the hope of once more walking in the garden.

Then one is the viewer who has become like a little child, enamoured of the screen, unable to tell shadow from flickering shadow. One has become like the most saintly character in *The Picturegoers*, who is envied for the 'primitive intensity of her dramatic experience' when at the pictures. Clare Mallory is a devout Catholic, who in church or cinema is a happy inhabitant of the cave. 'Any dramatic or cinematic performance, however crudely executed, seemed to draw from her the same rapt, child-like attention. To her, as to a child, what she saw on the screen was real'.[83] Only such a gaze can believe the beatitudes.

Notes

1 Genesis 1.11, King James Version.
2 Plato, *The Republic*, ll. 514a–521b.

3 Sigmund Freud, *The Interpretation of Dreams* (1900) in *The Penguin Freud Library*, vol. 4, translated by James Strachy, edited by James Strachy, Alan Tyson and Angela Richards (Harmondsworth: Penguin Books, 1976), pp. 684–5.

4 'It may sound like science fiction, but the technology is almost with us now. Virtual Retinal Display scans images directly onto the retina, without the intervention of anything so crude or conventional as a TV screen, computer monitor or even the latest active matrix LCD panel.' Jason Thomas, 'One in the Eye', *The Guardian* (Online), 29 July 1999, p. 8.

5 On the second-century apologists see Paul Corby Finney, *The Invisible God: The Earliest Christians on Art* (New York and Oxford: Oxford University Press, 1994), chs. 2 and 3.

6 Finney, *The Invisible God*, pp. 46–7.

7 See Clement, *Protreptikos*, bk 4; Finney, *The Invisible God*, pp. 42–3.

8 Antisthenes the Cynic cited by Clement, *Stromateis*, 5.14.108, 4.

9 Origen, *Contra Celsum*, translated by Henry Chadwick (Cambridge: Cambridge University Press, [1953] 1965), bk 6.63 (p. 378); Finney, *The Invisible God*, p. 45.

10 Finney, *The Invisible God*, pp. 47–53.

11 Athenagoras, *Legatio*, 26.1 and 27.2 in *Legatio and De Resurrectione*, edited and translated by William R. Schoedel (Oxford: Clarendon Press, 1972), pp. 65–7; slightly adapted after Finney, *The Invisible God*, p. 54. The Christian contention that the pagan deities were really demons persisted in Christian polemic. See Augustine, *The City of God*, bk 2.

12 Finney, *The Invisible God*, ch. 5.

13 Reported by William Peter Blatty to Mark Kermode in 1990 and 1998. See Mark Kermode, *The Exorcist*, 2nd edn, BFI Modern Classics (London: British Film Institute, 1998), p. 110 and p. 112 n. 2.

14 Kermode, *The Exorcist*, p. 68.

15 Kermode, *The Exorcist*, pp. 76–7.

16 Kermode, *The Exorcist*, p. 72.

17 Quoted in Pauline Kael, *Reeling* (London: Marion Boyars, [1976] 1977), p. 320.

18 Kermode, *The Exorcist*, p. 85.

19 Kermode, *The Exorcist*, pp. 86–7. Pauline Kael – who did not like the film – noted that 'the movie may be in the worst imaginable taste – that is, an utterly unfeeling movie about miracles – but it's also the biggest recruiting poster the Catholic Church has had since the sunnier days of *Going My Way* and *The Bells of St Mary's*'. Pauline Kael, 'Back to the Ouija Board', in *Reeling*, pp. 247–51 (p. 249).

20 Kermode, *The Exorcist*, pp. 43–4.

21 Plato, *The Republic*, translated with introduction and notes by F.M. Cornford (Oxford: Oxford University Press, 1941), ll. 514–15 (pp. 227–9).

22 Plato, *The Republic*, edited by Cornford, p. 228 n. 2. See further Ian Jarvie, *The Philosophy of Film: Epistemology, Ontology, Aesthetics* (New York and London: Routledge & Kegan Paul, 1987), pp. 44–55.

23 For Plato, knowledge is an ethical category.

24 Plato, *The Republic*, ll. 377d–378e (pp. 69–70).

25 Quoted in James C. Robertson, *The Hidden Cinema: British Film Censorship in Action, 1913–1972* (London: Routledge, 1989), pp. 143–4.

26 Vincent LoBrutto, *Stanley Kubrick* (London: Faber and Faber, [1997] 1998), p. 337. Lieberson went on to produce Nicholas Roeg's and Donald Cammell's *Performance* (UK 1970), starring Mick Jagger; and Russell turned his attention to filming Aldous Huxley's *The Devils* (UK 1971) with Oliver Reed and Vanessa Redgrave (see further chapter 4 below).

27 Like *The Exorcist, A Clockwork Orange* reputedly produced devilish effects in some of its audience, with a number of copycat crimes reported in England. These, together with various press attacks on the film, led Kubrick in 1974 to request Warners to withdraw the film from Britain, where it was not shown again until after Kubrick's death. In the USA, Arthur Bremmer, who attempted to assassinate Governor George Wallace in 1972, recorded in his diary that he thought of shooting the governor throughout his viewing of *A Clockwork Orange*. Bremmer's diary was one of the sources on which the writer Paul Schrader drew for the character of Travis Bickle (Robert De Niro) in Martin Scorsese's *Taxi Driver* (USA 1976). In turn that film, and in particular the actress Jodie Foster (who plays the preteen prostitute Iris) came to obsess John Hinckley III, who tried to shoot President Ronald Reagan in 1981.

28 This is the name Alex gives in the film, but not in the novel. As Kevin Jackson notes ('Real Horrorshow: A Short Lexicon of Nadsat', *Sight and Sound*, 9/9 (September 1999): 24–7), Alex's self-appellation derives from the passage in the book where 'two young ptitsas' have to 'submit to the strange and weird desires of Alexander the Large' (Anthony Burgess, *A Clockwork Orange*, introduction by Blake Morrison (Harmondsworth: Penguin Books, [1962] 1996), p. 39). Later in the film, however, newspaper articles give his name as Alex Burgess. This inconsistency need not be either 'Kubrick letting his attention wander' or a 'half-hidden dig about Burgess's identification with his terrible hero', as Jackson suggests (p. 27), since the identification of author and hero is already established in the book through Alex's namesake, victim and nemesis, F. Alexander, who is identified as the author of *A Clockwork Orange* (Burgess, *A Clockwork Orange*, p. 124). Burgess wrote of his hero's terrible violence that 'I was sickened by my own excitement at setting it down, and I saw that Auden was right in saying that the novelist must be filthy with the filthy'. Anthony Burgess, *You've Had your Time: Being the Second Part of the Confessions of Anthony Burgess* (London: Heinemann, 1990), p. 61.

29 Burgess, *A Clockwork Orange*, p. 22.
30 Burgess, *A Clockwork Orange*, p. 18.
31 John King, 'Recollections of Wittgenstein' in *Recollections of Wittgenstein*, edited by Rush Rees (Oxford and New York: Oxford University Press, 1984), pp. 68–75 (p. 71).
32 Burgess, *A Clockwork Orange*, p. 67.
33 Burgess, *A Clockwork Orange*, p. 81. Horrorshow is formed after the neuter form of the Russian for 'good' (*kharashó*) and used in the same way as 'wicked' in 1990s English slang. Blake Morrison, 'Introduction' to Burgess, *A Clockwork Orange*, pp. vii–xxiv (p. ix).
34 See Burgess, *A Clockwork Orange*, pp. 81–2 for the passage on which this piece of the screenplay is based. The necessity of photography for true sight was remarked as early as 1901 by Emile Zola, himself an amateur photographer. 'In my view you cannot claim to have really seen something until you have photographed it.' Quoted in Susan Sontag, *On Photography* (London: Penguin Books, [1977] 1979), p. 87.
35 Burgess, *A Clockwork Orange*, p. 82. Alex is forced to endure images that are considerably more sadistic and horrifying in Burgess's novel than the stylized, almost pantomimic renditions in Kubrick's film. Kubrick sought a balletic quality in the film's violent scenes, answering to Burgess's invented slang, its seventeenth-century rhythms derived from the King James Bible, and intended to act 'as a kind of mist half-hiding the mayhem and protecting the reader from his own baser instincts' (Burgess, *You've Had your Time*, p. 38). See LoBrutto, *Stanley Kubrick*, p. 338. If the film, because visual, is more horrifying than the book, it is yet less violent, and Burgess's protestations at its 'highly coloured aggression' can seem disingenuous. See Burgess, *You've Had your Time*, pp. 244–5. For Burgess's reaction to Kubrick's film and his part in its promotion see also Anthony Burgess, *The Clockwork Testament or Enderby's End* (London: Hart Davies, MacGibbon, 1974).
36 Burgess, *A Clockwork Orange*, p. 88.
37 Burgess, *A Clockwork Orange*, p. 80.
38 Burgess, *A Clockwork Orange*, p. 99.
39 Anthony Burgess, *A Clockwork Orange: A Play with Music* (London: Methuen, [1987] 1998), p. 51.
40 Arthur Freed and Nacio Herb Brown's song 'Singin' in the Rain' (sung by Gene Kelly as the title song of Stanley Donen's 1952 film) is first whistled and then sung by Alex as he sets about the rape of Mrs Alexander, the writer's wife (Adrienne Corri). The song later proves to be his undoing, when his idle singing of it in the bath reveals his identity to the now widowed and deranged writer, Mr Alexander (Patrick Magee). Malcolm McDowell claims to have thought of singing the song during the three or so days that were spent improvising the scene of the rape. See LoBrutto, *Stanley Kubrick*, p. 366.
41 Burgess, *A Clockwork Orange*, p. 147.

42 These were made by Liz Moore, and based on furniture-sculptures by the London artist Allen Jones. See John Baxter, *Stanley Kubrick: A Biography* (London: HarperCollins, 1997), p. 249.

43 This sculpture, together with that of four naked dancing Christs, was made by the Dutch artists Herman and Cornelius Makkink. Baxter, *Stanley Kubrick*, p. 255.

44 Plato, *The Republic*, l. 517 (p. 231).

45 Plato, *The Republic*, translated with an introduction by Desmond Lee, 2nd rev. edn (Harmondsworth: Penguin Books, 1987), p. 317 n. 1.

46 Plato, *The Republic*, l. 507a (p. 217). There is a play on the Greek *tokos*, meaning both 'offspring' and 'interest'.

47 Luce Irigaray, 'The Analysis of that Projection Will Never Take (or Have Taken) Place', *Speculum of the Other Woman*, translated by Gillian C. Gill (Ithaca, NY: Cornell University Press, [1974] 1985), p. 310.

48 Irigaray, *Speculum*, p. 287.

49 Camille Paglia quoted in E. Jane Dickson, 'The Wicked Queen', *The Independent* (Monday Review), 7 June 1999, p. 1.

50 Dickson, 'The Wicked Queen', p. 1.

51 Camille Paglia, *Sexual Personae: Art and Decadence from Nefertiti to Emily Dickinson* (Harmondsworth: Penguin Books, [1990] 1992), p. 346.

52 Paglia, *Sexual Personae*, p. 32.

53 Edward Rees, 'Rosalie Street and "the Pictures"', *The Manchester Guardian*, 26 February 1913.

54 David Lodge, *The Picturegoers* (Harmondsworth: Penguin Books, [1960] 1993), p. 125. A thematically related novel is Walker Percy, *The Moviegoer* (New York: Alfred A. Knopf, 1961), also a first novel.

55 Lodge, *The Picturegoers*, p. 107.

56 Lodge, *The Picturegoers*, pp. 108–9.

57 In both North America and Britain film going was at its height in 1946, with 1,635 million cinema admissions in Britain alone. Cinema attendance declined markedly in the 1950s with the growth of TV ownership, and continued to decline throughout the 1960s and 70s, reaching a low point in 1984 with only 54 million British admissions. However, since then there has been a steady increase in cinema admissions, with 123 million in 1996 (UK). See *BFI Film and Television Handbook 1998*, edited by Eddie Dyja (London: British Film Institute, 1997), p. 42.

58 On the ecclesial origins of the medieval theatre see Glynne Wickham, *The Medieval Theatre* (London: Weidenfeld and Nicolson, 1974) and John Wesley Harris, *Medieval Theatre in Context: An Introduction* (London: Routledge, 1992). See also Francesca Aran Murphy, *The Comedy of Revelation: Paradise Lost and Regained in Biblical Narrative* (Edinburgh: T. & T. Clark, 2000), ch. 6, especially pp. 254–80.

59 See Miri Rubin, *Corpus Christi: The Eucharist in Late Medieval Culture* (Cambridge: Cambridge University Press, 1991), pp. 243–71.

60 See Rubin, *Corpus Christi*, pp. 271–87.

61 Eamon Duffy, *The Stripping of the Altars: Traditional Religion in England 1400–1580* (New Haven and London: Yale University Press, 1992), p. 581.

62 Murphy, *Comedy of Revelation*, p. 254.

63 See William Tydeman, *The Theatre in the Middle Ages: Western European Stage Conditions c.800–1576* (Cambridge: Cambridge University Press), p. 190.

64 See Wickham, *The Medieval Theatre*, pp. 39–40.

65 See Lloyd Baugh, *Imaging the Divine: Jesus and Christ-Figures in Film* (Kansas City: Sheed and Ward, 1997), pp. 8–9. For an overview of the 'Christ film' see William R. Telford, 'Jesus Christ Movie Star: The Depiction of Jesus in the Cinema', in *Explorations in Theology and Film: Movies and Meaning*, edited by Clive Marsh and Gaye Ortiz (Oxford: Blackwell, 1997), pp. 115–39.

66 Baugh, *Imaging the Divine*, pp. 9–10.

67 Baugh, *Imaging the Divine*, pp. 12–13. On *King of Kings* (1927) see Bruce Babington and Peter Evans, *Biblical Epics: Sacred Narrative in the Hollywood Cinema* (Manchester and New York: Manchester University Press, 1993), pp. 110–26.

68 Lodge, *The Picturegoers*, p. 110. The worshipping community is the 'screen' on which God appears, and worship is to be a daily undertaking.

69 Thus censorship is not so much about denying people the right to view images, as judging the context of their showing. This is why film censorship is always a judgement on audiences, rather than films; and why what is deemed passable changes with time. Censorship also assumes that there is at least one audience with clear vision, the censors; and it is their implied judgement on the rest of us that causes affront.

70 For Gilles Deleuze, also, there is a kinship between church and cinema, between what we might see in the cult (liturgies) of the cathedrals and in the films of the great directors (Eisenstein). Cinema is twentieth-century piety. But unlike the 'grand *mise-en-scène*' of Catholicism, which seeks to show the God in whom the world no longer believes, cinema can show us the world in which we have ceased to have faith. 'The link between man and the world is broken. Henceforth, this link must become an object of belief: it is the impossible which can only be restored within a faith . . . The cinema must film, not the world, but belief in this world, our only link.' (Gilles Deleuze, *Cinema 2: The Time-Image*, translated by Hugh Tomlinson and Robert Galeta (London: Athlone Press, [1985] 1989), pp. 171–2.) *Pace* Deleuze, the Christian ecclesiacinema shows us the world through showing us our creatureliness in Christ; forming his/our body as the film of our only link to the world. On Deleuze, religion and film see further, Paolo Marrati, '"The Catholicism of Cinema": Gilles Deleuze on Image and Belief', in *Religion and Media*, edited by Hent de Vries and Samuel Weber (Stanford, CA: Stanford University Press, 2001), pp. 227–40.

71 Sigmund Freud, *Introductory Lectures on Psychoanalysis* (1915–17), in *The Penguin Freud Library*, vol. 1, translated by James Strachy, edited by James Strachy and Angela Richards (Harmondsworth: Penguin Books, 1973), pp. 189–90.

72 See Sigmund Freud, 'Leonardo da Vinci and a Memory of his Childhood' (1910), in *The Penguin Freud Library*, vol. 14: *Art and Literature*, translated by James Strachey and edited by Albert Dickson (Harmondsworth: Penguin Books, 1985), pp. 145–231.

73 Though St Francis of Assisi (1181/2–1226) may not have been the first to develop the Christmas crib, his use of it at Greccio in 1223 points to a growing desire to participate in Christ's life by means of symbolic portrayal; to make the life of Christ real through play-acting. See Bonaventure, 'The Life of St Francis' in *Bonaventure: The Soul's Journey into God*, translated by E. Cousins (New York: Paulist Press, 1978); and David Brown, *Tradition and Imagination: Revelation and Change* (Oxford: Oxford University Press, 1999), pp. 72–105.

74 Freud, *Interpretation of Dreams*, p. 212.

75 The child was really dead, the corpse laid out in a room adjoining the father's bedroom. The dream was occasioned by the falling of a candle, igniting the bed clothes where the child lay; but the father, rather than awakening, dreams that he is awakened by his (dead) child – 'Father, don't you see I'm burning?' – so fulfilling his wish that the child were still alive. 'If the father had woken up first and then made the inference that led him to go into the next room, he would, as it were, have shortened his child's life by that moment of time.' See Freud, *Interpretation of Dreams*, pp. 652–3.

76 Sigmund Freud, *The Future of an Illusion* (1927), in *The Penguin Freud Library*, vol. 12, *Civilization, Society and Religion*, translated by James Strachey, edited by Albert Dickson (Harmondsworth: Penguin Books, 1985), pp. 179–241 (p. 212).

77 Freud, *Future of an Illusion*, p. 213.

78 Freud, *Future of an Illusion*, p. 214.

79 Freud, *Future of an Illusion*, pp. 237 and 329.

80 Freud, *Interpretation of Dreams*, pp. 241–2.

81 Robert J.C. Young nicely notes that 'the claim that dreams are the fulfilment of a wish is something of a tautological joke in the context of a book whose overriding wish is to discover the secret of dreams.' See 'Freud's Secret: *The Interpretation of Dreams* was a Gothic Novel' in *Sigmund Freud's The Interpretation of Dreams: New Interdisciplinary Essays*, edited by Laura Marcus (Manchester: Manchester University Press, 1999), pp. 206–31 (pp. 220–1).

82 These themes are further explored in chapters 5 (God's Sex) and 6 (Sex Slaves) below.

83 Lodge, *The Picturegoers*, p. 54. For a Thomistic account of the childish vision nurtured in the ecclesiacinema see Denys Turner, *How to Be an Atheist* (Cambridge: Cambridge University Press, 2002), especially pp. 34–9.

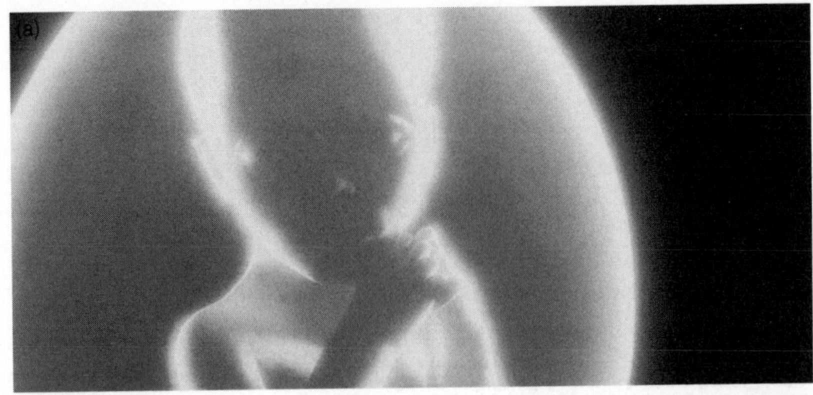

Figure 3 Seeing the Cinematic Apparatus

(a) The star-child and (b) the monolith in *2001: A Space Odyssey* (Stanley Kubrick, USA 1968). Photos: The Kobal Collection.

Chapter 3

VISIONARY SCREENS

In Stanley Kubrick's *2001: A Space Odyssey* (USA 1968), the dawn of a new millennium is heralded with the conception of a new being. As the film closes, there comes into view the foetal form of a 'star-child', formed from the last surviving crew member of the spaceship *Discovery*. He has been reborn as a second, celestial Adam. Previous to this closing scene, the film has told the story of how a primal horde of 'man-apes' became human – through learning the use of tools and weapons – and how their twenty-first century descendants were able to use machines to venture beyond the earth to other worlds among the stars. In one of the most remarkable of narrative ellipses, however, the entire history of this human development – from the first murder to the technological marvel of space flight – is covered by Kubrick's now famous jump cut, from a bone, as it flies up in the air, to the weightless fall, down screen, of a space craft, floating in the void to the strains of Johann Strauss's *Blue Danube* waltz.[1]

This chapter, even more than the last, will involve a number of jump cuts between theological, cinematic and other texts. These cuts, like Kubrick's, aim to effect a transport between different worlds, allowing each to resonate in the other. The intended final effect is one of layered meanings, superimposed images, a parodic palimpsest of ideas, that will allow the cinema to appear in the church, the practice of looking in one to inform that in the other, and to raise the question of what it is to see in either.

Kubrick's Child

The central section of *2001* is concerned with the journey from Earth to Jupiter of the spaceship *Discovery*, which has been occasioned by the finding on the moon of a black monolith, clearly of alien construction, and the source of a radio signal directed to the planet Jupiter.[2] It was the appearance of the same or similar monolith at the beginning of the film that led the early man-apes to first manipulate their world for their own interests. But while *2001* is framed by an originary and anticipated encounter between humanity and an alien presence, the major section of the film concerns only three characters: the two spacemen, David Bowman (Kier Dullea) and Frank Poole (Gary Lockwood), and the *Discovery*'s on-board computer, the HAL 9000 (voiced by Douglas Rain).[3]

It is a commonplace of commentary on the film to say that it exemplifies a recurring theme in Kubrick's work, namely the destruction of humanity by the institutional and technological machines that humanity itself produces. Thus, to take but two examples, in Kubrick's early First World War drama, *Paths of Glory* (USA 1957), Kirk Douglas plays Colonel Dax, striving to retain some sense of humanity for himself and his troops in the face of the remorseless logic of the French military machine, and the vanity of its generals. In Kubrick's later period drama, *Barry Lyndon* (USA 1975), Ryan O'Neill plays the eponymous hero, Redmond Barry, whose attempt at social mobility is eventually defeated by the aristocratic apparatus to which he aspires. In both films the social mechanisms are graphically realized in the use of confined, hermetic spaces, whether trenches or enfilades of rooms in town and country houses. Indeed, in nearly all Kubrick's films, his characters are constrained by grids that are both spatial and social, materializations of psychic confinement: the corridors of the Overlook Hotel in *The Shining* (USA 1980); the barracks in *Full Metal Jacket* (USA 1987); and the grid of New York streets in *Eyes Wide Shut* (USA 1999).

For Gilles Deleuze, Kubrick's films exemplify a cinema of the brain in which the world itself is a brain, and the brain the films' recurring *mise en scène*, rigorously formal and fastidiously executed. 'The black stone of 2001 presides over both cosmic states and cerebral stages: it is the soul of the three bodies, earth, sun and moon, but also the seed of the three brains, animal, human, machine.'[4] In *2001*, the human crew of *Discovery* have become brain machines, calmly rational and passively formal, cogs in a venture of which they know nothing, while the computer, through a conflict of directives, becomes emotional, unstable and murderous. All of Kubrick's films display violence erupting from creatures constrained by social formalities and rational mechanisms; the raging of caged animals, trapped in systems they have built but barely understand and cannot control.

The screenplay for *2001* was written by Stanley Kubrick and Arthur C. Clarke, who also produced a novel with the same title as the film. The idea derived from an earlier short story by Clarke, 'The Sentinel'.[5] In Clarke's novel, the star-child is the regressed astronaut, David Bowman, returned to a new, cosmic childhood, no longer earthbound but celestial. 'In an empty room, floating amid the fires of a double star twenty thousand light-years from Earth, a baby opened its eyes and began to cry.'[6] The mind of this child is woven anew by the entity of the double star, so that the child, in its mind's eye, can encompass the entire universe, and see what lies 'behind the back of space'.[7]

While the film's final scenes of Bowman's transformation into the star-child are serene and majestic, an altogether more chilling scenario arguably closes Clarke's novel, where the astronaut-become-child is indeed new born, being a capricious, self-centred creature, ignorant of life and death, good and evil. The world to which the star-child returns, across the void of twenty thousand light-years, is encircled by a nuclear arsenal, an orbiting, 'slumbering cargo of death'.[8]

> The feeble energies it contained were no possible menace to him; but he preferred a cleaner sky. He put forth his will, and the circling megatons flowered in a silent detonation that brought a brief, false dawn to half the sleeping globe.[9]

Admittedly, Clarke's text is ambiguous. Might a 'silent detonation' be a harmless one? Clarke has written that when he wrote the novel he thought so, the star-child clearing the world's skies, not the sky of the world. But noting in 1972 that many readers had interpreted the text as signalling the destruction of the earth, Clarke was now less sure of how to read his own novel. Perhaps, he mused, in view of our treatment of the earth, a returning star-child would 'judge all of us as ruthlessly as Odysseus judged Leiodes, whose "head fell rolling in the dust while he was yet speaking" – and despite his timeless, ineffectual plea, "I tried to stop the others"'.[10] When Clarke's darker reading of his novel is allowed to inform the final scene of the film, the embryonic star-child, filling the cinemascope screen and returning the gaze of a bemused audience, looks down upon them without sympathy. On this interpretation, the star-child is not 'one of cinema's most extraordinary images of hope and wonder', looking upon us with benevolence, wisdom and compassion.[11] Instead, it is the look of the demon, whose desire is to be seen, so as to return and destroy the gaze of the audience (figure 3a).

Indeed, as the camera pans around the star-child, so that it comes to look the viewer full in the face, its left eye is caught by the light, while the other is cast into shadow, so that for a few moments, it seems to have only one large glowing eye. This recalls the film's other demonic eye, the unflinching lens of the computer HAL, monoscopic but multiplied throughout the spaceship *Discovery*, the small world HAL rules and destroys. HAL's eyes glow red; the star-child's glow steely blue turning to white. As the star-child comes to face the audience, one can almost see the skull beneath the face of the foetal infant. While it is only the novel that ends with the destruction of the world, the cinema audience may yet feel a chill from the look that holds its gaze.[12]

Transcendent Sight

2001 is of course a millennial meditation, and thus already an occidental, socio-Christian venture. Ending with the coming to earth of a celestial being, which is also the second coming of human being, a remaking of humanity, the film is named after the first year of the third Christian millennium, and thus evokes, however faintly, the hope for a return that will remake the world, issuing in judgement and salvation. It is not evident that Kubrick intended his picture to have any religious resonance, though he is recorded as joking that 'MGM don't know it yet, but they've just footed the bill for the first six million-dollar religious film'.[13] For John Baxter, the religious or 'mystical' sense of the movie is that of 'man as God-in-waiting'.[14] As such, the film's 'religious' sense resonates against the Christian story of a God-become-human (God as man-in-waiting) who has already appeared in embryonic form, having grown quietly, secretly in his mother's womb.

Kubrick's film disdains to encode an interpretation of its images, though the final section of the film is entitled 'Jupiter: Beyond the Infinite'. Thus if Kubrick's child is not Clarke's infant, playing with the world's most deadly toys, it may yet be a symbol of infinite life, infinite vision, a being with a transcendent gaze, a god's-eye view of the world and its denizens. If nothing else, Kubrick's child – emerging out of the darkness of the cinema screen, its eye catching the light and looking on the audience with a gaze that portends life and death – signifies cinematic vision: seeing in the dark (of space and the movie theatre).[15] And we, watching the film, share in this vision, having travelled with Bowman through the 'star-gate' to his fateful rendezvous with the monolith in a white luminous room. Bowman's intergalactic journey is vividly presented through six minutes of fleeting, dizzying coloured patterns, strange shapes and chromatic landscape negatives. They mesmerize the eye, as György Ligeti's *Atmosphères* the ear,[16] and are intercut with shots of Bowman's eye, a single one, that fills the screen: a traumatized, terrified camera.[17]

Kubrick's *2001* ends by breaking the classic rule against characters in a film looking directly at the camera, that is, at the audience, for to do so draws attention to the artifice and convention of the cinematic space, and the audience's collusion in its fabrication. At the end of the film the star-child looks directly at us from the screen, across the divide between 'stage' and auditorium, between cinematic and real space. We are confronted with the eye of the cinema itself, with the god-like gaze that it bestows upon its viewer. If *2001* is a religious film, it is the religion of cinema itself, the transcendent vision of the camera's eye.

In order to suggest how cinema produces a sense of transcendence for the viewer, Christian Metz has famously drawn on Jacques Lacan's theory of the 'mirror stage' in the process of ego formation.[18] According to Lacan, the sense of the 'self' is formed in the young child when he or she comes to identify with an image of his or her own body; with, as it were, a self-reflection in a mirror.[19] Thus begins the process by which one comes to oneself as 'oneself', as an objective subject. In the cinema, however, the viewer's ego has already been formed, and the screen reflects no image of that ego; and yet for the film to be intelligible there must be something in the film with which the viewer can identify. One might identify with a character or actor, but not in those films, or stretches of films, where no actors appear, as in the long sequences of *2001* where there is only landscape, or the stately movement of spaceships. For Metz, the film viewer identifies with the camera, eliding its vision with his or her own.

> At the cinema, it is always the other who is on the screen; as for me, I am there to look at him. I take no part in the perceived, on the contrary, I am *all-perceiving*. All-perceiving as one says all-powerful (this is the famous gift of 'ubiquity' the film makes its spectator); all-perceiving, too, because I am entirely on the side of the perceiving instance: absent from the screen, but certainly present in the auditorium, a great eye and ear without which the perceived would have no one to perceive it, the *constitutive* instance, in other words, of the cinema signifier (it is I who make the film).[20]

Cinema endows its viewers with superhuman vision, an ability to see whatever they will, from vast panoramas to secluded intimacies, from past scenes to visions of the future – as indeed in *2001*. When cameras are light enough to be handheld, cinema can move as the human eye moves, walking, running or riding along the road. But such pictures are often jerky or nauseous, betraying their manufacture.[21] It is the camera on wheels, running on tracks, mounted on cranes, and, more recently, on the steadicam, that produces the ecstasy of the fluid, sinuous shot, that soars up or swoops down, or follows characters in and out of rooms, across roads, passing through otherwise impenetrable objects, to deliver an effortless constancy of vision; a spectator who sees all while remaining unseen.[22]

But since film viewers know that they are not the camera/projector, that what they see is a kind of hallucination, and yet that they are seeing with their own eyes what the film is showing, they identify themselves as all-perceiving, thus constituting the cinematic illusion, a 'religious' or transcendental state. The viewer, Metz contends, identifies him or herself as a 'pure act of perception (as wakefulness, alertness): as condition of possibility of the perceived and hence as a kind of transcendental subject, anterior to every *there is*.'[23] Cinema's constitution of the viewer as an all-perceiving, all-powerful, 'transcendental subject', has long been noted. Siegfried Kracauer (1889–1966), in his last work on *Theory of Film* (1960), discussed transcendent vision as one of cinema's gratifications. He noted how, in Wolfgang Wilhelm's 1940 study of filmgoers, one correspondent declared that in the cinema 'I can be everywhere, standing above as the god of this world'; while for another, one becomes 'like God who sees everything and one has the feeling that nothing eludes you and that one grasps all of it'. 'In the cinema', Kracauer remarks, 'the frustrated may turn into the kings of creation.'[24]

Something similar can be said of the church. Critics of religion – Nietzsche or Freud – declare the church a place for the projection of compensatory delusions, apparent fulfilments of childish wishes for omnipotence in the face of psychological and social degradation. Like cinema, the church offers escapist fantasies, temporary respites from the fears and frustrations that it yet engenders, solace for social impotencies that it simultaneously ensures. But believers must say something similar, since for them the church shows the God who became human so that humans might become God. This is what people go to church to see, to pray, to become: the glory of God in a human face.

From the church's point of view, the transcendence of the cinema is a snare and a delusion, being its pleasure and peril. For it grants an earthly omnipotence that is always, finally, fleeting, fragmentary and unfulfilling. It is God's point of view as imagined by beings who cannot see what is behind them without turning their heads, and so losing sight of what is in front of them. Yet cinema's ability to offer an apparent 'transcendence' of normal sight, to see what is behind as well as what is in front, through doors and around corners, to see everything and 'grasp all of it', is cinema's promise to show us what we would not otherwise see. Cinema can extend our vision, imagination and sympathy by presenting other worlds, past and future, near and far, real and fictional. It can show us what is around the corner, in parts of the city we never visit, in places where we fear to tread, in ways of living and feeling we dread or desire; in short, cinema can take us 'out of ourselves' and into other, alien domains, strange habit(u)ations. In cinema we can redream the world.

If Kubrick's *2001* is about cinematic transcendence – the sublimity of the vision machine – it is also about the danger, if not the futility of such dreaming. For the film's final epiphany – in this masterwork by the most bleak, most observant and quietly comic of film-makers – shows the star-child looking at us looking at it. Having travelled to the edge of the universe and beyond, Kubrick's Odysseus is still looking, but what does he (it) see?[25]

The Eye of the Monolith

What first disappears from view in Kubrick's film, though in a sense returning only to disappear again, is the alien, the 'entity' of the 'double star', as it is called in Clarke's novel. At its most prosaic, Clarke and Kubrick's tale is of humankind's tutelage by an unseen, unknown reality, an alien, off-world presence. Clarke and Kubrick considered picturing this extraterrestrial being or beings, but in the end decided against doing so. Instead we are shown the machine by which the alien(s) first influenced human enterprise and then tempted humanity beyond the earth's moon to a fateful rendezvous in the orbit of the planet Jupiter. This machine appears as a black, light-seducing monolith.[26]

In its abstract formality the monolith is, as it were, a *via negativa*, both incomprehensibly dark, unyielding of any interiority, and yet at the same time an object that deforms space, that draws people towards it, imperceptibly changes their world, marking an unknown they can acknowledge but not understand. It is the purely empty sign of that which makes the star-child possible, the matrix or womb of the film's final vision, the child's sight of the world's good and evil. Just before his apotheosis, Bowman is lying on his bed, in a neoclassical but modern antiseptic room, presumably created by the alien(s), perhaps inspired by television images of grand accommodations, suitable for important guests. Suddenly the monolith is standing at the foot of the bed (figure 3b). We see it almost from Bowman's point of view, from just behind the head of the bed, and then the camera tracks forward, so that the monolith comes to fill the whole screen, as if we were entering it, as it engulfs our vision. It is as if Bowman were in an inverted cinema, where the house lights are up, intensely bright, and only the screen is dark, the one place where light is absent when it should be present. It is in the vast, unmeasurable darkness of the monolith-screen, that the star-child comes to be. Though, more strictly, the embryonic star-child first appears on the bed, as a glowing conceptus that has replaced Bowman, or that Bowman has become, or that has been formed – conceived – between Bowman and the monolith, the human and the alien(s), the projector behind the head and the screen in front.

This is the only moment in the film when, fleetingly, the alien monolith gains subjectivity through the use of a shot/reverse shot. An example of 'classic' (Hollywood) cinematic grammar, the shot/reverse shot typically functions to establish the subjective relationship between two characters, as we see one person's view of the other, and then the other's reverse view of the first person. Because the spectator sees what each of the characters see, the characters gain 'subjectivity' from the viewer, and the viewer comes to feel what the characters feel, the viewer's subjectivity being, as it were, sutured into the space of the film. In *2001*, there are no shot/reverse shots between the human characters, though there are some that come close, as in the conversation between Heywood Floyd (William Sylvester) and Smyslov (Leonard Rossiter) on the earth-orbiting space station. But the camera remains on the other side of the table from the two interlocutors, with the other characters fore-grounded in the reverse shots. It is only between the computer HAL and the astronauts Bowman and Poole that the shot/reverse shot is used to establish HAL's subjectivity, the sense that the computer is a living, thinking and feeling entity. We see the astronauts through the fisheye lens of HAL's 'eyes', placed at various points throughout the *Discovery* spaceship, and, in the reverse shots, we see those eyes, unblinking and glowing red, with a yellow pupil. Each lens is placed in the lower half of a rectangular panel, which, in miniature, recalls the monolith itself. Bowman and Poole are for HAL characters in a film, playing before his lenses; while for them, and for the audience, HAL is a camera that mediates their lives, and finally their deaths. If HAL is in some way related to the monolith – which, though it did not kill, taught the man-apes how to do so – then it is entirely fitting that there is at least one shot/reverse shot between the monolith and Bowman-become-the-star-child.

Michel Chion offers a careful analysis of the narrative structure and kinds of shot in *2001*. He too, however, quickly declares that 'there is no monolith's point of view . . . no shot "seen" by it (when a single shot would be enough to subjectivize it)'.[27] The aged Bowman, lying in his bed, is seen first in a point-of-view shot, over the left shoulder of his younger self, seated at a table in his bedroom. There is then a cut to a close-up of Bowman in the bed, shot from the side. He slowly raises his right arm as if, perhaps, in greeting or entreaty, and the film cuts to the point-of-view shot described above – of the monolith standing at the foot of the bed, seen from behind the bed, not so much over the shoulder as over the head of Bowman. This is followed by a narratorial long shot of the entire room, with Bowman in his bed on the left, and the monolith standing on the right. The film then cuts back to Bowman's point of view, properly shot from his position in the bed, looking at the monolith, and then comes the reverse shot that Chion misses, of Bowman in the bed, from the monolith's point of view. But in the space of the reverse cut, Bowman has been transformed into the embryonic star-child, contained in a glowing orb. The film cuts to a close-up of the child, on the bed, again taken from the right side of the bed, as with the previous close-up of the aged Bowman. This is followed by a final point-of view shot, that of the star-child's, as we again see the monolith from the bed. But now the camera tracks forward, as if the child – as if we the viewers – were entering into the monolith's unmodulated darkness, as its perfect, unreflective surface fills the screen. The opening bars of Richard Strauss's *Thus Spake Zarathustra*, unheard since the film's opening titles, herald the film's final sequence: the star-child's encounter with planet earth and the movie audience. Briefly and obliquely, *2001* shows us an encounter with an alien subjectivity, but one that is hardly recognizable as such, not least because this alien is eyeless. If it has an eye, it can only be like HAL's, the eye of the cinema itself, as it returns the gaze of its own projection. The monolith is thus the presence on the screen of the cinematic apparatus, in which we – its viewers – are already caught.

The monolith is a wonderful conceit, for it both evokes an alien presence at the same time as it denies us sight of that which is thus evoked. It is the presence of an alien absence. As it fills Bowman's room it withdraws, and in leaving yet remains, absenting itself as it constitutes a space for the star-child that comes to shine in the darkness of the monolith's emptiness. But it is a cinematic conceit, for turn the monolith on its side, and one has the letterbox of the cinemascope screen, the blank rectangle on which the star-child appears, as does the entirety of Kubrick's film. The screen is white until light is shone upon it and it paradoxically becomes the darkness of space, in which glimmer the innumerable stars of the cosmos. The screen is the necessary matrix for the appearance of any film, that which must be in place, but which must also withdraw so that the moving picture can appear as its own reality, its own substantial thing. The viewer should not be aware of the screen or the projector, or the celluloid passing in the projector's gate, a frame at a time, held still for a fraction of a second. All these must be there, yet as if absent, for the film to be. It helps of course that the viewer can be immensely tolerant of imperfections in the screen, scratches on the film, and too slow to see that what appears to move is in fact standing still. For the star-child to appear, the cinematic apparatus must be annihilated, as also the alien if it is indeed to be alien; and yet not really annihilated, but suspended, absently present.

As if to accentuate the paradox of the screen's necessary invisibility, screens are multiplied throughout *2001*, and in one way or another appear in nearly every scene. The human inhabitants of the twenty-first century are surrounded by them, both explicitly, as televisions for communication and as displays of machinic functions, but also implicitly, since the many views in and out of the windows of various spaceships and the moon base were created by projections on to screens built into the sets and models. As Dr Heywood sits in the videophone cubicle on board the space station, talking to his daughter back on earth, we see the planet through a window, apparently turning somersaults as the space station spins on its axis in order to produce centrifugal gravity. But both earth and daughter are screen projections within the film.[28]

More covertly the vast panoramas of prehistoric earth that open the film, and against which the early hominids learn to kill, were created from photographs taken in south-west Africa, turned into 8 in. by 10 in. slides and projected from in front of the actors onto a huge curved screen, 100 ft wide and 40 ft high, designed to reflect as much of the projected light as possible, and on axis with the projector, so that the light returns almost along the same path of its projection. Through the use of a half-silvered and tilted mirror, camera and projector shoot from the same point of view, so that the actors precisely mask their shadows.[29] Only the shot of a leopard, as its sits by its dead prey (a horse painted to look like a zebra), gives the game away. As the leopard turns its head, its eyes catch the projected light, and shoot it straight back at the audience.[30] It is a complex moment: a knowing wink, because the highly reflective material of the front projection screen was developed by the 3M company for motorway signs and 'cat's eyes'; a cinematic conceit, because in this method of front projection, it is as if the camera projects the image it photographs, just as in the ancient tradition of extramission, it is the eye that projects the light by which it sees, an ability that Descartes attributed to the cat;[31] and it is, at the beginning of the movie, metaphoric of other eyes in the film, which also seem to emit light: the soft red glow of the murderous computer HAL, and the glint of the perhaps equally murderous star-child at the end of the film.

Screening the Maternal

It is not only the screen that disappears with the appearing of the star-child, as with the appearing of any cinematic image. Also effaced is the womb in which the star-child is formed, the mother on which it depends. In the depths of space, other forms of human life would seem to require a uterine matrix, whether the carapace of a spaceship or spacesuit, the latter connected by an umbilical cord to the former. But where is the umbilicus of the star-child? Perhaps, within the world of the film, at the diegetic level, the star-child's mother is the universe, the void become a maternal home, a productive no-thing.[32] But if its mother is not on the screen, perhaps she is the screen itself, with an umbilicus of projected light attaching her to the star-child. Then, at the level of the conceit, it is not the vastness of space that produces the child, but the fecund dark of the movie theatre. But in concealing the productive apparatus, Kubrick's celestial embryo, suspended in the darkness of space and cinema, is emblematic of that more general effacement of the maternal that Luce Irigaray finds at the beginning of the western philosophical tradition, in Plato's flight from the cave.

We have become so used to photographic images of the embryonic child, serenely floating in its amniotic waters, that it is easy to forget how novel they were in 1968, when Kubrick's steely blue embryo first turned its gaze upon its viewers, 'mutely imploring the audience to ponder its mystery'.[33] It was then almost as impossible an image as that of the earth from the moon, for it was only in 1965 that *Life* magazine had published a series of photographs by Lennart Nilsson showing the process of foetal development in the womb, the 'Drama of Life before Birth'.[34] Nilsson's photographs were indeed impossible images, for all but one of them were taken after death, being pictures of 'surgically removed' (aborted) foetuses. On the cover of *Life* was a picture of a 'living 18-week-old foetus shown inside its amniotic sac', but it was in fact post-mortem. Nilsson's impossible image was produced by highly technical means, involving the surgical removal and manipulation of the foetus, and its suspension in a carefully prepared tank of clear fluid, that was artfully back-lit. Thus a foetus could be shown moving 'freely in its capsule – weightless as an astronaut in space'.[35] Kubrick's foetal star-child is similarly free floating, and the product of hidden, technical skill.

Modelled on Nilsson's pictures, it also is an image of life in death, but doubly dead, since it was actually a resin mannequin, sculpted by Liz Moore. Its ten seconds or so of screen life were the product of 8 hours filming, as the effect of haloed light, apparently radiating from within the child, required the extended exposure of each frame of film.[36]

Already in Nilsson's remarkable but fraudulent photographs, prior to Kubrick's film, the womb of the mother, and the mother herself, have been made to disappear, in order to present an autonomous foetal identity that is the essence of human life: the utterly self-possessed individual, the superman.[37] But the image of the disembodied foetus, floating in the void, inside its amniotic capsule, has a long genealogy, greatly predating its photographic realization in the 1960s. As traced by Karen Newman, it is in the early modern period, in the sixteenth and seventeenth centuries, in an ever-increasing number of obstetrical manuals, that the foetus was shown as a cavorting infant in the jar of its mother's womb.[38] This infant stands (sometimes on its head), bends, kneels, raises its arms, and generally stretches to the limits of its environment, which is sketched in the most rudimentary, abstract of fashions. These images transcribed much earlier pictures, which can be found in manuscript editions of Muscio's Latin treatise on gynaecology, and, before that, in Soranus's second-century *Gynaecia*.

Whether standing or lying in their jar-wombs, these embryos are already little men, unconstrained by an umbilicus, apparently autonomous of their mothers, who have been reduced to the lines drawn around their progeny. Though later eighteenth- and nineteenth-century illustrations achieve a greater verisimilitude in displaying the uterine world, it remains an isolated domain, free of any maternal body. The womb is pictured as a fleshy casket on the page, with muscle and membrane folded back so as to reveal its slumbering occupant. The womb has become a monstrance for the embryo. The infant is still in its womb, but the womb itself has been ripped from the mother's body, or her body butchered so as to leave only her child-bearing midriff. In one of Jan van Rymsdyk's strikingly detailed images for William Hunter's *The Anatomy of the Human Gravid Uterus* (1774), most of the woman's torso has been cut away and her legs severed, leaving just stumps, showing their bone, flesh, fat and skin. But the now exposed child is apparently unaware of the butchery by which it is surrounded. It still sleeps, though it is perhaps dead, like its mother, who will never walk again. When, as sometimes, these obstetrical wombs are maternally located, they are placed in classical nudes, who, standing or reclining, seem unconcerned by their disembowelling. On occasion they will helpfully hold apart the flaps of their skin, so that we can gain a better view of their interior room.

This tradition of gynaecological illustration continued into the twentieth century, but now with photographs and electronic imaging, as with the ultrasound picture, from which the mother is entirely eliminated. While the images of this tradition were intended as maps for the apprentice doctor, schematics for tending the body's machinery, they betray an objective gaze that even as it seeks to serve the interests of survival, disentangles the life of the child from that of its mother, and reduces the latter to an indifferent, abstract receptacle. What matters is the little man within, who is already the measure of his cosmos.

> The autonomous human child represented in midwifery manuals, obstetrical atlases, anatomical sculpture, modern medical dictionaries, and new medical specialities is independent of the woman's body, whole and undivided, always male, and virtually never dissected, opened, wounded, or permeable; it is the image par excellence of rights-bearing Enlightenment Man ferociously rendered in the fabled state of nature.[39]

The obstetrical tradition doubly screened the mother, displaying the child-bearing womb, the very synecdoche of motherhood, while obscuring the mother herself, who was present only as a body-part. This double screening, revealing and hiding the mother, is continued in Kubrick's film, the last shot of which is one of the twentieth century's quintessential images of absent maternity. It is shown on a screen that itself must withdraw, go unseen, for the cinematic illusion of the wombless, all-perceiving foetus to appear. If cinema produces a transcendent gaze that escapes the limitations of the human eye, it is still dependent on the materiality of the screen. Kubrick's display of this maternal absence is futuristic, but continuous with an ancient tradition, predating modernity, that obscures the materiality of vision, the maternity of knowledge. The forgetting of the corporeal screen, that blocks our sight so that we might see, can be traced back to that most prestigious, because most primordial, cinema: Plato's 'kingdom of the shadows'.[40]

The Platonic Womb

The prisoner's flight from the cave, as recounted in Socrates' parable, is not only an allegory of the philosopher's journey from darkness to light – from ignorance to true knowledge – but also, on Luce Irigaray's reading, of his escape from the maternal earth, the material womb of the mother.[41] Plato's cave is, in detail, a womb. The upward passage, out of the cave, is repeated within it by the path that cuts it in two, and along which the puppeteers make their way, as they carry the figures whose shadows play on the back wall of the cave. But it is the other path that is the more important, since it leads out of and into the underground chamber. According to Irigaray, it is the path that Plato forgets, that he hurries along so as not to notice its passage, so as to forget the womb he flees, along this vaginal way.[42]

The cave doubles within itself the division between itself and its supposed outside; for in the cave are two screens, the curtain wall or hymen that separates the prisoners from the puppeteers, and the screen on which the shadows appear. It is between these two inner screens that the show of reality is produced, a vision machine that Irigaray also likens to the 'cinematographic apparatus'.[43] Irigaray offers a complex, many layered reading of Plato's parable, noting among other things the paradoxes that arise from supposing, as does Socrates, that the story of the cave and its outside is told from within, from between the two screens of the cave.[44] Irigaray, however, is not really interested in Plato's deconstruction of his story, holding, with most commentators, that what matters in Plato is his supposed theory of the forms. She is more concerned with the denigration of the maternal that follows from Plato's avowal of the sun as the single source of being and truth, an avowal that can be maintained only by looking into the sun, oblivious to the shadow that is cast upon the ground behind one.

The prisoner making his way out of the cave, 'must walk, without stopping, toward the "sun", taking no notice of the shadow that it still projects, *behind*. That double (of the self) must be neglected if one is to persevere with the climb. Leaving it to the still material extension of the path that one is following and ascending, in the *inverse direction*'. Thus the prisoner 'goes on with his "ordeal", the success of which is gauged by his blindness to everything around him'.[45] It is as if one were to look into the dazzling light of Kubrick's camera-projector, that both shows and sees the reality projected behind one, unable to see your own shadow that you perfectly mask, and oblivious to the materiality of the screen, that yet makes possible the showing and seeing of the camera-projector. Looking into the light of the camera-projector, supposing it the source of reality, one is blinded to the truth of one's situation. Thus the mother, the womb of reality, is left in darkness.

> Providing the basis for the wise man's auto-logical speculations, she lives in darkness. At/as back of the scene of representation which she props up by not/without knowing it. She makes no show or display. For if she were

> to shine, then the light would no longer, simply, belong to the sameness. The whole of the current economic system would have to be recalculated. And if she is granted the life of appearance, it will be a darkling affair. Underground shadow theatre, lunar reflection of the star that makes everything light and fertile. A lack-lustre double of the self-duplication that man carries within him, his 'soul', when 'she' doesn't stand in the way with her 'body'.[46]

For the escaping prisoner to turn his head and look backward, to see his shadow and remember from whence comes the materiality of his body, that casts the shadow, is to once more see what the sun, in dazzling the eye, does not show. But to look backward may not be enough, for even if the screen is recalled, one may yet envisage its function as merely reflecting the light straight back at the camera-projector, without variance of degree or diminution of brightness, and so once more confirm the camera-projector's self-sufficiency for the production of reality. We need a more complex apparatus, of mutually interdependent parts, a cinema cave where it is the circulation of light that produces vision; a light that does not move in one direction only, from behind to in front, or from in front to behind, but in all directions at once. We need a circulating, ambient light, that is the glowing of the screen, the fire of Pentecost.[47]

Virginal Light

Plato's flight from the cave is not quite as it seems, for as discussed in the previous chapter, it is imagined within the cave, and is thus a shadow-flight that never leaves the cave. It is a vision that the cave itself makes possible, and Irigaray's critique has purchase only when the condition of that possibility is forgotten, when the cave does not show itself in itself. It is then that vision becomes monocular, 'patriarchal', imagining a gaze that constitutes but is not constituted, that alone creates what it sees; an extramissive eye.

Such is the condition of the church, the ecclesiacinema, when it forgets itself; forgets *herself*. The church is not only the community that is formed by and witnesses to Christ, whom it seeks to follow. It is also the community, the body of people, who make Christ visible, seeable and followable. The church is a 'personal' community, all the members of whom are both projector and screen, a complex interanimative apparatus, all the parts of which are necessary for vision. The name of this community is also Mary, the Mother of God, Theotokos. For as mother, it was Mary who formed the Christ of God in her womb, held him in her arms and gave him to be seen – having been the first to see.

It is well established in the traditions of the church, though perhaps more in the East than in the West, that Jesus cannot be named apart from his mother, since she gave him her flesh, his humanity. It was her willingness to bear the Christ in her womb and in her arms, to bear him in her heart, that allowed God to appear in the world. Christ is to be seen in the Marian church. But Mary and her son are not isolated individuals, but are themselves parts of complex relationships, familial and social, ecclesial; forming and formed by friendships, known and unknown, an ever extending network that must finally include everyone. The person of Christ is one with his entire, multiple body.[48] In each appearing of Christ – in image and word, icon and scripture, in the bread and wine of the Eucharist, in each stranger who befriends another – it is Christ himself who arrives, entire and undivided, as if all other appearings were infinitely folded within each one, available to the mystic eye.

The church was identified with Mary by Ambrose, as early as the fourth century. Indeed, it is already implicit in the New Testament, in John's gospel, when, from the cross, Jesus gives his mother into the care of the beloved disciple, and thus the disciple into the care of Mary, who is to be his 'mother'.[49] In later figural readings of the text, mother and disciple became the maternal church and filial soul respectively, and as such stand at the foot of the cross in countless reredoses. It is she who produces and brings forth Christ, and shows him to the world. Without her, there would be nothing to see. This is wonderfully figured in those small medieval statuettes of the virgin and child that open to reveal not just Christ but the Trinity, as well as scenes from the life of Christ.[50] These 'opening virgins' (*Vierges ouverantes*) are miniature caves, little theatres, in the apses of which the divine is displayed. They contain a vision of Christ, just as the Virgin contained him in her womb, in the darkness of her cave. In the figure of Mary and her child, as he sits on her lap, or feeds at her breast, we see divinity dependent, succoured and nurtured, encompassed by the hands of a woman. In the figure of Mary and her child we see what Plato seems to forget, the cave upon which we depend, the screen which must be present if the cinematic vision is to appear. But this screen reflects light in all directions, because illuminating with its own light, with the radiance of mother and child. Moreover, as *ecclesia*, Mary is not only the mother on whom the church gazes, but also the gazing church, each and every one of whom is called to encompass Christ in his or her own life, to be the bride to his bridegroom.[51]

The cinematic screen gives rise to images through reflecting light, and in the cave a fire burns for the casting of shadows. So also in the Marian church, light is needed for vision in the womb. As the parallels with cave and cinema suggest, this cannot be an exterior light, penetrating the darkness from outside, since the 'outside' is that which appears 'inside'. It is the flickering fire that lights the cave and the projector that lights the cinema. They are 'inside' lights. So also in the church, in the virgin's womb, it is an interior light that gives rise to vision; the light of the Spirit. As such, it is a virginal and conceptive light. Virginal because it burns within, of itself; and conceptive because it produces vision. The light has no single origin, since it is the light of the Spirit that shines from, in and between Father and Son, and so also in the mother of the Son, from whom he takes his flesh, and in all those who partake of his flesh, drawn into the light of his body.

In the ancient church, in the Syrian tradition, Mary was the light by which the light of the world was made visible. She was the burning bush in whom God was manifested, burning without being consumed, bringing forth the very 'I am' of God, who would save his people from captivity (Exodus 3.1–15). 'In the fire Moses saw thy beauty in Shadow, O daughter of David, in whose bosom dwelt the Flame, and thou wert not consumed, O Mother of God, and full of grace.'[52] Mary is luminous because glorious, transfigured from within by grace, by the light of the Spirit. She is not merely a screen that reflects light, but shines herself, radiant with the Word she bears into the world. When Christ was transfigured on Mount Tabor, with his face shining like the sun, he showed the glory, the luminosity to be enjoyed by all the saints, and thus by Mary.[53] It is because she bore the Word that the saints can bear his glory. As the epitome of the church, Mary shines with a solar light, the brightness of the arc lamp in the projector: 'a woman clothed with the sun, with the moon under her feet, and on her head a crown of twelve stars'.[54]

Night Vision

The renaissance artist Raffaello Sanzio or Raphael (1483–1520) is said by Donato Bramante to have been blessed with a vision of the Virgin, who came to Raphael one night, at a time when he was struggling to paint a picture of the Madonna. She appeared to him in a self-illumined image; indeed, in a kind of movie playing on the wall of his bedchamber.

> In the night darkness, he looked at the wall across from his bed and saw that it was bathed in light, and the light was hanging on the wall, and it was the unfinished image of the Virgin shining in soft radiance, perfect, an image and yet living! and divinity was shining everywhere from it! Tears filled his eyes as he looked into Her indescribably tender face, and it was as if every least mistake he had made as an artist was being erased by this living vision of Her face; it even seemed to him that She was quite literally moving. And most wonderful of all, Raphael found in this bright vision precisely that for which he had searched all his life and that which he had for so long experienced only in dark haziness. He could not now remember how he had fallen back asleep, but upon arising in the morning, he felt as though he had been reborn.[55]

Indeed, Raphael's night-time vision might have been an early 'cinematic' image. It is now well established that the Dutch artist Johannes Vermeer (1632–75) used the *camera obscura* to produce the optically 'correct' images that we see most strikingly in his paintings of domestic interiors. The photographically unfocused highlights in Vermeer's *Girl with a Red Hat* (1660–1) can almost convince us that we are looking at a seventeenth-century photograph. Philip Steadman postulates that Vermeer's camera was his studio, or more properly a cubicle within it. The light from the room would enter this enclosure, focused through a 'pin hole' lens, perhaps set within a moveable tube poking through curtains. Standing or sitting in the dark, in his little man-made cave, Vermeer could trace the image that appeared on the back wall of the cubicle, the back wall of his studio. There, in his private cinema, he would see a young woman at her music lesson or making lace, writing a letter or drinking with friends, and transcribe and transmute these scenes with his artistry.[56]

As postulated, Vermeer's shadowy camera images would have been upside down and laterally reversed. He may have accepted this, and simply turned his tracing paper over, before transferring its outlines to his canvas, by the standard means of pinpricks and chalk. Alternatively, he might have traced the camera image from its other side, from outside the camera cubicle, with its back wall serving as a screen, either as a partition inside the cubicle or as the glowing wall of another room, beyond the cubicle. As with the glass screen in a plate camera, the image would still be upside down but laterally correct. A more technical solution would be to suppose the use of a plane mirror or two convex lenses for correcting the image before it fell upon the tracing wall. Whatever the means used by Vermeer to contrive his images, the evidence that he was an early master of the photographic image is compelling.[57] Like Raphael before him, Vermeer's paintings repeat a vision that appeared on the wall of a darkened chamber, glowing with the intensity of a cinematic image.

The use of a room or tent as a *camera obscura* is more akin to the modern cinema than were later box cameras developed in the eighteenth and nineteenth centuries, the images of which were viewed in shaded light. The image in the room or tent is not diminished by other light sources, but appears to shine with its own peculiar power. Seventeenth-century viewers were fascinated by what they saw in the *camera obscura*, and Steadman observes that even modern viewers are captivated by its images. 'The colours can seem richer, more intense, more concentrated than in direct vision – despite the general dimness of the image – particularly when the light comes from behind a translucent viewing screen.' Like Alex in the cinema-cave, for whom the 'colours of the real world only seem really real when you viddy them on the screen', viewers of the *camera obscura* see the world intensified, more real for being differently rendered, for being imaged in light and *moving*. In the *camera obscura* 'it comes as a shock – given one's preconceptions about photographic prints and slides – to see the objects in the picture move. A cloud floats across the sky, the branches of trees sway in the wind, a person innocent of being watched walks across the field of view.'[58] As today, so in the past, it is the life and movement of the camera's image that entrances, as, indeed, it had compelled Raphael, who in the dark saw 'an image and yet living'.

The British painter David Hockney wants to push the date for the first use of optical aids back to the early fifteenth century. He argues that in Flanders, at some point in the 1420s and 30s, artists such as Robert Campin (1378/9–1444) and Jan van Eyck (c. 1395–1441) inaugurated the realistic, 'photographic' way of picturing the world that we now think of as peculiarly modern.[59] Campin and Van Eyck had started to see the world through lenses; through the use, perhaps, of concave mirror-lenses, if not yet the apparitional images of the *camera obscura*. Hockney's claims are largely dependent on the evidence of the artists' pictures. Slight mismatches of perspective suggest the use of something other than the rules of geometric projection, developed in Florence at the beginning of the fifteenth century (by Filippo Brunelleschi and Leon Battista Alberti). The perfect delineation of foreshortened objects, the virtuoso rendering of folded cloths, and the production of portraits that we can only read as 'photographic', all suggest the use of optical aids. Among later fifteenth and sixteenth-century artists who show evidence of having seen the world optically – such as Hans Memling (c. 1430/40–94) and Hans Holbein (1497/8–1543) – Hockney includes the Italian Raphael. Raphael's 1518–19 portrait of Pope Leo X shows the pontiff holding in his left hand a small magnifying glass, perhaps an allusion to Raphael's use of some optical device in producing the portrait, the realism of which amazed Raphael's contemporaries.[60]

Raphael most likely used a concave mirror-lens, if he used any optical device at all. With his subject in bright sunlight, seated or standing by a small window or opening, the artist, on the other side, in a darkened chamber, could view and trace the subject's image, as it was caught at the window and cast by a concave mirror on to paper or canvas. Though the image would be upside down, the artist could exactly note the alignment of facial features, the hang of cloth and the curvature of rounded objects. And all the time the image would glow with the softened light of such transmission and gently move, as when a breeze might catch the subject's hair or s/he would blink or cough, or breathe deeply.

Raphael's dream-like vision of the Virgin, appearing as a moving picture on his bedroom wall, suggests the optical transfiguration of some living woman, a model whose features were transmuted by the lens, and fixed in paint. Raphael's Madonnas have seemed so serene and authoritative, that for many they became prototypical of the Virgin, as if Raphael had indeed seen and photographed the Mother of God. Pavel Florensky cites the story of Raphael's night-time vision as evidence that even in the West it is known that true religious art is informed by spiritual experience, by a vision or 'mystical dream'.[61] What makes for the truth of the picture – of the icon – is not whether it faithfully follows some prior representation, as when later artists strove to repeat Raphael's seraphic Madonnas, but whether it renders the artist's own apprehension of the mystical reality s/he is seeking to show. (Though of course, the eastern iconic tradition seeks to repeat a privileged, historically contingent Byzantine style of (re)presentation, and resists the use of human models, which it views as a modern aberration.[62])

The mystical reality that the icon seeks to evoke is the eternal prototype, of which all images, no matter how wondrous, are merely types. On this account, Raphael's paintings are truly iconic because they show the soul's vision of the Virgin, and it is no matter if the technical means for doing so involved the use of a model and a lens, since the cinematic (because moving) image cast by the latter might have been the icon by which Raphael was vouchsafed to see into the heart of the mystery. Yet this mechanism for fixing light, for conveying vision, is also a perfect figure or analogy for thinking about the relationship between what is seen and what is shown in the cinema-cave of the church. It is the relationship of the eternal prototype to the temporal type in the eastern iconic tradition; the relationship between the two sides of a window, when drawing with a concave-mirror lens. Thus by attending to the bearing of reality in the still or moving photograph, we can glimpse, by analogy or parody, the appearing of the real inside the cave, the showing of truth in the life and liturgies of the church.

Visionary Ontology

If the vision of the church is analogous to that of the cinema, and thus also to Plato's shadows, is it not finally an illusion? A shadow of a shadow, and so always susceptible to a reductive critique that will and should lead one from the shadows to the puppets and then on to something else, outside the cave, to 'reality' and 'truth'? In order to discover the real and the true must we not leave the cinema and the church, and go outside? If we remain within, are we not trapped in a space of fantasy, that is not merely illusory, but delusory in Freud's sense?

That would be the case if one supposed a non-paradoxical reading of Plato's parable, if that were possible. But if one holds that the venture of the 'outside' is always made from 'inside', is always a venture upon a 'shadow', then the latter is always its own thing; the 'original' of any reality it is said to represent. Reality precedes the shadow, but as the latter's reverse projection, as its belated presupposition.

For many, the photographic image achieves that to which all art tends, for which it has yearned, the direct representation of reality; an image without medium, that undoes absence and remakes the past. Mechanically produced, the photograph simply shows what was there. It is like no other forms of representation, which must always bear witness to their substance and making; to the chiselling of stone, the carving of wood, the brushing of paint. The photograph, on the other hand, is the real, to which it cleaves, losing itself in its referent. Thus for Roland Barthes, 'whatever it grants to vision and whatever its manner, a photograph is always invisible: it is not what we see'.[63] We see the thing.

In the motion picture we see the moving thing. We see its animation and duration, its life; and we cannot doubt that it lives. Yet the photographic process is deathly. This is most evident in the case of the still photograph, the freeze-frame that embalms a single moment for posterity. The subject is rendered as an object that has always already passed away.[64] No one is as they are in a photograph, or in a moving picture. No matter how vivacious or captivating are those who appear on the screen, they come to us out of the past, appearing as ghosts. There is no one more alive than Jeanne Moreau in *Jules et Jim* (France 1961), when in an oversized plaid cap, and with painted Chaplin moustache, she runs toward the camera across the bridge, racing her lovers Oskar Werner and Henri Serre. But the air of melancholy with which François Truffaut inflects this most vibrant and entrancing of his films, betokens not only the death that concludes the story, and the past age in which it is set, but the pastness of all celluloid life. When I look at a photograph of myself I see my passing, an anterior post-mortem.[65]

For Roland Barthes, it is the sign of death that constitutes the essence or *noeme* of (still) photography. For what the photograph shows 'has been'. 'Photography's inimitable feature (its *noeme*) is that someone has seen the referent (even if it is a matter of objects) in *flesh and blood*, or again *in person*.'[66] And it is the intractable 'this-has-been' of the photograph that marks its nature or genius, and difference from other forms of representation. The portrait painting can never convey the 'this-has-been' of its subject. This then is the mark of life *and* death in the photograph, that its subject has lived, and living, was, in a sense, always already dead. Of a photograph:

> These two little girls looking at a primitive airplane above their village (they are dressed like my mother as a child, they are playing with hoops) – how alive they are! They have their whole lives before them; but also they are dead (today), they are then *already* dead (yesterday). At the limit, there is no need to represent a body in order for me to experience this vertigo of time defeated.[67]

The photograph is the 'living image of a dead thing', an alive corpse.[68] It is this living mortality of the photograph, and the means of its production, that Barthes uses to differentiate photography from cinema, the still from the moving image, the historical 'snapshot' from the fictional film. Already in fiction cinema the 'this-has-been' of the actors is combined with the pose of the characters, diluting the melancholy of seeing the dead live.[69] Moreover, the 'trickery' that attends even the most straightforward of filmed sequences, the combination of lights, lens, apertures and framing, taken together with the 'fakery' of sets and costumes, means that what appeared before the camera is transfigured in the film, so that elements of what we see never were. As a consequence, the characters in a film are less ghostly than the subjects in a photograph. In the cinema, 'there is always a photographic referent, but this referent shifts, it does not make a claim in favour of its reality, it does not protest its former existence; it does not cling to me: it is not a *specter*'.[70]

Barthes can so distinguish cinema from (still) photography because he holds a resolutely 'realist' view of photographic transcription. Scorning those 'sociologists and semiologists' who argue for the fabricated nature of the photographic image, Barthes insists that the photograph is always 'analogical' of a preceding reality, because it is 'literally an emanation of the referent'.[71] 'From a real body, which was there, proceed radiations which ultimately touch me, who am here; . . . A sort of umbilical cord links the body of the photographed thing to my gaze: light, though impalpable, is here a carnal medium, a skin I share with anyone who has been photographed.'[72] Photography is 'magical' or 'religious', for 'might we not say of it what the Byzantines said of the image of Christ which impregnated St. Veronica's napkin: that it was not made by the hand of man, *acheiropoietos*?'[73] No doubt Barthes – a master semiologist – is being a little teasing, a little fanciful. The photographs he finds most radiant of the 'this-has-been' of the past, were nearly all carefully posed, and all were made by the hands of men, and he does not deny that all photographs are 'inflected' by the socio-semantic codes within which they are encountered.[74] Yet his analysis points to that which does indeed 'astonish' in the photograph, and – *pace* Barthes – in the cinema.

André Bazin (1919–58), the great French film theorist, was a 'realist' regarding both photography and cinema, arguing that film is most itself when showing us the 'this-has-been' of our world. As with Barthes' argument regarding photography, so for Bazin it is the mechanical production of the film image that assures its verisimilitude. Cinema achieves a pure mimesis, a zero degree of dissonance between reality and image.

> The objective nature of photography confers on it a quality of credibility absent from all other picture-making. In spite of any objections our critical spirit may offer, we are forced to accept as real the existence of the object reproduced, actually *re*-presented, set before us, that is to say, in time and space. Photography enjoys a certain advantage in virtue of this transference of reality from the thing to its reproduction . . . The photographic image is the object itself, the object freed from the conditions of time and space that govern it. No matter how fuzzy, distorted, or discoloured, no matter how lacking in documentary value the image may be, it shares, by virtue of the very process of its becoming, the being of the model of which it is the reproduction; it *is* the model . . . The photograph as such and the object in itself share a common being, after the fashion of a fingerprint.[75]

Cinema produces a moving fingerprint of mobile life, dragging the world into the theatre, so that the train hurtling toward the camera had early audiences jumping out of their seats.[76] The story may be apocryphal, but in a film like *L'Arrivée d'un train* (France 1895), Louis Lumière aimed at the facticity of life, natural and social. 'The cinema', declared Felix Mesguich, one of Lumière's cameramen, 'is the dynamism of life, of nature and its manifestation, of the crowd and its eddies. All that asserts itself through movement depends on it. Its lens opens on the world.'[77] When, in Lumière's *L'Arroseur arrosé* (France 1895), the hapless gardener is squirted with water from his hose, Maxim Gorky was so startled that he thought the spray was going to hit him too, and shrank back from the screen.[78]

Due to the automatic nature of the photographic machine, the image is not merely a representation, but a trace, a relic of the thing represented. This is what Barthes would call the fatality of the photograph, that its referent always comes with it, undetachable. Object and image are laminated together, perpetually coupled – an 'eternal coitus' – and cannot be separated without destroying both.[79] One might want to say that it is only light that is so fixed in the photograph, but for Barthes – as for Bazin before him – light is part of the apparatus, transubstantiating the object in the image. Yet Bazin, despite his rhetoric, was not a naïve realist. Like Barthes, Bazin's elision of the model with its image, comes from quietening the 'critical spirit' and giving in to the peculiar power of the photograph. Bazin knew as well as anyone that the appearance of reality in the still or moving photograph, is an effect of its process, its apparatus.

Bazin celebrated the development of the 'shot in depth', which allowed the movie camera to encompass a scene in a single take, with everything in focus, so that the movement of actors, rather than a montage of shots, produces the dramatic effect.[80] In this way dramatic space and duration is respected, and the structure of the image is more 'realistic'.[81] As with the world, the viewer's eye can range across the cinematic scene, which thereby gains an element of ambiguity, or at least the possibility for such.[82] Yet the fact that Bazin's favoured example of such a cinema is Orson Welles' *Citizen Kane* (USA 1941), alerts us to the fact that this 'realism' is as artificed as any cinema can be. Indeed, Bazin insisted that the single shot in depth is not, as one might think, merely a matter of removing the fourth wall from a room, but involves the careful placing of 'objects and characters' so that it is 'impossible for the spectator to miss the significance of the scene'.[83] Thus the apparent freedom of the viewer to interpret the drama is as constrained by the arrangement of objects and the placing and angle of the camera, as it is by a montage of shots.

Today, most informed cinemagoers know that much of what they see on the screen has never appeared before the lens of a camera, that the 'live action' of real life performers, acting against 'blue screens', has been digitally composited with other elements, either filmed elsewhere or generated from computer software, in order to produce images that appear to be mere reproductions of a pre-existing reality. Such 'special effects' are at their most effective, not when we cannot miss them, because then they are nearly all there is to see, as in George Lucas's *The Phantom Menace* (USA 2000), but in films where they go unnoticed, used to tweak otherwise straightforward scenes. Film trickery is as old as cinema itself. While Lumière was using his camera to record daily life, or tell simple stories, as in *Teasing the Gardener* (*L'Arroseur arrosé*), Georges Méliès would point his camera, not at real locomotives but at toy ones, using them to document a train that takes flight to the moon, in *Voyage à travers l'impossible* (France 1904).

At the outset of cinema, Lumière and Méliès established what Siegfried Kracauer saw as its two main tendencies: the 'realistic' and the 'formative', the one seeking to depict the world and the other to explore the imagination. Méliès, the fabulist, is the antithesis to Lumière's realist thesis, the one pursuing illusion and the other the mundane.[84] In which case, we might suggest Kubrick's *2001* as their synthesis, if not by intent at least in appearance, since it is an illusion that appears to be absolutely real, a sublime documentary of banal space flight. Indeed, some of its tricks are absolutely real, a matter of simply recording what was in front of the camera, as with Lumière recording the arrival of a train in the station. An example of such realism would be the shot of the stewardess on board the Aries spacecraft, as she walks slowly up the wall until she is completely upside down and able to exit along another corridor, the floor of which we might have thought the ceiling. This beautifully executed stunt was simply achieved by fixing the camera to the floor of the set, which was then made to rotate very slowly. As long as the actress kept walking on her treadmill, the illusion was flawless, since the camera was as honest as a camera can be.[85] Kubrick's pursuit of realism in science fiction, shows us that cinematic verisimilitude is as much a matter of artifice as the 'special effect' that attempts to deceive the eye. What, after all, was so 'realistic' about Lumière's silent, black and white, two dimensional images, when the world appears to us in three tactile dimensions, coloured and full of noise?

Bazin was the most theological of film theorists, but he needs to be pushed a little bit further in order to arrive at an ontology of the film image that will suffice for the ecclesiacinema. For Bazin still keeps open a homogeneous space between the image and its model, so that the reality of one resides in that of the other. 'The photograph as such and the object in itself share a common being, after the fashion of a fingerprint'.[86] Bazin needs to be more of a surrealist (a kind of realist), for whom, he tells us, '[e]very image is seen as an object and every object as an image'. For the surrealist, according to Bazin, photography 'produces an image that is a reality of nature, namely, an hallucination that is also a fact'.[87] It is in this way, which is not quite Bazin's way, that we should take him when he says that the 'photographic image is the object itself', that the image '*is* the model'. Model and image are collapsed into one another, but the being of the cinematic image has its own existence, which is not reducible to either an objectivity prior to the image, nor to a subjectivity that persists after the passing of the image, in the mind of the viewer. The reality of the image is to be found moving between all of these, excessively, transforming and producing each in turn. Its location is indeterminate, its being only in its becoming, appearing in the working of the cinematic apparatus, which includes the labour of looking and learning to see.[88]

Cinematic images are like other artistic representations; they are representations of nothing other than themselves. They are their own thing, their own presentation. They do not come after some other thing, that they repeat; they repeat only themselves. Here we tend to be fooled by the means of their production, by the automatic and machinic nature of their making, whereby we place the camera in front of the object – whether thing or person, still or moving – and expose the film, which then, after due processing, delivers the reality of the object, inscribed by light on the plane of the film. But though object and image are related by light, they are at the same time separated by that very relationship; and it will need the gaze of the viewer, who has learned how to look at the image, to see its disclosure of a reality. Without the looking and seeing, the vision of the viewer, the vision of the image will not show itself. Raphael had to awaken in the night and look with desirous eyes in order to see the tender smile of the Virgin.

Iconostasis

At one point in *Camera Lucida*, Roland Barthes likens the photograph to the icon, or rather he suggests that it is only by refusing to look at a photograph, that it can gain a power of disclosure similar to that of the icon when it is venerated but not viewed. For then the photograph's denotation – with all the power of the 'this-has-been' – no longer overwhelms the eye, and its (non)viewer is able to see its connotations and allusions, in his or her mind's eye.

> I cannot place [the photograph] in a ritual (on my desk, in an album) unless, somehow, I avoid looking at it (or avoid its looking at me), deliberately disappointing its unendurable plenitude and, by my very inattention, attaching it to an entirely different class of fetishes: the icons which are kissed in the Greek churches without being seen – on their shiny glass surface.[89]

The photograph's 'unendurable plenitude' is the strength with which it imposes the being of its referents upon us, the violence with which 'it fills the sight by force'. In the photograph 'nothing can be refused or transformed'.[90] We must believe what we see, even when we do not quite know what it is, for 'this-has-been'. Icons are different, but not, as Barthes suggests, because they are refused sight, but because they show us their subjects in a different way, in a different economy of looking. And they do this by barring our vision.

In the first instance the icon is the painted image of Christ, or of the Virgin, or of one of the saints, as produced in the Byzantine manner, in the Eastern Orthodox tradition.[91] But it is also any image used in a Christian church to convey sight of spiritual truths, including the verbal pictures of scripture, themselves often repeated in visual form. More essentially, the icon is anything that gives sight of the one true image who is Jesus Christ. Icons are scriptural images, not painted but 'written', and not completed until signed with their names;[92] and scriptural images only live in their performance, in the life of Christ's body.[93] Thus it is not just words or paintings, but also people who are icons of the image, and most truly the icon of Christ when, forgiving and forgiven – forgiving because forgiven – they gather at the Eucharist to again receive and become the body of Christ.

In the liturgies of the church, the icon in its various forms enlivens all the senses. Though seen with the eyes, it is also heard with the ears, touched with the hand or lips, tasted in the bread and wine, and inhaled in the encircling incense. This is a richer presentation than the cinema can provide, and one that is more intense, because more truly a transcendent vision than the ecstasy of the all-seeing, all grasping camera-projector. Moreover, the icon allows us to see by refusing us that 'unendurable plenitude' that Barthes finds in the photograph. There is no violence akin to the photograph's 'this-has-been'. For the icon offers a vision that requires our looking as much as its showing, a vision that is pacific to the eyes of faith, and so not really our looking at all, but a participation in the seeing of that on which we look. And this is possible because the icon bars our sight.[94]

In the Orthodox Church the icon is not one but many, gathered together and displayed on the *iconostasis*, the screen that shows the meaning of history, from creation to judgement, and that separates the sanctuary from the nave.[95] This arrangement is itself a kind of icon, a model of that which the iconostasis permits, since the altar hidden behind the screen figures the prototype that the icons present and conceal. By barring our sight, the iconostasis shows us into the mystery of God. It shows us the saints, not as they were, but as they are in glory, irradiated with a light that shines from within, the circling light of heaven, figured in the gold that closes off the icon's visual field, and from which its colours emerge. 'Gold, which combines a radiating luminosity with opacity, adequately expresses the divine light – an impenetrable light, that is, something essentially different from natural light, the opposite of darkness.'[96] The icons shows us Christ transfigured, not simply the man who was, the 'this-has-been' that a camera might have caught, but the Word-in-the-man, who *is*; the glorious Christ on Mount Tabor, portrayed in scriptural and visual icons. 'And he was transfigured before them, and his clothes became dazzling white, such as no fuller on earth could bleach them.'[97]

> In actuality the iconostasis is a boundary between the visible and invisible worlds, and it functions as a boundary by being an obstacle to our seeing the altar, thereby making it accessible to our consciousness by means of its unified row of saints (i.e. by a cloud of witnesses) that surround the altar where God is, the sphere where heavenly glory dwells, thus proclaiming the mystery.[98]

The icon is a type of the prototype, an image that precisely because it resists a photographic 'realism' – through the manners of artistic convention and liturgical parlance – stops us from imagining that we might simply see the unseeable, the ineffable mystery of those in glory. Yet at the same time as our vision is stopped, brought up against figures of speech and paint, liturgical repetition, our eyes may be opened to that which the icons have to show, and which appears to the eyes of faith as their depth or intensity.

In the church there is a passage through the iconostasis, the royal doors, the gates of paradise, that allow what is within to come forward, so that the iconostasis serves and finds its elucidation in that which is the church's truest icon: the receiving of the consecrated bread and wine. 'Christ does not show himself in the holy gifts: he *gives* himself. He *shows* himself in the icon.'[99] In the eucharistic 'memorial' there is no pathos of the photographic 'this-has-been', since what was, *is now*; arriving now, becoming now, the body given once and for all, eaten and drunk now. The eucharistic icon is entirely saturated with the body it presents; an abundant plenitude that we can receive again and again, excessively. All icons are ordered to this reception, offering their surfaces – written, painted and acted – as screens on which we can see the mystery, yet only by that looking which participates in the seeing of that on which we look, lit by the glory of the triune God, eternity's dancing light. If we do not see by the light of the Spirit, the icons remain merely painted boards, empty gestures, antique tales.[100] (Churches without an altar screen lack a certain propaedeutic for learning how to look at the eucharistic icon, and so must train their vision more immediately through the performance of the liturgy.)

Unlike the photograph, which is always belated, filled with the pathos of the 'this-has-been' (though less so in the cinema), the icon does not come *after*, but always *ahead* of its referent, which is not presupposed as its ground, but evoked as its fulfilment, its transcendent condition of possibility. The icons are not denied a historical reference, indeed they are almost exclusively concerned with what has happened. But these past happenings are never simply past, pathetic with the sense of the never-to-be-recovered, since their participants, caught up into the glory of the living God, are living now. The icons show us what will be, and in this do not simply oppose the 'this-has-been' of the photograph, since the promise of the future is its arriving, already now in the vision of the icon. At the Eucharist – the truest icon – the church does not call for Christ to come forth from the past, dredged into present memory, but from the future, from whence he is already arriving in the church's incomprehensible power to call him to the eucharistic table; which is Christ's call to us, to come and eat and see that the Lord is good.

*

For Roland Barthes, unlike David Hockney, the invention of photographic vision was not a matter of lenses but of chemicals, for only with the latter was it possible to fix light on a surface, as an emanation of the object photographed. This renders the photograph immensely affecting, overpowering us with a melancholy for what has been, since in the photograph those who are past appear to us as the living dead. This power is weakened in the cinema, where theatrical and technical artistry produce something less automatic and more akin to painting, the fabricating of images through the manipulation of lights, chemicals – and now – computers. Yet, as already suggested, there is something knowingly fanciful in Barthes' account of photographic realism, which is intensified with the replacement of celluloid by video-tape, and tape by digital discs, and so on. The fixing of light was always its manipulation, its use for human ends, and it doesn't so much matter if this was once done by eye and hands, placing paint upon board and canvas.

The icon finds its analogy in the *camera obscura*, because the latter produces an image by blanking out that which would be seen, setting up a wall between the viewer and the viewed. However, it is the wall that allows the image to appear, just as it is the iconostasis that allows us to see the truth of the altar, the glory of God in Christ's body. The secret of the *camera obscura* is the aperture, the tiny hole or lens that transforms light into an image. It has to be precisely placed in a darkened enclosure, within which the viewer once had to take up residence, as in the cinema, becoming part of the apparatus. So in the church, the icon has traditionally been pictured as a window through which divine light streams, making the icon both aperture and screen. The viewer of the icon must also be participant in the apparatus, practised in seeing with the eyes of faith, of ritual performance, and illumined – given vision – by the very light that is to be seen, shining from the icon. This vision is a moving one, as in the cinema, for its truest form is the living icon of the Eucharist, the celebration of reception and return, of being for/given, again and again; of Christ-with-us, once more, as the church prays.

Light shines from the face of the icon, illuminating those who participate in the iconic/cinematic apparatus, who view its moving scenes. It is this flow of light, from the shining icon-screen inside the cave-become-temple, illuminating all who are within, that shows us that what they go to see is not simply a glorious vision – an angelophania – of what is and will be, but themselves, their own lives, in the light of that vision. They go within in order to see what is without, to see into all the corners of our sunlit, neon-lit world, that yet is still in darkness. It is this searching light that constitutes the church's ontological catechesis, which shows us how we do and might live by showing us lives shaped in and after Christ, in the light of his life.[101] The Paul of Ephesians enjoins us to 'live as children of light',[102] that is to dwell in Christ as he dwells in us, to live in the body-temple called Christ.[103] 'Sleeper awake! Rise from the dead, and Christ will shine on you'.[104]

When we enter the commercial cinema-temples of our age, we find ourselves looking at other glowing screens, parodically different from those in the church, and yet themselves a kind of angelophania, showing us visions of how we do and might live, how we might imagine ourselves in the world. The theology of the cinema is required to consider these rival screen-visions in the light of the church's own iconostasis, which itself is plural and internally contested. The church learns to see from the looking of all her members, no matter how differently they see from one another. It cannot be that other visions are only a kind of darkness, since the light of Christ shows us that these other lights might also shine with his radiance. In other cinemas we may see what we have missed in the church, either because the church has yet to produce the icon, or because looking, we have yet to see what is before our eyes. Thus a theology of the cinema is also a discerning of lights, of screen-visions, and that is what is attempted in the rest of this book with regard to visions of the body and its desiring. For it is from desire that we learn of divine eros, the love that comes to us in the flesh so that we might enter into the triune mystery, the embrace of God, and with our bodies see the beatific vision.

Notes

1 On Kubrick's brilliant use of music and sound – or its absence – in *2001* see Michel Chion, *La Musique au cinéma* (Paris: Fayard, 1995), pp. 345–52; and Michel Chion, *Kubrick's Cinema Odyssey*, translated by Claudia Gorbman (London: BFI Publishing, 2001), pp. 90–101. This book is the best single text on *2001* in English.

2 It was to have been Saturn, but Kubrick felt that the available special effects technology was not adequate for imaging Saturn's rings.

3 The computer was first imagined as a robot, named Athena – after Odysseus's divine protectress – then Socrates, before becoming HAL, the on-board computer in charge of all of the *Discovery*'s systems. Many noted that HAL was but one letter away from IBM, the giant American computing company; but the official story was that HAL is an acronym for Heuristic and Algorithmic. In the French language version of the film, HAL is CARL (Centre analytique de recherche et de liason) and voiced by Jean-Louis Trintignant; and, in the scene where HAL faces 'death' and recalls his 'childhood memories', instead of singing 'Daisy' he sings 'Au clair de la lune' ('My candle has gone out, I have no more flame . . .'). See Chion, *Kubrick's Cinema Odyssey*, pp. 4–5, 28.

4 Giles Deleuze, *Cinema 2: The Time Image*, translated by Hugh Tomlinson and Robert Galeta (London: The Athlone Press, [1985] 1992), pp. 205–6. On Deleuze and Kubrick see further Bill Krohn, 'Full Metal Jacket' in *Incorporations*, edited by Jonathan Crary and Sanford Kwinter (New York: Zone Books, 1992), pp. 429–35.

5 'The Sentinel' was written in 1948 but not published until 1951. It is reprinted in Arthur C. Clarke, *The Lost Worlds of 2001* (London: Sidgwick & Jackson, 1972), pp. 19–28.

6 Arthur C. Clarke, *2001: A Space Odyssey* (London: Arrow Books, 1968), p. 251.

7 Clarke, *2001*, p. 253.

8 Clarke, *2001*, p. 255. Film and novel were produced in the period of the 'cold war' between the capitalist West and the Communist East, and one of the arenas of that 'war' was the 'space race' between the United States of America and the Union of Soviet Socialist Republics. The Russian Yuri Gagarin was the first man in space (12 April 1961); the American Neil Armstrong was the first man on the moon (20 July 1969); and in between came Kubrick's film. See further Chion, *Kubrick's Cinema Odyssey*, pp. 32–4.

9 Clarke, *2001*, p. 256.

10 Arthur C. Clarke, *The Lost Worlds of 2001*, p. 239. See Homer, *The Odyssey*, translated by E.V. Rieu (Harmondsworth: Penguin Books, 1946), p. 336 (bk XXII, l.306–82).

11 Piers Bizony, *2001: Filming the Future* (London: Aurum Press, 1994), p. 16. Alexander Walker finds *2001* a hopeful film, which he contrasts with Kubrick's previous film, *Dr Stangelove* (1964), 'weighted with pessimism' (*Stanley Kubrick, Director*, revised edition (London: Weidenfeld & Nicolson, 1999), p. 162). Thomas Allen Nelson also offers a hopeful reading of the film, paying attention to its doubling of characters and events (*Kubrick: Inside a Film Artist's Maze*, revised edition (Bloomington and Indianapolis: Indiana University Press, 2000), pp. 103–35). Even Gilles Deleuze suggests that the murderous violence of HAL's brain-world may be overcome, in the creation of a 'world-brain as a whole in the harmony of the spheres', as foetus and earth enter 'into a new, incommensurable, unknown relation, which would convert death into a new life' (Deleuze, *Cinema 2*, p. 206).

12 Zoë Sofia does not hesitate to read the film in this way, as closing with a vision of the 'exterminating fetus', revenging the aborted. When 'we see the Earth-fetus dyad replaced by the fetus alone, we are to read the move literally: the Star Child bumps off (i.e., exterminates) the Earth, fulfilling the nuclear project by disappearing life into the circle of megadeath.' Zoë Sofia, 'Exterminating Fetuses: Abortion, Disarmament, and the Sexo-Semiotics of Extraterrestrialism', *Diacritics*, 14 (1984): 47–59 (p. 53).

13 John Baxter, *Stanley Kubrick: A Biography* (London: Harper Collins, 1997), p. 210.

14 Baxter, *Stanley Kubrick*, pp. 209–10.

15 Kubrick likened the star-child's ambiguous appearance to the enigmatic Mona Lisa. See Walker, *Stanley Kubrick, Director*, p. 192.

16 'Ligeti's *Atmosphères*, composed in 1961, is an astonishing orchestral piece on the threshold of formlessness, close to what could be imagined as the

sound of matter in continual transformation.' Chion, *Kubrick's Cinema Odyssey*, p. 96.

17 A similar resonance between the eye and the world it beholds and the camera and the world it creates, opens Ridley Scott's *Bladerunner* (USA 1982), with its haunting panorama of twenty-first century, smog bound Los Angeles, reflected in the eye of the film's chief protagonist (Harrison Ford). His vision proves to be as unreliable as that of any camera. But the elision of eye and camera appears early in film history, for example in Dziga Vertov's powerfully inventive *Man with a Movie Camera* (USSR 1929).

18 Christian Metz, 'The Imaginary Signifier', translated by Ben Brewster, *Screen*, 16 (1975): 14–76; variously reprinted, but here cited from *Film and Theory: An Anthology*, edited by Robert Stam and Toby Miller (Oxford: Blackwell, 2000), pp. 408–36.

19 See Jacques Lacan, 'The Mirror-Stage as Formative of the I as Revealed in Psychoanalytic Experience' in *Écrits: A Selection*, translated by Alan Sheridan (London: Tavistock, 1977).

20 Metz, 'The Imaginary Signifier', pp. 412–13.

21 Kubrick would endlessly re-shoot tracking shots that he thought too bumpy, reputedly taking three days to capture the 'dolly' shot that concludes *The Shining*.

22 Robert Altman and Brian de Palma are modern masters of the fluid shot, the sinuous long take, as in the opening of Altman's *The Player* (USA 1992) or De Palma's *Snake Eyes* (USA 1998), the latter aided with a little trickery. From the earliest days of cinema, film makers sought to mobilize their cameras, sometimes to astounding effect, as in Dziga Vertov's *Man with a Movie Camera* (USSR 1929) or F.W. Murnau's *Sunrise* (USA 1927).

23 Metz, 'The Imaginary Signifier', p. 413.

24 Siegfried Kracauer, *Theory of Film: The Redemption of Physical Reality* (Princeton, NJ: Princeton University Press, [1960] 1997), p. 171.

25 For Michael Herr, the last shot of *2001* is 'the single most inspired spiritual image in all of film, the Star Child watching with equanimity the timeless empty galaxies of existence-after-existence, waiting patiently once again to be born.' See Michael Herr, *Kubrick* (London: Picador, 2000), p. 71.

26 'A heavy wooden monolith was sanded, rubbed, sanded again. Then a mixture of black paint and pencil graphite was applied – and rubbed down, applied and rubbed down, over and over, till the slab glowed with an eerie blackness. It shone like silk, yet sucked up light like a black hole . . . Touching this immaculate surface on set with greasy fingers was proclaimed a capital offence'. Bizony, *2001*, p. 105.

27 Chion, *Kubrick's Cinema Odyssey*, p. 88.

28 Heywood's daughter was played by Kubrick's own, Vivian Kubrick. Later she would film her father in *The Making of the Shining*.

29 Bizony, *2001*, pp. 130–1.

30 Baxter, *Stanley Kubrick*, p. 219.
31 René Descartes, *Discourse on Method, Optics, Geometry and Meterology*, translated by Paul J. Olscamp (Indianapolis: Bobbs-Merrill, [1637] 1965), p. 68.
32 Zoë Sofia finds that the 'fertilization of a womb-like space by a spermatic emission is played out at several moments: monoliths generate ideas in ape-men's brains; tools fly off and fertilize high-tech wombs; the Discovery crosses space and time to come into Jupiter Space and generate a cyborg fetus.' ('Exterminating Fetuses', p. 51) However, the womb of 'Jupiter Space' is precisely nothing, so answering to that forgetting of womb and mother which is prevalent in much Pro-Life rhetoric, which imagines a kind of motherless, spermatic womb ('Exterminating Fetuses', pp. 56–7).
33 Nelson, *Kubrick*, p. 135.
34 Lennart Nilsson, 'Drama of Life before Birth', *Life* (30 April 1965). See also Lennart Nilsson, *A Child Is Born*, revised edition (London: Faber and Faber, [1965] 1977).
35 Nilsson, 'Drama of Life before Birth', p. 54.
36 Bizony, *2001*, p. 131.
37 Sofia, 'Exterminating Fetuses', p. 49. The romance of foetal life informs films like Steven Spielberg's *Close Encounters of the Third Kind* (USA 1977 and 1980 for the extended Special Edition), which presents its magic aliens – sci-fi fairies or guardian angels – as walking, elongated embryos, shining with benevolence, the so-called 'greys' of countless abduction scenarios. Their dark eyes, over-large foreheads and glowing white skin, establish the 'white man' as primordial in the universe, innocent of all politics.
38 Karen Newman, *Fetal Positions: Individualism, Science, Visuality* (Stanford, CA: Stanford University Press, 1996).
39 Newman, *Fetal Positions*, p. 67. For Newman, the gynaegraphical history she so extensively illustrates, supports an anti-abortion rhetoric that she seeks to ironize, apparently unperturbed that much 'pro-choice' rhetoric must repeat a similar abstraction of foetus from mother, establishing the autonomy of the rights bearing woman over against that of her child. For nuanced theological reflection on the question of abortion see Ann Loades, 'On Abortion: Some Feminist and Theological Reflections', in *Faithfulness and Fortitude: In Conversation with the Theological Ethics of Stanley Hauerwas*, edited by Mark Thiessen Nation and Samuel Wells (Edinburgh: T. & T. Clark, 2000), pp. 233–55; Rowan Williams, *Lost Icons: Reflections on Cultural Bereavement* (Edinburgh: T. & T. Clark, 2000), pp. 31–47.
40 This is Maxim Gorky's description of the Lumière film-world he first encountered at the Nizhny Novgorod Fair in 1896. 'If only you knew how strange it is to be there. There are no sounds, no colours. There everything – the earth, the trees, the people, the water, the air – is tinted in a grey monotone: in a grey sky there are grey rays of sunlight; in grey faces, grey eyes, and the leaves of the trees are grey like ashes. This is not life but the shadow of life and this is not movement but the soundless shadow of movement.'

Maxim Gorky, 'The Lumière Cinematograph' in *The Film Factory: Russian and Soviet Cinema in Documents 1896–1939*, edited by Richard Taylor and Ian Christie (London: Routledge and Kegan Paul, 1988), pp. 25–6.

41 Luce Irigaray, 'Plato's Hystera' in *Speculum of the Other Women*, translated by Gillian C. Gill (Ithaca, NY: Cornell University Press, [1074] 1985), pp. 243–364.

42 Irigaray, *Speculum*, pp. 247–48.

43 Irigaray, *Speculum*, p. 271.

44 Irigaray, *Speculum*, pp. 278–83.

45 Irigaray, *Speculum*, p. 314.

46 Irigaray, *Speculum*, p. 345.

47 We need to be caught up into the rotating light of the Trinity, when, as Gregory of Nyssa has it, we will see 'the revolving circle of the glory moving from Like to Like . . . For with what shall the Father be glorified, but with the true glory of the Son: and with what again shall the Son be glorified, but with the majesty of the Spirit? In like manner, again, Faith completes the circle, and glorifies the Son by means of the Spirit, and the Father by means of the Son.' Gregory of Nyssa, *On the Holy Spirit*, in *The Nicene and Post-Nicene Fathers*, edited by Philip Schaff and Henry Wace (Edinburgh: T. & T. Clark, 1994), vol. 5 (Gregory of Nyssa), p. 324.

48 1 Corinthians 12.12–13.

49 John 19.26–7. For a meditation on this text see Tina Beattie, *Rediscovering Mary: Insights from the Gospels* (Tunbridge Wells: Burns & Oates, 1995), ch. 10; and for a relevant discussion of the text see Gavin D'Costa, *Sexing the Trinity: Gender, Culture and the Divine*, (London: SCM Press, 2000), pp. 68–72.

50 See Caroline Walker Bynum, *Fragmentation and Redemption: Essays on Gender and the Human Body in Medieval Religion* (New York: Zone Books, 1992), pp. 212–17.

51 Ephesians 5.22–4.

52 St Ephrem (c. 306–73) quoted in Thomas Livius, *The Blessed Virgin in the Fathers of the First Six Centuries* (London: Burns & Oates, 1893), p. 605.

53 See Leonid Ouspensky, *Theology of the Icon*, translated by Anthony Gythiel and Elizabeth Meyendorff, 2 volumes (Crestwood, NY: St Vladimir's Seminary Press, 1992), vol. 1, p. 159. Mount Tabor is the traditional name for the site of the transfiguration. The Eastern Orthodox tradition has disputed the nature of the taboric light, as to whether it was created or uncreated. Generally it has been understood as an 'energy' of divinity, and so one with the divine essence. For St Gregory Palamas (c. 1296–1359) it is the 'unchangeable beauty of the prototype, the glory of God, the glory of the Holy Spirit, a ray of divinity' (quoted in Ouspensky, *Theology of the Icon*, vol. 2, p. 238). Here I have more closely associated the light of glory with God-the-Spirit, which, in a further move, one might associate with Wisdom/Sophia.

54 Revelation 12.1. Mary was identified with the 'woman clothed with the sun' from the fourth century onwards (as in Epiphanius's *Panarion*), but

the identification was firmly established by Bernard of Clairvaux in the twelfth century. Margaret Barker identifies the 'woman clothed with the sun' as the ancient – sixth century BC – Goddess of Jerusalem, the Queen of Heaven, Wisdom/Sophia. 'The Queen of Heaven in all her aspects is central to the Book of Revelation. She returns to her city, first giving birth to the divine child. The harlot who had replaced her as the genius of Jerusalem is destroyed, and the bride can then return from heaven as the heavenly Jerusalem. She gives herself as the gift of resurrection, and her children become citizens of the heavenly city, restored to Eden and eating from the tree of life.' Margaret Barker, *The Revelation of Jesus Christ* (Edinburgh: T. & T. Clark, 2000), p. 211.

55 Donato D'Angelo Bramante, quoted in Pavel Florensky, *Iconostasis*, translated by Donald Sheehan and Olga Andrejev (Crestwood, NY: St Vladimir's Seminary Press, 1996), p. 77.

56 Philip Steadman, *Vermeer's Camera: Uncovering the Truth behind the Masterpieces* (Oxford: Oxford University Press, 2001). See also Lawrence Gowing, *Vermeer*, second edition (London: Faber, [1952] 1970). The *camera obscura* should not be confused with the *camera lucida*, that uses a prism to allow the artist to view his or her subject with one eye and the paper with the other, thus superimposing one upon the other.

57 Steadman, *Vermeer's Camera*, pp. 112–13.

58 Steadman, *Vermeer's Camera*, p. 15.

59 David Hockney, *Secret Knowledge: Rediscovering the Lost Techniques of the Old Masters* (London: Thames and Hudson, 2001).

60 Hockney, *Secret Knowledge*, pp. 52–3.

61 Florensky, *Iconostasis*, pp. 75, 79–80.

62 Ouspensky, *Theology of the Icon*, vol. 2, pp. 501–2.

63 Roland Barthes, *Camera Lucida: Reflections on Photography*, translated by Richard Howard (London: Vintage, [1982] 1993), p. 6.

64 Barthes, *Camera Lucida*, pp. 10–15.

65 Barthes, *Camera Lucida*, p. 97.

66 Barthes, *Camera Lucida*, p. 79.

67 Barthes, *Camera Lucida*, p. 96.

68 Barthes, *Camera Lucida*, p. 79.

69 Barthes, *Camera Lucida*, p. 79.

70 Barthes, *Camera Lucida*, p. 89.

71 Barthes, *Camera Lucida*, pp. 88 and 80.

72 Barthes, *Camera Lucida*, pp. 80–1.

73 Barthes, *Camera Lucida*, pp. 88 and 82. Some seventeenth-century Orthodox writers argued for a 'photographic' understanding of iconic representation, as 'mirroring' reality, for which the fourteenth-century legend of St Veronica's veil – the *vera icon* (true image) – was exemplary. However, this is not the theology of the icon as generally developed in the Orthodox tradition, which is not so much concerned with the outward appearance as with the inner

truth of the saints, the 'intensity' or glory of their lives. See Ouspensky, *Theology of the Icon*, vol. 2, pp. 344–5.

74 Barthes, *Camera Lucida*, p. 88.

75 André Bazin, 'The Ontology of the Photographic Image', in *What Is Cinema?*, translated by Hugh Gray (Berkeley: University of California Press, 1967), pp. 9–16 (pp. 13–15).

76 'It darts like an arrow straight towards you – watch out! It seems as though it is about to rush into the darkness where you are sitting and reduce you to a mangled sack of skin, full of crumpled flesh and splintered bones, and destroy this hall and this building, so full of wine, women, music and vice, and transform it into fragments and into dust. But this, too, is merely a train of shadows.' Maxim Gorky, 'The Lumière Cinematograph', p. 26. Gorky's film hall – with its wine, women, music and vice – can be seen in Francis Ford Coppola's *Bram Stoker's Dracula* (USA 1992), when Prince Vlad (Dracula) takes Minna to the London cinematograph, apparently showing the Lumières' train. How-ever, though the Lumières exhibited in London from 1896 onwards, Dracula and Minna are shown watching Thomas 'Wizard' Edison's Vitascope, which first exhibited in New York in the same year, and was briefly brought to London. See Charles Musser, *The Emergence of Cinema: The American Screen to 1907*, History of the American Cinema Volume 1 (Berkeley: University of California Press, 1990), pp. 109–32. Coppola's film is set in 1897, the year when Bram Stoker published his novel, and the film wonderfully weaves together the invention of the cinema with that of one of its most enduring characters, Count Dracula. For more on the vampire see chapter 7 (Want of Family) below.

77 Quoted in Kracauer, *Theory of Film*, p. 31.

78 Maxim Gorky, 'You Don't Believe your Eyes', *World Film News* (March 1938), p. 16.

79 Barthes, *Camera Lucida*, p. 6.

80 André Bazin, 'The Evolution of the Language of Cinema', in *What Is Cinema?*, pp. 23–40 (p. 33).

81 Bazin, *What Is Cinema?*, p. 35.

82 Bazin, *What Is Cinema?*, p. 36.

83 Bazin, *What Is Cinema?*, pp. 34–5. On Welle's cinema see further André Bazin, *Orson Welles: A Critical View*, translated by Jonathan Rosenbaum (London: Elm Tree Books, 1978).

84 Kracauer, *Theory of Film*, p. 30.

85 See *The Making of Kubrick's 2001*, edited by Jerome Agel (New York: New American Library, 1970).

86 Bazin, *What Is Cinema?*, p. 15.

87 Bazin, *What Is Cinema?*, pp. 15–16.

88 The indeterminate location of the artwork is not of course peculiar to cinema, being a condition of all artistic performances; and all viewing is a kind of participative performance, since we must *look* in order to *see*.

89 Barthes, *Camera Lucida*, pp. 90–1.
90 Barthes, *Camera Lucida*, p. 91.
91 For a short history and critique of the ideology of the icon see Alain Besançon, *The Forbidden Image: An Intellectual History of Iconoclasm*, translated by Jane Marie Todd (Chicago: University of Chicago Press, [1994] 2000), ch. 3.
92 Besançon, *The Forbidden Image*, p. 134.
93 See Gerard Loughlin, *Telling God's Story: Bible, Church and Narrative Theology* (Cambridge: Cambridge University Press, [1996] 1999), ch. 4.
94 The icon bars sight in order to show what cannot be seen, to show the unseen in the seen. This 'barring' of sight should not be confused with the idol, which terminates the gaze. 'In the idol, the gaze is buried.' Jean-Luc Marion, *God without Being: Hors-Texte*, translated by Thomas A. Carlson (Chicago: University of Chicago Press, [1982] 1991), p. 13. The icon bars vision in the sense that it renders the invisible visible, as invisible in the visible. 'The icon . . . attempts to render visible the invisible as such, hence to allow that the visible not cease to refer to an other than itself, without, however, that other ever being reproduced in the visible . . . The gaze can never rest or settle if it looks at an icon; it always must rebound upon the visible, in order to go back in it up the infinite stream of the invisible. In this sense, the icon makes visible only by giving rise to an infinite gaze.' Marion, *God without Being*, p. 18. See also Jean-Luc Marion, *The Idol and Distance: Five Studies*, translated by Thomas A. Carlson (New York: Fordham University Press, [1977] 2001) and Gerard Loughlin, 'Breezes: Religious Images in the Age of Mechanical Reproduction', *Louvain Studies*, 27 (2002): 265–79.
95 Ouspensky, *Theology of the Icon*, vol. 2, pp. 275–85.
96 Ouspensky, *Theology of the Icon*, vol. 2, p. 496. On the use of gold see further Florensky, *Iconostasis*, pp. 121–31.
97 Mark 9.2–8; Matthew 17.1–8; Luke 9.28–36.
98 Florensky, *Iconostasis*, p. 62.
99 Ouspensky, *Theology of the Icon*, vol. 2, p. 283.
100 Florensky, *Iconostasis*, pp. 64–6. Marion presents the economy of iconic vision in terms of the intentional gaze. 'The essential in the icon – the intention that envisages – comes to it from elsewhere, or comes to it as that elsewhere whose invisible strangeness saturates the visibility of the face with meaning . . . Contemplating the icon amounts to seeing the visible in the very manner by which the invisible that imparts itself therein envisages the visible – strictly, to exchanging our gaze for the gaze that iconistically envisages us.' Marion, *God without Being*, p. 21.
101 Florensky, *Iconostasis*, pp. 157–60. See further Williams, *Lost Icons*, pp. 184–7.
102 Ephesians 5.8.
103 Ephesians 2.21–2.
104 Ephesians 5.14.

Part III

COPULATIONS

I opened to my beloved . . . (Song of Songs 5.6)

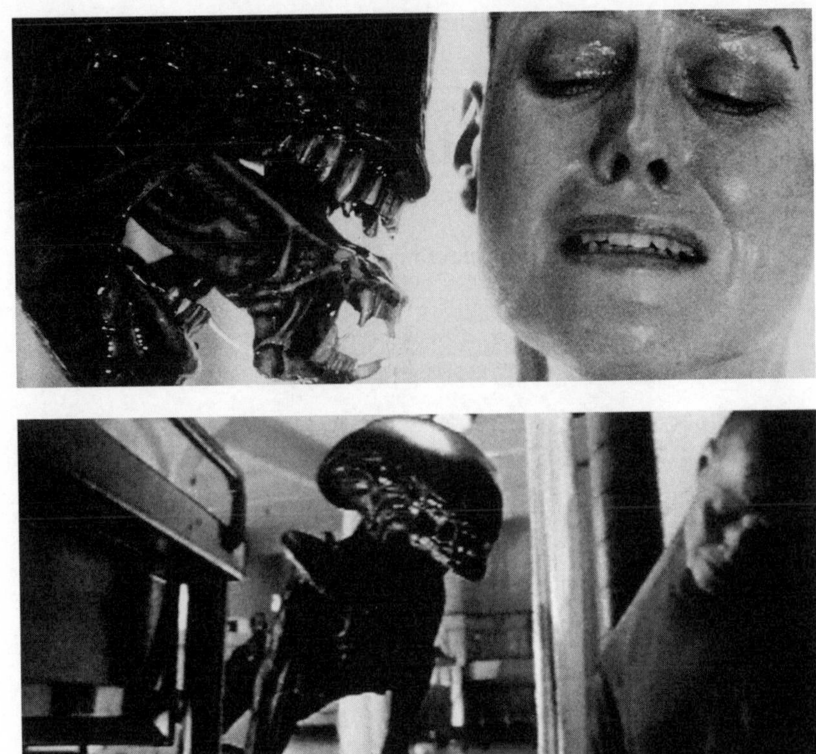

Figure 4 Announcing a Birth/Death

The alien and Ripley (Sigourney Weaver) in *Alien3* (David Fincher, USA 1992).
Photo: British Film Institute

Chapter 4

ALIEN SEX

At the end of Jean-Pierre Jeunet's *Alien Resurrection* (USA 1997) – the fourth in the *Alien* film series – Ripley and Call, the film's two surviving female characters, look out from the window of their spacecraft, astonished at the play of light on earth's oceans, passing beneath them. 'It's beautiful', Call gasps. 'I didn't expect it to be.' Turning to look at Ripley she asks, 'What happens now?' Ripley smiles. 'I don't know. I'm a stranger here myself.'

Ripley has never been to earth before. It's her first visit. An extra-terrestrial, she was conceived and born in the depths of space, where only electric light disturbed the darkness. Yet she is coming home, for Ripley is Ripley's clone, created from a few surviving cells of warrant officer Ellen Ripley, who had left earth many years before, prior to the opening of *Alien* (UK/USA 1979), the first in the *Alien* film series. Thus, for the film viewer, Ripley has always been extra-terrestrial. She almost got back to earth in James Cameron's *Aliens* (USA 1986), the second film of the series, but not quite; and she was still trying to get home when she died at the end of the third film, David Fincher's *Alien3* (USA 1992).

The Ripley who looks down on planet earth, as if on a long lost Eden, is a resurrected Ripley, a still fleshly but transformed Ripley, a Ripley into whose wounds you could put your finger. But you would have to be quick, for now her wounds heal almost instantly. The scientists who have brought Ripley back to life are not interested in her for herself, but for the alien that had been incubating within her, and that was just coming to birth at the time of her death, at the end of Fincher's film. Through genetic cloning the scientists have resurrected both Ripley and her 'baby', which they hope to develop as the ultimate killing machine. But in the period of incubation, or in the cloning process itself, the DNA of human and alien – mother and child – has somehow intermingled, so that each has inherited some of the characteristics of the other.

The resurrected Ripley is like the dead seed of St Paul's analogy for the resurrected body. Having died in the earth, she has returned in new flesh.[1] 'What is sown is perishable, what is raised is imperishable. It is sown in dishonour, it is raised in glory. It is sown in weakness, it is raised in power.'[2] Like Paul's old Adam, the first Ripley was 'of the dust'; but the second, cloned Ripley, is, like the new Adam, 'of heaven'.[3] She has a human's grace and wit, but the senses, strength and agility of an alien; she is a creature between, transcendent of both. 'Not all flesh is alike', Paul tells us. 'There are both heavenly bodies and earthly bodies, but the glory of the heavenly is one thing, and that of the earthly is another. There is one glory of the sun, and another glory of the moon, and another glory of the stars; indeed, star differs from star in glory.'[4] Ripley has the glory of one such star.[5]

Bad Dreams

Ripley has been coming home for a long time. Almost 20 years in real time – narrative time – the time it has taken to tell her story, from the release of the first *Alien* film in 1979 to the fourth in 1997; but much longer in story time, in Ripley's own time, the time of her dreaming.[6] The story of Ellen Ripley and her monster began with Ripley awakening from cryogenic 'hypersleep' at the beginning of Ridley Scott's *Alien*. The spaceship *Nostromo*, named after Joseph Conrad's eponymous novel, is homeward bound, carrying some 20 million tons of mineral ore.[7] Her seven crew are sleeping out the long voyage in a form of suspended animation, each within a glass-fronted pod or casket. It is this hypersleep which permits Ripley to travel across the interminable distances of space and between each film in the series; 57 years between the first and second films, an unidentified period of perhaps a few weeks or several months between the second and third, and 200 years between the third and fourth.[8] If Ripley was in her late twenties when she first encountered the alien – Sigourney Weaver's age when she first played the part – then the cloned Ripley is a good 300 years old, though born only yesterday (with Weaver herself being 47).

These are nocturnal films, each set between periods of long, dreamless sleep. During a lull in the frantic pace of *Aliens*, Ripley persuades the little girl Newt to have a nap. But Newt suffers from 'scary dreams', for she is the only survivor of the human colony destroyed by the aliens. 'My mommy always said there were no monsters, no real ones. But there are.'[9] Ripley tells her to sleep, but not to dream. At the end of the film, Newt asks Ripley if she can now dream in hypersleep, 'Yes honey', Ripley replies,

'I think we both can'. But indeed, it is the film itself that is the dream, the nightmare, a succession of which have come to punctuate Ripley's sleeping. As James Cameron remarks, a 'film like *Aliens* is basically one long bad dream'. But while the audience gets to 'wake up at the end and leave the cinema', Ripley must continue to sleep until visited by her next nightmare.[10]

The last shot in *Alien* is of Ripley asleep in her cryotube, one hand resting on her chest. 'I wanted her to be the sleeping beauty', Ridley Scott has remarked; and indeed she is, a princess awaiting her prince, serenely sleeping in her glass coffin.[11] The image is repeated in all the subsequent films; at the beginning and ending of James Cameron's *Aliens*, at the beginning and ending of Fincher's *Alien3* – except that with Ripley having died, the coffin is empty; and, in a way, at the beginning of Jeunet's *Alien Resurrection*, except that now it is Ripley's clone who stands upright in a glass tube, naked, with her arms crossed over her chest, serene. *Alien Resurrection* is the only film of the four to end without Ripley falling asleep, though she is still shown behind glass. But it is the window of the spaceship, in which we can see reflected earth passing beneath, as if superimposed on Ripley and Call. Earth has appeared only once before in the four films, near the beginning of *Aliens*, when it is the backdrop to the orbiting space station in which Ripley has been hospitalized after her adventures in the previous film. We see the earth, but Ripley is oblivious to its proximity, fighting her own inner demons in the antiseptic white confines of hospital ward and flat. In one of the film's deleted scenes (but available on the DVD 'director's cut'), we come upon Ripley sitting on a park bench, looking out between trees on verdant fields. But it is only a projection on the wall of a waiting room, a simulacrum of a breathable outside, which Ripley switches off when the Company's agent, Carter Burke (Paul Reiser), comes into the room. Earth, for Ripley, is only a memory, a dream, a fleeting shadow on the wall. Though we ourselves must be in the cave to see it, it is only at the end of Jeunet's film that Ripley emerges from the cave into the sunlight, looking upon the earth beneath her, as had another newborn, some 30 years previously, at the end of Stanley Kubrick's *2001: A Space Odyssey*.

Bodily Fluids

> They kept saying, 'there's no sex in this movie.' I said, 'you don't need any . . . but . . . there's a good opportunity here to have a little hint of . . . you know . . . hinted at sexuality, and Sigourney is certainly the person to project that.'[12]

Ridley Scott is talking about the last scene of *Alien*, when Ripley, thinking that she and Jones the cat are the only survivors of the now destroyed *Nostromo*, prepares for hypersleep in the sanctuary of the *Sulaco*, the *Nostromo*'s 'lifeboat'. Having put Jones in the cryotube, she undresses down to her skimpy vest and pants, and with a touching vulnerability, completes preparations for the long journey home. This is the most obviously voyeuristic scene in the film, when the pleasure of watching Weaver's young body distracts the audience from what it fears is about to happen, for it knows that it cannot yet be bedtime. The destruction of the alien has not been witnessed, and everyone knows that monsters jump out when characters are least vigilant. Sure enough, part of the cabin's shiny metallic piping is in fact the grey carapace of the alien's elongated head, with its body tucked between the ducting pipes behind the control panel over which Ripley is leaning. Suddenly, as if stretching in its sleep, the monster puts out an arm and almost hits Ripley in the face. Terrified, she retreats across the cabin and hides in a glass-fronted cupboard, from where she watches the alien yawn, bear its teeth and uncurl its limbs, its movements fragmented by strobe lighting. Ripley clambers into a spacesuit that is conveniently hanging in the cupboard. Shot from a low angle, we watch as she places her naked limbs into the protective clothing of the suit. The entire sequence that begins with Ripley preparing for sleep and ends with the expulsion of the alien through the airlock is erotically handled. But it is not, as Scott suggests, the only hint of sexuality in the film. *Alien* reeks of sex.

From the first sighting of the alien pods lying on the ground like so many detumescent phalloi, the alien, in all its transformations, is presented as an obscene sexual organ, the horror of flesh that engorges with blood, flows with fluids and forces itself into the orifices of the human body. It rapes those it embraces, utterly indifferent of their sex. The alien 'face-hugger' – constructed from sheep intestines and the stomachs of cows – pulses in its pod, before leaping at Kane's (John Hurt's) face and inserting its egg-laying tube down his throat. Later, when it has released its grip and fallen from Kane's face, we see its soft underside, fabricated from oysters and mussels. Later still, at dinner, the child of this incubus, rips through Kane's chest, rising out of his entrails as a hungry screeching phallus, covered in blood. Growing swiftly, the monster embraces its next victim – Brett (Harry Dean Stanton) – before killing him, holding his head in its now humanoid hands (Bolaji Badejo in a rubber suit), as if to kiss him, while inserting its sinuous tail between his legs, as if about to rape him.[13]

When aliens kiss they kill, their inner jaws shooting out of their mouths, puncturing holes in the bodies of their lovers.[14] Those they do not kiss they impregnate, making them wombs for their children. They are the horror of the male sexual organ for the prepubescent child who has read his Freud, who can hardly imagine the transformations that will befall his own body, and who (mis)interprets his parents' lovemaking as a violent and sadistic encounter, 'something that the stronger participant is forcibly inflicting on the weaker'.[15] Presented as a voracious phallus, the alien's indifference to the sex of its victims, all but one of whom are men in *Alien*, threatens the horror of male homosexual copulation. In *Alien* this is carried over to the character of Ash, whose 'strangeness' is conveyed by Ian Holm's subtly prissy performance, and, in a deleted scene, the knowledge that neither of the women – Lambert or Ripley – have had sex with him. 'I never got the idea he was particularly interested', says Lambert.[16] This suggests his homosexuality, though quite how strange Ash is only becomes apparent when he turns on Ripley and tries to kill her by inserting a rolled up pornographic magazine into her throat. Like the alien, Ash kills through penetration, or would if he could, but his murderous attack on Ripley is stopped by the intervention of Parker and Lambert. In the ensuing struggle, Parker delivers a blow to Ash's head that sends him rolling against the wall, white liquid spurting from his mouth, and then, with another blow, Ash's head is broken from his neck, revealing him to be an android, 'a Goddamn robot', as Parker puts it. In his violent death throes, Ash's broken neck reveals a squelchy interior, with hydraulic fluids ejaculating onto the floor. Ash, his arms flailing, knocks Parker onto his back, and with his half-severed head hanging down his back, Ash thrusts himself between Parker's legs, as if in a frenzied sexual act, only dying when, with a shower of sparks, Lambert spears him in the back with an electric prod.

This remarkable scene of entangled, writhing bodies is so sudden and unexpected that a shocked audience may hardly recollect its obscene conjunction of limbs, enacting a primal scene of grotesque animal congress. Ash, whose job is to bring the alien home at whatever cost, is sexualized like the alien: polymorphously perverse, insatiably hungry, penetrating and killing without consideration of gender.[17] Yet, with this parallel in mind, Ash as a monstrous feminized 'man', points to another way of construing the alien. For if a feminized man, he might also be understood as a masculinized 'woman', and thus parallel Barbara Creed's reading of the alien as the monstrous-feminine, the concretion, not of the male sex, but of the all devouring mother, the vaginal mouth.[18]

Drawing on the work of Julia Kristeva, Creed argues that the alien represents the maternal, which the child must deny in order to enter into the social-symbolic of the paternal world, the domain of order and reason, the body under control.[19] The flesh, with all its strange desires and excretions, its entrances and exits, becomes the horror of the pre-social and uncontrolled, of a purely animal existence. Within the social, in the cultural-symbolic, the mother's body becomes this horror, with her metonymic womb its most monstrous part. This 'archaic' mother pervades the *Alien* films; indeed they are all set within her, in her dark, twisting, sometimes writhing, tunnels, coated in emulsions and ejaculates, dripping with bloods and acids, and harbouring strange, violent births, destructive of bodily composure and sensibility. *Aliens* shows us the archaic mother herself, an alien queen laying her eggs, excreting each pod from her huge elongated ovipositor. But in *Alien Resurrection*, we actually enter within her body, which at times seems to lose all distinction between inside and outside. The film's opening titles appear over shots of strange undulating flesh, as if shot from within the fat and muscle of a body, a butchered but palpitating animal. The alien mother is monstrous because she devours, a terrifying, castrating *vagina dentata*.[20] Thus the alien is not only the horror of the phallus/penis, or of its absence, but also of its loss. As fetish, the alien substitutes for both a primordial lack and a threatened loss.[21]

But films and their psychoanalytic interpretations are all too labile, and the sexual horror of the *Alien* films may be understood in a more fluid manner, as a more generalized horror, as of a disembowelled body, with its insides on the outside. The *Alien* films are about the horror of the inside, and of what happens when it gets out, or worse, when it gets back in again. These films have a mythic resonance because they are a kind of psychic pornography, fascinating us with the horror of our own flesh, the terror of our embodiment, of what lies beneath the skin. This terror arises when we realize that the distinction between our self and what is not our self, is already crossed. What we would exclude in order to constitute our self is already within; and what we think most our self, most interior, is already without.

> The concept of inside/outside suggests two surfaces that fold in on each other; the task of separating inside from outside seems impossible as each surface constitutes the 'other' side of its opposite. The implication is that the abject can never be completely banished if 'inside', the abject substance forms a lining for the outside; if 'outside', it forms a skin for the inside. The womb represents the utmost in abjection for it contains a new life form which will pass from inside to outside bringing with it traces of its contamination – blood, afterbirth, faeces.[22]

Our interiority is entirely dependent on a preceding exteriority from which we have emerged, and the alien figures the distance we are from ourselves, the stranger within.[23] The aliens of the *Alien* films figure this denial of our dependence in terms of bodily permeability, the fleshly desires that constitute our carnality. When abjected, these desires appear utterly horrific, purely monstrous. But – as we will see – the *Alien* films, as they proceed from the first to the fourth, also teach us how to own our flesh through surrendering to its fluidity, its wants and flows. When shown in the ecclesiacinema this becomes the venture of surrendering to a yet more fundamental desire, that precedes all others; a desire that flows through us when we no longer abjure the alien, but open – because opened – to our beloved.

Hurting

David Fincher's films are remarkable not least because, as products of a culture that trades in the want of the body beautiful, they dwell upon the body *in extremis*. Fincher's films take lustrous Hollywood 'stars' – Sigourney Weaver, Brad Pitt, Michael Douglas, Helena Bonham Carter, Jodie Foster[24] – and not merely bring them down to earth, but subject them to earth's powers of corruption. Their bodies visibly collapse before our gaze: Pitt increasingly covered in cuts and bruises, Weaver – her head shaven because of lice – reduced to the appearance of a death-camp inmate. Far from celebrating the plastic body of desire, of fulfilment through physical intimacy and sexual coupling, Fincher's films articulate the dreadful fear that sex finds its ending – its *telos* – not in life, in the body enhanced, renewed and burgeoning; but in death, in the defilement, decay and destruction of the body.[25]

One might think of David Fincher's films as neo-medieval texts. *Alien3* dresses its prisoners in monk-like garb, provides them with candles to light their way, and leaves them with little more than fire and water for defence. *Seven* (USA 1995) refers to Aquinas and Dante, with the latter's *Divine Comedy* providing the pattern of material descent leading to possible moral ascent, certainly to self-knowledge, no matter how bleak. This pattern also structures both *The Game* (USA 1997) and *Fight Club* (USA 1999). In both of these last films, Fincher's characters are gradually deprived of the accoutrements of modern living, the products and systems – material, economic and social – that insulate them from their bodies and their souls. Above all, his films are concerned with that most medieval of interests: the display of spiritual poverty in the decrepitude and corruption of the body. In the horror science-fiction film *Alien3* and the neo-noir detective story *Seven*, characters descend into the circles of hell, into the decay and ending that is the body, which, even as it harbours life, destroys and is destroyed. The opening credits of *Fight Club* are played over a bravura tracking shot from deep within the synapses of the narrator's deranged brain, out through his skin and up the barrel of the gun that is stuck in Tyler Durden's mouth. Edward Norton and Brad Pitt (again) provide the bodies that in the course of the film become increasingly bruised and battered, as they seek redemption through pain. Some of the film's funniest sequences concern therapy groups for the terminally ill, for people dying of tuberculosis and various forms of cancer, bowel and testicular. As Fincher's characters learn what it is to have a soul through having a body that decays, his camera lingers on rotting, gouged or otherwise mutilated flesh, or, in startling close-ups, shows us body-parts variously invaded or caressed. Fincher's films look with a certain tenderness on the perishability and defeat of the body: on the presence of death in life.

The third of the seven victims in *Seven* is discovered lying on his back, bound to a bed, where he has been cruelly cosseted so as to prolong his dying. Representing the vice of sloth, he has become a figure of death, a sore-ridden emaciated corpse, the skin so shrunken upon the face that it hardly remains more than a skull, ligaments contorted into a frozen visage of agony. It might be a *transi*, a cadaver tomb,[26] or a vision of the dead Christ, as shown to Mother Julian of Norwich, with Christ's nostrils shrivelling and drying before her eyes, his body turning black and brown. His 'dear body was so discoloured and dry, so shriveled, deathly, and pitiful, that he might well have been seven nights in dying'.[27] The poor soul in *Seven* has been a year about it, though even as the detectives talk over him – taking samples of blood and faeces – some life still remains, and the cadaver suddenly jolts and coughs, unexpectedly and grotesquely animated, become a mobile *memento mori*. Julian and Fincher well understand that putrefaction is a truth of the body, in life as in death. It is the ending to which all bodies tend; the *telos* that awaits every engendering.

Falling

Images of descent and fall recur throughout Fincher's films, so dominating *Seven* that its end-titles go down rather than up the screen. *Alien3* opens with the sudden descent of its heroine, warrant officer Ripley (Sigourney Weaver) into hell. Sleeping soundly in cryogenic suspension, homeward bound from her adventures in the preceding film of the *Alien* series, *Aliens*, an onboard fire leads her and her fellow crew members – Newt and Hicks – to being placed in an evacuation craft and sent hurtling to the nearest planet, Fiorina 161.

Ripley awakens to find herself the sole survivor, rescued by the planet's only inhabitants, the inmates of an isolated penal colony. From then on her journey is forever downwards, descending to ever deeper levels of what is quite literally an inferno, since the prison is also a mineral ore refinery and foundry, capable of making lead sheeting for nuclear waste containers. But this hell into which she has fallen is also our world, in which that more primal fall of the first man and woman has already occurred. And she comes to it as a reminder of that first couple and their fallen, lustful coupling by which their degradation was passed to each of their offspring, down the long line of years, and across the deserts of the universe.

The men of Fiorina or Fury 161 are not only criminal recipients of society's punishment, but the subjects of a self-imposed bodily discipline, which serves to control their fleshly desires, while orienting them to the ultimate void – the *nihil* – that encompasses their captivity. Five years before the story opens, Dillon (Charles S. Dutton) and other 'alternative people' among the prisoners, embraced an 'apocalyptic, millenarian, Christian-fundamentalist' kind of religion. It is these 'brothers' who now comprise the inhabitants of the prison foundry, together with two 'minders' and a 'medical officer'. The 'brothers' have taken a vow of celibacy and bound themselves into a semi-monastic community, seeking spiritual solace through self-regulation in the midst of damnation. They know that sin enters through the eye. Sight of forbidden fruit – the flesh of the other – can elicit bodily desires that destroy proper order. On being told of Ripley's arrival, one of their fellows reminds them that they have all taken a vow of celibacy, which includes women. This suggestion of a sexualized fraternity among the inmates is left unexplored in the film, though Amy Taubin takes Dillon to be a 'homosexual', and finds the 'alien's basement lair, with its dripping pipes and sewerage tunnels' to represent fear of the homosexual as well as the monstrous-feminine; the entwining of uterine and 'anal plumbing'.[28] To the order of the male penal body – each member of which is a YY chromosome multiple murderer – Ripley appears as a new Eve, bearing forbidden and – as it transpires – rotten fruit. She is warned not to go unaccompanied among the men, and at one point in the story, when she is in an isolated part of the prison, she is set upon by a group of prisoners who are intent upon raping her. They have forgotten their vow of celibacy. She is saved by Dillon, who had, on first meeting her, described himself as a 'murderer and rapist of women', and who now lays about her attackers with an iron bar, while informing her that he has to 're-educate some of the brothers'. They have to discuss 'some matters of the spirit'.

In this way Fincher's film evokes the Augustinian thematic of lust, which for Augustine is the 'general name for desire of every kind',[29] though most particularly that desire which 'arouses the impure parts of the body',[30] overcoming the control and regulation of the will. After the fall, Adam and Eve had to sew together fig leaves and make aprons to cover their *pudenda*, in order that each might hide from the gaze of the other those organs which had become the site of an instinct beyond their control.[31] It is as if their 'sexual organs' had 'somehow fallen so completely under the sway of lust that they have no power of movement at all if this passion is absent, and unless it has either arisen of its own accord or been aroused by another'.[32] For Augustine the sexual organs have become an alien within the body; the very sign of that disobedience which constitutes our fallen world.

Augustine, writing at the end of his life, but perhaps remembering his own youthful ardour for the embrace and excitement of flesh, both evokes the pleasure of fallen sex – the intensity of which can breach the city-walls of body and mind from without and within[33] – and imagines the possibility of a sexual act without lust; an embrace without passion. He admits the difficulty of conceiving such an act, since we have no example of such obedient members as the sexual organs would then be; not even Adam and Eve, for whom such sex was available, experienced it, since 'their sin happened first'.[34] But if they had embraced and coupled before their disobedience, the seed 'would have been sown by the man and received by the woman at the time and in the quantity needed, their genital organs being moved by the will and not excited by lust.'[35]

> Then, not needing to be aroused by the excitement of passion, the man would have poured his seed into his wife's womb in tranquility of mind and without any corruption of her body's integrity. For, though this cannot be proved by experience, there is no reason for us not to believe that, when those parts of the body were not driven by turbulent heat but brought into use by the power of the will when the need arose, the male seed could have been introduced into the womb with no loss of the wife's integrity . . . so the two sexes might have been conjoined for the purpose of impregnation and conception by a natural use of the will, and not by lustful appetite.[36]

Such a sexual scene must seem strange to us, who are now so deeply fallen into disobedience that we cannot imagine such a calm integrity of mind and body. To us it will seem like alien sex; like the sex that – in a hideous parody of Augustine's paradisal and lustless coupling – opens David Fincher's *Alien3*. The main titles of the film are intercut with the primal scene of sexual penetration that sets the story of the film in motion. As Ripley lies passively upon her back, asleep and unaware that the security of her 'cryotube' has been breached – a hapless Eve, a sleeping princess[37] – the hand of an alien sex covers her face and places its seed within the earth of her breast.

The reproductive cycle of the alien is the central fascination and horror of all the *Alien* films. First appearing as a face-hugging, mucous-dripping and bony-fingered creature, in Ridley Scott's *Alien*, it jumps from a plant-like pod onto the face of its victim, rendering him insensible while secretly laying its seed within his chest, through his mouth: patient of alien oral-rape. Only later will the growing alien child suddenly and terribly rip through the chest of its host-mother, killing the latter in the very moment of birth.[38] That this alien biology – so carefully and explicitly rendered in the film – represents a male-identified fear of penetration, gestation and birth, is a commonplace of commentary on the film, not least because the rape victim is a man. For Amy Taubin, the film plays on 'anxieties set loose by a decade of feminist and gay activism', embodying the 'return of repressed infantile fears and confusions about where babies come from and the anatomical differences between the sexes'.

> [The alien's] toothy, dripping mouth was hermaphroditic: while the double jaws represented the inner and outer labia of the *vagina dentata*, the projectile movement of the inner jaw was a phallic threat. Granted that the terror of being raped and devoured by the monster loomed large for both sexes, *Alien* was a basically male anxiety fantasy: that a man could be impregnated was the ultimate outrage.[39]

This thematic is played down in Cameron's *Aliens*, where we witness a woman rather than a man giving 'birth' to an alien, and where an egg-laying alien 'queen' is introduced, a mother every bit as protective of her offspring as is Ripley of her adopted child, Newt. As Taubin notes, the climactic fight between Ripley and the alien queen is 'structured as a cat fight between the good mother and the bad'.[40] Thus in *Aliens* sexual difference is properly ordered and the audience invited to side with the good against the deviant mother, who is, of course, a single parent.[41] Its object of fear is woman out of place, rather than the body of woman as such. It is the latter fear that *Alien3* again thematizes, with renewed force.

For Taubin *Alien3* is 'all about the AIDS crisis and the threat to women's reproductive rights'.[42] The film graphically plays on the fear of an invisible enemy within the individual and the social body: the alien embryo within Ripley, herself an alien within the penal colony, a woman among men. The film is about bodily control and its loss, the body given over to another life, another body. Life grows within Ripley and she seeks its abortion. But she can do so only at the cost of her own life. At the end of the film, the 'pro-life' representative of The Company – which desires the alien for military research purposes (as the ultimate phallic aggressor) – urges her to save the 'child', and herself. But in the inverted world of *Alien3* such an act would be to give death and not life. However, while the film can be read as Taubin suggests, it is also, as we have seen, about sex more generally, and about the fear that to engage in sexual congress is to engage death, to inaugurate the end of life, even as another life begins within or from you: that to conceive is to die. In Fincher's film, death is the end of sex, the *telos* to which it moves.

Redemption

Alien3 affirms the possibility of life in death, but what sort of life is ambiguous. This is didactically expressed in the scene of the funeral service that is held for Ripley's shipmates, Hicks and Newt. The words of the service are ironically counterpoised with the birth of an alien out of the body of a dog, elsewhere in the prison. Andrews (Brian Glover), the prison superintendent, first commits the dead to the keeping of the Lord. They have been 'taken from the shadow of our night, they have been released from all darkness and pain'. They 'have gone beyond our world, they are forever eternal and everlasting. Ashes to ashes, dust to dust'. But then Dillon, the leader of the 'brothers', comes forward to make his own, more impassioned and questioning speech. 'Why? Why are the innocent punished? Why the sacrifice? Why the pain? There aren't any promises. Nothing is certain, only that some get called, some get saved'. Then he also commits the bodies, but this time to the void, and does so with a glad heart, because 'for within each seed there is a promise of a flower, and within each death, no matter how small, there is always a new life, a new beginning.' It is this last expression of faith in the natural cycle of birth and death – to which all the 'brothers' respond 'Amen' – which is intercut with the scene of a hideous alien life emerging from the small death of the dog. Neither Andrews nor Dillon expound a theology of resurrection.

As already indicated, *Alien3* is replete with religious resonance. The story of Ripley's descent into hell, which is also the story of a birth, can be read as a horribly inverted Christian nativity play, with Ripley taking the part of the Virgin Mary. As already noted, she comes among the men of Fury 161 as Eve the temptress, but she also appears as the second Eve, bearing their destiny within her. The conception she bears has left her 'virginal', her child having been conceived among the stars, through the mouth, by an alien being. Her child has no human father. Furthermore, her child, like that of the earlier virginal conception, will bring the men of Fury 161 a genuine – though pagan – redemption through heroic struggle with the monster; a parody of the Christian hope of life through death with Christ. Against the common enemy each man must risk his own life in the hope that he may thereby save it.

But what is the common enemy that at one and the same time destroys and makes possible a certain moral heroism? There are two aliens in the film: the one that emerges from the prisoner Murphy's dog – the ravaging beast, the 'dragon' as the prisoner Golic (Paul McGann) will call it – and the one that secretly grows unseen within Ripley. Indeed, one can read the first as a prolepsis of the second, an extrapolation of the gestating embryo, enacting the horror that is the secret of pregnancy: the fear that in sex is death. These themes and others are complexly brought together in a central scene of the film, which concludes its first part and inaugurates its second.

Alien Annunciation

Ripley has been confined to the prison hospital by superintendent Andrews, who does not believe her story about the alien creature she believes responsible for the violent deaths that have occurred among the prisoners. She is being tended by Clemens (Charles Dance), the medical officer, with whom she has established a (sexual) relationship. The now deranged prisoner Golic, who witnessed the 'dragon' dispatching the prisoners he is suspected of having murdered, is tied to the bed beside the one on which Ripley is seated. Clemens gives Ripley an injection of pain-killer, and explains the crime that first brought him to Fury 161, not as a doctor, but as a prisoner: a morphine addict, he killed eleven patients with the 'wrong dosage' of pain-killer. This is the most tender and, as Amy Taubin notes, erotic scene in the film, with Clemens taking Ripley's arm and carefully injecting her with one of his own 'special cocktails'. It is, as it were, the missing scene from an earlier sequence in which we saw him with Ripley, before and after sex. Then the scene of their sexual coupling was replaced with one showing the first slaying of a prisoner by the alien. Death was already present at their union.

As Clemens prepares to give Ripley her injection, Golic suddenly asks her if she is married. He tells her that she should be, that she should have children.[43] Then he tells her that she is going to die. Clemens draws a curtain between the beds, shutting Golic out, but repeats Golic's question to Ripley: is she married? She responds by asking about his past, which he explains, and then he administers the injection; his fluid passing into her body. It is at this moment that the alien strikes. Suddenly looming behind the rubber curtain, it grasps Clemens and lifts him away before puncturing his skull. It then approaches Ripley, who is now cowering on the floor; while all the time Golic, strapped to his bed, watches terrified, as do we. What we see is the annunciation of an impending birth.

In many medieval paintings of the angel Gabriel's visit to the Virgin Mary,[44] as in the *Annunciation* (1333) by Simone Martini (c. 1284–1344), painted for an altarpiece in Siena,[45] the angel is placed on the left of the picture, leaning towards Mary, while she, on the right, is seated or kneeling, and cowering away with fright. Sometimes she has lifted a hand, as if to ward off the angel's advance. Uncannily, Fincher's alien also approaches Ripley from the left of the screen. She is recoiling on the right, her averted face tight up against the edge of the widescreen picture frame (see figure 4). The gilded background of Martini's painting is darkly echoed in the subdued browns, golds and ambers of Fincher's palette, the coppery sheen of the alien stretching out from behind a chromed medical trolley towards Ripley, as she retreats in terror. The alien approaches to within an inch of Ripley, opening its mouth and projecting its inner phallic jaw towards her, as if perhaps to kiss rather than destroy her face. But then it shuts its mouth and leaves her, as swiftly as it came. It has sensed the presence of the alien embryo, silently growing within her. She is with child.

As with Mary and the angel, Ripley and the audience are perplexed by the behaviour of the alien, and ponder what its arrival and departure might mean. An attentive audience, that followed the events so abruptly fragmented between the film's opening credits, may have understood that Ripley was impregnated with an alien while asleep on the *Sulaco*. But more likely, as David Thomson notes, an audience 'may have preferred to read the credit sequence as a vague preview, no matter its miserly exactitude'.[46] At the start of the film, Ripley fears that the dead Newt had been impregnated by an alien while asleep on the *Sulaco*. She persuades Clemens to carry out an autopsy in order to be sure that there is no alien growth around Newt's heart. Disturbed by the arrival of Andrews and Aaron (Ralph Brown), Ripley does not insist on searching for the alien in the cadaver of her other dead companion, Corporal Hicks, and nor does she pause to consider her own body. But the idea that the alien is hiding in Ripley must surely occur to her as it will to an audience, except that Ripley is Sigourney Weaver, the heroine of the film. Her destruction is unthinkable, an unconscious fear that the scene of the autopsy has nevertheless lodged in the basement minds of both protagonist and viewers.[47]

Fincher's annunciation is a demonic parody of Martini's, not least because Fincher's angel has come from hell not heaven, and the child it presages will not be the saviour, but the destroyer of humanity. Moreover, Ripley has no choice in this conception, being already the recipient of an alien donation, already the monster's mother. Unlike Mary, on whose answer – 'let it be with me according to your word'[48] – God had to wait, Ripley is vouched no such freedom; her body is already colonized.[49] Ripley will only regain her autonomy at the end of the film, but then she will have only one choice: to birth salvation through the death of herself and of her monstrous child.

Phallic Mother

Sigourney Weaver is both star and co-producer of *Alien3*, and Amy Taubin suggests that we should not underestimate Weaver's 'contribution to its authorship'.[50] Does it then present us with a woman's view of sex – of the fear, as Taubin suggests, of 'being pregnant with a monster, or being forced to carry a foetus you don't want to term, or never being able to have a baby though you desperately want one'?[51] Or is it a masculine view of sex – a (heterosexual) man's fear of what he thinks sex means for women: an impregnation, gestation and birth that destroys the body? Or is it the fear that to engage in sexual congress is to court death: the very fate that befalls Clemens?

In certain respects the film may be viewed as feminist, in the sense of claiming equality for women; but it nevertheless remains within a patriarchal imaginary, in the sense that the equality claimed for women is an equality with men. All four *Alien* films make a woman – warrant officer Ripley – their central character; and there is little doubt that her success lies in being more resolute, resilient and courageous than any of the other, largely male, characters. In short, one could argue that Ripley survives because she is more of a man than are the men. In Cameron's *Aliens*, Ripley and the other women among the soldiers are the equal of their male counterparts in handling the massive phallic armoury with which they are supplied. In *Alien3*, Ripley's masculinization is further marked by her clothing and shaven head. The difference of her sex is not marked by bodily adornment. Yet she remains sexually different. The men, despite everything, insist upon it. They mark her out as not one of them; all that is, except Clemens, who seems to have more in common with her than he does with any of his fellow males. It is with him that she establishes a sexual relationship. In this way, perhaps, one can read the film as contesting the price of masculinization that Ripley has to pay in order to survive in the fraternal society of the penal colony. It would then be this tension – of the feminine body within a masculine economy, and the question of female identity within such an economy – that is complexly articulated and disturbingly explored at the level of the film's sexual symbolic: the biology of alien sex.

As already suggested, Ripley comes to Fury 161 as Eve, and as Mary, but she also comes as Christ or Christa, descending into the maw of hell in order to announce the possibility of life in the very place of death itself. But she descends, not as Christ risen in glory, but as Christ fallen, headlong, into an underworld whose gates she cannot unlock. Growing within her is the alien, whose import is proleptically announced by the adult alien which devours the prisoners, a foretaste of the death to which Ripley will give birth. But at the same time Ripley, in leading the men to fight the alien, will give their lives a purpose; the possibility of a heroic, sacrificial death for the good of the fraternity, and indeed of the world. And even before that comes to pass, Ripley comes among the prisoners as someone who accepts them as they are; someone who – like Christ – eats with sinners. Her act – which is not without challenge to the men – is perhaps more radical than that of any in the gospel stories: for she is a woman who sits down to eat with rapists.

The scene of Ripley's eschatological meal with the prisoners opens with her coming to stand in front of a cross-shaped structure, which is on the wall behind her. This allusion to Ripley's eventual sacrificial death, and to the death of Christ, is picked up as she crosses the room by a prisoner in the foreground, who covertly makes the sign of the cross on his chest, while at the same time placing his fingers on his neck. Why does he cross himself? Perhaps against the temptation of the flesh that has just entered the room. Perhaps because he dimly senses the alien life within her – the presence of death – that even now comes to eat (with) them. Perhaps because he obscurely recognizes the Christic import of the newcomer.

The alien growing inside Ripley is, we are told, a 'queen', capable of producing thousands of alien eggs. The Company's man – Bishop (Lance Henriksen) – offers to release Ripley from her predicament. The alien child will be removed from her body, saving both it and her. But if the alien child lives and grows, people will die. Thus Ripley, at the very end of the film, having, with Dillon, destroyed the adult alien that was devouring the prisoners, chooses to sacrifice her life, as has Dillon sacrificed his. Before the Company's men can get to her, Ripley falls backwards into the furnace, her arms outstretched, as if on the cross of Christ. As Barbara Creed notes, 'the close-up shot of Ripley's face, with shaven head and expression of blissful resignation, bears a striking resemblance to the face of [Renée Jeanne] Falconetti in Carl Dreyer's *The Passion of Joan of Arc* [France 1928], as she, too, is consumed by the flames'.[52] Ripley is figured not just as an 'androgynous god or religious saint', as Creed suggests,[53] but as Christ, for Ripley is saving the world. As she falls, the alien bursts out of her chest and she holds it, as if holding a child to her breast. Mother and baby disappear into the all-consuming fire – as it fills the screen from one side to the other.

There are at least two senses in which this climactic moment, to which the whole film labours, is a scene of life in death. The alien queen comes to birth in the very moment that she and her host-mother are consumed by the fire; and Ripley's death gives life to all those who will not now be devoured by the alien body she has harboured within her. But these mythic and religious themes are crossed by a more disturbing symbolic, suggested by the image of the alien birth itself.

What, if anything, has Ripley gained by the end of the film? Has she secured an identity as a woman over against the 'brothers' or the Company? Or is she, at the end as at the beginning, possessed rather than possessing, invaded by an alien life that makes her its own, from without and within? The phallic nature of the alien has been noted by most commentators on the *Alien* films, and it is at its most penis-like when still an 'alien baby (or as one 42nd Street moviehouse denizen exclaimed, 'little-dick-with-teeth')' – bursting from the chest of John Hurt in *Alien* and from the chest of Sigourney Weaver in *Alien3*. What is at one level a scene of birth in *Alien* is also a scene of castration, since the penile alien rips away from Hurt's body and disappears into the dark labyrinth of the spaceship. Could it then be that in the last birth scene of *Alien3*, Ripley does not lose but gains a phallus/penis; so that as she holds her baby/fetish to her breast, we witness her complete masculinization by an ultimate phallic aggressor? Might she even have secretly desired this most feared event? If so, we may suppose that at the last Ripley remains within patriarchy, within the Freudian imaginary.[54] Once more Hollywood, in its myth making, has been unable to imagine an identity for woman that is not given by man.

Yet our earlier discussion of Creed's reading of *Alien* and *Aliens* suggests the possibility of moving beyond so tight a Freudian reading of the scene, to one that makes better sense of the Dreyeresque look of 'blissful resignation' that appears on Ripley's face as she falls towards the flames. For if the alien represents not so much the fear of an absence as of a presence one cannot avow, then perhaps the look on Ripley's face is the beginning of an acknowledgement, a welcoming of the stranger who was always already within, and so a transformation of herself. 'You've been so long in my life, I cannot remember anything else', Ripley once told the alien. Her identity had been formed through her disavowal of the alien, so that when she now embraces the alien 'child' she is freed to pass beyond her former identity and become something else altogether. Admittedly, this is an entirely figural reading of the scene, departing from the diegetic level of the narrative. But the film's imagery does not refuse such a reading, and it finds a confirmation in Jean-Pierre Jeunet's *Alien Resurrection*.

Alien Resurrection

However one reads the scene of Ripley's death at the end of *Alien3*, it is not one of resurrection. Fincher's films do not release us from hell, or suggest the radical remaking of the body, individually or socially. At best, there is the struggle, and learning about one's frailty and dependency, about the pain and contingency of life. When Fincher's protagonists survive their ordeals they gain a sense of their own guilt and the world's anguish, and their fortitude in the face of suffering. But though they are redeemed from ignorance and complacency, they are hardly resurrected.

In the last book of the *City of God*, Augustine appropriately turns to the resurrection of the body, and to the questions by which pagans seek to ridicule the idea. Will abortions rise? Will all bodies be the same height and size? Will all our hair be restored, including that which was cut off throughout our lives? Will the same happen with our nail-clippings?[55] For Augustine, the most difficult question concerns cannibalism.

> [T]o whom will the flesh of a dead man be restored at the resurrection if it has been made into the flesh of a living one? Suppose that someone, consumed and compelled by hunger, has eaten the bodies of men . . . And could

> anyone contend, with truth or reason, that the whole of a body so eaten simply passes through the digestive tract without any of it being changed or converted into the flesh of the eater? The mere fact that the eater was thin and is so no longer shows clearly enough that what he lacked has now been made good by such food.[56]

Among the other questions that Augustine considers is this one: will women keep their sex in the resurrection, for some say that 'women will not be resurrected as female in sex, but that all are to be men, because God made only man of earth, and the woman from the man'?[57] On the contrary, Augustine argues, women will rise as women, in their essential nature; a nature that is not defined in terms of motherhood, of sex and birth.

> [T]hen there will be no lust, which is now the cause of confusion. For before they sinned, the man and the woman were naked, and were not ashamed. Vice will be taken away from those bodies, therefore, and nature preserved. And the sex of a woman is not a vice, but nature. They will then be exempt from sexual intercourse and childbearing, but the female parts will nonetheless remain in being, accommodated not to the old uses, but to new beauty, which, so far from inciting lust, which no longer exists, will move us to praise God, who both made what was not and redeemed from corruption what he made.[58]

For Augustine, the making of woman out of the rib of man is not an indication that she is part of him, to whom she is destined to (re)turn, but an allegory of the relationship between the church and Christ, emphasizing the unity between them. The woman-church is born in the flow of blood and water out of the side of the man-Christ. This symbolic reversal of the sexual roles in biological birth is certainly problematic, but it is clear that in contemplating the resurrection, Augustine begins to imagine men and women, not as they stand in relation to one another, but as they stand in relation to the divine wisdom and compassion, and thus beyond the social symbolics of a fallen world.

In the resurrection we 'shall enjoy each other's beauty without any lust'.[59] We will not desire the other to meet our need, but desire him for himself, her for herself, as herself, as himself, in her or his own beauty. In this imagining of the resurrection there is no more lusting after the flesh, and so an end to sex, or sex as we have known it; but sexuation – our difference from one another as sexed bodies – is maintained, enhanced and celebrated. As sexual beings, we will be more ourselves than we are now.

If we think of heavenly bodies as both sexed and beyond sex – so that the eschaton represents not a denial, but an intensification of our sexuate nature – then the church may even now begin to allow our future bodies to inform present practice, just insofar as the church shapes bodies fit for heavenly fulfilment. For the vision of what we will be shows us what we are already, but cannot fully see with our fallen eyes. Therefore the church is right to insist on sexual difference, and to mark, enhance and celebrate this difference, while resisting those tendencies in modernity which would deny sexual difference in the name of a neuter or egalitarian sex, which is always finally a male sex. Yet at the same time the church must also seek to enact that heavenly family in which all are equally different or differently equal in virtue of their relationship to the one who has called them to the heavenly banquet, as sisters or brothers.[60]

The church must begin to see and show heavenly bodies, no matter how alien they now seem to us. When not abjected, such bodies will appear as angels, for – as Augustine taught – 'we already begin to belong to those angels with whom we shall dwell in fellowship in that holy and most delightful City of God'.[61] What will the desire of such angel-aliens be like, whose sex is beyond sex? They will see with the 'eyes of the heart',[62] desiring the God who is beyond all things, but in all things, bodied forth in the spiritual flesh of the heavenly communion.

In heaven there are no strangers, for each other constitutes the peaceful harmony of the whole, which depends upon distance, united in the intimacy of difference. Indeed, the divine distance itself will be seen in and between our bodies, the glory of the Other in the other's spiritual flesh. By the body we shall see God in every body. We shall see God 'in ourselves, in one another, in Himself, in the new heavens and the new earth, and in every created thing which shall then exist'.[63] In heaven we will recognize that what we thought most different from us was already most intimate to us, infinitely far because infinitely near, just the other side of our skin. If now we try to see the inner truth of the other behind rather than in the other's face, we find only the other side, the equally baffling surfaces of bone, flesh and blood. They in turn will only send us back to their other side, outside; where we first sought the interiority that we mistakenly thought inside. Thomas wanted to put his hand into Christ. But blessed are those who only have the flesh of one another for their belief.[64] We cannot catch the other – or ourself – behind or within the body, but only between bodies.

Jean-Pierre Jeunet's *Alien Resurrection* does not resurrect Ripley in the sense of the Christian hope for a world remade. It merely returns her to more of the same; to the same hell, though to a different circle. Yet the film does begin to presage a different form of life for Ripley, an intensification of that 'blissful resignation' that suffused her face at the end of *Alien3*, as if she were tasting resurrection life in the moment of her death. Jeunet's film has even more abstract moments than Fincher's, scenes disconnected from narrative space, especially in the images of Ripley as she is mysteriously, voluptuously swallowed into an all-encompassing alien maternity, an uncanny, uterine domain of undulating flesh.[65] It is the point at which Ripley comes to accept her own animality, her own desires and strange sensibilities. When she is consumed – but not destroyed – by the alien without, she learns to embrace the alien within herself.

Within the alien queen, whose flesh is everywhere, Ripley witnesses a second birth of a second hybrid like herself, but one that is more alien than human, a monstrous child, craving affection. At the level of the narrative, this creature provides the necessary return of the monster just when the audience thinks that all is secure, but suspects that it is not. Hollywood is rigorously traditional, and Jeunet's film repeats the endings of *Alien* and *Aliens*, with Ripley once more casting the alien out into the void. But now she does so with a certain pity, for the creature cannot answer for its own monstrosity, and in some sense it is her own offspring – arguably her 'grandchild', its mother being the alien queen to which Ripley gave birth at the end of *Alien3* and birthed again (by caesarian section) at the beginning of *Alien Resurrection*. Moreover, the creature treats Ripley as its mother. The pity that Ripley experiences when she aborts this child indicates the weakening, if not the overcoming, of her fear of the alien within, the terror of her own sexual body. Ripley's continued abjection of her flesh suggests to Stephen Mulhall that 'Jeunet's inflection of the alien universe has only transposed its essential thematic coordinates – it has not transcended them'.[66] Perhaps. But this is the only *Alien* film at the end of which Ripley is awake, and standing in solidarity with a being as strange as herself. It suggests some kind of reconciliation with the alien within, some kind of blessing.

*

At the end of *Alien Resurrection*, Ripley and Call – alien and android – look down on planet earth passing beneath them: the promise of a new Eden. We cannot tell if they are demons or angels, but perhaps they are more the latter than the former. For they have learned that there is nothing so strange or foreign as they are to themselves, nothing so alien as the distance within that constitutes their own intimacy and identity. These aliens are ourselves: struggling proto-angels, the fallen children of Adam and Eve.

Over against the myths of our time – which find in the body and its sex the seeds of death, powerfully resonating with Augustine's ancient vision of a world fallen into corruption – the ecclesiacinema must still strive to show the latter part of Augustine's tale, which modernity denies, but which for Augustine is the point and purpose of the story, its ending and fulfilment. It is the vision of a body – individual and social – that no longer abjects its flesh, but finds in all its parts a perfect peace and harmony. This multiple body will see God in every body, for then God will be all in all.

> God will be the end of our desires. He will be seen without end, loved without stint, praised without weariness. And this duty, this affection, this employment, will, like eternal life itself, be common to all.[67]

Notes

1 1 Corinthians 15.36–8.

2 1 Corinthians 15.42–3.

3 1 Corinthians 15.47–8.

4 1 Corinthians 15.39, 40–1. In the course of these verses Paul moves from flesh (*sarx*) to body (*soma*), and the glory (*doxa*) of the latter. This provides a nice analogy for Ripley's clone because Paul's contrast between earthly and heavenly bodies is not between material and spiritual (non-material), but between different kinds of material body ('stuff'), the psychic (*soma psychikon*) and the pneumatic (*soma pneumatikon*). The latter has no flesh and blood (*sarx kai haima*) or soul (*psyche*), but it is a body. See further Dale B. Martin, *The Corinthian Body* (New Haven: Yale University Press, 1995), pp. 123–9.

5 'Sigourney Weaver's performance [in *Alien Resurrection*] is a marvel of economy, intelligence and physical fluidity; her subtle incarnation of genetic hybridity, her capacity to accommodate wild shifts of tone from sarcastic, adolescent one-liners to agonized psychic struggles, and her undeniably charismatic physical presence, hold together a film that is sometimes in danger of losing its grip on its audience, and together declare that she is at the peak of her powers.' Stephen Mulhall, *On Film* (London: Routledge, 2001), p. 136. We all love Sigourney.

6 On the distinction between narrative time and story time see Gerard Loughlin, *Telling God's Story: Bible, Church and Narrative Theology*, second edition (Cambridge: Cambridge University Press, 1999), pp. 52–63.

7 Joseph Conrad, *Nostromo: A Tale of the Seaboard*, edited by Martin Seymour-Smith (Harmondsworth: Penguin Books, [1904] 1983). Conrad's novel also provides the name for the *Nostromo*'s escape ship, the *Sulaco*, named after the south American seaport – an 'inviolable sanctuary' – in which the novel opens (p. 39).

8 David Thomson is so astounded, outraged, that so little has changed in such a long time, and so disappointed with the fourth film that he rewrites it as a soft-porn encounter between Ripley and Bishop (a character from the second and third films), who one suspects is standing in for Thomson himself. See David Thomson, *The Alien Quartet* (London: Bloomsbury, 1998), pp. 139–69.

9 These words are repeated by Ripley (more properly Ripley's clone) at the beginning of *Alien Resurrection*.

10 James Cameron interviewed by Don Shay, 1986 (*Aliens* DVD, 20th Century Fox, 2000).

11 Ridley Scott in his commentary on the film (*Alien* DVD, 20th Century Fox, 2000).

12 From Ridley Scott's commentary on the film (*Alien* DVD).

13 These shots were cut from the theatrical release of the film, but can be seen on the *Alien* DVD. The sexual nature of the alien's embrace can still be seen in the theatrical film, when it attacks Lambert (Veronica Cartwright), its tail sliding across the floor and rising between her legs.

14 Jeunet's *Alien Resurrection* plays on the perverse sexuality of the alien's embrace by having the mad scientist Gediman (Brad Dourif) kiss an alien by kissing the glass window between them. The scene is deliciously horrific for seasoned viewers, since they know what Gediman has yet to find out.

15 For Freud, the 'sadistic view of coition' is the third of the 'typical sexual theories' that children form if 'through some chance domestic occurrence, they become witnesses of sexual intercourse between their parents.' Though Freud allows that girls may also form this view, he really thinks it a theory for boys, who compare their parents' humping with their own 'romping', which is not without a 'dash of sexual excitation'. See Sigmund Freud, 'On the Sexual Theories of Children' (1908) in *The Penguin Freud Library*, 15 volumes, translated by James Strachey and edited by Angela Richards (Harmondsworth: Penguin Books, [1977] 1991), vol. 7: *On Sexuality*, pp. 183–204 (pp. 198–9). See also Freud's discussion of the 'wolf man' in 'From the History of an Infantile Neurosis' ([1914] 1918) in *The Penguin Freud Library*, vol. 9: *Case Histories II*, pp. 227–366.

16 This scene is available on the *Alien* DVD, and differs from the scene as scripted. See *Alien: The Illustrated Screenplay*, edited by Paul M. Simmon (London: Orion Books, 2000), pp. 182–3.

17 According to Freud, anyone may be seduced into polymorphous perversity, but the child and the 'average uncultivated woman' are especially prone. If

the woman is 'led on by a clever seducer she will find every sort of perversion to her taste, and will retain them as part of her own sexual activities'. See Freud, 'Three Essays on the Theory of Sexuality', in *The Penguin Freud Library*, vol. 7, pp. 45–169 (p. 109).

18 See Barbara Creed, '*Alien* and the Monstrous-Feminine' in *Alien Zone: Cultural Theory and Contemporary Science Fiction Cinema*, edited by Annette Kuhn (London: Verso, 1990), pp. 128–41; and Barbara Creed, *The Monstrous-Feminine: Film, Feminism, Psychoanalysis* (London: Routledge, 1993).

19 See Julia Kristeva, *Powers of Horror: An Essay on Abjection*, translated by Leon S. Roudiez (New York: Columbia University Press, [1980] 1982).

20 For this inflection of Freudian theory see Creed, *Monstrous-Feminine*, pp. 22–3, 105–21.

21 On the 'fetish' as substitute for the penis see Sigmund Freud, 'Fetishism' (1927) in *The Penguin Freud Library*, vol. 7, pp. 347–57.

22 Creed, *Monstrous-Feminine*, p. 49.

23 See further Julia Kristeva, *Strangers to Ourselves*, translated by Leon S. Roudiez (London: Harvester Wheatsheaf, [1988] 1991); Timothy K. Beal, *Religion and its Monsters* (London: Routledge, 2002) and Richard Kearney, *Strangers, Gods and Monsters* (London: Routledge, 2002).

24 Weaver in *Alien3*; Pitt in *Seven* and *Fight Club*; Douglas in *The Game*; Bonham Carter in *Fight Club*, which also brutalizes Edward Norton; and Jodie Foster in *The Panic Room* (USA 2002).

25 See further Amy Taubin, 'The Allure of Decay', *Sight and Sound*, 6/1 (January 1996): 22–4.

26 See Philippe Ariès, *Western Attitudes toward Death: From the Middle Ages to the Present*, translated by Patricia M. Ranum (London: Marion Boyars, [1974] 1976), pp. 39–46.

27 Julian of Norwich, *Revelations of Divine Love*, translated by Clifton Wolters (Harmondsworth: Penguin Books, 1966), ch. 16 (pp. 87–8).

28 Amy Taubin, 'Invading Bodies', *Sight and Sound*, 2/3 (July 1992): 8–10 (p. 10).

29 Augustine, *The City of God against the Pagans*, edited and translated by R.W. Dyson (Cambridge: Cambridge University Press, 1998), bk XIV, ch. 15 (p. 613).

30 Augustine, *City of God*, bk XIV, ch. 16 (p. 614).

31 Augustine, *City of God*, bk XIV, ch. 17 (p. 615).

32 Augustine, *City of God*, bk XIV, ch. 19 (p. 619).

33 'This lust triumphs not only over the whole body, and not only outwardly, but inwardly also. When the emotion of the mind is united with the craving of the flesh, it convulses the whole man, so that there follows a pleasure greater than any other: a bodily pleasure so great that, at the moment of time when he achieves his climax, the alertness and, so to speak, vigilance of a man's mind is almost entirely overwhelmed'. Augustine, *City of God*, bk XIV, ch. 16 (p. 614).

34 Augustine, *City of God*, bk XIV, ch. 26 (p. 630).
35 Augustine, *City of God*, bk XIV, ch. 24 (pp. 625–6).
36 Augustine, *City of God*, bk XIV, ch. 26 (p. 629).
37 The version of the story of the sleeping beauty in Basile's *Pentamerone* (1636) makes explicit what is at most implicit in Perrault's latter telling of the tale in *Histoires ou contes du temps passé* (1697). The 'beauty' is found by a prince who 'cannot rouse her, yet falls in love with the insensible body as did the prince who came upon Snow White laid out in her coffin; but being less courteous, he rapes her, and forgets her'. It is only when one of the two children to whom she gives birth nine months later sucks the poisoned splinter from her finger that she is restored to life. See Iona and Peter Opie, *The Classic Fairy Tales* (London: Oxford University Press, 1974), p. 81. The Opies find an earlier version of the story in a fourteenth-century prose romance, *Perceforest*, and locate its origin in the story of Brynhild in the *Volsunga Saga* (p. 83).
38 In *Aliens* the otherwise unexplained seed-pods of the first film are revealed to be the eggs of an alien 'queen'. They are capable of lying dormant until a suitable host-victim comes into proximity with them.
39 Taubin, 'Invading Bodies', p. 9.
40 Taubin, 'Invading Bodies', p. 9.
41 Taubin suggests that as well as representing the 'monstrous feminine', the alien queen 'bears a suspicious resemblance to a favourite scapegoat of the Reagan/Bush era – the black welfare mother, that parasite on the economy whose uncurbed reproductive drive reduced hard-working taxpayers to bankruptcy' ('Invading Bodies', p. 9).
42 Taubin, 'Invading Bodies', p. 9. 'Aids is everywhere in the film. It's in the danger surrounding sex and drugs. It's in the metaphor of a mysterious deadly organism attacking an all-male community. It's in the iconography of the shaven heads. Exhorting the prisoners to defy The Company, Ripley shouts, "They think we're scum and they don't give a fuck about one friend of yours who's died", an Aids activism line if ever there was one' ('Invading Bodies', p. 10).
43 In *Aliens* we learned that Ripley did indeed have a daughter, who, in the director's cut, had grown up and died an old woman while Ripley was in hypersleep between the first and second films.
44 Luke 1.26–38.
45 The painting is co-signed by Martini's brother-in-law, Lippo Memmi, but his work is most likely confined to the two side panels of the altarpiece, which was one of the earliest to depict the Annunciation.
46 Thomson, *Alien Quartet*, p. 106.
47 Thomson finds this aspect of the film unsatisfactory, the point in the quartet when it becomes 'less than good enough'. Ripley's pregnancy should come as a surprise, but now cannot, and so is turned into 'some sort of ritual in which the process of gestation is fulfilled (or not) with a concomitant spiritual

discovery'. (Thomson, *Alien Quartet*, p. 114.) But Fincher's film is more subtle than Thomson allows, since the extremely brief exposition of Ripley's impregnation, interleaved between the credits as the audience is still settling in its seats, followed by the scene of Newt's autopsy, establishes the still unspoken fear of the film. Thus the horror, though unstated and hardly shown, takes up residence in the mind of the viewer. Fincher developed this game to perfection in his next film, *Seven*, where the viewer alone, in his or her mind's eye, stages scenes of appalling sadism, tricked into imagining what is never shown in the film, and thus made complicit with the murderer.

48 Luke 1.38.

49 On Mary's freedom see Tina Beattie, *Rediscovering Mary: Insights from the Gospels* (Tunbridge Wells: Burns & Oates, 1995), ch. 1.

50 Taubin, 'Invading Bodies', p. 10. *Alien* was made for an estimated $10 million, of which $33,000 were paid to Sigourney Weaver; but for *Aliens* (which cost $20 million) she was paid $2 million, and for *Alien3*, $5.5 million, out of an estimated $50 million that the film cost to make. Her fee for *Alien Resurrection* was an estimated $11 million. See Thomson, *The Alien Quartet*, pp. 11, 59, 100, 143.

51 Taubin, 'Invading Bodies', p. 9.

52 Creed, *Monstrous-Feminine*, p. 52. On Dreyer's film see Paul Schrader, *Transcendental Style in Film: Ozu, Bresson, Dreyer* (New York: Da Capo Press, [1972] 1988), pp. 121–6.

53 Creed, *Monstrous-Feminine*, p. 53.

54 See Sigmund Freud, 'On Transformations of Instinct as Exemplified in Anal Erotism' (1917), in *The Penguin Freud Library*, vol. 7, pp. 294–302.

55 Augustine, *City of God*, bk XXII, ch. 12 (pp. 1139–41).

56 Augustine, *City of God*, bk XXII, ch. 12 (pp. 1150–1). Nothing, of course, is impossible for God. 'For, clearly, all the flesh which hunger has removed from the starving man will have evaporated into the air; and, as we have said, Almighty God has power to recall what has thus fled. The flesh of the man who was eaten, therefore, will be restored to him in whom it first began to be human flesh. For it must be regarded as borrowed, as it were, by the person who ate him, and, like a loan of money, it must be repaid'. Augustine, *City of God*, bk XXII, ch. 20 (p. 1151).

57 Augustine, *City of God*, bk XXII, ch. 17 (p. 1144).

58 Augustine, *City of God*, bk XXII, ch. 17 (p. 1057). We already have some indication of the useless beauty we will acquire in the resurrection, for now we enjoy such useless adornments as the nipples and beards of men. Nipples are useful in women, and they, as the weaker sex, would find beards useful for hiding behind. Augustine, *City of God*, bk XXII, ch. 24 (p. 1164).

59 Augustine, *City of God*, bk XXII, ch. 24 (p. 1164).

60 'No one will wish to have what he has not received, and he will be bound in a bond of uttermost peace to one who has received it; just as, in the body,

the finger does not wish to be the eye, since both members are contained within the ordered composition of the whole body. Thus some will have greater gifts than others; but each will have the gift of not wanting more than he has.' Augustine, *City of God*, bk XXII, ch. 30 (p. 1179).

61 Augustine, *City of God*, bk XXII, ch. 29 (p. 1172).

62 Augustine, *City of God*, bk XXII, ch. 29 (p. 1175).

63 Augustine, *City of God*, bk XXII, ch. 29 (p. 1177).

64 John 20.29.

65 '*Alien Resurrection* exhibits the appearance and logic of dreams and fairy tale rather than of the real world (even the world of the future, the reality of science fiction).' Mulhall, *On Film*, p. 126.

66 Mulhall, *On Film*, p. 135.

67 Augustine, *City of God*, bk XXII, ch. 30 (p. 1179).

Figure 5 Kissing Christ

Urbain Grandier (Oliver Reed) and Jeanne des Anges (Vanessa Redgrave) in *The Devils* (Ken Russell, UK 1971). Photo: The Kobal Collection.

Chapter 5

GOD'S SEX

Clad only in a garter and sparkling boots, strings of pearls and three golden cockle shells, covering breasts and pudenda, the king of France, Louis XIII (Graham Armitage), rises onto the stage as Venus, born from the waves.[1] Three young men in baroque tutti enter, and together with three maidens join the king in a lively but stately dance, pointing toes to Renaissance rhythms (provided by David Munrow's Early Music Consort of London). The show is watched by Cardinal Richelieu (Christopher Logue), attended by his nuns. He is seated amidst the courtiers, many of them in drag, who are more concerned with who is sleeping with whom, and who with the king, than with the king's performance on the stage. Thus begins Ken Russell's darkly camp production of *The Devils* (UK 1972), a free but concise amalgam of John Whiting's play of the same name and Aldous Huxley's highly imaginative study, *The Devils of Loudun* (1952).[2]

Though based on historical events, Russell's film is not historically fastidious. Its opening scene is more redolent of the court of Louis XIV than that of the sun king's predecessor.[3] Moreover, the decadence of the court is merely a backdrop for the central action of the film which concerns the downfall of Urbain Grandier, priest of Loudun; and Grandier's story is merely a pretext – one might think – for Russell to indulge his fascination with religious erotics, with the conjunction of wimples and writhing bodies. Nevertheless, with music by Peter Maxwell Davies (performed by his band The Fires of London), that is by turns plaintive and percussive, and with stark, expressionist sets by Derek Jarman, *The Devils* is Russell's finest film, an extravagant but compelling exploration of carnal spirituality.[4]

Theatre of Demons

By the 1630s, Loudun's population consisted of both Huguenots and Catholics, living in an uneasy alliance within the walls of their common city. While there were more Huguenots than Catholics, the latter were increasingly prominent, building new churches and houses for various religious orders: Jesuits, Discalced Carmelites, Capuchins, the Daughters of Calvary, and, from 1626, the Ursulines.[5] That year also saw the completed restoration of Loudun's fortress and defensive walls, representing the town's relative autonomy with regard to the state, which under Cardinal Richelieu was fast encroaching on all areas of civic life.[6] But the days of Loudun's independence were fast closing, and in 1632, the Baron de Laurbardemont, on the orders of the king, began the demolition of the walls, and eventually of the castle keep. Russell's film is staged against this event, as also against the plague that came to Loudun in 1632. During May and September of that year an estimated 3,700 people died out of a total population of 14,000.[7]

In order to defeat the plague, public gatherings – including religious ceremonies – were banned, and people retreated behind their doors; the nuns behind their convent walls. It was then, in September 1632, that the Ursuline prioress, Jeanne des Anges (Vanessa Redgrave), witnessed the apparition of the convent's recently dead confessor, prior Moussant, and then, a little later, the phantom of the still living parish priest of Saint-Pierre, Urbain Grandier (Oliver Reed). '[A]ltering his words and behaviour at the same time as his figure', Grandier 'talked to her of amours, plied her with caresses no less insolent than unchaste, and pressed her to grant him what was no longer hers to dispose of, that which, by her vows, she had consecrated to her divine Bridegroom.'[8] Thus began the possession of the prioress and her nuns by the demons that, as it would transpire, the sorcerer-priest of Saint-Pierre had conjured out of hell.

Grandier was arrested in December 1633 and after being held in Angers was brought back to Loudun in the following Spring. Meanwhile, the possessed women were held in various houses throughout the town, from which they would be taken to nearby churches and chapels for their exorcising, which continued throughout the Spring of 1634. Their exorcisms were publicly staged on specially constructed platforms. The possessed sisters would be bound to bunk beds, and then set free as the exorcists got to work, enticing the demons to manifest and name themselves. But off-stage the nuns appeared untroubled by their devilish inhabitants, quietly going about their normal routines and exercises.

> Visit them privily when they have goodly intervals. You will see well-behaved, modest religious who do some needlework or spin before you, who take pleasure in hearing God spoken of, and in learning ways to serve Him well. They perform their examination of conscience, confess exactly, and take communion, when they are not agitated, with as much peace and repose of mind as if they were not possessed.[9]

For Michel de Certeau, the story of Loudun – caught between sorcery and a newly 'objectified world'[10] – figures the indeterminate moment when medieval Europe gave birth to modernity. Previously, the exorcist spoke in Christ's name in order to drive out the demon. But at Loudun the demon – along with everyone else – must be cajoled to speak the truth of possession, and so of Christ, who alone can combat such devilry. But since by definition the demon is a liar, the truth he speaks is beset by an interminable ambiguity. The exorcist must conjure the demon to speak the truth of the exorcist's conjuration, and by this very act defeat the object of his exercise.[11] Thus the truth and power of the church is at stake in the possession at Loudun, and it is only by staging the routing of the demons and the destruction of their conjuror, Grandier, that the church's power can be re-established. 'The representation of power is all the more spectacular in that it betrays the anguish of losing it – or of having lost it.'[12]

There were those who doubted the authenticity of the possession, and wondered if the audience of doctors and exorcists were not as much the cause as the remedy of the sisters' plight.[13] Marc Duncan noted that Sister Agnès claimed 'that she was not possessed, but that they wanted to make her think she was, and that they forced her to let herself be exorcised'. When some burning sulphur fell on Sister Claire's lip, she cried out 'that since they said she was possessed, she was willing to believe there was some truth in it, but that she didn't deserve to be treated like that because of it'.[14] Despite these testimonies, most observers were convinced that devilry was afoot, and were prepared to believe the claim that the priest Grandier was the culprit whose sorcery had brought this spiritual infection upon the town. At one point Grandier himself was brought on to the stage before his accusers, and invited to exorcise them of the demons he had conjured. The meeting ended in bedlam.

> All the said energuments were shaken by the most violent, extraordinary, and frightful convulsions, contortions, movements, cries, clamours and blasphemies that one can imagine, it being impossible to describe or in any way represent them, unless by saying that it seemed to all present that they were seeing on that occasion all the fury of hell.[15]

In due course, Grandier was found guilty of sorcery, and on 18 August 1634 he was burned alive, after having first been put to the 'question ordinary and extraordinary'.[16] It was held against him that during the torture he shed no tears, but repeatedly prayed: 'My God of heaven and earth, give me strength.'[17] Whether by accident or design, Grandier was not discreetly strangled, as was customary, but abandoned to the flames. 'For the fire or the Devil cut the rope in an instant, and so quickly that the fire was scarcely lit before he fell into it and was burned alive without crying out. Only a few heard that he said: "Ah, my God." '[18] Thousands came to watch the demise of the sorcerer of Loudun, and no doubt the demons he had conjured were among them.

> I saw him at the stake speak boldly, I even saw the fire lit without his showing any apprehension of it, but he rather said aloud: 'Lord Jesus, I commend my soul to thy hands.' A witness asked for his pardon, as well as that of the others. He answered in these terms: 'My friend, I pardon you as willingly as I believe firmly my God will pardon me and receive me today in paradise.'[19]

It was thus that Loudun became a theatre of demons, a staged madness that Russell's film can barely indicate, for all its extravagance and orgiastic embellishments.[20] Some audiences were shocked by the lewdness of the exorcism scenes in the film. Shaven naked nuns debauch themselves with one another and with visiting dignatories, or masturbate with candles, or receive clysters, rectal and vaginal enemas, at first forcibly and then voluntarily, enthusiastically, with ever-larger syringes. Aldous Huxley notes that the Marquis de Sade would later make use of such devices for sexual purposes, and, following Huxley, Russell's film shows a scene in which the exorcist Pierre Barré subjects Jeanne to a public purging that is more or less 'a rape in a public lavatory'.[21] Derek Jarman's white-tiled, lavatorial convent materializes Huxley's description. Jarman reports that the filming of such scenes were 'fuelled with champagne', and filmed on a closed set with Russell banging away on a set of drums in order to 'whip up fervour'.[22] Russell admits to playing 'the most barbaric bit of [Stravinsky's] Rite of Spring . . . flat out' during the shooting of the film's most notorious scene, when the possessed nuns, in their abandon, 'rape' a life-size figure of the crucified Christ, with Father Mignon looking on from the rafters, masturbating.[23] Unfortunately this sequence was considered too strong by the film's producers, and, on the advice of the British film censor, John Trevelyan, it was removed from *The Devils* before the film was submitted to the British Board of Film Classification, who gave it an X certificate. The sequence has remained 'lost' until recently.[24]

Devilish Visions

Even before he died, Grandier's story and that of the possessed Ursulines was being told by contemporaries, in letters and pamphlets, and for some time after his death people came to Loudun to see the bewitched Jeanne, and hear her own account of what had transpired. The story enthralled then as it does now, for the story of Loudun – as Michel de Certeau notes – offers 'the participants in more recent conflicts' a means for 'entering into a dialogue with their own devils'.[25] In Russell's film, Grandier and Jeanne exemplify different attempts to marry spiritual and carnal yearning. The historical Grandier authored a *Treatise on Celibacy* in which he argued for the legitimacy of married priests. He concluded, with Saint Paul, that those who remained virgins did better than those who did well, and married; but he was content to do well.[26] He wrote the *Treatise* for Madeleine de Brou (Gemma Jones), who was said to have been his mistress, and Russell, after Huxley, follows this story in the film. Unlike Grandier's previous liaisons – as with Phillipe Trincant (Georgina Hale), whom he beds and discards – his feelings for Madeleine challenge his cynicism and lead him to seek the reconciliation of his physical and spiritual passions. 'Oh God help me', he prays. 'I love this woman. Let us find a way to you together.'

It was rumoured that Grandier officiated at his own marriage to Madeleine de Brou. 'As priest he asked himself whether he took this woman to be his wedded wife, and as bridegroom he answered in the affirmative, he slipped the ring upon her finger. As priest he invoked a blessing, and as groom he knelt to receive it.'[27] In Russell's film the marriage takes place at night, celebrated with a nuptial mass. 'With my body I thee worship', Grandier avows, and offers Madeleine the chalice of Christ's blood. Drinking from it, they kiss over it, united together with Christ, who is the third in their union. Eucharistic imagery is consistently associated with their love for one another. In one scene Grandier, who is on his way to Paris to entreat the King to save Loudun's walls, stops by a lake, surrounded by mountains. At the lakeshore he blesses and breaks the bread of communion, of his union with Christ and with Madeleine, with the people he is called to serve, and with the God who gives all.[28]

> Strange thoughts come to me. I am like a man who has been lost, who has always been lost. Now, for all kinds of reasons I have a vague sense of meaning, and can think of myself as a small part of God's abundance, which includes everything. And I know I want to serve it. I want to serve the people of Loudun. I want to serve you.

The scene ends with Grandier again sharing Christ's blood with Madeleine, who has now joined him on the lakeshore, and drinks with him from the chalice. The bread and wine, the body and blood of Christ, signifies the mystical in Grandier and Madeleine's carnal union, the love that draws them together, and together draws them to Christ. The film explicitly contrasts their communion with that of Jeanne and her phantasmatic Christ/Grandier by intercutting between the scene of the lakeshore Eucharist and the increasingly sexual cavorting of the possessed nuns, which originally ended with the now excised 'rape of Christ'.

> The naked nuns tear down a wooden figure of Christ and throw themselves on it, having it in every possible way. Then Mignon goes up into the roof rafters and masturbates looking down on the orgy below. Both Warner Brothers and the censor thought it was too strong so I took it out. Short of burning the entire film I had no choice. But it was really central to the whole thing, intercut as it was with Grandier finding both himself and God in the solitary simplicity of Nature. Over-ripe, perverted religion going as bad and wrong as it can possibly become, with the eternal truth of the bread and the wine and the brotherhood of man and God in the universe. Try getting the Hollywood heavies or the Festival of Light swallowing *that*![29]

Christ's lakeside communion with Grandier and Madeleine also signifies their impending participation in Christ's suffering, in the breaking of his body and the spilling of his blood. Grandier's and Madeleine's clandestine wedding does not go unobserved, and when its rumour reaches the Ursuline convent, the younger nuns enact a bawdy parody of the wedding – 'they shall be one flesh' – and of the wedding night. It is when the besotted Jeanne sees this, that she conceives of Grandier's nocturnal visitations to her cell.

Before his meeting with Madeleine, Russell's Grandier is vain but world-weary, a self-destructive cynic, and this perhaps explains why he is not more astute at recognizing the political interests that are growing against him. Jeanne's fatal naming of Grandier as the conjuror of her demons is explained by her sexual obsession for him, which she confuses with her devotion to Christ, so that in her visions Christ becomes Grandier, and Grandier her way to union with Christ.[30] Near the beginning of the film, we see Jeanne spying from behind the convent walls on Grandier, as he passes by in the funeral procession for the governor of Loudun. In her ecstasy she has a vision of Christ walking toward her, across water, and herself as Mary Magdalene falling at his feet, covering them with her hair. But Christ is Grandier, and as he looks at Jeanne, she becomes aware of her humped back, and the jeering of her sister nuns who now surround her. Tormented by her unnameable desires, Jeanne calls on Christ: 'Let me find a way to you. Take me in your sacred arms. Let the blood flow between us, uniting us. Grandier! Grandier!' But it will be her own and Grandier's blood that unites her to Christ.

Jeanne's second vision comes to her while she is leading her sisters in the recitation of the fifth sorrowful mystery of the rosary, meditating on Christ's death. As she kneels before the crucifix, she sees herself as the Magdalene before the cross, with a malignant crowd baying at both her and the dying Christ, who now looks at her, and it is again Grandier – in Christ's place – who looks at her. He descends from the cross and takes her in his arms, and she kisses the wounds on his hands. Kneeling, she licks the wound in his side, inserting her tongue and tasting his blood (figure 5). Then they passionately embrace, rolling together on the ground. As Jeanne imagines being penetrated by Grandier's Christ, she beats her head with the black beads of her rosary, and drives its crucifix into the palm of her hand, gouging a bloody hole. By this self-wounding Jeanne is freed of her vision, and she flees the chapel in terror.

Angelic Raptures

The film critic, Tony Rayns, is not alone in finding *The Devils* 'overwrought', a 'diabolical comedy' at best. And perhaps, as he says, it is 'more redolent of a camp revue than a cathartic vision'.[31] But Jeanne's visions are not so far from those of other well-attested 'mystics', and, in particular, not so far from the spiritual writings of her sixteenth-century predecessor Teresa of Avila (1515–82), who was canonized in 1622 and whose *Life* was a model for Jeanne des Anges' own *Autobiographie*.[32] Amorous discourse was, for Teresa, the language of the Holy Spirit, the tongue in which the divine love was expressed.[33] It is this language that Teresa speaks in her *Meditations on the Song of Songs* (1566–7).

> In the interior of the soul a sweetness is felt so great that the soul feels clearly the nearness of its Lord . . . He enters the soul and does so with wonderful sweetness. He pleases and makes it happy, and it cannot understand how or from where the blessing enters . . . But when this most wealthy Bridegroom desires to enrich and favour the soul more, He changes it into Himself to such a point that, just as a person is caused to swoon from great pleasure and happiness, it seems to the soul it is left suspended in those divine arms,

> leaning on that sacred side and those divine breasts. It doesn't know how to do anything more than rejoice, sustained by the divine milk with which its Spouse is nourishing it and making it better so that He might favour it, and it might merit more each day.[34]

But unlike Teresa, the protagonists in Russell's comic vision have confused their sexual desires with spiritual yearnings, deflecting the latter into perverse parodies of their carnal cravings, confusing their piety with obscene visions. This might seem a twentieth-century, post-Freudian, reading of the events at Loudun, but at the time, the doctor Claude Quillet diagnosed the outbreak of demons among the Ursulines as a case of hysteromania or erotomania. 'Those poor she-devil religious, finding themselves shut up between four walls go crazy, fall into a melancholic delirium, tortured by the urges of the flesh, and in reality what they need is a carnal remedy in order to be perfectly cured.'[35]

Then, as now, the panting soul was suspect of a baser hunger, a purely bodily want, that needs only carnal satisfaction, and Teresa of Avila would not necessarily have disagreed with Quillet's diagnosis. In 1580, Teresa was ordered to destroy her *Meditations on the Song of Songs*. She at once threw her book into the fire, though she knew that several other copies were in circulation.[36] The spiritual – amorous – interpretation of the Song, as opposed to the ecclesiological, had become suspect of erotic interests. Friar Luis de Léon had made the mistake of translating the Song into an all too obvious vernacular, and was imprisoned by the Inquisition from 1572–5. One witness at Luis' trial complained that the translation had turned the Song into 'nothing but a love letter, in no way spiritual, differing hardly at all from the love poems of Ovid'.[37] The spiritual rendering of the Song was suspect of legitimating debauched devotions, for Spain in the 1570s was again visited by the Illuminist heresy, that supposedly advocated an all too carnal communion with the humanity of Christ. Thus many came to associate erotic encounters with ecstatic prayer, and made this association with regard to Teresa's *Meditations* and *The Interior Castle* (1577).[38]

In 1578 – in a strange prefiguring of Jeanne and Grandier – two nuns at the Seville convent accused Teresa of carnal contact with her confessor, Jerónimo Gracián. He also was said to have consorted with other nuns, and 'danced naked before them'.[39] The Inquisition, however, did not act on these accusations, and Teresa forgave the penitent nuns, especially Beatriz de Chávez, whom she thought 'a weak-minded person who had been led astray . . . by the devil . . . for he is very good at taking advantage of temperamental and unintelligent people.' She enjoined her sisters to pray for Beatriz, 'for many of the saints have fallen and then become saints again'.[40] As this story indicates, Teresa was aware of the temptations to which cloistered nuns, engaged in contemplative prayer, were prone. Teresa did not doubt the possibility of demonic possession, but she became aware – and argued the point – that some discover a devilish illness when all that is present is a physiological perturbation, a 'melancholy' brought on by excessive devotion and lack of food.

> There was a nun who . . . [by] dint of much discipline and fasting . . . had become so weak that, whenever she communicated or had occasion to be enkindled in devotion . . . would fall to the ground and remain there for eight or nine hours: both she and the other nuns thought it was a case of rapture . . . Her confessor, who was a great friend of mine, came to tell me about it . . . I told him he must forbid her fasting and discipline and provide her with some distraction. She was obedient and did as he said. Soon she became stronger and stopped thinking about raptures.[41]

This attitude – that should have prevailed at Loudun – was adopted by Teresa in the face of growing hostility toward the contemplative life in late sixteenth-century Spain. But she did not abandon her belief that genuine rapture is possible, that the soul can be embraced by divinity in the seventh dwelling places or mansions (*moradas*) of the interior castle, and that the proper language for this ecstatic encounter is that of eros. As Noel O'Donoghue notes of Teresa's most famous vision, it is 'erotic precisely because it is mystical'.[42]

> I would see beside me, on my left hand, an angel in bodily form – a type of vision which I am not in the habit of seeing, except very rarely.[43] . . . He was not tall, but short, and very beautiful, his face so aflame that he appeared to be one of the highest types of angel who seem to be all afire. They must be those who are called cherubim[44] . . . In his hands I saw a long golden spear and at the end of the iron grip I seemed to see a point of fire. With this he seemed to pierce my heart several times so that it penetrated to my entrails. When he drew it out, I thought he was drawing them out with it and he left me completely afire with a great love for God. The pain was so sharp that it made me utter several moans; and so excessive was the sweetness caused me by this intense pain that one can never wish to lose it, nor will one's soul be content with anything less than God. It is not bodily pain, but spiritual, though the body has a share in it – indeed, a great share. So sweet are the colloquies of love which pass between the soul and God that if anyone thinks I am lying I beseech God, in His Goodness, to give him the same experience . . . But, when this pain of which I am

> now speaking begins, the Lord seems to transport the soul and to send it into an ecstasy, so that it cannot possibly suffer or have any pain because it immediately begins to experience fruition.[45]

Russell's tortured souls never learn the amorous language of mystical encounter, the happiness of the soul's embrace by its divine lover, of its ecstatic fecunding. This is especially true of Jeanne, who is last seen in her cell, administering yet another vaginal enema. 'I am purging my own devils' she tells Laubardemont, who has come to tell her that now Grandier is dead, the show is over. 'There will be a few tourists occasionally to brighten things up. But that won't last long. Soon the town will die. You'll be left in peace and oblivion.' As a parting gift he throws her a souvenir, one of Grandier's charred black bones.[46]

The film ends with Madeleine clambering out of Loudun, over its broken walls, taking a lonely, desolate road, which has only gibbets for trees. Yet the story of Grandier and Madeleine points to the possibility of finding the mystical in the erotic, and not only the erotic in the mystical. It points to the idea that the sexual relationship, as well as providing the language for the soul's divine desire, can also be the means of the soul's ascent when caught in the divine descending, 'suspended in those divine arms, leaning on that sacred side and those divine breasts'.[47] The divine eros, the 'energy of creation', sweeps the soul 'onwards towards the fullness of self-giving' towards another, so that together each might in the other discover the depths of the desire by which they are held and moved.[48]

The face of the angel – the cherubim – that appears to Teresa is 'aflame' with a light that is so bright that it is as if the angel were 'all afire', a burning flame like the tip of his 'long golden spear', itself a 'point of fire'. The vision is radiant with the light of the triune God that, in the seventh mansions of the soul, enkindles the spirit to burn with a vision beyond vision, to 'see' the divine mystery, the three 'persons' of one substance, power, knowledge and divinity. Then the soul 'knows in such a way that what we hold by faith, it understands . . . through sight – although the sight is not with the bodily eyes nor with the eyes of the soul, because we are not dealing with an imaginative vision'.[49] In this 'seeing' the three persons 'speak' to the soul a sweet colloquy of love, of how all three – Father, Son and Spirit – will dwell in the soul that loves them, that embraces the heavenly bridegroom. Thus the angel plunges his fiery spear into the very entrails of the soul, the fire of God's threefold presence causing 'greater bliss than any that can come from the whole of creation'.[50] By this 'fire in the heart' – in the very fundament of the body – God comes to the soul so that the soul, its flesh opened to God, can come to dwell, to dance, in the life of the triune mystery.[51]

That the angel's fiery spear penetrates not only the souls of sequestered celibates but also those of concupiscent couples is the concern of the remainder of this chapter. Here our guide will be the Swiss theologian, Hans Urs von Balthasar (1905–88) and his sexual parody of God's triune relationships. For Balthasar, like Teresa, believes that the Spirit speaks an erotic tongue, and, in the figures of Dante and Beatrice, Balthasar finds a human love that is by Love inspired, a union that is also an ascent, caught up into the circling glories of cherubim and seraphim. This is to imagine a mystical union that does not take place in the secret interior of the soul, but in the exteriority of the body, in the amorous colloquies of the flesh.

Erotic Parodies

'It is clear' – Georges Bataille (1897–1962) asserts at the beginning of his essay 'The Solar Anus' (1927) – 'that the world is purely parodic, in other words that each thing seen is the parody of another, or is the same thing in a deceptive form'.

> Ever since sentences started to *circulate* in brains devoted to reflection, an effort at total identification has been made, because with the aid of a copula each sentence ties one thing to another; all things would be visibly connected if one could discover at a single glance and in its totality the tracings of an Ariadne's thread leading thought into its own labyrinth. But the *copula* of terms is no less irritating than the *copulation* of bodies.[52]

For Bataille's parodic thought everything in the world is ultimately relatable to everything else, everything can be substituted for another thing, in a ceaseless process of metaphoric exchange. It is the circulation of language that makes this possible; and since it is possible in language it is possible in the world(s) that language constitutes. The coupling of words performs the copulation of bodies. For Bataille, parody utterly eroticizes the world, so that in the running of the 'locomotive's wheels and pistons' he sees the world's 'two primary motions' of 'rotation and sexual movement'. In the image of the steam engine's pounding pistons and turning wheels, Bataille sees the coupling of animals and the movements of the planets, always moving from 'their own position in order to return to it, completing their rotation'. These 'two motions' – the thrusting of sexual frenzy and the circling of the stars – are 'reciprocally transformed, the one into the other', so that the turning of the earth 'makes animals and men have coitus' and – since 'the result is as much the cause as that which provokes it' – the coupling of animals and men turns the earth.[53] For Bataille, the earth and its motions are enfolded in the erotic embrace of the cosmos.

> The simplest image of organic life united with rotation is the tide. From the movement of the sea, uniform coitus of the earth with the moon, comes the polymorphous and organic coitus of the earth with the sun. But the first form of solar love is a cloud raised up over the liquid element. The erotic cloud sometimes becomes a storm and falls back to earth in the form of rain, while lightening staves in the layers of the atmosphere. The rain is soon raised up again in the form of an immobile plant.[54]

A similar parodying of the erotic can be found in the work of the great Swiss theologian Hans Urs von Balthasar. While Bataille couples the sun and moon with the sea, with clouds and plants, with the coitus of animals and the 'amorous frenzy' of men and women,[55] Balthasar couples the processions of the divine Trinity with the birthing of a maiden's child, with the kiss of a bride and groom who are also mother and son – bone of bone and flesh of flesh – and with the embrace of every couple in Christ, and of every soul by God. Balthasar's 'copulations' are no less startling than Bataille's 'torrid and blinding sun' that 'exclusively loves the Night and directs its luminous violence, its ignoble shaft, toward the earth', whose 'nocturnal terrestrial expanses head continuously toward the indecency of the solar ray'.[56]

By thinking the parallels between the motions of Trinity, Christ and church (Mary) as parodic transformations, we unveil the 'body', the ancient cultural biology, which Balthasar both exposes and conceals in his 'suprasexual' erotics. The use of 'parody' rather than 'metaphor', 'symbol' or 'analogy', does not deny the propriety of the latter terms for the linkages and connections – including the copula(tion)s of human bodies, one with another, and with the divine flesh – that are the subject of this chapter. But the use of parody – as metaphoric substitution (in the quite precise and somewhat peculiar sense offered by Bataille) – disturbs the ease with which we tend to pass over such analogical exchanges in theology. If one thinks of simile as metaphor footnoted and explained, rendered less provocative and dangerous, one can think of analogy/parody as simile extended, elaborated, intensified, stressing the greater dissimilarity (*maior dissimilitudo*) of the analogously/parodically conjoined, copulated similars.

Analogy – as John Saward puts it – sets a 'certain likeness' within a 'greater unlikeness'.[57] But since analogy, particularly in theology, does not measure the distance between the analogues, one is left only with the 'certain likeness', which then gains in intensity from the silence of the unmeasured space – the 'greater unlikeness' – in which it is set. The shock of calling analogy 'parody' may remind us that in using analogies/parodies – even one as hallowed as the fatherhood of God – we do not escape the historical and the cultural, from which the 'certain likeness' is taken. Thus I do not intend to divest parody of burlesque, which is certainly still present in Bataille's usage, when he couples the polite with the vulgar, the metaphysical with the indecent. The analogical burlesque reminds us that there is always something comic about theology, something absurd in trying to speak of that which we do not know but by which we are known.[58]

The 'Dance of Dispossession'

By means of the parodic copula Bataille relates sexual rhythm with planetary motion; Balthasar – in what may be considered a no less surreal manner – relates the economic with the immanent Trinity. It is not the relation as such, baldly stated, that constitutes the surreal in Balthasar, for as much is asserted by other theologians, most notably Karl Rahner, for whom it is axiomatic that the ' "economic" Trinity is the "immanent" Trinity and the "immanent" Trinity is the "economic" Trinity'.[59] Christian theology can hardly say otherwise, unless it is to entertain a second God, hidden and undisclosed behind the showing of divinity in Christ.

Balthasar's surreal move is to suppose that in the economic Trinity, in the scriptural story of Christ's ministry, death and resurrection, we see the inner-economy of the immanent Trinity, its fundamental dynamic, a drama that has, as it were, always-already occurred before its expression in the history of the world.[60] Thus the mission of Christ is the historical concretion of the Son's procession from the Father, and Balthasar's 'great insight', as John Saward puts it, is to see that 'the "kenosis" of the Incarnation is made possible by and lays open a preceding and underlying kenosis within the Trinity'.[61] Thus the incarnation as kenosis – as a radical donation of the self, the self-gift of Christ unto death, an utter dispossession – is the non-identical repetition or parody of the intratrinitarian kenosis, the Father's eternal dispossession and donation of himself to the Son.

It is the nature of God to be endlessly abundant, perpetually effusive, overflowing with fecund love; an unceasing donation of self to other; 'not another God but an other in God'.[62] The one who is thus given – eternally – is constituted as gift and reception, and thus can only in turn give again, thereby establishing the circulation, the rotation, of the eternal charity. This spinning love is the act of the Trinity, spinning so fast, with such joy, that – for no other reason than its sheer goodness – there flows the world, which, caught in the circling draft, is drawn back into the eternal rotation.

> The life of the Trinity is an eternally self-fulfilled circle, which does not need the world . . . The act of creation has its source in the freedom of the Trinity; it is a 'selfless' sharing of [the Trinity's] life of blessed selflessness with needy creatures.[63]

It is then out of this circling dynamic, this 'dance of dispossession', as John Saward calls it,[64] that there flows a series of relationships, each one of which, like the figures or sets of a dance, differently repeats the preceding one, joined only by a parodic copula. This is the flow of the divine mission which repeats, *ad extra* and non-identically, the preceding procession of the Son from the Father.

Continuum and Indeterminacy

The foregoing description of Balthasar's parodic kenotic theology is open to at least two related objections. First, Bataille's parodic copula presumes a continuous domain in which to operate. No matter how fanciful or shocking his connections, they take place within the single space of the cosmos; they do not presume a radical discontinuity between any of the terms, such as the infinite distance that theology presumes to separate the creator from the creature, and which requires some concept of analogy for its bridging, if not indeed a strategy of negation. Bataille's parodic world is the pre-Christian cosmos that Balthasar describes as the 'all-embracing context' of 'being as a whole, which always includes the *theion*'.[65] This ancient cosmos – as in Plato's *Republic* – is already one of parodic substitution, in which the rightly ordered soul is the rightly ordered polis is the rightly ordered cosmos, exhibiting what Balthasar terms a 'fluid *analogia entis*'. He notes that such a cosmos, embracing both human and divine being, 'survived, in a Christian transposition, right into modern times, in spite of the fact that now there was a far more abrupt distinction between the divine, absolute world and the contingent world freely created by God'.[66] But if Balthasar's kenotic repetitions are to be read as a continuum of parodic substitutions, it would seem that we have to assume the survival of just such a cosmos in Balthasar's theology. But then how far do Balthasar's analogies/parodies have to travel? What is the distance between the terms that his copulas hold together?

The second objection to applying Bataille to Balthasar, concerns the reversibility or inversions of Bataille's parodies, since on Bataille's account the pistons drive the wheels and the wheels power the pistons; copulation turns the planet and the planet moves the copulators, and so we are asked to imagine a perhaps perpetual motion with an indeterminate cause. In an economy of radical substitution there can be no fixed priority or stable hierarchy. But then this raises a second question to Balthasar. Is it so certain that he can establish the priority presumed in his parodic account of trinitarian kenosis? Might the procession of Son from Father be the parody of creation, or of incarnation, or of redemption, or of the relationship – which has yet to be discussed – between man and woman, rather than that they are parodies of a prior intratrinitarian kenosis? In short, are matters not more fluid, more 'uncanny', as in the way of ancient cosmology?[67]

It is these two questions – how analogical/apophatic is Balthasar's *analogia entis*, and how can he preserve the Trinity from contamination by its human parodies – that must be brought to a consideration of Balthasar's body theology.[68]

Sexual Womb

Mary Timothy Prokes defines human sexuality as the capacity 'to enter into love-giving, life-giving union in and through the body in ways that are appropriate'.[69] Human sexuality is not 'animalistic', but '*person-al*, involving the giving and receiving of person-gift'. As a 'capacity', this self-giving is not 'restricted to certain bodily organs and activities, nor is it confined to a certain portion of life'.[70] It pervades all of life. Like Balthasar, Prokes sees this bodily capacity to give oneself and in return receive the self of the other, as a result of our 'being created in the image and likeness of God', thus parodying, as it were, 'the Trinity of Persons who are in constant perichoretic union through total Self-Gift to the other Persons'.[71]

> The theology of God's inner life (and thus, of human life in that image) is a 'gift theology', a faith reflection upon the irrevocable givenness and receptivity among the divine Persons. Faith-based understandings of human sexuality take their starting point in the trinitarian mystery.[72]

Prokes pictures both the inner trinitarian relations, and the relations between divinity and humanity, after the pregnant body; the body of the woman with child. For Prokes, the child in the womb experiences sexuality in 'an elemental but profound manner', in the sense that at 'no time in later life will there be the same capacity to *reside – to live within another physically* or to share flesh and blood with such an enduring immediacy'.[73] The intimate residence of the child in the womb is for Prokes an image of that residence in Christ – and of Christ in us – to which all Christians are called.

> Womb-life is a prelude to the mature capacity of living within one another in the manner that Christ prayed for in his Last Discourse: 'May they be one in us, as you are in me and I am in you, so that the world may believe it was you who sent me' (John 17.21).[74]

In a similar way, Balthasar likens the triune circumincession to that of the Christ-child in the womb of his mother. Mary's consciousness of the child growing within her is 'like an imitation, within the economy of salvation, of the mystery of the Trinity, and, no less, like an imitation (the first and closest imitation) of the mystery of the two natures in the one Person'. She feels the child within her, as she is felt by the child. And just as this circumincession of mother and child is an imitation of the triune life, so also is it of the individual soul in relation to God.

> [T]he experience of self . . . open[s] out, through faith, to an experience that encompasses both oneself and the other – oneself and the burgeoning Word of God, which at first seems to be growing in the self until in this growth it becomes evident that it is rather the other way around and that it is the self that is contained in the Word of God. [75]

Enraptured Bodies

Unlike their predecessors, many modern theologians have wanted to draw a sharp distinction between the love that is proper to God and to the Christian imitation of God, and that which enthrals the flesh, which elicits touch, caress and embrace, the stroking of skin and the meeting of lips.[76] For Karl Barth this latter love (*eros*) is but a rapacious 'intensification and strengthening of natural self-assertion'.

> It is hungry, and demands the food that the other seems to hold out. This is the reason for its interest in the other. It needs it because of its intrinsic

> value and in pursuance of an end. As this other promises something – itself in one of its properties – there is the desire to possess and control and enjoy it . . . For all the self-emptying on the part of the one who loves, union with the beloved as the supreme goal of this love consists in the fact that this object of love is taken to himself, if not expressly swallowed up and consumed, so that even in the event he alone remains, like the wolf when it has devoured, as it hopes, both Red Riding Hood and her grandmother.[77]

Barth contrasts eros – ravenous desire – with agape, the properly Christian love which 'turns to the other purely for the sake of the other'.

> In Christian love the loving subject gives to the other . . . that which it has, which is its own, which belongs to it. It does so irrespective of the right or claim that it may have to it, or the further use that it might make of it . . . It does so with a radically unlimited liberality. For in Christian love the loving subject reaches back, as it were, behind itself to that which at the first it denies and from which it turns away, namely, itself: to give itself . . . away; to give up itself to the one to whom it turns for the sake of this object. To do this the loving man has given up control of himself to place himself under the control of the other, the object of his love.[78]

There can be little doubt that the opposition Barth posits between agape and eros is overwrought, rhetorical, misleading. From the point of view of classical philosophy it ignores the 'concern for the other' that is present in Plato's account of erotic love. 'It makes Eros selfish or self-interested at the expense of ignoring happiness as consisting in justice and friendship, the works of Eros as issuing in creation not only according to the body but the soul, and the termination of Eros in contemplation of the *summum bonum*.'[79]

From the theological side, Barth's account pays insufficient attention to what he nevertheless notes, namely that eros 'can claim some of the greatest figures in the history of the human spirit'.[80] And indeed, in another part of the *Church Dogmatics*, Barth does envisage, if not a synthesis of eros and agape – as he thinks was attempted in the medieval concept of *caritas*[81] – then at least the possibility of locating eros within agape; desire ordered by self-giving ordered by understanding.

> As the desire of love, of true *eros*, desire is legitimate . . . when it is preceded by self-giving and thus controlled, not by the need of the other, but by the joy of being his and of willing to belong to him, the confidence of being well-placed with him, the willingness to make common cause with

> him. Again, this self-giving, as that of love, of genuine *eros*, is legitimate, because free, when it is preceded by understanding, so that it is not a blind surrender to the other, but he is seen in his totality to be [a] partner to whose being in its totality one can honourably give oneself, and whom one may honourably desire in the totality of one's being.[82]

But for a more enthralling, passionate desire – one that might just get carried away with the object of its love – we have to turn back to Balthasar. For the ordering of eros by agape, of desire by dispossession, is one of Balthasar's central concerns. This is not least because he is much more open than Barth to being instructed by some of those figures in the 'history of the human spirit' who have been claimed by divine and human eros, namely Dante, and, before him, the Pseudo-Dionysius.

For Balthasar, the content of dogmatic theology is the divine ecstasy (*ekstasis*), the venture of God to us and we to God, the traversal of the infinite distance between human and divine. This venture is *rapture*, a transport of delight at the beauty of the divine glory.[83] Here Balthasar follows the Pseudo-Dionysius, for whom the venture of delight is eros, the desire that draws God out into creation, revelation and incarnation, and in turn draws us into God.

> We must dare to affirm (for this is the truth) that the creator of the Universe himself, in his beautiful and good Eros towards the Universe, is, through his excessive erotic Goodness, transported outward of himself in his providential activities towards all things that have being, and is overcome by the sweet spell of goodness, Love and Eros. In this manner, he is drawn from his transcendent throne above all things to dwell within the heart of all things in accordance with his super-essential and ecstatic power whereby he nonetheless does not leave himself behind. This is why those who know about God call him 'zealous', because he is vehement in his manifold and beneficent Eros towards all beings, and he spurs them on to search for him zealously with a yearning eros, thus showing himself zealous for love inasmuch as he allows himself to be affected by the zeal of all beings for which he cares.[84]

Acknowledging that this may appear too neoplatonic for some, Balthasar nevertheless insists that it is consistent with the 'most authentic covenant-theology of either Testament', and that there is simply nothing to be done for those who fail to see that all revelation is 'impregnated' with 'enthusiasm'. The Pseudo-Dionysius is even more direct when he says that those who object to talk of God's yearning, of God's eros or desire, are people 'concerned with meaningless letters and lines, with syllables and phrases which they do not understand'.[85] Such people do not meditate on the meaning of scripture or contemplate the mystery toward which it gestures. But for those who attend properly, in the depths of their soul, 'the name "love" is used by the sacred writers in divine revelation with the exact same meaning as the term "yearning".'[86] The teaching of the Pseudo-Dionysius simply points us to the 'jealous and consuming love of the divine Bridegroom doing his work in his bride in order to raise her up, invite her, and bring her home to the very same answering love'.[87]

> What is signified is a capacity to effect a unity, an alliance, and a particular commingling in the Beautiful and the Good. It is a capacity which preexists through the Beautiful and the Good. It is dealt out from the Beautiful and the Good and through the Beautiful and the Good . . . This divine yearning [*eros*] brings ecstasy so that the lover belongs not to self but to the beloved . . . This is why the great Paul, swept along by his yearning for God and seized of its ecstatic power, had this inspired word to say: 'It is no longer I who live, but Christ who lives in me.'[88] Paul was truly a lover and, as he says, he was beside himself for God,[89] possessing not his own life but the life of the One for whom he yearned, as exceptionally beloved.[90]

Nor is the Pseudo-Dionysius afraid to acknowledge the parallel between carnal and spiritual desire. He notes the 'lovely verse' in which David celebrates the love between himself and Jonathan: 'Love for you came on me like love for women'.[91] For the Pseudo-Dionysius, carnal love teaches spiritual desire. Thus Urbain Grandier – in Ken Russell's film – can defend his marriage to Madeleine de Brou. 'It was a real ceremony. A simple act of committal done with my heart, in the hope of coming to God through the love of a woman.' Whether or not Grandier comes to God, the attempt to do so was already ventured by Dante, who, according to Balthasar, performed the 'daring act of taking before the throne of God the earthly love between man and woman and of purifying Eros so as to make of it something akin to Agape'.[92] In the *Divina Commedia*, the love of man and woman is made the means, rather than the obstacle, for ascent to God. 'This is utterly unprecedented in the history of Christian theology'.

> [T]he principle is established for the first time, and never again so magnificently: for the sake of infinite love, it is not necessary for the Christian to renounce finite love. On the contrary, in a positive spirit, he can incorporate his finite love into that which is infinite . . . Eros and Agape . . . for Dante are but two names for the same thing: Amor, God's most truly proper name.[93]

Male and Female He Created Them (Genesis 1.27)

According to Balthasar, the riddle of humanity is constituted by a three-fold polarity, of spirit and body, man and woman, and of individual and community. These constants are part of the human essence, 'three fundamental human tensions'.[94] 'In all three dimensions, man seems to be built according to a polarity, obliged to engage in reciprocity, always seeking complementarity and peace in the other pole'.[95] None of the three polarities can be treated completely without reference to the other two, but here we will focus on the second polarity of sexual difference.

The polarity of spirit and body suggests two models, one of a natural process ascending to spirit, the other an incursive descent already realized by spirit into nature. The human person, 'formed out of existing clay by the hand of God *and* directly endowed with the breath of divinity', couples these alternatives together.[96] But for Balthasar the two – earthly clay and heavenly breath – are not simply conjoined, but set against one another. The human condition is essentially dirempted, torn, broken. Or, to put it another way, it is that of being on and of the boundary, the *metharion* between two regions. This opens us to three possibilities: to remain in this condition or to seek to move beyond it, upwards or downwards. For Plotinus, life on the boundary can have only a negative meaning, for the soul, midway between the intelligible and the sensible, is unable to obtain precise knowledge of either.[97] For Gregory of Nyssa, however, it is possible and necessary to choose, and the right choice is the spiritual; but that which so chooses is, Balthasar reminds us, 'unthinkable apart from its physiological infrastructure'.[98] In choosing the spiritual, therefore, we cannot wish to leave behind the physical. 'Pure spiritualization . . . must appear as hubris, as wanting to be like God. And yet the fundamental demand must be for an upward movement, involving control of the physical and embodied, the natural and mediate'.[99] There is then, a need for an almost impossible synthesis of the contrary movements, and this, Balthasar insists, is possible only in terms of a 'dramatic engagement'.[100] Again, for Balthasar, we are not absolved from the need to fashion ourselves as 'responsible spiritual-physical' beings.[101] But in order to become such beings – inhabiting, as it were, a middle which is not poised between two extremities, but where both extremities interpenetrate, folded upon and inside one another – we need a model, a 'blueprint', which can only be Christ.

> Such a blueprint would have to execute fully both movements without hubris and without degeneration: it would have to come down into flesh 'from above', as the pure breath of God, plumbing the dimensions of 'world' and 'flesh' to the very bottom. And this descent must not imply a (Buddhist, Platonic or Gnostic) 'fall' from God: rather, it must undergird and embrace every possible declension from God. And from below, on the basis of a perfected fleshly being, it must go beyond the realm of the 'world' so as to bring both world and flesh with it, in its transcendence, up to God, 'transfiguring' it, not 'spiritualizing' it in some incorporeal manner.[102]

The tension between the two movements, upward and downward, is repeated in the second fundamental polarity of human existence, that of man and woman, which at the same time introduces the tension between individual and community, since, following Genesis, Eve is created in order to establish community for Adam, as his helpmate, counter-image and complement.[103]

One might think that Eve is but a second, though differentiated, Adam, since Adam recognizes her as bone of his bones and flesh of his flesh,[104] and Balthasar insists that they share 'an identical human nature'. Nevertheless, Balthasar also insists on their near absolute difference. Their identical nature does not, as Balthasar puts it, 'protrude, neutrally, beyond the sexual difference, as if to provide neutral ground for mutual understanding'.

> The male body is male throughout, right down to each cell of which it consists, and the female body is utterly female; and this is also true of their whole empirical experience and ego-consciousness . . . Here there is no *universale ante rem*, as all theories of a nonsexual or bisexual (androgynous) primitive human being would like to think.[105]

Thus, just as Balthasar wants to think body and spirit as a unified difference, and do so by way of the incarnation, so also with man and woman, individual and community. The poles of all three tensions are not denied or synthesized, but held within a differentiated unity, which must be thought according to the drama of the incarnation which, as we have seen, is already the drama of the Trinity. It must also be understood as the drama of the church. The unified difference of Christ and church is variously parodied: as head and members of one body, as the nuptial embrace of bridegroom and bride, and of mother and child. Indeed it is Mary who attains to the pitch of parodic substitution, since she is both the mother of Jesus and, as mother-church, of each member of his body; but as the church she is also the bride of Christ, not only the mother but the wife of her son. (Here we are reminded that parodic substitution allows Christianity to place certain cultural taboos – against cannibalism, incest and homosexuality – at its symbolic centre and there break them.)

Balthasar, however, does not really succeed in thinking difference-in-unity, and in particular the differentiated unity of man and woman. He fails to think sexual difference, not because he stresses unity at the expense of difference, but because the unity he does stress is finally, and only, male: a difference within the male. Needless to say, this failure is also present in his account of Jesus and Mary, and of the Trinity.

(Relative) Masculine Priority

Balthasar's insistence – in which he is followed by John Paul II[106] – that sexual difference is to be traced 'right down to each cell' of the male and female body, so that one can speak of male and female cells, is a particularly modern notion. It is dependent – as Thomas Laqueur has shown – on the invention at some time in the eighteenth century of two human sexes; a model which gradually replaced the more ancient idea – dependent on Aristotle and Galen – of one sex with two genders.[107] For the ancient and medieval medical worlds, all bodies were in some sense male and female; the woman being but a weaker, cooler, more imperfect form of the man. 'Women were merely less of what men were more.'[108]

Balthasar's notion of male and female cells may be traced to the eminent nineteenth-century biologist Patrick Geddes (1854–1932), who argued that males were constituted of *catabolic* cells, that expended energy, whereas females were composed of *anabolic* cells, that conserved energy. On the basis of this evolutionary difference Geddes maintained the typical gender roles of his day, arguing that what 'was decided among the pre-historic Protozoa cannot be annulled by an act of Parliament'.[109] Whatever the origin of the idea in Balthasar, it would seem – when taken with his opposition to the idea of an androgynous human being – to indicate a firm resistance to a monological account of humankind. Nevertheless, it is possible to read Balthasar as finally purveying a covert androgyny.

For Balthasar, a human being is dipolar, but one of the poles has priority. In the order of creation they do not arrive simultaneously, but sequentially; and in this they parody the order of incarnation: 'Jesus Christ can only enter the human sphere at the one pole, in order, from that vantage point, to go on to fulfil the other pole'.

> This becomes concrete in the man/woman relationship: because of the natural, relative priority of the man (given an equality of both persons), the Word of God, on account of its absolute priority, can only enter the world of the human in the form of a man, 'assimilating' the woman to itself (Ephesians 5.27) in such a way that she, who comes from him and is at the same time 'brought to him' by God, is equal to him, 'flesh of his flesh'.[110]

This text is tense with the indeterminacy of parodic direction. It just keeps in check the potential of each parody to turn around and go in the opposite direction to that intended. Balthasar wants equality of male and female but the text displays the priority of the male; he wants the priority of the male but the text insinuates an equality with the female. So we have the 'relative priority of the man', which only whispers the relative equality of the woman. The Word has absolute priority and so must have the (relative) priority of the man, rather than the posteriority of the woman. But if the Word's priority follows that of the man, whose priority does the man's follow? Who gives priority to the man if not the Word? The priorities would seem to rotate, chasing one another. Why can the Word only enter the world of the human as a man, why can it not adopt the form of a woman, the posterior position? Surely the Word is not constrained by the created order which is but a parody of a preceding heavenly one? Or if it is so constrained – constrained by itself, by its 'nature' – must we not suppose the Word already masculine?

Imagine reversing the order of creation – of Adam and Eve, man and woman – so that Adam comes from Eve and is brought to her, and the Word can only enter the world of the human in the form of a woman; so that Ephesians 5.21–7 now reads:

> Be subject to one another out of reverence for Christ. Husbands, be subject to your wives, as to Christ. For the wife is the head of the husband as Christ is the head of the church, her body, and is herself its saviour. As the church is subject to Christ, so let husbands also be subject in everything to their wives. Wives, love your husbands, as Christ loved the church and gave herself up for him, that she might sanctify him having cleansed him by the washing of water with the word, that she might present the church to herself in splendour, without spot or wrinkle or any such thing, that he might be holy and without blemish.

In keeping with the overall reversal, the gender of the church's pronoun has been changed, so that instead of a male Christ with a female body, as in Ephesians, we have a female Christ with a male body. The reversal allows us to imagine a different world, but does it require us to imagine a different theology, different kinds of relationship between the persons of the Trinity (Mother, Daughter and Holy Spirit), different kinds of relationship between the Daughter and her church? If the answer is yes, then it is clear that we are thinking the Trinity a parody of creation. Change the order of the sexes, the relative priority of one to the other, and we have to change heaven. But if the answer is no, then we can see that creation is properly a parody of the Trinity, a non-identical repetition in the order of created being of the trinitarian relations, which are now seen to be determinative of human bodies, but not of human sexes. We can leave heaven as it is because we do not have to adopt Balthasar's ancient, pagan biology.

Eve's Flesh

Here is another take on the problem. Does Eve have her own flesh? Adam recognizes her as bone of his bones, flesh of his flesh.[111] In short, she has the bones and flesh of a man, and Balthasar does not demur from this. His reference to male and female cells is only a gesture, as also his appeal to genetics as providing a supporting parody for the idea that human being is understood more properly as feminine than as masculine, as Marian rather than Christic. For according to the flow of the trinitarian parodies, Marian flesh is already male flesh, since as the bride of the groom – the second Eve – Mary is flesh of his flesh.[112]

This is confirmed by another passage in the *Theo-Drama*, in which Balthasar follows Augustine and couples the coming forth of the church from Christ with the coming forth of Eve from the wound in Adam's side, the extracted bone. The second Eve is born from the second Adam, the bride from the husband, the mother from the Son. This confirms the eternal (relative) priority of the masculine.

> The reciprocal fruitfulness of man and woman is surpassed by the ultimate priority of the 'Second Adam', who, in suprasexual fruitfulness, brings a 'companion', the Church, into being. Now the 'deep sleep' of death on the Cross, the 'taking of the rib' in the wound that opens the heart of Jesus, no longer take place in unconsciousness and passivity, as in the case of the First Adam, but in the consciously affirmed love-death of the *Agape*, from which the Eucharist's fruitfulness also springs. The relative priority of the man over the woman here becomes absolute, insofar as the Church is a creation of Christ himself, drawn from his own substance. All the same, the first account of creation is over-fulfilled here, for in the mind of God the incarnate Word has never existed without his Church (Ephesians 1.4–6).[113]

However, perhaps Christ's flesh is itself womanly, since as I have already mentioned, the Christ of Ephesians is transsexual, a male with a female body; a bearded woman. The answer to this supposition is already given in Genesis, where, as we have seen, there is really only one kind of flesh – Adam's – from which Eve's flesh derives. This parodies – or is parodied by – the ancient biology that posited two genders upon one sex, the female being a cooler version of the male. It is this biology that really informs Balthasar's theology (rather than the more recent, nineteenth-century biology of Patrick Geddes), and it is this ancient biology that Balthasar parodies in the Trinity.

Why 'Father'?

Balthasar understands God's intratrinitarian being according to two reciprocal acts, the giving and receiving of love, the outpouring of divine agape/eros and its return, an eternal circulation of charitable desire that constitutes creation and incarnation. But giving and receiving are parodied as masculinity and femininity, informing both human flesh and trinitarian being, so that sexual difference is parodied in heaven. But since there is no sex in God – to suppose which would be to fall into gnostic mythology – heavenly masculinity and femininity are suprasexualities: supramasculinity and suprafemininity.

David L. Schindler notes that 'Balthasar's carefully qualified treatment of the question of gender in God follows the processions in God'.

> That is, the Father, as the begetting origin-with-out-origin, is primarily supramasculine (*übermännlich*); the Son, as begotten and thus receptive (*der Geschehenlassende*) is suprafeminine (*überweiblich*); but then the Father and the Son, as jointly spirating the Spirit, are again supramasculine; the Spirit then is suprafeminine; finally, the Father, who allows himself to be conditioned in return in his begetting and spirating, himself thereby has a suprafeminine dimension.[114]

Here masculinity is associated with giving, as begetting and spirating, as generating; whereas femininity is associated with receiving. In other words, and according to a certain kind of biology, masculine and feminine parody the active and passive partners in the act of insemination or fertilization.[115] As Schindler notes, the trinitarian processions or relations, which are represented temporally, must be understood simultaneously, so that both supramasculinity and suprafemininity are 'somehow shared' by all the divine 'persons'. In other words – and again according to a certain biology – the Trinity is parodied as a self-inseminating, self-fertilizing womb.

Balthasar warns us against the error of projecting 'the difference between the sexes upon God', so that we might see the Spirit as feminine, 'the "womb" in which generation occurs'. Nevertheless, he allows that for those who wish to 'go further', the feminine is best sought in the Son, who in his earthly existence 'allowed himself to be led and "fertilized" by the Father', while yet at the same time representing the 'originally generative force of God in the world'. And since the Son – the inseminated icon of the inseminator – proceeds from the Father, 'the different sexes are, in the end, present in the latter in a "preternatural" way'.[116] It is only at the end of this remarkable passage from Balthasar's meditations on the Apostles' Creed – in which he has imagined the incestuous pederastic coupling of Father and Son – that he reminds us that God remains 'more dissimilar than similar to everything created'.[117]

> It is not the case that the Father and the Spirit each possess one 'gender' to the exclusion of the other, or that the Son alone possesses both 'genders'; it is rather the case that all three persons share both 'genders' (share in some sense both generativity and receptivity), but *always by way of an order that remains asymmetrical.*[118]

Thus, as Schindler brings out, the Son is both supramasculine and suprafeminine. He is suprafeminine in relation to what he receives from the Father, yet supramasculine in what he gives, both to the Father and to the Spirit, and to the world, in creation and incarnation. And what he gives is his own giving, his suprafemininity, given both to Mary, and, in her, to the church. At the same time he is also the icon of the Father's supramasculinity, which he has received by way of his preceding suprafemininity, which suggests to Balthasar and Schindler a certain priority of the suprafeminine, in Christ and in creation. Yet, as before, this supposed precedence of the suprafeminine conceals an always prior supramasculinity.

Neither Balthasar nor Schindler ask the question: why 'Father'? Why, beyond a certain historical contingency, should we suppose the primal *paternity* of the Godhead? Neither does Balthasar or Schindler ask why – given the name – the Father's primary act should be considered supramasculine rather than suprafeminine? Why not think donation suprafeminine and reception supramasculine? In a sense, of course, Balthasar has already done this, in that both Father and Son are alike suprafeminine and supramasculine, that is, conceived androgynously or hermaphroditically. Nevertheless, in

Balthasar, they are male hermaphrodites. Balthasar – for whom theological agnosticism is almost utterly foreign – does try to say why the simple origin of all is 'Father'.

> That he is Father we know in utmost fullness from Jesus Christ, who constantly makes loving, thankful, and reverent reference to him as his Origin. It is because he bears fruit out of himself and requires no fructifying that he is called Father, and not in the sexual sense, for he will be the Creator of man and woman, and thus contains the primal qualities of woman in himself in the same simultaneously transcending way as those of man.[119]

Needless to say, the Father's bearing of fruit out of himself without need of fructifying does not explain why he is named 'Father'. On the very same ground, one might as well, if not better, name him 'Mother'. Balthasar's *non sequitur* is indicative of a failure to maintain the 'greater unlikeness' between God and humankind. In the passage just quoted we are told that God's fruitfulness, his self-fructifying nature, is not to be understood in a sexual way. Elsewhere, as we have seen, he refers to the suprasexual. But that the addition of 'supra' fails to measure the infinite distance between ourselves and the Trinity – whose relations Balthasar describes in such resolutely sexual terms – is indicated by the ancient biology that informs Balthasar's Trinity, and which the latter parodies. The man gives to the woman, who is but an extension of his body. She takes what she is given and returns it, enhanced, to his greater glory, having become the mother of his child. This is the drama of the Trinity, of its processions and missions.[120]

Cultural Biology

Breandán Leahy, in his study of the Marian principle in Balthasar's theology, has a curious footnote in which he tells us that Balthasar 'guards' against any 'false implication' that might arise from identifying God with generativity, understood as a 'masculine' principle, and of woman with receptivity, 'maternal fecundity'.

> Von Balthasar writes [Leahy doesn't tell us where] that, prescinding from any and every social system, be it patriarchal or matriarchal, and from all theories of procreation, be they ancient, scholastic or modern, it remains true that in the act of sexual intercourse the man is the initiator, the one who shapes, while the woman's active role is essentially receptive. In this act the woman is awakened to the fullness of her feminine self-awareness.[121]

Leahy supposes that the woman – all women? – comes to fully know herself only when sexually penetrated by the man. (Thus, one must suppose, consecrated virgins live in a kind of daze, unaware of their full femininity.) Both Balthasar and Leahy are seemingly unaware of the masculinist culture that shapes their understanding of sexuality, of masculinity and femininity. Despite Balthasar's advocacy of 'dramatics', he is unaware that sexuality is culturally constituted and performed. Our sex/gender identities are given to us in and by our cultures, which are often religious ones, and the instability of these identities is evidenced and overcome by their repeated performance, the constant reiteration of their norms, postures and sensibilities.[122] It is just one such set of scripts that Balthasar enacts in his trinitarian theology.

Like Karl Barth before him, Balthasar fails to recognize the import of his understanding of the trinitarian relations for human coupling. This is because Balthasar, like Barth, is too influenced by what Luce Irigaray calls the culture of hom(m)osexuality. That is a culture in which the only significant relationships are those of men, bonded by their exchange of women. 'Reigning everywhere, although prohibited in practice, hom(m)osexuality is played out through the bodies of women, matter, or sign, and heterosexuality has been up to now just an alibi for the smooth workings of man's relations with himself, of relations among men.'[123] Though such men suppose themselves heterosexual, their use of women as tokens of exchange betrays an underlying hom(m)osexuality, in the sense that only men desire while women are desired. Thus true reciprocity can exist only between men, but never really achieved, or if achieved – by heterosexual or homosexual couples – achieved in despite of the culture; as momentarily achieved by Grandier and Madeleine in Russell's film. In such an economy of desire, the practice of male homosexuality becomes taboo, because it too clearly gives the lie to compulsory heterosexuality as the alibi or dissembling of hom(m)osexual yearning.

Even more than Karl Barth, Balthasar – because of his failed *analogia entis* – is unable to realize the fluidity of sexual symbolics when applied to the bodies of actual men and women.[124] Indeed, it is because Balthasar's Trinity so excessively parodies Irigaray's hom(m)osexual culture – as an all-male affair in which the Son plays the part of the woman[125] – that when it comes to earth in the parodies of Adam and Eve, Christ and Mary/church, the feminine poles of these pairs can only be momentary extensions of a single sex. The ancient masculinist biology Balthasar nowhere questions is indeed both product and producer of an hom(m)osexual culture.

Indeed it may be suggested that it is possible to think sexual difference only when we start from the paradigm of the homosexual couple. For then we are not burdened by the power asymmetries that have infected the heterosexual relationship from at least Aristotle onwards. Then women can be construed as desiring subjects in their own right, and not merely as the alibis for a desire that can never really exist, because never really returned. When we start with the same-sex couple it becomes possible to think of a genuine reciprocity, constituted by the desire that at one and the same time unites and differentiates bodies. Theology can think of heterosexual love *for the first time*.[126]

Such a way of thinking about sexual difference is indeed already partly present in both Barth and Balthasar as the relationship of donation, reception and return. But the relationship of desire needs to be thought more radically, as that which establishes sexual difference, so that whether it plays between Father and Son, man and man, woman and woman, or woman and man, it remains always constitutive of sexual difference. In this way, what our culture may dictate as our sex and gender will no longer be determinative of our freedom to give and receive love. For truly in Christ there is no male and female, only the reciprocation of bodies; beautiful parodies of the trinitarian donation.

Dancing

Earlier in this chapter we encountered Bataille's 'locomotive', the thrusting pistons of copulating animals turning the world; a parody of the love that in Dante 'moves the sun and the other stars' (*l'amor che move il sole e l'altre stelle*).[127] From the century of the steam engine, Gustave Dore's illustrations of Dante's *Commedia*, first published in 1861, provide wonderful images of the celestial wheels that empower the world's pistons. The heavens through which Dante – with Beatrice – ascends, are shown in perpetual motion, filled with rotating lights, turning and circling, with saints and angels performing round dances, 'measure with measure matching, strain with strain'.[128]

Dante attains sight of God's throne at the centre of the celestial rose, the encircling flower of the redeemed. Dore gives us a picture of Dante, with a figure standing by his side. Perhaps it is Beatrice, just before she slips away to take her seat 'In the third circle from the highest place, enthroned where merit destined her to be'.[129] Or perhaps it is St Bernard, sent by Beatrice to guide Dante's sight, first to the Virgin, and then with the Virgin's aid, to the dazzling, unapproachable 'light supreme' of the three-fold God.[130] I would like to think it is a picture of Dante with Beatrice, before his gaze sees into the light.

We can think the picture a parody – an analogy – of the heart's yearning, of its desiring for that divine donation and dispossession which already gives to the heart its restless want of beatitude: eros in the order of agape. Or is it agape in the order of eros; desire teaching dispossession? Dante and Beatrice stand in the foreground, looking toward the rose; Dante transfixed, standing at a distance, fallen into a silent stupor before the 'living light'.[131] It is the moment before Beatrice merges, as it were, with the light, taking her place in the circling glory. It is the moment before Dante begins his final ascent that will lead him to see into the light, to see the 'three spheres, which bare three hues distinct' and occupy 'one space', the first mirroring the next, 'as though it were rainbow from rainbow', and the third seeming 'flame breathed equally from each of the first pair'.[132]

The image of Dante with Beatrice, their love ordered by and toward the celestial charity, is also a parody or analogy of the final argument of this chapter. We will better think eros the more we remember that an infinite distance stretches between the clouds on which Dante and Beatrice stand and the glory of the celestial rose on which they look.

Notes

1 Not Louis XV, as stated in Ken Russell, *Directing Film: From Pitch to Première* (London: Batsford, 2000), p. 41.

2 John Whiting's *The Devils* was first performed in 1961 by the Royal Shakespeare Company at the Aldwych Theatre, London. The play is published in *New English Dramatists 6*, edited by Tom Maschler (Harmondsworth: Penguin Books, 1963). On Russell's sources and his use of them see Joseph A. Gomez, *Ken Russell: The Adaptor as Creator* (London: Frederick Muller Limited, 1976), pp. 114–64. Aldous Huxley's *The Devils of Loudun* (London: Chatto & Windus, 1952) also informed Krzysztof Penderecki's 1969 opera of the same name. The story of Jeanne des Anges has also been told in Jerzy Kawalerowicz's film *Matka Joanna od Aniołów* (Poland 1961), but with the events relocated in Poland. It is more concerned with the relationship between Jeanne and her exorcist, Jean-Joseph Surin (1600–65), who came to Loudun after Grandier's execution, and with whom she developed a lasting friendship. See Michel de Certeau, *The Possession at Loudun*, translated by Michael B. Smith (Chicago: University of Chicago Press, [1970] 1996), pp. 199–226; and Michel de Certeau, 'Surin's Melancholy' in *Heterologies: Discourse on the Other*, translated by Brian Massumi (Manchester: Manchester University Press, 1986), pp. 101–15.

3 For Louis XIV's interest in the staging of his own glory see Gérard Corbian's film *Le Roi Danse* (France 2000), which explores the relationship

between Louis and the composer Lully. For Louis XIII see Elizabeth Wirth Marvick, *Louis XIII: The Making of a King* (New Haven: Yale University Press, 1986) and A. Lloyd Moote, *Louis XIII, The Just* (Berkeley: University of California Press, 1989).

4 Surprisingly, but not unreasonably, the film director Alex Cox and film critic Mark Kermode chose *The Devils* as one of their top ten greatest films of all time. See *Sight and Sound*, 12/9 (September 2002): 31 and 41. Jarman cites 'Ledoux, Boulée, and Piranesi's prison series' as influencing his designs. 'All detail is sacrificed to scale as I want the sets as large as possible, and as forceful as the sets from an old silent.' Derek Jarman, *Dancing Ledge*, edited by Shaun Allen (London: Quartet Books, 1984), p. 100.

5 See de Certeau, *The Possession at Loudun*, p. 25. The Ursuline Order was founded in 1535, and granted rights of enclosure and strict vows by Pope Paul V in 1612.

6 See Huxley, *The Devils of Loudun*, pp. 66–7.

7 De Certeau, *Possession at Loudun*, p. 11.

8 Huxley, *The Devils of Loudun*, p. 125.

9 An 'ecclesiastic from Tours' quoted in de Certeau, *Possession at Loudun*, pp. 86–7.

10 De Certeau, *Heterologies*, p. 107.

11 De Certeau, *Possession at Loudun*, pp. 144–5.

12 De Certeau, *Possession at Loudun*, p. 151. The changing relationship of church and state is also figured at Loudun. Grandier is tried and executed by the state, but the state's agent, Laubardemont, also plays the role of exorcist, extracting the demonic truth he needs in order to convict his victim, whose real crime is his supposed opposition to Richelieu's interests, which were indistinguishable from the king's. On the latter point see Marvick, *Louis XIII*, pp. 220–4.

13 'But let us suppose there is no trickery or fabrication in this affair. Does it necessarily follow that these girls are possessed? Can it not be that, through folly and error of imagination, the women believe themselves to be possessed without being so? This happens frequently to spirits that are predisposed to folly, if they are closed up in a convent and become confused in meditation'. From Marc Duncan, *Discours sur la possession des religieuses ursulines de Loudun* (1634), quoted in de Certeau, *Possession at Loudun*, pp. 135–6.

14 Duncan quoted in de Certeau, *Possession at Loudun*, p. 136.

15 From a report by Laubardemont, quoted in de Certeau, *Possession at Loudun*, p. 108.

16 'The torture consists in driving a series of increasingly large wedges between the boards within which the legs are enclosed and the legs, until the bones break.' De Certeau, *Possession at Loudun*, p. 173. The thieves executed with Christ had their legs broken *after* their crucifixion (John 19.31–2), but the

legs of the Renaissance malefactor are broken *before* his final destruction. But this anterior breaking of the body – both in the 'question' and in other forms of judicial execution – was often read back into artistic representations of Calvary. See further Mitchell B. Merback, *The Thief, the Cross and the Wheel: Pain and the Spectacle of Punishment in Medieval and Renaissance Europe* (London: Reaktion Books, 1999), pp. 101–25. Mitchell also discusses (pp. 150–57) how Calvary was read forward into the scene of contemporary execution, with the martyr-criminal imitating the good thief, or even Christ himself, as does Grandier in several accounts of his death.

17 The notary d'Angevin writing on 19 August, and quoted in de Certeau, *Possession at Loudun*, p. 174.

18 Father Du Pont quoted in de Certeau, *Possession at Loudun*, p. 178. 'Strangling the victim beforehand in secret became more common in the self-consciously "civilized" eighteenth century, as authorities sought ways to balance the conflicting aims of minimizing the actual pain of the convict, while still providing a terrifying spectacle for the populace who watched.' Merback, *The Thief, the Cross and the Wheel*, p. 160. In the yet more civilized twentieth and twenty-first centuries, cinema provides the means for maximum spectacle and minimum pain in the staged death of the villain(s) at the climax of the movie. See for example John Woo's *Face Off* (USA 1997). Such a film also proffers the pleasure of watching the crimes that are avenged at its conclusion.

19 Ismaël Bouilliau to Gassendi (7 September 1634), quoted in de Certeau, *Possession at Loudun*, p. 180.

20 '*The Devils* is a harsh film – but it's a harsh subject. I wish the people who were horrified and appalled by it had read the book, because the bare facts are far more horrible than anything in the film.' Ken Russell in John Baxter, *An Appalling Talent/Ken Russell* (London: Michael Joseph, 1973), p. 202. As with Stanley Kubrick's *A Clockwork Orange*, Russell's *The Devils* censors its source material, while appearing to exaggerate its excesses. For the image, as Russell remarks, is 'immediate, irrefutable.'

21 Huxley, *The Devils of Loudun*, p. 132. Russell claims that the film's white-tiled convent was inspired by this line. See Ken Russell, 'Three Cuts and You're Out', *Sight and Sound*, 7/10 (October 1997): 69.

22 Jarman, *Dancing Ledge*, p. 102.

23 Baxter, *An Appalling Talent*, p. 188. Elsewhere, Russell recalls that he had 'big loud speakers playing Prokofiev's opera *The Fiery Angel*, which is about the possession of nuns'. Russell, 'Three Cuts and You're Out', p. 69.

24 The lost footage of the 'rape of Christ' was found by Mark Kermode and shown again in his TV film of its making and rediscovery, 'Hell on Earth' (25 November 2002, Channel 4). See further Mark Kermode, 'Hell on Earth', *Sight and Sound*, 12/12 (December 2002): 29–31.

25 De Certeau, *Possession at Loudun*, p. 6.

26 De Certeau, *Possession at Loudun*, p. 62.
27 Huxley, *The Devils of Loudun*, p. 51.
28 Russell astutely remarks that despite all the things about his religion that Grandier does not take seriously, 'he *does* take the Eucharist seriously – that's why I had the scene where he blesses and breaks bread out in the mountains – because, as you know, the Mass is the core of Catholicism. The sacrament is greater than the man.' Russell in Baxter, *An Appalling Talent*, p. 204.
29 Russell in Baxter, *An Appalling Talent*, p. 210.
30 'The poor Prioress had nothing to do, no husband, no children and no vocation. What wonder if she too fell in love with the delicious monster! . . . The thought of the parson haunted her continuously. Her meditations, which should have been a practice of the presence of God, were a practice, instead, of the presence of Urbain Grandier, or rather of the obscenely fascinating image which had crystallized, in her fancy, around his name. Hers was the unobjective and therefore limitless and insane desire of the moth for the star, of the schoolgirl for the crooner, of the bored and frustrated housewife for Rudolf Valentino.' Huxley, *The Devils of Loudun*, pp. 121–2. See further Ken Russell's *Valentino* (UK 1977), with Rudolf Nureyev as the impossible object of desire.
31 Tony Rayns in the *Time Out Film Guide*, tenth edition 2002, edited by John Pym (Harmondsworth: Penguin Books, 2001), p. 290. On the erotic union between Christ and the soul see above chapter 1 and below chapter 9.
32 De Certeau, *Possession at Loudun*, p. 223. See Teresa of Avila, *The Life of St Teresa*, translated by E. Allison Peers (London: Sheed & Ward, [1944] 1979); and Jeanne des Anges, *Autobiographie*, edited by G. Legué and Gilles de la Tourette (Paris, 1866). Huxley suggests that Jeanne's life is a parodic, 'long-drawn out impersonation of St Teresa.' Huxley, *The Devils of Loudun*, p. 117. For an introduction to Teresa's life and theology see Rowan Williams, *Teresa of Avila* (London: Geoffrey Chapman, 1991).
33 Teresa of Avila, *Meditations on the Song of Songs*, in *The Collected Works of Teresa of Avila*, translated by Kieran Kavanaugh and Otilio Rodríguez (Washington DC: Institute of Carmelite Studies, 1976–1980), vol. 2, ch. 4 (p. 217).
34 Teresa, *Meditations*, ch. 4 (pp. 243–4).
35 Claude Quillet cited in a letter from Naudé to Guy Patin, quoted in de Certeau, *Possession at Loudun*, p. 135.
36 Alison Weber, *Teresa of Avila and the Rhetoric of Femininity* (Princeton, NJ: Princeton University Press, 1990), p. 117.
37 Quoted in Weber, *Teresa of Avila*, p. 118. St John of the Cross wrote his poems on the Song of Songs in 1577, while he was in prison at Toledo.
38 Weber, *Teresa of Avila*, pp. 120–1.
39 Weber, *Teresa of Avila*, p. 154.

40 Teresa of Avila, *The Letters of Saint Teresa of Jesus*, translated by E. Allison Peers, 2 volumes (London: Burns, Oates and Washbourne, 1951), vol. 2, pp. 647–8; quoted in Weber, *Teresa of Avila*, p. 154. Despite Teresa's magnanimity, Beatriz did not retract her accusations until 1580.

41 Quoted in Weber, *Teresa of Avila*, pp. 137–8.

42 Noel O'Donoghue, *Mystics for our Time: Carmelite Meditations for a New Age* (Edinburgh: T. & T. Clark, 1989), pp. 13–14. 'The Carmelite or other religious who is not a passionate man or woman, should try to summon up enough energy to jump over the wall, and become a civil servant or politician. There is no place for such a one in the vital and colourful world of Teresa.' (p. 15).

43 Teresa distinguishes between corporeal, imaginary and intellectual visions, seen respectively with the eyes of the body, soul and intellect.

44 Teresa wrote cherubim, but from Fray Luis de Léon's edition onwards, it has usually been given as seraphim, the highest of the angelic orders. It is a fallen seraphim – Léviathan – who lodges in Jeanne des Anges's forehead. See de Certeau, *Possession at Loudun*, p. 90.

45 Teresa, *Life*, ch. 29 (pp. 192–3). The pleasurable pain of the angel's penetrating dart is the wound of love that Teresa discusses in *The Interior Castle*. The soul 'feels that it is wounded in the most exquisite way . . . It knows clearly that the wound is something precious, and it would not want to be cured . . . And the pain is great, although delightful and sweet'. Teresa of Avila, *The Interior Castle*, in *The Collected Works of Teresa of Avila*, translated by Kieran Kavanaugh and Otilio Rodríguez (Washington DC: Institute of Carmelite Studies, 1976–80), vol. 2, VI.2.2 (p. 367).

46 This was not the end of Jeanne's career, and Russell would like to have filmed the rest of her story. 'At the end de Laubardemont says "You're stuck in this convent for life", but as soon as he'd gone Jeanne set about getting out because her brief moment of notoriety had whetted her appetite for more. So she gouged a couple of holes in her hands and pretended she had stigmata, saw "visions" and, with the help of Sister Agnès, gulled some old priest [Jean-Joseph Surin] into thinking she was the greatest lady since the Virgin Mary. So she and Agnès went on a jaunt all over France and were hailed with as much fervour as show biz personalities and pop stars are received today. In Paris thirty thousand people assembled outside the hotel just in the hope of getting a glimpse of her. She became very friendly with Richelieu, the King and Queen wined and dined her, and she had a grand old time. When she died – I particularly wanted to include this scene – they cut off her head and put it in a glass casket and stuck it on the altar in her own convent. People came on their knees from miles around to pay her homage.' Russell in Baxter, *An Appalling Talent*, pp. 201–2. Russell has the gist of the story, but for a more hesitant account see de Certeau, *Possession at Loudun*, pp. 199–26.

47 Teresa, *Meditations*, p. 244.

48 The quoted phrases are from O'Donoghue's description of the 'deep feminine *eros*' that confronts us in Teresa's vision. But I have extended O'Donoghue's thought of God's self-giving *eros* – the 'holy force' whose 'truth is always creativity, whose joy is true to itself only when it is creative' – in the direction of the sexual relationship. See O'Donoghue, *Mystics for our Time*, pp. 14–15. There are times, of course, when the 'holy force' seems to depart. The soul finds itself destitute, as if deserted by its bridegroom, who may also depart the married couple; the dark night in which a marriage is lost.

49 Teresa, *The Interior Castle*, VII.1.6 (p. 430). Teresa has an intellectual vision of the Trinity. 'Obviously there is some floating or attendant imagery here, but essentially the vision at this level is conceptual. It becomes focused in the theological concepts available to Teresa, and this is not difficult since these concepts are in any case points of luminosity within the general radiance of the Divine presence . . . These theological concepts are servants of the light not masters of it.' O'Donoghue, *Mystics for our Time*, pp. 47–8.

50 Teresa, *Life*, ch. 29 (p. 193).

51 See O'Donoghue, *Mystics for our Time*, pp. 48–52.

52 Georges Bataille, *Visions of Excess: Selected Writings 1927–1939*, translated by Allan Stoekl, Carl R. Lovitt and Donald M. Leslie Jr (Minneapolis: University of Minnesota Press, 1985), p. 5.

53 Bataille, *Visions of Excess*, p. 6.

54 Bataille, *Visions of Excess*, p. 7.

55 Bataille, *Visions of Excess*, p. 5.

56 Bataille, *Visions of Excess*, p. 9.

57 John Saward, *The Mysteries of March: Hans Urs von Balthasar on the Incarnation and Easter* (London: Collins, 1990), p. 18.

58 In this regard, Thomas Aquinas is the great comedian of the Christian faith, a theological Buster Keaton, whose jokes are made with deadpan precision.

59 Karl Rahner, *The Trinity*, translated by Joseph Donceel (London: Burns & Oates, 1970), p. 22; see also C.M. LaCugna, 'Reconceiving the Trinity as the Mystery of Salvation', *Scottish Journal of Theology*, 38 (1985): 1–23.

60 It is one of the great ironies of Balthasar's theology that his conception of God's drama – the *TheoDramatik* – is so very undramatic. Nothing ever happens in Balthasar's world, for it has always already 'happened' in God's eternity. Balthasar's drama is utterly spatialized, and any temporality it contains is always that of time past, with its eschatology always fully realized. For something on this see Lucy Gardner and David Moss's baroque essay, 'Something like Time, Something like the Sexes: An Essay in Reception', in *Balthasar at the End of Modernity* (Edinburgh: T. & T. Clark, 1999), pp. 69–137.

61 Saward, *Mysteries of March*, p. 28.

62 Hans Urs von Balthasar, *Credo: Meditations on the Apostles' Creed*, translated by David Kipp (Edinburgh: T. & T. Clark, 1989), p. 31.

63 Balthasar quoted in Saward, *Mysteries of March*, p. 31.

64 Saward, *Mysteries of March*, p. 31.
65 Hans Urs von Balthasar, *Theo-Drama: Theological Dramatic Theory*, vol. 2: *The Dramatis Personae: Man in God*, translated by Graham Harrison (San Francisco CA: Ignatius Press, 1990), p. 347.
66 Balthasar, *Theo-Drama*, vol. 2, p. 348.
67 Balthasar, *Theo-Drama*, vol. 2, p. 352.
68 On 'body theology' see what was said in 'In the Lobby' above.
69 Prokes, *Towards a Theology of the Body*, p. 95.
70 Prokes, *Towards a Theology of the Body*, pp. 95–6.
71 Prokes, *Towards a Theology of the Body*, p. 96.
72 Prokes, *Towards a Theology of the Body*, pp. 96–7.
73 Prokes, *Towards a Theology of the Body*, p. 97; original emphasis.
74 Prokes, *Towards a Theology of the Body*, p. 97.
75 Hans Urs von Balthasar, *The Glory of the Lord: A Theological Aesthetics*, vol. 1: *Seeing the Form*, translated by Eramo Leiva-Merikakis, edited by Joseph Fessio and John Riches (Edinburgh: T. & T. Clark, 1982), p. 339.
76 See Anders Nygren, *Agape and Eros*, translated by Philip S. Watson (London: SPCK, 1982); and more recently Francis Watson, *Agape, Eros, Gender: Towards a Pauline Sexual Ethic* (Cambridge: Cambridge University Press, 2000). For Watson, eros has to be limited and contained by marital agape (p. 250).
77 Karl Barth, *Church Dogmatics*, vol. IV.2: *The Doctrine of Reconciliation*, translated by G.W. Bromiley (Edinburgh: T. & T. Clark, 1958), p. 734.
78 Barth, *Church Dogmatics*, vol. IV.2, p. 733.
79 *The Dialogues of Plato*, vol. 2: *The Symposium*, translated by R.E. Allen (New Haven: Yale University Press, 1991), p. 97. For Barth's discussion of Plato see Barth, *Church Dogmatics*, vol. IV.2, pp. 738–9.
80 Barth, *Church Dogmatics*, vol. IV.2, p. 735.
81 Barth, *Church Dogmatics*, vol. IV.2, pp. 737–8.
82 Karl Barth, *Church Dogmatics*, vol. III.3: *The Doctrine of Creation*, translated by A.T. Mackay et al. (Edinburgh: T. & T. Clark, 1961), p. 219; adapted.
83 Balthasar, *The Glory of the Lord*, vol. 1, p. 126.
84 Pseudo-Dionysius, *The Divine Names*, translated by C.E. Rolt (London: SPCK, 1940), 4.13, pp. 105–6 (translation slightly altered by Erasmo Leiva Meriakis); quoted in Balthasar, *The Glory of the Lord*, vol. 1, p. 122.
85 Pseudo-Dionysius, *The Divine Names*, in *Pseudo-Dionysius: The Complete Works*, translated by Colm Luibheid and Paul Rorem (New York: Paulist Press, 1987), 4.11 (p. 80).
86 Pseudo-Dionysius, *The Divine Names*, 4.12 (p. 81).
87 Balthasar, *The Glory of the Lord*, vol. 1, p. 123. On the Pseudo-Dionysius see further, Balthasar, *The Glory of the Lord*, vol. 2: *Studies in Theological Style: Clerical Styles*, pp. 144–210.
88 Galatians 2.20.
89 2 Corinthians 5.13.

90 Pseudo-Dionysius, *The Divine Names*, 4.13 (p. 82).
91 'Greatly beloved were you to me; your love to me was wonderful, passing the love of women' (2 Samuel 1.26); Pseudo-Dionysius, *The Divine Names*, 4.12 (p. 81).
92 Hans Urs von Balthasar, 'In Retrospect', in *The Analogy of Beauty: The Theology of Hans Urs von Balthasar*, edited by John Riches (Edinburgh: T. & T. Clark, 1986), pp. 194–221 (p. 215).
93 Balthasar, *Glory of the Lord*, vol. 3 (1986), pp. 32 and 81.
94 Balthasar, *Theo-Drama*, vol. 2, p. 358.
95 Balthasar, *Theo-Drama*, vol. 2, p. 355.
96 Balthasar, *Theo-Drama*, vol. 2, p. 359.
97 Balthasar, *Theo-Drama*, vol. 2, p. 360.
98 Balthasar, *Theo-Drama*, vol. 2, p. 362.
99 Balthasar, *Theo-Drama*, vol. 2, p. 363.
100 Balthasar, *Theo-Drama*, vol. 2, p. 364.
101 Balthasar, *Theo-Drama*, vol. 2, p. 363.
102 Balthasar, *Theo-Drama*, vol. 2, p. 364.
103 Balthasar, *Theo-Drama*, vol. 2, p. 365; see also Balthasar, *Theo-Drama*, vol. 3, pp. 284–7.
104 Genesis 2.23.
105 Balthasar, *Theo-Drama*, vol. 2, p. 365–6.
106 John Paul II, *Original Unity of Man and Woman* (Boston: St Paul Books, 1981), pp. 155–6.
107 Thomas Laqueur, *Making Sex: Body and Gender from the Greeks to Freud* (Cambridge, MA: Harvard University Press, 1990), pp. 149–92.
108 Bynum, *Fragmentation and Redemption*, p. 109.
109 Patrick Geddes and J. Arthur Thompson, *The Evolution of Sex* (London: W. Scott, 1889), p. 266; quoted in Laqueur, *Making Sex*, p. 6. See also Thomas Laqueur, 'Orgasm, Generation and the Politics of Reproductive Biology', in Catherine Gallagher and Thomas Laqueur (eds.), *The Making of the Modern Body: Sexuality and Society in the Nineteenth Century* (Berkeley, CA: University of California Press, 1987), pp. 1–41.
110 Balthasar, *Theo-Drama*, vol. 2, p. 411.
111 Genesis 2.23.
112 Balthasar, *Theo-Drama*, vol. 2, p. 411.
113 Balthasar, *Theo-Drama*, vol. 2, p. 413.
114 David L. Schindler, 'Catholic Theology, Gender and the Future of Western Civilization', *Communio*, 20 (1993): 200–39 (p. 206).
115 Biology bemuses even the most radical of theologians, in whose work it can appear as a strange intrusion of the 'real' into an otherwise utterly mediated, cultural domain; except that the latter shows itself all too clearly in the observed sociobiology. 'In general the clichés do hold . . . men are more nomadic, direct, and abstractive; women are more settled, subtle, and particularizing

– though they are both equally innovative, legislative, and conservative within these different modes.' John Milbank, 'The Gospel of Affinity' in *The Strange New World of the Gospel: Re-Evangelizing in the Postmodern World*, edited by Carl E. Braaten and Robert W. Jenson (Grand Rapids, MI: Eerdmans, 2002), pp. 1–20 (p. 16).

116 Balthasar, *Credo*, p. 78.

117 Balthasar, *Credo*, p. 79.

118 Schindler, 'Catholic Theology', p. 207.

119 Balthasar, *Credo*, p. 30. A similar *non sequitur* 'explains' why the Word is Son and not Daughter: 'We call him Son, and not Daughter, because he will appear in the world as male, and will do so in order to represent to us the authority of the fruitful fatherly Origin' (p. 37).

120 That the Father and the Son are really male is also implied by Balthasar's argument for reserving the priesthood to men. The argument goes something like this. Priests must be men because they symbolically represent Christ's maleness, and Christ was a male not for contingent, socio-historical reasons, but because, in representing the Father, Christ's maleness represents, is analogous to – parodies – the Father's self-gift of himself to the Son. As receptive of the Father the Son is feminine, as representing the Father he is masculine. And one has to speak like this because the revelation of God in the Christ-event shows that the relationship of the man to the woman is (analogous to/parodies) that of Christ to his church, which is (analogous to/parodies) that of the Father to the Son. But the only way in which this argument can be grounded – properly motivated – is to assume a false Aristotelian biology (in which the man gives and the woman receives), and to assume that the Father, like the Son, has a 'suprapenis'. This is required if the argument is not to be a series of *non-sequiturs* (which of course it is). For Balthasar's argument – but without its critique – see Robert A. Pesarchick, *The Trinitarian Foundation of Human Sexuality as Revealed by Christ According to Hans Urs von Balthasar: The Revelatory Significance of the Male Christ and the Male Ministerial Priesthood* (Rome: Editrice Pontificia Università Gregoriana, 2000).

121 Breandán Leahy, *The Marian Principle in the Church in the Ecclesiological Thought of Hans Urs von Balthasar* (Frankfurt am Main: Peter Lang, 1996), p. 85 n.187.

122 See further Judith Butler, *Bodies that Matter: On the Discursive Limits of 'Sex'* (London: Routledge, 1993). 'The category of "sex" is . . . a regulatory ideal whose materialization is compelled, and this materialization takes place (or fails to take place) through certain highly regulated practices . . . [T]he regulatory norms of "sex" work in a performative fashion to constitute the materiality of bodies and, more specifically, to materialize the body's sex, to materialize sexual difference in the service of the consolidation of the heterosexual imperative.' (pp. 1–2) Against this, church performances should seek to materialize the differencing of bodies through dispossessive desire, charitable practices, consolidating the cut that connects.

123 Luce Irigaray, 'Women on the Market' in *This Sex which Is Not One*, translated by Catherine Porter with Carolyn Burke (Ithaca, NY: Cornell University Press, [1977] 1985), pp. 170–91 (p. 172). See further Elizabeth Grosz, 'The Hetero and the Homo: The Sexual Ethics of Luce Irigaray' in *Engaging with Irigaray: Feminist Philosophy and European Thought*, edited by Carolyn Burke, Naomi Schor and Margaret Whitford (New York: Columbia University Press, 1994), pp. 335–50.

124 On Karl Barth and the flow of sexual symbolics see Gerard Loughlin, 'Baptismal Fluid', *Scottish Journal of Theology*, 51/3 (1998): 261–70.

125 For an analysis of trinitarian theology along these lines see Gavin D'Costa, *Sexing the Trinity: Gender, Culture and the Divine* (London: SCM Press, 2000), ch. 1.

126 For the development of this and related arguments see Gerard Loughlin, *Homosexuality and Christian Ethics* (Cambridge: Cambridge University Press, forthcoming).

127 Dante, *The Divine Comedy*, translated by Dorothy L. Sayers and Barbara Reynolds (Harmondsworth: Penguin Books, 1962), vol. 3 (*Paradise*), Canto 33, l. 145 (p. 347).

128 Dante, *Paradise*, Canto 12, l. 6 (p. 157).

129 Dante, *Paradise*, Canto 31, ll. 68–9 (p. 329).

130 Dante, *Paradise*, Canto 33, l. 67 (p. 345).

131 Dante, *Paradise*, Canto 31, l. 46 (p. 328).

132 Dante, *Paradise*, Canto 33, ll. 116–20 (p. 346).

Figure 6 Matrimony

Jan (Stellan Skarsgård) and Bess (Emily Watson) in *Breaking the Waves* (Lars Von Trier, Denmark 1996). Photo: British Film Institute.

Chapter 6

SEX SLAVES

Dante and Beatrice didn't do it. Hans Urs von Balthasar supposes that with Dante's *Divina Commedia* the Christian tradition acknowledges the compatibility of earthly and heavenly desire, with Dante lured from carnal to celestial bliss by divine eros, by the angelic Beatrice.[1] Diotima, in Plato's *Symposium*, supposed that the attraction of boys would give way to the delights of more abstract beauty, until finally the truest lovers would seek only the beautiful itself. In Dante's tale, it is a girl's beauty that first captivates, and it is a beauty that is not relinquished in favour of something more ethereal, but is itself enhanced, haloed by the celestial beauty in which it participates. This is indeed a development of the platonic tradition, made possible by an incarnational thought that finds the material to be not a passing means, but the very place in which God's glory shines forth, a corporeal radiance. Yet Dante and Beatrice didn't do it. Flesh is glorified, made to participate in the divine effulgence, but only so long as it is not touched, fondled or caressed.

If Dante had bedded Beatrice, could he have come to see her in the celestial rose? Could she have led him to heaven if she had thrown her arms around him, and enticed him between the sheets of her bed? Would this have occluded the heavenly light, restricting the reach of Dante's gaze? Or would he have found in Beatrice's embrace the presence of a mystery that, in its withdrawing, drew him on into the darkness that is also an unbearable light? Perhaps such a corporeal revelation was not impossible for Dante, who loved more than one woman, and who married Gemma Donati, with whom he had at least three children. Though Beatrice is from the first a more than earthly creature, appearing as a divine, angelic being, she yet appears naked in the opening vision of the *Vita Nuova* (1292), wearing nothing but a crimson cloth. She is held in the arms of Love, who feeds her with Dante's fiery heart.[2] Thus from the first, Dante's spiritual love is sexually coded. Whether or not Dante's Beatrice would still have been an angel, a 'thing from Heaven sent', if she had been his wife, his bed companion, this seems a much more unlikely proposition for Balthasar, whose Dante approaches heaven through yearning for an always distant, untouched Beatrice. And Dante and Beatrice didn't do it, they didn't touch.

Waves

In Lars von Trier's *Breaking the Waves* (Denmark/Sweden/France/Netherlands/Norway 1996), Bess is Beatrice to Jan's Dante, except that he is also her Beatrice. In him she sees the shining of God's glory. Wanting love, God has given her Jan so that in loving him she might love God all the more. When, at the beginning of the film, the church elders ask Bess if she knows what matrimony is, she replies firmly that of course she does. 'It's when two people are joined in God.' Bess's relationship with Jan is always part of her relationship with God, the form that her loving God takes in her life. After gaining permission to marry Jan, Bess comes out of the church and raises her head to the sun. In close-up she turns to the camera and smiles. At once we are complicit in her theological confidence.

Lars von Trier's story of matrimonial love and lovemaking – 'a curious mixture of religion and eroticism and possession' – has the form of a fable, a fairytale.[3] He himself has said that it is based on a folktale remembered from childhood, the story of Golden Hearted (Guld Hjerte), who gives away all of her possessions to whoever asks, until she has nothing, no clothes and no food. But in Trier's telling, the tale of Golden Hearted is crossed with that of Justine, the eponymous heroine of the Marquis de Sade's story of innocence uncorrupted. De Sade's Justine undergoes all manner of sexual degradations, but throughout maintains her faith in goodness, that in the end all will be well, until finally she is hit by a bolt of lightning and dies. Trier thought this very funny.[4] For him Justine and Golden Hearted epitomize the steadfastness of the Christian saint, losing herself for the other.[5] Together with *The Idiots* (1998) and *Dancer in the Dark* (2000), *Breaking the Waves* is the first in what Trier calls his Golden Hearted trilogy.

The world of *Breaking the Waves* is completely constructed, a purely cinematic reality, a stage for Trier's heightened psychodrama. Set in the 1970s, it conjures a remote Scottish community in the Outer Hebrides, with a dour Presbyterian Free Church, in which women are not permitted to speak and the sinful dead are committed not to God's mercy but to his wrath, to the flames of hell.[6] Yet into this world descend the 'outsiders' who work on the offshore oil-rigs, alighting from their helicopter. The film's narrative is divided into seven chapters, with a prologue and an epilogue, each framed by a digitally realized panorama, highly coloured tableaux of Scottish scenery. These are accompanied by a variety of 1970s pop songs by David Bowie, Procul Harum, Mott the Hoople and Elton John, among others. Yet the credulity of the acting, especially that of Emily Watson as Bess, who 'seems to empty herself out onto the screen',[7] together with the hand-held camera work, fabricate an intense emotional reality.[8] By encoding the melodrama in a cinéma-vérité style, the film renders the potentially risible as raw, elemental savagery. Only the most truculent of viewers will be undisturbed by the film. Most are weeping by its end, caught in Trier's emotional machinations.[9] He claims to cry every time he sees the film; as do I.[10]

Bess is an innocent; 'very susceptible', as her sister-in-law says. At the cinema Bess is enthralled by the film, which she watches with a child-like rapture, and Jan watches her.[11] Like a child, she has not learned how to conceal her emotions, expressing love, fear and rage with equal intensity. Bess was so grieved at the death of her brother that her mother had her sectioned. As her sister-in-law, Dodo, says, 'she's not right in the head'. She lives what she feels. Being an innocent she loves purely, passionately, physically. She loves greedily, obsessively. 'Everyone says I love you too much', she tells Jan. She has prayed to God for love, and when Jan comes to love her, she loves everything about him. Once married, she cannot wait for him to make love to her, and takes him to the hotel restroom, where, with her white dress hoisted up around her waist, he fucks her for the first time, up against the wall. The camera stays in close-up on Bess's face throughout the scene, registering her uncertainty and bemusement, her wordless wonderment at what bodies might do. Later she will giggle when Jan invites her to explore his naked body, and when he makes love to her on the bed she will gasp out 'Thank you, thank you.' Jan thinks she is thanking him, but her gratitude is first to God, whom she was really addressing. She has thanked God previously, when alone in the church – 'I thank you for the greatest gift of all, the gift of love. I thank you for Jan. I'm so lucky to have been given these gifts.' And now in bed with Jan, making love to Jan, she thanks God again, fervently. Thanking God for the bliss of the body, their bodies, for the waves of her pleasure. Amazingly, Trier contrives to make screen sex seem both utterly banal – the awkward, sweaty negotiation of naked bodies – and the occasion for an intense but simple, sincere gratitude. *Laudate Dominum.*

As with saints, God is more intimate with Bess than with the men who dominate the church, who know only God's word and law, and not his compassion, his love of human beings. Being innocent, Bess has a direct relationship with God, with whom she holds daily converse. Always knowing what she should be doing, what others would say to her, Bess's God addresses her through her own mouth, when she closes her eyes and speaks more slowly and sternly, with a deeper voice. Bess cannot endure that Jan must leave her to work on the oil-rig, and when he has gone she wants him back. Bess prays to God that Jan will be returned to her. 'Are you sure that's what you want?' God asks. 'Nothing else matters, I just want Jan home.' And so God answers her prayer, and Jan comes home. An accident on the oil-rig paralyses him from the neck down, and he is brought back to Bess.

God's cruel joke opens the second, longer part of the film, in which Bess will not leave Jan's bedside, in which she argues with God and hopes for a miracle. 'Your love for Jan is being put to the test', God tells Bess, and with this thought she looks through her tears at the camera. God makes her a deal. He will do what she asks, if she will do what Jan asks, and he asks that she should take a lover, and tell him about her love-making. Jan's request is a misguided attempt to save Bess, to suggest that she should forget Jan and find a new life with someone else, someone who can be a real husband to her. 'I'm finished Bess. You could take a lover without anyone noticing. But you can't divorce me. They'll never let you.' But when Bess refuses to countenance such a suggestion, Jan's request becomes more manipulative. He knows that Bess will do anything for him, if not for herself. 'Love is a mighty power', he tells her.

> If I die, it will be because love cannot keep me alive. But I can hardly remember what it's like to make love. And if I forget that, then I'll die. Remember when I phoned you from the rig. We made love without being together . . . Bess, I want you to find a man to make love to, and then come back here and tell me about it. It will feel like you and me being together again. And that, that will keep me alive.

Knowing that Bess will not take a lover for herself Jan asks her to take one for him, to keep him alive. 'Because I don't want to die. I'm afraid . . . It will be you and me Bess. Do it for me.' Whatever Jan's intention, his request destroys Bess, for finally she cannot but acquiesce. 'Prove to me that you love him, and then I'll let him live', God tells her. In order to love Jan she must give herself away to others, prostituting her flesh for love of another's crippled body: the horror of an utterly dispossessive desire. There is a strange logic here, for, as Stephen Heath notes, love and sex are treated as 'consubstantial', so that Jan is still a 'great lover' even when he can no longer make love to Bess.[12] And yet Bess is having sex with other men whom she does not love. 'I don't make love with them, I make love with Jan'. But perhaps they are being loved, the recipients of an agapeistic fallout from the eros by which Bess is consumed. Out of love for God's gift – living in God's gift – Bess gives away her body, and it is destroyed, like Christ's on the cross. Like Christ, like Abraham, Bess's sacrifice is beyond the ethical, beyond any sane measure of giving and receiving.[13]

When Dr Richardson (Adrian Rawlins) refuses Bess's advances, she turns to complete strangers, to a lonely man at the back of a bus, to the sailors in the fishing port: 'How much darling?' Revolted by these sordid encounters, Bess relates invented, more titillating tales to the drugged Jan, as he lies in his hospital bed.[14] 'I come to the back of the bus and you're there. And you're so huge that you're almost bursting out of your pants. And I undo your fly and I touch you. I'm touching your prick.' When Jan shows signs of recovery, Bess believes that it is due to her sacrificial devotion – 'I've saved Jan' – and seeks ever more degrading opportunities for bodily dispossession, in order to hasten Jan's full recovery. 'I don't make love with them, I make love with Jan and I save him from dying', she tells Dr Richardson. 'Sometimes I don't even have to tell him about it.'

When Bess, who has been cast out of the church, learns that Jan is dying, she tells Dodo to go to him and 'pray for him to be cured and to rise from his bed and walk'. And Dodo does. She prays and Jan subsequently rises from his bed. But Bess goes back to the 'big boat', the offshore trawler that is shunned by the other prostitutes, and where before Bess was nearly raped. And this time she is raped and badly beaten, and dies from her wounds shortly after being admitted to hospital. Her fate is as funny as that of de Sade's Justine. At the subsequent inquest, Dr Richardson suggests that Bess died from goodness. The church elders, however, condemn her to hell as they lower her coffin into the grave. But Bess has passed beyond their ability to hurt her. Jan, who is now fully recovered, has removed her body from the coffin and with the help of his friends has taken it to the oil rig where they give Bess over to the keeping of the sea, to the dark waves of the night. But the following morning Jan and the other riggers are brought up on to deck by the sound of bells, ringing in the sky. The film cuts to a shot looking down on the rig from the clouds, with two large bells tolling in the foreground, the film's final digital vision, a *visio Dei*.

For many viewers, Bess is a pathetic figure. She is a child in an adult body, whose naïveté allows her to be brutalized by those around her, and not least by Trier himself, whose camera – on this reading – takes a sadistic interest in her degradation.[15] She is, as Dr Richardson puts it in his official report, 'an immature and unstable person. A person who due to the trauma of her husband's illness gave way in obsessive fashion to an exaggerated perverse form of sexuality.' But for others she is as the doctor later describes her at the inquest, someone who is so good that her attempts to love in a fallen world cannot but seem naïve and blameworthy. She must be judged and found wanting lest her total dispossession should judge our more circumspect charity. Viewed one way, Bess is a psychologically damaged child, possessed by the foolish idea of a God who responds to her entreaties. Viewed another way, she is possessed of a love that knows no limits, that gives itself away without thought of the cost – giving 'anything to anyone', as Dodo says of Bess near the beginning of the film.[16] She is simply a saint who loves as Christ loves.

Prostitution

> After I became a prostitute, I had to deal with penises of every imaginable shape and size. Some large, others quite shrivelled and pendulous of testicle. Some blue-veined and reeking of Stilton, some miserly. Some crabbed, enchanted, dusted with pearls like the great minarets of the Taj Mahal, jesting penises, ringed as the tail of a raccoon, fervent, crested, impossible to live with, marigold-scented. More and more I became grateful I didn't have to own one of these appendages.[17]

Thus begins the narration of another modern saint, number 271 in Tama Janowitz's *Slaves of New York* (1986). A collection of short stories, Janowitz's tales are about male egos and the women who service them, the slaves who tidy the men's apartments, cook their food and tend their vanities in return for habitation and – sometimes – protection from other slave owners. These women are interchangeable, functions without identities. Thus in one story, the narrator tells us that first you must 'dispose of his wife'. You lobotomize Mrs Springsteen with an ice pick and send her on her way to Hollywood, then dress in her 'nightie' and lie in bed, 'looking up at the ceiling', waiting for the return of the 'boss'. 'Bruce strips down to his Jockey shorts and gets into bed with you. "Good night, honeybunch", he says. In the morning he still doesn't seem to realize there's been a change of personnel.'[18]

He never does, and nor does anyone else; and this is not surprising, for as he tells you, '"There's only one thing I'm interested in". "Me"? you say. Bruce looks startled. "My music", he says'.[19] Though you have sex with Bruce – 'he likes you to pretend to fight him off'[20] – you are never more than an adjunct to his ego, an object in his world.

Matters are slightly different for modern saint number 271. She has a 'boss', a writer, a 'double Ph.D. candidate in philosophy and American literature at the University of Massachusetts', for whom she keeps house, though not very well, fetches food and otherwise cossets; working the streets – 'crouched in dark alleys, giggling in hotel rooms or the back seats of limousines'[21] – while he lies on his bed reading Kant or Heidegger, or 'dreamily eating' whatever she brings him.[22] But he is also her friend, Bob, with whom she has long and intense conversations. 'When I was near Bob, with his long graceful hands, his silky moustache, his interesting theories of life and death, I felt that for the first time in my life I had arrived at a place where I was growing intellectually as well as emotionally'.[23] On the nights when she cannot sleep, feeling herself 'adrift in a sea of seminal fluid', he softly ties up her arm and injects her with a 'little heroin', or if none is available, 'a little something else'.[24] Bob is also her pimp, though somewhat inadequate as her protector on the streets.

> Sometimes I wished Bob was more aggressive as a pimp. There were moments on the street when I felt frightened; there were a lot of terminal cases out there, and often I was in situations that could have become dangerous. Bob felt that it was important that I accept anyone who wanted me . . . Still, I could have used more help from him than I got. But then Bob would arrive at the hospital, bringing me flowers and pastrami on rye and I realized that for me to change pimps and choose a more aggressive one, one who would be out there hustling for me and carrying a knife, would be to embrace a lifestyle that was genuinely alien to me, despite my middle-class upbringing.[25]

We may presume that Janowitz does not intend her readers to admire and emulate the modern saint; on the contrary, we are to discern in her a distressing internalization of the slave condition: complete abjection. 'My clients', she tells us, 'had a chunk of their body they wanted to give away; for a price I was there to receive it. Crimes, sins, nightmares, hunks of hair: it was surprising how many of them had something to dispose of'.[26] But it is she who gives herself away, handing herself over to anyone who wants her, who needs her; dispossessing herself, so that 'now at night, cruising the great long avenues of the city, dust and grit tossed feverishly in the massive canyons between the skyscrapers, it often occurs to me that

I am no more and no less'.[27] But above all she hands herself over to Bob, to his fantasizing of her as 'madonna and whore'.[28]

> I could have written a book about my experiences out on the street, but all my thoughts are handed over to Bob, who lies on the bed dreamily eating whatever I bring him – a hamburger from McDonald's, crab soufflé from a French restaurant in the theater district, a platter of rumaki with hot peanut sauce in an easy carry-out container from an Indonesian restaurant open until 1:00 a.m., plates of macaroni tender and creamy as the sauce that oozes out from between the legs of my clientele.[29]

This modern saint, refusing no one who wants her, thinks of herself as 'like a social worker for lepers',[30] or like a nun in the convents she used to read about as a child. Since 'there are no convents for Jewish girls', she has created her own in the cloisters of New York, in the canyons between the skyscrapers, in the back seats of limousines; places of holy devotion, where the poor are tended, their bodies caressed and pleasured. Afterwards she returns to Bob, her confessor, who dreamily consumes the stories of her abasement along with his hamburger or soufflé.

But the modern saint's devotions are not pure, since she exacts a price for her body. She does not give herself away for nothing: dollars are exchanged for flesh. This modern saint makes money in order to buy the things that money can buy. 'Even saints have human flaws'.[31] She does not give her body as a pure gift, without recompense or return. Yet it is her willingness to give herself away, to make her body available for the want of others, that permits the conceit of saintliness. One may recoil from this idea of saintly prostitution – this prodigality of the body – yet is this not the very practice that St Paul enjoined upon those Corinthians who burned for want of sexual gratification?[32]

Bodily Dispossession

St Paul advised the Corinthians that while lack of sexual congress is a good, its want should not lead to fornication, and therefore every man should have a wife and every woman a husband.

> The husband should give to his wife her conjugal rights, and likewise the wife to her husband. For the wife does not have authority over her own body, but the husband does; likewise the husband does not have authority over his own body, but the wife does.[33]

Husband and wife are to be as slaves to one another, each giving his or her own body to the other, for his or her use, each ready to receive what the other gives and to give what the other wants. This dispossession of one's body includes giving up, at least for a time and by consent, one's claim on the body of the other, in order to give oneself to prayer, before coming together again in order to avoid incontinency.[34] Such radical dispossession is possible for husband and wife because in Christ they already stand within a yet more radical relation of dispossession. They are already the recipients of a body totally given away, given over to the satisfaction of their want, their lack and desire; a body that will receive anything they give it, and accept anyone who wants it. This is the body of Christ.

In 1 Corinthians 7.3–4 Paul does not describe husband and wife as each other's 'slave', but in the context of the chapter and the letter, it is a warranted interpretation. It is quite likely that the Corinthian disputes in which Paul intervened were influenced by Stoic and Cynic teachings on marriage, and that in 7.3–4 Paul advocates a moderate Stoicism that sees marriage as the mutual sharing of power over the body of one's spouse, as against a stricter Cynicism that advocated celibacy and sexual renunciation within marriage ('It is well for a man not to touch a woman'[35]). Marriage as slavery was a common enough conceit in philosophical discourses of the time, not least in Stoic and Cynic teachings, and this may have led some Corinthians to understand marriage between a Christian and an unbeliever as the latter's enslavement of the former, which Paul denies in 7.15 – 'in such a case the brother or sister is not bound'. However, Paul does not so much deny as subvert the Stoic-Cynic construal of marriage as slavery. In 7.17–24 he insists that one's material circumstances do not affect one's relationship to Christ, who spiritually frees the slave and enslaves the free. Here we should fold Paul's notion of enslavement to Christ[36] – which again is arguably influenced by Stoic teaching – back onto his idea of marriage as mutual authority or ownership,[37] for such ownership will be dispossessive if it is indeed mutual and non-coercive, owning through disowning one's self.[38]

Husband and wife are able to give themselves to one another, to be one another's sex slave, because they are already the slaves of Christ – 'bought with a price'[39] – and thus no longer the slaves of this world. For Paul – as for most of the Christian tradition – one is never the owner of oneself, but always the slave of other powers. It is really only with the project of Enlightenment – and subsequent modernity – that Christians have been tempted to suppose autonomy a possibility for themselves. For Paul there is no real possibility of freedom from slavery; rather it is a matter of becoming the slave of that master whose service *is* freedom. In Christian marriage, as Paul imagines it, husband and wife are completely the slaves of Christ, in body and spirit, to be trained in the practice of dispossession, which is the very price by which they have been purchased. They own one another only to the extent that they are owned by a third, whose ownership constitutes the relationship of dispossession between them. They become the slaves of a slave, and must act as he does; giving themselves away in the way that he disposes of himself.

> Do you not know that your body is a temple of the Holy Spirit within you, which you have from God, and that you are not your own? For you were bought with a price; therefore glorify God in your body.[40]

Thus Paul, at his most radical, imagines marriage as a partnership between sex slaves, where each disposes of his or her body for the use of the other, in imitation of their mutual master, who is the slave of all: a body entirely dispossessed for the want of the other. Thus the modern saints in Trier's film and Janowitz's story – Bess and modern saint number 271 – are already performing, however imperfectly, the Pauline ideal; imperfectly because their bodies are purchased for a price which is not that of a reciprocal dispossession. Their sexual relationships are not married ones in the Pauline sense, but fornicatory. However, this observation does not so much call into question their saintliness as invite the suggestion that their sex slavery opens unto the possibility of a yet more radical invention of 'marriage' than Paul ostensibly envisaged.

But surely we are not meant to emulate such 'saints'? Tama Janowitz's modern saint is not proffered for admiration but rejection, as a satiric example of women's subjugation to male want in modern society. Surely the condition of the modern saint is precisely that which is to be overcome? And a first move in doing so would be to overcome the Pauline concept of marriage, as advocated by some feminist theologians.

After Slavery

Elizabeth Stuart has questioned the idea that Paul understood Christian marriage as a relationship of 'mutuality between husband and wife', and has done so by drawing attention to the use of slavery in his theology. She argues that in the Pauline texts marriage is understood as an asymmetric slave relationship, in which the wife is always subordinate to the husband, notwithstanding that Paul imagines an equal reciprocity between the two partners.

> In Paul the language of mutual authority obscures notions of ownership in which the wife will always be disadvantaged because of the web of power relations she has to exist in, which cannot be conveniently unspun in a marriage bed.[41]

Stuart insists that the Pauline ideal of reciprocal sex slavery precludes mutual love and respect because it involves the having of power over another, which in itself is objectionable, but which moreover can never be truly reciprocal between husband and wife in a society where men have power over women. Furthermore, as Stuart reminds her readers, women's authority over their own bodies has been 'the first and most symbolic and controversial aim of the feminist movement'.[42] Thus she concludes that the idea of reciprocal slavery is 'simply an unacceptable one to those who take the pain and struggle of women seriously'.[43]

A similar conclusion is reached by Adrian Thatcher, who, having noted the integration of marriage and slavery in the Pauline texts, argues that once the institution of slavery has been repudiated, so must the theology of marriage built upon it. 'It is inadmissible to appeal to biblical teaching on marriage while at the same time rejecting slavery since marriage and slavery are as indissolubly linked as a man and a woman are linked in marriage'.[44] There is certainly no question today of the church endorsing slavery, the use of people as objects, the failure to love as God loves.[45] But it might still be suggested that Stuart's and Thatcher's criticisms of the Pauline texts pay insufficient attention to the way in which those texts start to turn or subvert the idea of slavery away from violent power toward pacific charity. If Christ's dispossession is made the model of true slavery, its repetition within a mutual relationship constitutes an economy in which power is constantly circulating, given away in order to return, and only returning because given away. But for this suggestion to be at all persuasive one must first repudiate the notions – neither of which Paul nor much of the Christian tradition would accept – that one can be the self-sufficient author of one's life, and that a contrary ideal can make no headway against a persistent social order.

Thus even if it is the case that men have power over women in society, this is not a sufficient reason for giving up on an ideal which gives equal power to both men and women; though it is a power that neither possess. The church itself is constituted as the witness to the promise of a hoped for future which is the 'impossible' contrary of all known societies. Thus the ideal nature of the Pauline conception can be a problem only for those who have no such hope, and do not pray for the coming of such a future. One might therefore suggest that the practice of the ideal – as construed above – should not wait upon the reform of society, but be practised in order to hasten that reform.

The Pauline ideal contests Enlightenment notions of autonomy, of powers rightly possessed, and thus does put certain questions to women's right to author their own bodies – as also to men's control of their own and other bodies. However, the Pauline ideal does not so much deny women – or men – authority over their own bodies, as relocate that authority within the slavery of Christ, so that – again – one comes to self-possession through dispossession, to having through being had, to getting through giving.

After Complementarity

In *After Christianity* (1996), Daphne Hampson seeks to articulate what comes after the demise of Christianity and goes after Christianity in order to hasten its demise. Following Simone de Beauvoir, she argues that under patriarchy 'woman' is constructed as the other of 'man', that is, as the 'slave' of the 'master'. In Western societies women become slaves by internalizing an image or images of woman projected by men, and the chief means for projecting such images – and presumably internalizing them – has been and is religion: the 'over-arching framework through which men have projected their understanding of reality'.[46] Hampson discerns a threefold construction of woman as 'other' in Western religion: 'woman as ideal, woman as slut, and woman as complement to the male'.[47] The most pertinent of these three images is the third, since it most closely resembles the Pauline concept of reciprocal slavery, and most clearly articulates Hampson's own definition of sex slavery as the systematic projection of the other by the same; of 'woman' by men.

For Hampson, 'woman as slave is socialized to conform' to a male construct of the 'feminine', understood as the ' "complement" of the male and never *vice versa*'.[48] The feminine is constructed as that which man is not: gentle, receptive, humble, nurturing and obedient. While this image is normally projected onto women, real or imaginary, it is also applied to social groups such as the church in relation to Christ or God, and can even be applied to men. This mobility of the feminine allows men to explore what they envisage as the 'female or maternal', but their exploration does not lead them to respect women, because while the image is adulated, actual women are despised. More importantly, the male projection of the feminine denies women the possibility of developing their own subjectivity, their own image of femininity.[49] 'Woman' is made according to the imagination of men.

Hampson's critique is chiefly aimed at ideological constructions of the feminine in various Christian traditions, and especially in Catholicism, for which she appears to have a particular *animus*, not least because of the 'astonishing' extent to which 'Catholicism has distorted its symbolism . . . in order to construct a place for the feminine'.[50] Hampson has much less to say about the idea of complementarity itself, beyond noting some of the ways in which it 'quickly translates into giving woman an inferior position to the male'.[51] This seems to suggest the possibility of a genuine 'complementarity', which Hampson would seem to understand as a radical equality between man and woman, for she writes that the 'patriarchal imagination substitutes for woman as the equal of man, a male projection of "woman" '.[52] But Hampson does not discuss the difference that is man and woman, and the relation between them, which is surely the burden of the idea of complementarity. Hampson supposes that there are significant differences between men and women,[53] and moreover that woman has her own essential identity, which needs to be set free from the 'suppression' of patriarchy.[54]

> It need not follow from the fact that there are manifestly differences [between men and women] that we should set up dualisms around gender (or anything else) which consign some members of humanity to something less than the status of being a full person. It could be possible simply to allow other persons to be themselves![55]

Yet it is of course the idea of an already existing but suppressed self, an essential identity as man or woman, which has been the subject of much criticism in recent feminist theory,[56] and which much Christian anthropology would want to question. For such anthropology, the self is called into being by God in Christ, and formed through the practices of that calling. The self is not that which, already made, awaits its release from oppressive structures, but that which has to be formed, over time, through habitual practices. This is to understand the self as the disciplining of a soul.[57] It arrives when we learn to let go of those identities that hinder the dispossessive flow of Christ's self/lessness. The self that arrives as it passes away is an activity rather than an achievement, a verb rather than a noun; a process of remaking through continual unmaking: un/selfing. It is in this context that we must consider what it is to have a sex, to be 'male' or 'female', and for these to be complementary modalities of the desiring body.

Gender Anxieties

Karl Barth – to take a theologian whom Hampson briefly discusses and dismisses[58] – sets before us a picture of man and woman as produced or constructed in Christ. What is of fundamental importance for Barth is the non-negotiable sexual difference of man and woman. Each one of us is either male *or* female, while at the same time being oriented to the sex we are not.

> [S]ince man has been created by God as male or female, and stands before God in this Either-Or, everything that God wills and requires of him is contained by implication in this situation, and the question of good and evil in his conduct is measured by it . . . We remember that the 'male *or* female' is immediately to be completed by the 'male *and* female'. Rightly understood, the 'and' is already contained in the 'or' . . . For how is it possible to characterize man except in his distinctive relation to woman, or woman except in her distinctive relation to man? But just because in the being of both it is so deeply a question of being in relation to the other, of duality rather than unity, the first principle must be stated independently that, in obedience to God, man will be male or female.[59]

Of course for Barth there is a sense in which the call to be man or woman before God is a call to be what one is always already, a call to realize an underlying and essential self. But for Barth this self is not known other than in our response to the call of God to become what we are already; the self is realized only through a process of becoming. Barth rejects 'every phenomenology or typology of the sexes', and indeed pours scorn on such ideas of the feminine as are to be found in Protestant as well as Catholic Christianity.[60] Furthermore, Barth – writing in the late 1940s and early 50s – is aware that women are increasingly seeking to determine their own identities.

> The question what specific activity woman will claim and make her own as woman ought certainly to be posed in each particular case as it arises, not in the light of traditional preconceptions, but honestly in relation to what is aimed at in the future. Above all, woman herself ought not to allow the uncalled-for illusions of man, and his attempts to dictate what is suitable for her and what is not, to deter her from continually and seriously putting this question to herself.[61]

Barth insists that however 'woman' constructs her own identity, she 'must always and in all circumstances be woman; . . . she must feel and conduct herself as such and not as man; . . . the command of the Lord, which is for all eternity, directs both man and woman to their own proper sacred place and forbids all attempts to violate this order'.[62] Yet this concern, which Barth might be thought to share with some feminists such as Luce Irigaray, betrays a certain anxiety regarding an implicit typology of the sexes. He wonders if Friedrich Schleiermacher, as a male, should have 'defined religion as the feeling of sheer dependence', and wonders even more about Schleiermacher's 'impossible wish' to have been born a woman.[63] Whatever man and woman are to become under God, they are not to deny or seek to overcome their fundamental difference from one another as male and female.

> That God created man as male and female, and therefore as His image and the likeness of the covenant of grace, of the relationship between Himself and His people, between Christ and His community, is something which can never lead to a neutral It, nor found a purely external, incidental and transient sexuality, but rather an inward, essential and lasting order of being as He and She, valid for all time and also for eternity.[64]

Thus while Barth allows for variability and new possibilities in the meaning of 'masculine' and 'feminine' – such that what it means to be a man or woman in society is always to be determined anew by each individual man or woman – he nevertheless insists on an underlying stability of sexual identity and orientation. 'All the other conditions of masculine and feminine being may be disputable, but it is inviolable . . . that man is directed to woman and woman to man'.[65] For Barth, man and woman are mutually constituting of one another, and this 'complementarity' (though it is not a term Barth uses) replaces all other typologies of the sexes.[66] But Barth is unable to maintain the distinction between inviolable sexualities and otherwise disputable conditions of 'masculine and feminine being'. Most obviously, the rigid polarity of male and female precludes homosexuality as a possible condition of masculine and feminine existence.

For Barth, homosexuality is that 'physical, psychological and social sickness, the phenomenon of perversion, decadence and decay', which emerges when God's fundamental ordinance is refused. Barth allows that homosexuality, in its early stages, 'may have an appearance of particular beauty and spirituality, and even be redolent of sanctity'. But he nevertheless insists that homosexuality is – as St Paul suggests[67] – a form of idolatry, in which the person – man or woman – thinks that he or she alone constitutes true humanity, having no need of the other sex, who is thus despised. The homosexual fails to recognize that 'as a man he can only be genuinely human with woman, or as a woman with man'.[68] This argument, like some of Balthasar's, rests on a *non sequitur*. Homosexuals, as such, do not think that their own sex, male of female, constitutes the whole of humanity. Nor are heterosexuals, as such, precluded from thinking that the whole of humanity is included within their own sex, male or female – though this is more often fantasized by men than women. Barth's argument is no argument at all, but a mere prejudice, and unacceptable to those Catholic and Orthodox traditions which value segregated sororal and fraternal communities, the formation of which Barth describes as 'obviously disobedience' and incipiently homosexual.[69]

It may be conjectured that Barth's argument arises from his thinking through of Paul's remark about idolatry in relation to Barth's own fear of homosexuality, albeit that the latter was unacknowledged and culturally constructed. Barth displays anxiety concerning sexual boundaries, such that Schleiermacher's theology – which both fascinated and repelled Barth – might be thought a symptom of Schleiermacher's wish to be a woman. That disputable genderings of male and female bodies are not disavowed but everywhere present in Barth's thought is even more obvious when he turns to consider the 'order' of man to woman. Here everything that Hampson and others have said about complementarity is confirmed.

Man and woman are equal but not equivalent: man comes first and woman second, subordinate to the superordinate male.[70] 'Properly speaking, the business of woman, her task and function, is to actualize the fellowship in which man can only precede her, stimulating, leading and inspiring'.[71] And when the man fails to act as he ought, it is no business of the woman to do likewise. For if 'there is a way of bringing man to repentance, it is the way of the woman who refuses to let herself be corrupted and made disobedient by his disobedience, but who in spite of his disobedience maintains her place in the order all the more firmly'.[72] It is a matter of keeping 'order', and, for the obedient man, of being 'strong'. 'He is strong to the extent that he accepts as his own affair service to this order and in this order. He is strong as he is vigilant for the interests of both sexes'. Woman, on the other hand, is to be 'mature', that is 'to take up the position which falls to her in accordance with this order, desiring nothing better than that this order should be in force'.[73]

While Barth opened the possibility of rethinking 'woman' in theology – and thus 'man' also, and moreover of women rethinking woman – he himself was unable to resist the culture of his day, which, more grievously, he presented as the minimal command of God, the 'order' that must be kept irrespective of what individual men and women hear as God's address to them. This 'order' is pernicious, as Hampson and others allege. Not only must women conform to the command of God and man, but if man fails in his obedience, woman's only redress is to be yet more obedient to her calling, namely obedient to the disobedient man; whereas if she fails, the man must chastise her for it. But it is not for this that we should read Barth today, which only confirms Hampson's critique of Christianity, but rather for what Hampson neglects, namely Barth's prior insistence that the address of God is a word of freedom to us, which calls into question the norms, orders and frameworks, the phenomenologies and typologies, that our culture would impose on us. If Barth's own attempt to delineate this freeing of our bodies merely reproduced a cultural order that we must now disdain, he nevertheless first maintained the power of the Word to open for us a space in which our bodily relations can be remade as tangible, fleshly promises of God's beatitude. For Barth – after Paul – this freedom is possible only as a certain form of obedience, a certain kind of slavery.[74]

Thus in the last part of this chapter we will consider a different conception of complementarity, one more suited to Barth's space of obediential freedom than Barth's own, one that takes further the idea of mutual sex slavery in Christ. Needless to say, it is as much a cultural product as Barth's own rendering of God's sexual order. But unlike Barth, it seeks to acknowledge the always unstable and culturally contingent meaning of such an order, of 'man' and 'woman', 'masculine' and 'feminine'. Moreover, it identifies this contingency as a final undecidability in the bodily relationship of gifted dispossession that Christ makes possible – as disclosed in the Pauline text.

Undecidable Bodies

The Slovenian philosopher, Slavoj Žižek, has ventured an understanding of complementarity based on his reading of quantum mechanics, and in particular of Heisenberg's 'uncertainty principle'. On certain readings of the principle, one cannot measure the mass *and* momentum of a particle simultaneously: one can measure only one or the other. It is a case of epistemological uncertainty. Žižek, however, insists on a 'stronger' reading of the principle, which accords an ontological status to the uncertainty of the particle's mass and momentum: it has mass *or* momentum, but not both. Thus uncertainty is a fundamental property of the particle itself, and this ontological uncertainty constitutes a form of oppositional complementarity: 'two complementary properties do not complement each other, they are mutually exclusive'.[75] This form of complementarity is like those pictures that can be seen in one of two ways – either as a vase or as two faces, either as a duck or as a rabbit – but which cannot be read in both ways at the same time. Both images are as it were present, but at any one time only one can be realized; mass and momentum are potentially mutual, but actually exclusive in the particle.

Žižek suggests that the counterpart to quantum complementarity in the human condition is a 'situation in which the subject is forced to choose and to accept a certain fundamental loss or impossibility'.[76] Thus, for example, a person who would be virtuous in certain ways – who would be forgetful of self and give without thought of return – must not so consciously seek, otherwise he or she will remember him or herself and receive a restitution in the knowledge of his or her generosity. A true gift or act of humility is accomplished only through ignorance of its actuality. Knowledge of the act – *in* the act – is impossible: if one knows what one is doing, one has not done it.[77]

Another example of this logic of complementarity is the relationship between an action and knowledge of its circumstances. We think that the more we know about the circumstances, the easier it will be for us to act; but the more we know the harder it becomes. With full knowledge, action becomes impossible. We must simply act. Žižek suggests that this condition is analogous to religious belief.

> [T]he decision to believe never results from a careful weighing of *pro* and *contra*, that is, one can never say: 'I believe in Christ because, after careful consideration, I came to the conclusion that reasons for prevail' – it is only the act, the decision to believe, that renders the reasons to believe truly comprehensible.[78]

This is why, of course, the gospels tell us stories of people who choose to follow Jesus for no reason. Another example that Žižek offers – the 'most pathetic' – is that of love: 'the decision to love somebody is free (compulsory love is no love), yet this decision can never be a present and conscious one (I can never say to myself: "Now I will decide to fall in love with this person . . .") – all I can do in the present is to ascertain that *the decision has already been taken* and that I am caught in the inexorable necessity of love'.[79] In order to act there is always something we must either not know or forget, and forget that we have forgotten.

This then is what is here meant by complementarity: the condition of forgetfulness for action, the very condition that is necessary for the Pauline idea of marriage as mutual dispossession or slavery. In order to turn the idea of slavery away from one of abject compliance with the will of another, one must choose to give oneself away to the other, and to do this utterly, as a pure gift of self without thought of reciprocation. But at the same time one must not know that this is what one is doing, even as one disposes of oneself. It is in this sense that one becomes the 'complement' of another; not in the sense that one is the other half that makes a whole, understood in an entirely biologistic manner, according to a certain cultural biology,[80] but in the sense that one's body is an unknown gift to the other, given as an utter gratuity, an absolute grace, to the point that in the relationship one can no longer say who gives and who receives, or even, whose body is whose.

No doubt this reading of the Pauline text has taken us far beyond its warrant, especially if – as may be suggested – we understand 'marriage' not in terms of a preceding legality, but precisely in terms of an undecidable complementarity, of that mutual sex slavery which I have read in the Pauline text. On such an account, real marriages may well exist in other than legally constituted unions, and such unions are not the confirmation but the undertaking of such slavery. Furthermore, it may be suggested that within the Christian symbolic, as already in Paul, the mapping of gender relations onto actual bodies is always contingent or pragmatic, so that the relation of 'husband' to 'wife' is applicable not only to heterosexual couples, but to all those bodies in Christ who seek to exercise their sexuality in the order of the gift.[81]

There is, however, another way in which this argument perhaps exceeds the text, and contradicts the Žižekian notion of complementarity. This is the way in which we have too easily spoken of the slave-body-become-gift as a realizable possibility. Does not the very fact of mutuality in the married relationship preclude the possibility of the pure gift of the body? Even as I give myself to the other, do I not know that I receive his body in return? Even if I forget – a forgetting that must surely seem impossible – that I am giving myself to the other, how can I forget that he is giving himself to me in return for myself to him? Thus we might think that it is only outside of marriage as mutual sex slavery that there can be true slavery in the sense of absolute gift; and thus it is only somebody like Trier's Bess or Tama Janowitz's modern saint who approaches the condition of true bodily dispossession. Admittedly, Trier's Bess gives her body for Jan's life and Janowitz's modern saint is a prostitute: she gives her body not gratuitously, as a grace poured out, but in return for money. Thus we might think that it is only the person who gives his body away without any thought of return, who simply makes his body available for the pleasure of others, who most truly achieves saintly slavery: a profitless prostitute.

In a sense it is such a person that Paul already invites us to imagine, since his married couples are not only mutual sex slaves, but enjoined to copulate without desire for each other's flesh.[82] Paul urges celibacy, but allows sex in marriage for the weak; but married sex is disciplined sex. It is sex without want, for marriage puts out the flames of desire. It was a commonplace of Greco-Roman culture that sexual desire was a kind of burning that heated the flesh. While such warmth was good for the body, too much was dangerous, and medical opinion warned against excessive passion, which it conceived as illness. Paul seems to have followed medical opinion in this regard, if for different reasons; but his cure would have perplexed contemporary physicians as it still offends today, because for Paul 'it is better to marry than to be aflame with passion'.[83] Marriage is not just an appropriate context for sexual desire, it is its remedy. This view would have seemed preposterous to many in the ancient world, since a certain amount of heat, of burning desire, was necessary for procreation; but procreation was not one of Paul's concerns. His concern was to eliminate fornication, which polluted the Christian body, individual and social, and which resulted from sexual desire. Marriage eliminates both.

> For this is the will of God, your sanctification; that you abstain from fornication; that each one of you know how to control your own body in holiness and honor, not with lustful passion, like the Gentiles who do not know God.[84]

If Paul's thought now seems bizarre, it did so also in his own day, when desire was considered the motive for sex, and marriage its constraint and discipline, rather than its extermination. Yet, as Dale B. Martin has argued, this seems to be Paul's view, that sex in marriage is a prophylaxis against desire.[85] The idea of sex without desire was not unique to Paul, but upheld as an ideal by later Christians such as Clement of Alexandria and Augustine of Hippo, who pictured paradisal sex – the kind of copulation that Adam and Eve might have enjoyed in Eden if they had not first eaten the fruit – as passionless sex, the flesh aroused by the will rather than by lust.[86] But this passionless, lustless sex, is not only paradisal, it is 'prostituted' sex, undertaken not from sexual desire, but as an act of the will. Just as Augustine pictures the unfallen Adam, so the prostitute, or the porn star, 'without feeling the allurement of passion goading him on', wills his flesh to perform, 'in tranquillity of mind and with no impairment of his body's integrity'.[87]

The idea of sex without desire, copulation without passion, is so strange that Dale B. Martin, who strenuously advocates this reading of Paul, suggests that Paul must nevertheless have had some concept of sexual motivation in order to explain why people had sex at all. Martin suggests that this may be an occasion when 'modern categories' fail us, and 'we need to invent or appropriate some other term to convey this necessary urge for sex without invoking Paul's rejected category of desire'. Martin suggests 'inclination'.[88] In Christian marriage there is to be no sexual desire, only the operation of sexual inclination. But this, as Martin acknowledges, leaves Paul's otherwise unnamed category almost incomprehensible. In line with the reading so far advanced of 1 Corinthians 7.3–4, we may better think not so much of inclination, as of inoculation. Against the temptation of the prostitute's body, union with which pollutes the body of Christ (1 Corinthians 6.15–16), Paul advocates a form of prostituted sex within the Christic body, as the poison that cures. If one allows that the prostitute, in his or her professional capacity, has sex without desire, then the Christian couple who have sexual intercourse without passion, copulate as prostitutes. They give themselves to one another not in order to fulfil their own want, but to satisfy the need of the other, thereby practising a desire for the other which is not born of any lack, but in imitation of that charitable excess which is God's alone; a giving to the other, for the other, without thought of return, other than to receive back again what was first given, in order to give again. And of course the giving of the body is an almost perfect analogue for this grace of God, since just as God's gift never leaves her hand – God is the gift of God – so the giver of the body is one with the body given.

It is in the married relationship – understood as a relationship of mutual sex slavery – that one receives, as a gift, the possibility of giving oneself; just as in giving oneself in the relationship one bestows the gift of giving to the other. It is in dispossessing oneself of one's body that one makes it possible for the other to approach, to dispossess himself, knowing that what he receives in return is in part the ability of such dispossession. The giving of oneself is itself a gift that one receives in the very act of so giving, just as in giving, the other receives the gift they return to you, and so on, infinitely. And because this gift of self is possible only as it is received, it is never purely in one's gift, but rather a movement that always precedes one, in which one is caught and moved, always already underway. It is like a current in the sea that moves the swimmer's body even before she recognizes that her motion is not the result of her strokes, of her arms embracing the swell of the sea, but of the sea embracing her, as she moves in its waves. Thus we may think Paul's married prostitution a radical instant of the logic of complementarity in Žižek's sense: the impossibility of fully knowing what one is doing in the act of doing it. Is one giving *or* receiving? Is one giving *and* receiving? Is one 'man' *or* 'woman', or 'man' *and* 'woman'? Or is one beyond these differences, falling fast into the different 'difference' of God?

Notes

1 The story of Dante's angelic infatuation is told by the poet in *La Vita Nuova*, translated by Barbara Reynolds (Harmondsworth: Penguin Books, 1969).

2 Dante, *La Vita Nuova*, III, ll. 24–9 (p. 31).

3 Lars von Trier in Stig Björkman, 'Naked Miracles', translated by Alexander Keiller, *Sight and Sound*, 6/10 (1996): 10–14 (p. 14). The shooting script is published in Lars von Trier, *Breaking the Waves* (London: Faber & Faber, 1996).

4 Jack Stevenson, *Lars von Trier* (London: British Film Institute, 2002), p. 90. Marquis de Sade, *Justine ou les malheurs de la vertu* (1791) (Paris: Union Générale d'Editions, 1969).

5 Stevenson, *Lars von Trier*, pp. 89–90. See also the interview with Trier in Björkman, 'Naked Miracles', p. 12.

6 In an early version of the film script, Bess was Caroline, a devout Catholic who entreats the Virgin Mary rather than Bess's Father-God. Stevenson, *Lars von Trier*, p. 91.

7 Lizzie Francke, Review of *Breaking the Waves*, *Sight and Sound*, 6/10 (1996): 36–7 (p. 36).

8 'I . . . remember that Emily [Watson] was the only one who came to the casting barefoot and with no make-up at all! There was something Jesus-like about her which attracted me. She had had no earlier film experience.' Trier in Björkman, 'Naked Miracles', p. 14. The part of Bess was to have been played by Helena Bonham Carter, but she withdrew from the project at the last moment (Stevenson, *Lars von Trier*, pp. 94–5). Though frustrating at the time, Bonham Carter's withdrawal was to prove a happy event, since it allowed Emily Watson to give what is undeniably one of the great film performances. Though shot on film, the images were transferred to video for editing, before being returned to film, having been drained of much of their colour.

9 Any doubt that Trier was not intending to manipulate his audience will be dispersed by viewing his later film, *Dancer in the Dark* (1998), in which he almost pulls off the same trick, by the same means. Emily Watson has described watching *Dancer in the Dark*, as 'like having someone walk over your grave'. Watson quoted in an interview with Melissa Denes, 'Coming Up for Air', *The Guardian Weekend* (11 January 2003): 22–4 (p. 24). Cinematic reality, including emotional reality, is always an artificial effect.

10 Stevenson, *Lars von Trier*, p. 101.
11 They are watching *Lassie Come Home* (USA 1943).
12 Stephen Heath, 'God, Faith and Film: *Breaking the Waves*', *Literature and Theology*, 12 (1998): 93–107 (p. 98).
13 'The love of God is irrational, anarchic, beyond norms, made real by Christ's passion and expressed in sacrifice, martyrdom, self-abandonment, goodness in the extreme it is.' Heath, 'God, Faith and Film', p. 99.
14 Jack Stevenson argues that the film would have been more unsettling for audiences if Bess had started to enjoy her degrading sexual adventures, as does Charlotte Rampling at the hands of her Nazi lover, Dirk Bogarde, in Liliana Cavani's *The Night Porter* (Italy 1973) – reportedly one of Trier's favourite films. Stevenson, *Lars von Trier*, pp. 92–3.
15 For a powerful critique of the film as replicating the social dominance of men over women, of phallic rigour over 'debilitating masochism', see Alyda Faber, 'Redeeming Sexual Violence? A Feminist Reading of *Breaking the Waves*', *Literature and Theology*, 19 (2003): 59–76. Faber not only offers a critique of the film, but of Stephen Heath's essay and two other important essays on the film: Kyle Keefer and Tod Linafelt, 'The End of Desire: Theologies of Eros in the Song of Songs and *Breaking the Waves*' and Irena S.M. Makarushka, 'Transgressing Goodness in *Breaking the Waves*', both in *Imag(in)ing Otherness: Filmic Visions of Living Together*, edited by S. Brent Plate and David Jaspers (Atlanta, GA: Scholars Press, 1999), pp. 49–60 and 61–80 respectively.
16 Stephen Heath notes that the film 'wagers' on the possibility of representing such seeming contradictions simultaneously. 'Bess is simple, not all there, deluded; *and* Bess is a demonstration of the confines and constraints of her community (constraining particularly on women, not allowed, for example, to speak in church gatherings); *and* Bess is a point of ultimate value, the genuine figure of the film's religious stakes.' Heath, 'God, Faith and Film', p. 95.
17 Tama Janowitz, *Slaves of New York* (London: Pan Books, [1986] 1987), p. 1. James Ivory's film of the book, with the same title, was released in 1989. While scripted by Janowitz, and retaining the conceit of slavery, the film finally opts for romance rather than the sense of quiet despair that pervades Janowitz's stories.
18 Janowitz, *Slaves*, p. 37.
19 Janowitz, *Slaves*, p. 40.
20 Janowitz, *Slaves*, p. 38.
21 Janowitz, *Slaves*, p. 6.
22 Janowitz, *Slaves*, p. 5.
23 Janowitz, *Slaves*, p. 3.
24 Janowitz, *Slaves*, p. 2.
25 Janowitz, *Slaves*, p. 3.
26 Janowitz, *Slaves*, p. 2.
27 Janowitz, *Slaves*, p. 5.

28 Janowitz, *Slaves*, p. 3.
29 Janowitz, *Slaves*, pp. 5–6.
30 Janowitz, *Slaves*, p. 2.
31 Janowitz, *Slaves*, p. 3.
32 For a brief overview of Paul and his anxious – 'even alarmist' – teaching on the body and its sex, in particular in 1 Corinthians 7, see Peter Brown, *The Body and Society: Men, Women and Sexual Renunciation in Early Christianity* (London: Faber & Faber, [1988] 1989), pp. 44–57.
33 1 Corinthians 7.3–4.
34 1 Corinthians 7.5.
35 1 Corinthians 7.1.
36 'For whoever was called in the Lord as a slave is a freed person belonging to the Lord, just as whoever was free when called is a slave of Christ' (1 Corinthians 7.22).
37 1 Corinthians 7.3–4.
38 For the historical background to this rhetorico-theological interpretation see Will Deming, *Paul on Marriage and Celibacy: The Hellenistic Background of 1 Corinthians* 7, Society for New Testament Studies Monograph Series 83 (Cambridge: Cambridge University Press, 1995), pp. 108–73. The metaphor of 'slavery', while deployed in church and theology at a symbolic, imaginary or phantasmatic level, nevertheless raises the question of actual slavery, and the rectitude of 'playing' at it when many people had (and have) no choice about doing so. See further I.A.H. Combes, *The Metaphor of Slavery in the Writings of the Early Church: From the New Testament to the Beginning of the Fifth Century*, Journal for the Study of the New Testament Supplement Series (Sheffield: Sheffield Academic Press, 1998) and Peter Garnsey, *Ideas of Slavery from Aristotle to Augustine* (Cambridge: Cambridge University Press, 1996).
39 1 Corinthians 6.20, 7.23.
40 1 Corinthians 6.19–20.
41 Elizabeth Stuart, *Just Good Friends: Towards a Lesbian and Gay Theology of Relationships* (London: Mowbray, 1995), pp. 125–6. Stuart also suggests that the understanding of marriage in Hosea is one of slavery: 'the woman whom the jealous but faithful husband passionately pursues is an object to be shamed, humiliated, starved and seduced, reduced to proper passivity' (p. 125).
42 Stuart, *Just Good Friends*, p. 123.
43 Stuart, *Just Good Friends*, p. 126.
44 Adrian Thatcher, *Liberating Sex: A Christian Sexual Theology* (London: SPCK, 1993), p. 16.
45 For an account of the respect due all God's creatures see Kathryn Tanner, *The Politics of God: Christian Theologies and Social Justice* (Minneapolis: Fortress Press, 1992), ch. 5.
46 Daphne Hampson, *After Christianity*, second edition (London: SCM Press, [1996] 2002), p. 169.

47 Hampson, *After Christianity*, p. 173.
48 Hampson, *After Christianity*, p. 192.
49 Hampson, *After Christianity*, pp. 192–3.
50 Hampson, *After Christianity*, p. 193. Hampson's admission that she 'grew up within Protestantism' (p. 203) may account for this curious criticism.
51 Hampson, *After Christianity*, p. 200.
52 Hampson, *After Christianity*, p. 206.
53 'There is every indication . . . that women tend to be more religious or spiritually inclined than men' (Hampson, *After Christianity*, p. 205).
54 Hampson, *After Christianity*, p. 206.
55 Hampson, *After Christianity*, pp. 207–8.
56 See *The Essential Difference*, edited by Naomi Schor and Elizabeth Weed (Bloomington and Indianapolis: Indiana University Press, 1994).
57 See further Rowan D. Williams, 'Interiority and Epiphany: A Reading in New Testament Ethics', *Modern Theology*, 13/1 (1997): 29–51. The idea that the Christian self or soul is formed in and through a slave relationship, raises the question of subjection as addressed in Hegel, Nietzsche and Foucault. See further Judith Butler, *The Psychic Life of Power: Theories in Subjection* (Stanford, CA: Stanford University Press, 1997). It may be suggested that the Christian subject is produced in and through subjection to Christ who, however, is always already subject to his disciple(s); and this is what it means to be born again of the Spirit. It is to be born again in the event of Christ-become-the-church, which birth is itself a further rebirthing of the church, just as each parent is reborn with the coming of a child.
58 Hampson, *After Christianity*, p. 195.
59 Karl Barth, *Church Dogmatics*, translated by A.T. Mackay, T.H.L. Parker, Harold Knight, Henry A. Kennedy, and John Marks (Edinburgh: T. & T. Clark, 1961), III/4, p. 149.
60 Barth, *Church Dogmatics*, III/4, pp. 152–3.
61 Barth, *Church Dogmatics*, III/4, p. 155. Barth praises Simone de Beauvoir's *Le Deuxième Sexe* (1949), noting that 'the description of the way in which man has made and still makes himself master of woman, the presentation of the myth with which he invests her in this process and for this purpose, and the unmasking of this myth, are all worthy of attention especially on the part of men and not least of Christian theologians' (III/4, p. 162).
62 Barth, *Church Dogmatics*, III/4, p. 156.
63 Barth, *Church Dogmatics*, III/4, p. 155. 'What are we to think when in the year 1804 we find him [Schleiermacher] writing to a woman friend: "Women are more fortunate than we in that their business affairs take up only a part of their thoughts while the longing of the heart, the beautiful inward life of the imagination, always dominates the greater part . . . Wherever I look, it always seems to me that the nature of women is nobler and their life happier, and if ever I toy with an impossible wish, it is to be a woman".' It may be suggested

that Barth's anxiety concerning Schleiermacher's masculinity betrays a deeper cultural anxiety which is, according to Mark Breitenberg, constituted by and constitutive of Western patriarchal society. See Mark Breitenberg, *Anxious Masculinity in Early Modern England*, Cambridge Studies in Renaissance Literature and Culture 10 (Cambridge: Cambridge University Press, 1996).

64 Barth, *Church Dogmatics*, III/4, p. 158.

65 Barth, *Church Dogmatics*, III/4, p. 163.

66 Barth, *Church Dogmatics*, III/4, p. 164.

67 Romans 1.25.

68 Barth, *Church Dogmatics*, III/4, p. 166.

69 Barth, *Church Dogmatics*, III/4, pp. 165–6.

70 Barth, *Church Dogmatics*, III/4, p. 169.

71 Barth, *Church Dogmatics*, III/4, p. 171.

72 Barth, *Church Dogmatics*, III/4, p. 172.

73 Barth, *Church Dogmatics*, III/4, p. 177.

74 'Barth presupposes that there is initially not-much-to-speak-of in the creature – all is owed to the positing work of the Holy Spirit. The creature becomes interesting as a subject only when he or she stands under the divine call or injunction and responds appropriately. But from this initial restriction of what we might think of as creaturely entitlements or faculties, there opens up a great domain of freedom in Christ – life in a dynamic and open space (which is how he envisages the church)'. Ben Quash, 'Von Balthasar and the Dialogue with Karl Barth', *New Blackfriars*, 79 (1998): 45–55 (p. 52). On Barth's obediential freedom more generally see Nigel Biggar, *The Hastening that Waits: Karl Barth's Ethics* (Oxford: Clarendon Press, 1993).

75 Slavoj Žižek, *The Indivisible Remainder: An Essay on Schelling and Related Matters* (London & New York: Verso, 1996), p. 211.

76 Žižek, *The Indivisible Remainder*, p. 211.

77 See further Jacques Derrida, *Given Time: I Counterfeit Money*, translated by Peggy Kamuf (Chicago and London: University of Chicago Press, 1992); and Gerard Loughlin, *Telling God's Story: Bible, Church and Narrative Theology* (Cambridge: Cambridge University Press, [1996] 1999), pp. 226–9.

78 Žižek, *The Indivisible Remainder*, p. 212.

79 Žižek, *The Indivisible Remainder*, p. 213.

80 See chapter 5 above (God's Sex) for an account of such a cultural biology in the theology of Hans Urs von Balthasar.

81 Indeed it may be suggested that once the church imagined its relation to Christ as that of a bride to her groom, the church had – if only phantasmatically and only for men – instituted same-sex marriage. Thus the contemporary theology of same-sex unions merely seeks to actualize what has already been thought, from the first, though disavowed until now. On same-sex unions see the following articles by David Matzko McCarthy, 'Homosexuality and the Practices of Marriage', *Modern Theology*, 13 (1997): 371–97; and 'The Relationship of

Bodies: A Nuptial Hermeneutics of Same Sex Unions', *Theology and Sexuality*, 8 (1998): 96–112. See also Eugene F. Rogers, *Sexuality and the Christian Body* (Oxford: Blackwell, 1999).

82 For the following argument see Dale B. Martin, *The Corinthian Body* (New Haven and London: Yale University Press, 1995), pp. 198–228.

83 1 Corinthians 7.9.

84 1 Thessalonians 4.3–5.

85 Martin, *Corinthian Body*, p. 217.

86 Martin, *Corinthian Body*, p. 215.

87 Augustine, *The City of God*, translated by Henry Bettenson (Harmondsworth: Penguin Books, 1972), bk XIV, ch. 26 (p. 591). For an illustration of the Augustinian ideal – the ever-obedient penis – see the performance of Dirk Diggler's (Mark Wahlberg) member in Paul Thomas Anderson's film *Boogie Nights* (USA 1997). Augustine imagines paradisal or edenic sex as purely instrumental, which is to say, as *perverse sex*, since it is precisely such sex – practised in pornography, prostitution and Pauline marriage – that the Law prohibits. The story of the Fall is then a phantasmatic narrative that institutes passionless instrumental sex (procreative/recreative/cultic) as that which is lost and subsequently forbidden. See Slavoj Žižek, *The Plague of Fantasies* (London: Verso, 1997), pp. 13–16.

88 Martin, *Corinthian Body*, p. 216.

Figure 7 The Unholy Family

Claudia (Kirsten Dunst), Louis (Brad Pitt) and Lestat (Tom Cruise) in *Interview with the Vampire* (Neil Jordan, USA 1994). Photo: British Film Institute.

Chapter 7

WANT OF FAMILY

> That morning I was not yet a vampire, and I saw my last sunrise. I remember it completely, and yet I can't recall any sunrise before it. I watched the whole magnificence of the dawn for the last time as if it were the first. And then I said farewell to sunlight, and set out to become what I became.

These lines are spoken by the vampire Louis (Brad Pitt) to the young journalist Malloy (Christian Slater) near the beginning of Neil Jordan's *Interview with the Vampire* (USA 1994). Vampires cannot live in sunlight; it burns them to ash. But it took more than light to kill a vampire at the end of the nineteenth century, in Bram Stoker's *Dracula* (1897). Then the offices and accoutrements of the church were also necessary; holy prayers, blessed crucifixes and consecrated hosts. But in more Godless times, the sun, a natural bleach, is sufficient.[1] However, while vampires shun the light, they may yet be in want of its comfort, of its warmth and illumination, its life. Louis is one such vampire, a dark angel with a human soul. He can still remember a different way of living.

As Louis describes the last sunrise he saw, we see him looking towards the faint outline of the sun, as it seeks to penetrate the mists of the Mississippi. It appears as a dismal orange orb, a clearly artificial light on a Pinewood sound-stage. A theatrical effect, photographically displayed, it is a nice conceit, for at the end of the film Louis will again have sight of the sun, when he goes to the cinema.

> A mechanical wonder allowed me to see the sunrise for the first time in two hundred years. And what sunrises! Seen as the human eye could never see them. Silver at first, then, as the years progressed, in tones of purple, red and my long-lost blue.

Louis goes within in order to see what is without, from F.W. Murnau's grey *Sunrise* (USA 1927) to Robert Towne's *Tequila Sunrise* (USA 1988).[2] In the darkness of the cinema-cave he again sees the sun, and more than the sun. For these solar rays are symbolic of a life before death, before and beyond the living death that is Louis' life. They show him another way of living, another way of being, seen as the human eye could never see it.

The story of Louis at the cinema provides us with a secular parable for the congregation in the church, for the people who have gone within in order to see what is without, to see the world as the human eye could otherwise never see it: as redeemed creation.[3] And if we watch the story of the vampire from within the ecclesiacinema, we will find in it another parable – at least one other parable – for family life in post/modern culture.[4] For above all, Louis yearns for the familiality of humankind, and Louis is the spirit of the age – as the vampire Armand tells him – 'at odds with everything'.[5]

Inversions

Armand reveals to Louis that most vampires are trapped in the time of their mortal death. Vampires are always as they were, but the world is not, it changes around them. It becomes unknown and unknowable. The vampire's 'immortality becomes a penitential sentence in a madhouse of figures and forms that are hopelessly unintelligible and without value'. Then 'nothing remains to offer freedom from such despair except the act of killing'.[6] And in despair the vampire will, one day, go out to die, to vanish away. Armand hopes to save himself from such despair through Louis, who will allow him to understand the modern world. 'I must make contact with the modern age . . . [a]nd I can do this through you . . . you are the spirit, you are the heart.'[7] Louis protests: 'I have never belonged anywhere with anyone at any time.' But such dislocation is the spirit of the age, of a world out of joint. 'Everyone else feels as you feel', Armand tells him. 'Your fall from grace and faith has been the fall of a century.'[8]

Armand and Louis are talking of the nineteenth century, but they might as well be talking of the twentieth, or indeed the twenty-first century; of the modern age that began to fragment as soon as it was formed.[9] If the hero is a character of the modern age, then so is the antihero. Modernity is both the project of making oneself and the failure to do so.[10] Louis' inability to understand himself is the inability of a culture. The condition of the vampire is the post/modern condition, for when the future has fallen into the present, we can have no sense of where we are going, and so no sense of whom we are or may be. There is no future from which the self can arrive. Now we, when we are post/modern, are all like Louis, endlessly feeding upon one another as of necessity, without hope of a different future. We seek solace in melancholia, a weakening regret for what has been. And the family does not escape this condition.

The vampire is in him or herself a parodic character, an inversion. The vampire figures the 'invert' of nineteenth-century sexology, who threatens to infect normal men and women with forbidden desires, unnameable lusts.[11] When, in Dracula's castle, Jonathan Harker is confronted by three strange women – with 'brilliant white teeth, that shone like pearls against the ruby of their voluptuous lips' – he finds himself both fearing and yearning for their embrace. 'I felt in my heart a wicked, burning desire that they would kiss me with those red lips.'[12]

> The fair girl advanced and bent over me till I could feel the movement of her breath upon me. . . . I was afraid to raise my eyelids, but looked out and saw perfectly under the lashes . . . There was a deliberate voluptuousness which was both thrilling and repulsive, and as she arched her neck she actually licked her lips like an animal, till I could see in the moonlight the moisture shining on the scarlet lips and on the red tongue as it lipped the white sharp teeth . . . Then the skin of my throat began to tingle as one's flesh does when the hand that is to tickle it approaches nearer – nearer. I could feel the soft, shivering touch of the lips on the supersensitive skin of my throat, and the hard dents of two sharp teeth, just touching and pausing there. I closed my eyes in a languorous ecstasy and waited – waited with beating heart.[13]

Just then, when Harker is on the tip of ecstasy, about to be penetrated, the scene of vampiric copulation is interrupted by the arrival of the Count himself, a furious and jealous lover. 'How dare you touch him, any of you? How dare you cast eyes on him when I had forbidden it? Back, I tell you all! This man belongs to me!'[14] Harker has unknowingly wanted what is most improper for his sex, to be ravished rather than to ravish, and, as Dracula's arrival insinuates, he has wanted to be taken by a man, by the vampire who is present in all his offspring.[15] 'Then horror overcame me, and I sank down unconscious.'[16] The Count carries Harker to his room, undresses him and puts him to bed.

The 'invert' vampire is coded by another inversion, in which he appears as the opposite of Christ and his offer of eternal life. For like Christ, the vampire's blood brings salvation, resurrection to everlasting life. When Dracula appears to Jonathan Harker's wife, Mina, and makes her drink the blood spurting from his breast, as many saints have drunk from the wound in Christ's side, it is clear that she is to be a new Eve, sprung from the side of Dracula. 'And you', Dracula says to her, 'are now to me, flesh of my flesh; blood of my blood; kin of my kin; my bountiful wine-press for a while; and shall be later on my companion and my helper.'[17] But vampiric life is a living death, a complete stasis, for the vampire cannot change. Vampire immortality is the very opposite of God's eternity, in which the desiring soul is drawn forever onwards, into the always transcendent mystery of the triune life. And this contrast between the static and the dynamic proves to be the contrast between the post/modern arrival of the future and the ecclesial anticipation of that which is still to come. Thus post/modernity is itself vampiric, and the vampire's inversion undone, since now we are all vampires, when we are post/modern.

Family in Post/modernity

It would seem that family and post/modernity have little in common. On the one hand, family would seem to be about affective relationships and bonds that are generational and irreversible, establishing a person in past and future as well as in the present. Post/modernity, on the other hand, would seem to be about the continual realignment of relationships, asserting an atomistic individuality which is free to rove an infinite web of connections, without need of past or future because situated within simultaneity: everything is always-already to hand. There is truth in this contrast. However, if with Fredric Jameson we understand post/modernity as the cultural logic of consumerist or late capitalism, we must allow that post/modernity has claimed the family for its own, as it claims everything else.[18]

Long before political parties sought to sell themselves on the back of 'family values', commercial advertising had understood that it could sell its products through want of the family, through people's desire for the family they feared they lacked. Contemporary society has want of family, and both commerce and politics have an interest in sustaining that want, for in a consumer society no want can be met unless replaced with another, more voracious hunger. Families are big business.

'Family' has been and is used of many different groupings. There is, as Wittgenstein might have said, and the *Oxford English Dictionary* will confirm, a family of family meanings. For Christianity, also, there is no one proper sort of family, or rather there is, but it includes all the other sorts of family. In the light of this proper family all actual families – as we know them in history – are 'pretend' families. We will come to this one proper family at the end of the chapter, after first re/viewing three films of family life, *Dick Tracy*, *Terminator 2* and the film with which we have already begun to enter the post/modern condition of the family, *Interview with the Vampire*. These films parody the family of which we are in want.

Cartoon Comforts

Hollywood projects various images of family,[19] among them the nuclear family of father, mother and child as a subordinated trinity offering safe haven from social chaos: a world at war.[20] These trios survive amidst urban decay, deprivation and death, constituting a territory of relative calm, support and mutuality. They alone are bonded. Such families are given to group hugs.

The image of the familial three against the world appears in many different genres and to differing degrees of imaginative depth. In Warren Beatty's *Dick Tracy* (USA 1990) – an expensively staged comic strip performed by real actors – Dick Tracy (Warren Beatty) is not only the fearless cop confronting the unlawful rule of the mobster, but a hero who gathers to himself an admiring and loving family. Already able to resist the temptations of wealth and power offered to him by the mobsters, the love of a good woman also enables him to resist the seductive charms of the mobsters' moll, Breathless Mahoney – even though she comes in the form of the pop singer Madonna.

Like everything else in the film, Tracy's family is the instant production of an artist's sketch. At one moment Tracy is alone in the world, a single action hero; the next moment he has a family. His 'son' comes to him on a stormy evening as an orphan rescued from an abusing thug. There is something about the kid that leads Tracy to take him into his own home, and something about Tracy that leads the streetwise scamp to trust his new 'father'. Almost as suddenly Tracy has a 'wife' and his 'son' a 'mother', Tess Trueheart (Glenne Headly), and the three are pictured in the local diner, discussing their problems and those of the city, their affection for one another inarticulate but palpable. It is a dream family conjured from nowhere, instantly produced without labour.

Tracy gathers his family to him because he is an action hero, able to fight violence with violence. The bond between father and son is established as the latter excitedly watches Tracy shooting numerous hoodlums, riddling their cars with bullets. The bond between husband and wife is ensured because she knows that while her man is gentle at home he is tough on the streets, able to secure desired domesticity. Mayhem reigns outside the home, and while Tracy will always be drawn out there – as he is at the end of the film – he will also always return, his venturing the condition of the home for which he fights.

Nuclear Territory

Similar themes are present in more adult action yarns – more adult because the terror that is society outside the home is portrayed more extensively, imaginatively and expensively, and because the terror now reaches into the home itself. The family visibly struggles to survive. A good example of this fearful fantasy is James Cameron's *Terminator 2: Judgement Day* (USA 1991). As the title suggests this is a sequel to Cameron's earlier film, *The Terminator* (USA 1985), in fact a remake of that film, with Arnold Schwarzenegger reprising his role as the cyborg T800 (now reprogrammed for 'good' rather than 'evil').[21] The new terminator of the second film, the cyborg T1000, is a virtually indestructible killing machine, brought into the present from the future, from beyond Armageddon. But this future – in which the world is laid waste, and the last remnants of humanity are hunted down by the machines of its own making – is already our present. The film not only projects the possibility of nuclear holocaust – scenes of which are some of the most spectacular in the film – but also shows us images of present social disorder as the condition of that holocaust. The killing machine from the future comes to a world already violent; the world we think already too real beyond the comforting warmth of the cinema's auditorium.

Against the terror, *Terminator 2*, like *Dick Tracy*, conjures an almost instantaneous family. But Schwarzenegger's family is materially grounded in a way that Tracy's family is not. The child is the fruit of his mother's womb, and we are left in no doubt that she has laboured to rear her offspring. But once joined by Schwarzenegger as their adoptive father/husband, they constitute a similar family territory to that in *Dick Tracy*, except that while Tracy remains the sole protector of his family, Schwarzenegger's 'wife', Sarah Connor (Linda Hamilton), is almost as violent as himself. In the world of the terminator all members of the family must fight if they are to maintain a territory in which the habits of the heart may be nurtured.

Cameron's film has mythic pretensions. His family is not set simply against a world of gangsterism, but against a world on its way to nuclear holocaust; nor does it stand simply for the territory of the familial, for home comforts, but for the whole world, perhaps even for the world as home and humanity as family. This is because Cameron's family has the possibility of changing the future that otherwise leads to the destruction of humanity. Cameron's family is the holy family that brings salvation. The conceit of time travel – of heroes and villains coming from the future – allows Cameron to place the holy family of Nazareth in a sci-fi world of the late twentieth century. Cameron's holy child, John Connor (Edward Furlong), is literally fathered from the future. The child will grow up to defeat the future killing machines, just so long as they do not kill him first. Thus they send a machine from the future to destroy him, as do the last survivors of humanity to protect him. It is the story of a child saviour, beset by demons and protected by angels.

The families of *Dick Tracy* and *Terminator 2* are without substance, not simply because they must finally serve the constraints of their genres – the comic-strip and the action-yarn – but because they have no basis or support outside of themselves. Set against a violent world, there is nothing in that world that can account for their appearance. As a consequence they offer no real alternative to it. They are unable to imagine any other way of being than as the world is: they cannot imagine an alternative to violence. This is most evident in Cameron's film, whose saviour and holy family contrast markedly with the family from Nazareth, which not only flees but finally refuses violence as a possibility.

While Cameron's film is not alone in failing to imagine any alternative to violence – it is perhaps impossible for Hollywood to do so – it nevertheless articulates the want of a such a possibility in western society, and constructs this want, this lack and desire, as the possibility of the nuclear family. An altogether more thoughtful and disturbing projection of such a want is found in Jordan's *Interview with the Vampire.*

At Home with the Vampire

Interview with the Vampire opens and closes in contemporary San Francisco and in between takes us from eighteenth-century slave-owning New Orleans to nineteenth-century bohemian Paris; the decadence of Huysmans' *Là-Bas* (1891).[22] It tells the story of Louis, who shortly after the death of his young wife in childbirth, meets the vampire Lestat (Tom Cruise). The vampire, having witnessed Louis' suicidal despair, offers him the choice of death or immortality; though it is no more a choice than the rest of us have about being born.[23] Louis accepts immortality, little comprehending that it is the stasis of life: a living death. Louis will remain forever as he was at the moment of his human death and vampiric rebirth. While he is now immortal he has no future, no possibility of change and thus no possibility of redemption. He is condemned to the endless repetition of death in life, surviving as he does on the blood of the living.

In the course of the story Lestat 'saves' the life of Claudia (Kirsten Dunst), an abandoned child of five years old in the novel, somewhat older in the film, who is in danger of dying from the plague. Lestat makes her like himself: an immortal vampire. The anguish of endless life without a future, without hope, is most poignant in her. As the years pass her body remains that of the child she was when she died to mortal life. She will never grow up, never become like one of the young women, the young whores, whose blood satiates Lestat's hunger. She will always look like one of the white-faced china dolls she avidly collects. In one scene she tries to deny her perpetual infancy by cutting off her hair, only to find her golden locks immediately regrown. She is terrifyingly trapped within her immature flesh. Like Wilde's Dorian Gray, her face will hardly show her atrophying, monstrous soul.[24] Only her interests and attitudes will betray her aging heart. '[M]ore and more her doll-like face seemed to possess two totally aware adult eyes, and innocence seemed lost somewhere with neglected toys and the loss of a certain patience.'

> There was something dreadfully sensual about her lounging on the settee in a tiny nightgown of lace and stitched pearls; she became an eerie and powerful seductress, her voice as clear and sweet as ever, though it had a resonance which was womanish, a sharpness sometimes that proved shocking.[25]

Lestat creates this strange girl-woman to be a companion for Louis, so that Louis will remain Lestat's companion. Soon after Lestat has made Claudia a vampire by giving her his blood to drink, and taught her how to drink from the living, he tells her that she is now his and Louis' daughter. 'One happy family.' He is the vampiric father, the fount of the other two, with his blood coursing through their veins. This vampire family is the bogey family of the 'moral majority': a homosexual couple with an adopted child – though they are of course blood relatives.[26]

Jordan's film considerably weakens the homoeroticism of Rice's novel, which explicitly renders the covert desire in Stoker's *Dracula*.[27] Her vampires penetrate (bite) men as well as women; and some of her men want to be bitten. 'For vampires, physical love culminates and is satisfied in one thing, the kill.'[28] But the kill is sex. In the novel Armand keeps a mortal and willing catamite, whom he shares with Louis.

> Never had I felt this, never had I experienced it, this yielding of a conscious mortal. But before I could push him away for his own sake, I saw the bluish bruise on his tender neck. He was offering it to me. He was pressing the length of his body against me now, and I felt the hard strength of his sex beneath his clothes pressing against my leg. A wretched gasp escaped my lips, but he bent close, his lips on what must have been so cold, so lifeless for him; and I sank my teeth into his skin, my body rigid, that hard sex driving against me, and I lifted him in passion off the floor. Wave after wave of his beating heart passed into me as, weightless, I rocked with him, devouring him, his ecstasy, his conscious pleasure.[29]

In the film this moment of weightless ecstasy is transferred to Lestat's seduction of Louis. As the vampire bites, he and his victim fly up into the air. But Pitt looks less than ecstatic at being bitten. Armand's catamite also remains in the film (played by Louis Lewis-Smith) – but he offers his hand rather than his neck for drinking, and he does not swoon in 'conscious pleasure'. Banderas does caress Pitt's cheek with the back of his hand, and tells him that he is beautiful. 'A vampire with a human soul. An immortal with a mortal's passion.' But though this signals the desire between Louis and Armand, it is barely shown. Instead the film focuses on what is also one of the central concerns of the novel, the familial relationships between the three central vampires, and especially between Louis and Claudia – father and daughter.

In Jordan's film, as in Beatty's and Cameron's, we have a family that constitutes a territory of affection and mutuality, set against a hostile world. And like the other families, the vampiric family is violent, destroying to survive. Yet unlike the other families, violence does not seem forced upon them through a necessary engagement with the world, but emerges from within the family as of its nature. Lestat seeks to ease Claudia's unhappy conscience by arguing that it is simply in the nature of the vampire to feed upon the living; it can do no other.

Jordan's film represents a distrust of the nuclear family that the other films do not. Here the family is the unholy family. Each of its members is born into immortal – but not eternal – life through his or her own death. It parodies not so much the family of Nazareth, as heaven's triune family, with Louis begotten of Lestat, and Claudia the love that proceeds from and between both. Just before Lestat turns Claudia into a vampire, he tells Louis that 'God kills indiscriminately and so shall we. For no creature under God is as we are. None so like him as ourselves.'[30] Then Lestat offers Claudia to Louis as a 'gift', as a companion to ease his loneliness, and perhaps Lestat's also. Though monstrous, the initial relationships between Lestat, Louis and Claudia, and then just between Louis and Claudia, constitute the only mutualities displayed in the film. That these relationships offer nostalgia in place of hope, suggests that even these last vestiges of humanity will soon disappear.

With Hollywood as our guide, the nuclear family in post/modernity appears as a nostalgic enclave, a haven against a violent and terrifying world, a territory in which mutual bonds of affection are still possible, but only just. In *Dick Tracy* the family is a confident possibility, in *Terminator 2* it has to struggle for survival; but in *Interview with the Vampire* it is already invaded by the forces it would resist. It is this recognition that makes the latter film more insightful than the others, since they display but do not recognize families predicated upon destruction. On this reading, post/modernity does not perceive the family as a real alternative to a feared and fearful society; at best it is a barricade against the wider terror. Where then might we look for an alternative family?

The Holy Family

In 1893 Pope Leo XIII instituted the Feast of the Holy Family on the third Sunday after Epiphany. It was reassigned to the first Sunday after Epiphany in 1920, and in 1969 it was moved again to the first Sunday after Christmas. The family feasted is that of Nazareth – Jesus, Mary and Joseph. But it is also the family as such, as an ideal of Christian life. Christian devotion to the Holy Family of Nazareth promotes and protects the family in society. This is evident, for example, in the work of the Sons of the Holy Family, a congregation of priests and brothers founded in 1864 to 'promote devotion to the Holy Family and to foster true Christian family life'. As the *New Catholic Encyclopaedia* notes, this apostolate is 'accomplished through the education of youth and the organization of a family movement consisting of instruction in the faith and in the management of the ideal Catholic home'.[31]

The nineteenth century saw the founding of many such congregations,[32] ecclesiastical sororities and fraternities that sought to foster family life through education and through care of those not otherwise supported by families. For them the Holy Family is the family of piety, both as pictured in devotion to Jesus, Mary and Joseph, and as practised in the care of others.

They promote the life of the Holy Family through their own in the life of others. Yet at the same time they refuse to constitute the sort of family they promote; they refuse marriage and the production of children. They themselves are family insofar as they are the brothers and sisters of Jesus, and thus members of the Holy Family; but they are not family insofar as they have denied themselves the possibility of producing children. They are devoted to the reproduction of a family that at the same time they refuse for themselves. Nor is this the only anomaly between the three families they seek to relate, for the Holy Family is itself unlike their own congregational families. While the Holy Family is celibate, as are the congregations, it remains heterosexual in a way that the homosocial congregations do not. The Holy Family also maintains a fleshly relationship between mother and son that is only figural in the ('spiritual') offspring of the mediating brother and sisterhoods.

As the dates for the founding of these brotherly and sisterly congregations suggest, the families they refuse for themselves are very much nineteenth century constructions, both the Holy Family of Nazareth and the ideal of Christian family. As such these families were not only in the province of the Catholic Church, but were more widespread in Christian society, as shown in the discussion of both families – the Nazarene and the ideal – in the work of the philosopher Hegel at the beginning of the nineteenth century.[33]

For Hegel, in his lectures on aesthetics (1823–9), the Holy Family is the 'absolutely ideal subject' for the concrete representation in art of 'love *reconciled* and at peace with itself'.[34] The Holy Family is the site of a spiritual love without taint of sensuous desire or self-interest. This is seen especially in the relation of the Virgin Mother to her child.

> The natural depth of feeling in the mother's love is altogether spiritualized; it has the Divine as its proper content, but this spirituality remains lowly and unaware, marvellously penetrated by natural oneness and human feeling . . . a pure forgetfulness and complete self-surrender which still in this forgetfulness is from the beginning one with that into which it is merged and now with blissful satisfaction has a sense of this oneness.[35]

In the *Philosophy of Right* (1821) loving union is central to Hegel's idea of the family as such. The family is 'characterized by love', such that in the family a person experiences individuality 'not as an independent person but as a member'.[36] Marriage, in its ethical and objective aspect, is that act of self-restriction in which a person is paradoxically liberated through union with another. It is the transformation of contingency – dynastic alliance or sexual desire – into substantive self-consciousness. As such it is a love like that of the Madonna for her child, a spiritual union that transcends self-interest.

> The ethical aspect of marriage consists in the parties' consciousness of . . . unity as their substantive aim, and so in their love, trust, and common sharing of their entire existence as individuals. When the parties are in this frame of mind and their union is actual, their physical passion sinks to the level of a physical moment, destined to vanish in its very satisfaction. On the other hand, the spiritual bond of union secures its rights as the substance of marriage and thus rises, inherently indissoluble, to a plane above the contingency of passion and the transience of particular caprice.[37]

In its essence, marriage is not a contract, since contract is a relation between individuals as 'self-subsistent units'. Marriage transcends such a relationship, forming one 'ethical mind': the family as 'one person', one substance, whose members are its accidents. It is in this unity that the 'religious character of marriage and the family, or *pietas*, is grounded'. This idea of marriage and family as an ethical unity does not deny or denigrate the physical or sensuous, but puts it 'into its ethical place as something only consequential and accidental, belonging to the external embodiment of the ethical bond, which indeed can subsist exclusively in reciprocal love and support.'[38]

For Hegel marriage is not simply one possibility among others, but an 'objectively appointed end', such that it is 'our ethical duty to enter the married state'.[39] This is because the difference and union of the sexes has a 'rational' basis in the ethical 'concept' as it 'internally sunders itself in order that its vitality may become a concrete unity consequent upon this difference'.[40] Thus the ethical concept, in its Hegelian history, dirempts itself between the two sexes. It is perhaps unremarkable that in this diremption between universality and particularity, there is found a philosophical basis for patriarchal gendering, so that 'man has his actual substantive life in the state, in learning, and so forth', while woman finds 'her substantive destiny in the family'.[41] In marriage these differences or personalities are surrendered to one another, such that each comes to know itself in knowing the other.[42] Hegel founds both monogamy and exogamy in the 'mutual, whole-hearted' surrender of one to another in the marriage union. It is an absolute and exclusive surrender of oneself to another, thus ruling out other partners and a partner like oneself: 'for individuals in the same circle of relationship have no special personality of their own in contrast with that of others in the same circle'.[43]

While the Hegelian idea of marriage as difference-in-unity seems to indicate a certain mutuality between the surrendering parties, it nevertheless remains skewed. As Hegel notes, the unity of marriage is 'only a unity of inwardness or disposition; in outward existence . . . the unity is sundered in the two parties'.[44] Man, labouring and struggling in the external world, may have to fight to gain a 'self-subsistent unity with himself', but he can always find a 'tranquil intuition of this unity' in the family, where 'he lives a subjective ethical life on the plane of feeling'. But there is no suggestion that woman, in her turn, might engage in the external world: her destiny is the family.[45] Thus the lines are drawn between world and family, public and private; and while man might labour in one and find haven in the other, woman knows only her domesticity.

The Hegelian philosophy both establishes the liberal division of public and private, and shows why the latter could never have the influence on the former that the former has on the latter. As Laura Gellott notes, in nineteenth-century liberal polity the family 'served not only as a counterweight to the vicissitudes and the amorality of public society, it was the source of moral formation, emotional satisfaction and renewal for individuals. Separate from the public sphere and sheltered within the walls of the home, the family would shape individuals equipped to venture forth daily to do battle in the marketplace and the political assembly.'[46] Here we are not so very far from the territory of the Hollywood family in *Dick Tracy*; and just as the cartoon family cannot finally resist the violence it holds at bay, so the bourgeois family succumbs to the marketplace outside its door. It becomes one more institution that serves, rather than counters 'the interests of atomistic individuals'.[47] This outcome is presaged in Hegel's idea of the family 'as person', as the unity of an unequal diremption.

Papal Families and Paranoia

Pope John Paul II, in his exhortation *Familiaris Consortio* (1981), presents a picture of the family in some conformity with the Hegelian unity, and thus the family of nineteenth-century liberalism. Like Hegel, the Pope is concerned to go beyond mere appearance and discern the innermost truths of marriage and family, but now rooted in the will of God rather than the motor of the Hegelian 'mind'. Like Hegel, however, these truths consist in the possibility of a man and woman so totally surrendered to one another that they constitute a harmonious unity and secure a real freedom in fidelity.[48] Marriage 'aims at a deeply personal unity, the unity that, beyond union in one flesh, leads to forming one heart and soul; it demands indissolubility and faithfulness in definitive mutual giving; and it is open to fertility'.[49] As with Hegel, the totality and exclusivity of this unity rules out polygamy;[50] and as with Hegel this unity is constituted between different but complementary personalities. This unity is rooted in the will of God, expressed in the Genesis creation story and in the analogy between the relation of Christ and church to that of husband and wife. Marriage is the type of Christ's 'spousal covenant' with his church.[51] This analogy means that the pope is in danger of reproducing that imbalance of man to woman that we find in Hegel's conceptuality.[52]

If both the Hegelian and papal families are finally patriarchal in structure, the family of the latter achieves a degree of openness lacking in the former. While both conceive the family as a unified territory, the Pope insists on the family as a community in a way that opens it to a wider conception of the family than the merely nuclear. 'In matrimony and in the family a complex of interpersonal relationships is set up – married life, fatherhood and motherhood, filiation and fraternity – through which each human person is introduced into the "human family" and into the "family of God", which is the Church.'[53] The idea of community allows the family to exceed the triangular structure of the nuclear family, and returns it to an earlier conception of family as household.[54] While the 'communion of the family, of parents and children, of brothers and sisters with each other, of relatives and other members of the household' is still rooted in 'conjugal communion',[55] the family is understood to be animated by a wider communality. 'The Christian family constitutes a specific revelation and realization of ecclesial communion, and for this reason too it can and should be called "the domestic Church".'[56] Reconceiving the family as household, and the household as a localization of the ecclesial community, serves to broaden the space of the familial, opening it to an indeterminate number of historically contingent instantiations. However, there is a darker side to papal thinking about the family, which, when taken with its patriarchalism, renders it seriously flawed.

Laura Gellott identifies the flaw as a lack of inclusivity.[57] Just as Hegel sought to render marriage and family as a metaphysical necessity, so papal teaching posits marriage and family as the divinely willed *telos* of human life. Of course it allows for certain exceptions, such as the Pope himself. 'Christian revelation recognizes two specific ways of realizing the vocation of the human person, in its entirety, to love: marriage and virginity or celibacy.'[58] Outside of these possibilities, love is not really love. Yet there is love outside of these possibilities, to which gay men and lesbian women testify. But their vocation to love is effectively denied by the church. Indeed, they may be called upon to 'sacrifice' their love in the name of love. Thus Cardinal Joseph Ratzinger urges 'homosexual persons' to 'enact the will of God in their life by joining whatever sufferings and difficulties they experience in virtue of their condition to the sacrifice of the Lord's Cross'.[59]

The idea of the Christian family turns sour when it ceases to promote the dispossession necessary for receiving God's gifts, including the gift of children, and is instead used to attack those whom the idea itself is supposed to exclude and construct as 'threat'. This is when the practice of familial virtues becomes the ideological promotion of 'family values'. Thus Cardinal Ratzinger constructs the homosexual as the enemy of the family, arguing that the equal valuing of homo- and heterosexual relations 'has a direct impact on society's understanding of the nature and rights of the family and puts them in jeopardy'.[60] In a similar – though more viciously paranoiac – way, the Ramsey Colloquium, an American group of Jewish and Christian writers, including priests and rabbis, constructs homosexuals as libertines, who, allied with proponents of abortion, adultery, divorce and feminism, threaten 'innumerable individuals' and 'our common life'.[61]

Faced with such shameful attitudes, shamelessly expressed, it is important to learn that the church has no long-term interest in the heterosexual family, either nuclear or extended. The family of which the Church is in want is altogether different. The pope's model of the extended conjugal community or household – as advocated in *Familiaris Consortio* – points us in the direction of this family. But it will only come into view when our idea of the family no longer starts out from the procreating heterosexual couple, but from the properly theological space of Christ's ever extending kin, the family of Christ's friends. And this space comes into view when we consider its fulfilment in the heavenly household, in which there are many mansions.[62]

Heavenly Families

Are there families in heaven? In Matthew 22.30, Jesus tells the Sadducees that in heaven there is no marriage, for people are then like angels. This has proved a protean text for speculation on post-mortem existence. The medieval mind was much concerned with the nature of the resurrection body, and in this followed Augustine, who worried about what would and would not be raised. Caroline Walker Bynum provides a useful conspectus of his questions:

> Will aborted foetuses rise? Will Siamese twins be two people or one in the resurrection? Will we all be the same sex in heaven? the same height and weight? the same age? Will we have to eat? Will we be able to eat? Will deformities and mutilations appear in heaven? Will nail and hair clippings all return to the body to which they originally belonged? Will men have beards in their resurrected bodies? Will we 'see' in heaven only when our eyes are open? Will we rise with all our internal organs as well as our external organs?[63]

It would seem that Augustine thought we might all be raised aged thirty, and that we will be raised with our internal and external organs, including our sexual organs, they being part of our perfection.[64] But while we will have our genitals, we will not enjoy the use to which we put them at present, for while the body, in all its particulars is important for our salvific identity, its processes must be arrested, for process is change and change is decay. Tertullian was certain that we will have mouths but not eat, genitals but not copulate. 'Such organs will have no function in the resurrection, but they will survive for the sake of beauty. We will not chew in heaven, but we will have teeth, because we would look funny without them.'[65] Origen, on the other hand, said that we will not have age or sex, for in heaven there is no growth, excretion or copulation. We may not even remember the relationships we have enjoyed or endured in this life.[66]

Speculation on our future state is not an idle exercise, for thinking about how we will be is thinking about how we are, from the perspective of our eternal destiny. Christian thought on the present is not complete until it is thought from the future, as if retrospectively, eschatologically. Karl Barth's theology of marriage and family is an attempt to think these realities from the future, from the eschatological event of Jesus Christ. In doing so, Barth displays a very different view of these matters from that of John Paul II. For the latter marriage is given for procreation, for biological family. 'The biblical account [in Genesis] speaks of God's *instituting marriage* as an indispensable condition for the transmission of life to new generations, the transmission of life to which marriage and conjugal love are by their nature ordered: "Be fruitful and multiply, and fill the earth and subdue it" (Genesis 1.28).'[67] For Barth, however, marriage is commanded for some as their vocation to love. 'There is no necessity of nature nor general divine law in virtue of which every man is permitted or commanded to take a wife, or every women a husband. If this is permitted and commanded, it is a special distinction, a special divine calling, a gift and grace.'[68] And procreation, though natural, is an inessential part of marriage. The latter is not given for the former.

> In the sphere of the New Testament message there is no necessity, no general command, to continue the human race as such and therefore to procreate children . . . *Post Christum natum* there can be no question of a divine law in virtue of which all these things must necessarily take place. On the contrary, it is one of the consolations of the coming kingdom and expiring time that this anxiety about posterity . . . is removed from us all by the fact that the Son on whose birth alone everything seriously and ultimately depended has now been born and has now become our Brother. No one now has to be conceived and born . . . Parenthood is now only to be understood as a free and in some sense optional gift of the goodness of God.[69]

For Barth there is finally only one proper family: the extended space of the church. This family space is constituted by Christ, who acts as brother and friend to all. His father is everyone's father, and his mother – at least in a non-Barthian Catholic rendition – is everyone's mother also. Thus while Barth devotes many pages to the subject of parents and children, he refuses to discuss the 'family' as such.

> In the more limited sense particularly the idea of the family is of no interest at all for Christian theology . . . When the New Testament speaks of a 'house', it means the *familia* in the comprehensive sense of a household fellowship which can become the centre of the message heard and reproduced in the wider life of the community . . . Parents and children are still emphasized, like men and women, masters and servants, but as persons and for the sake of their personal connections and duties. The family collective as such plays no further part at all.[70]

Barth's teaching on the family reminds us that in Christian thought the territory of the family, especially the nuclear family, is already passing away with the coming of Christ and the one family of heaven. Or, to put it more vividly, the vampiric family is ceasing to parody the nuclear family – as in the fevered imaginations of sacred congregations and holy colloquia – and is becoming an analogy for the Christian family which grows through sharing the bread and passing the cup; eating the flesh and drinking the blood.

There are two points to stress about the coming heavenly family. The first is that it is precisely that, a family that is *arriving but is not yet here*, just as the old world, with its various earthly families, is *passing but has not yet gone*. It is only in the proleptic presence of the heavenly household in Jesus Christ that we begin to live ahead of the future that is not yet fully arrived. The Church, as has often been said, lives in the interim, in the Saturday between the Friday and the Sunday, between the ascension and the parousia. It lives in hope.

Christians are always seeking new ways to live the coming household now, new ways of being the heavenly family on earth, one of the most striking of which has been the monastic movement, which has sought to recognize all as brothers or sisters in Christ, and to imitate that asexuality which the medievals, following the teaching of Jesus, believed part of heavenly joy. Thus what Pope John Paul II calls 'consecrated virginity or celibacy' is not so much a renunciation for the sake of the Kingdom as the enactment of the Kingdom in the sphere of sexuality. As the Pope writes, the celibate 'anticipates in his or her flesh the new world of the future resurrection'.[71] Such celibacy is denial only because heavenly life is not now natural to us, who still live in the old, unreal world.

The church has always deemed celibacy more perfect than conjugality, being a more perfect living of heavenly life. As John Paul II writes, the church 'has always defended the superiority of this charism [celibacy] to that of marriage, by reason of the wholly singular link which it has with the Kingdom of God'.[72] And yet we might still wonder about this 'wholly singular link'. Why is asexuality deemed such an important aspect of heavenly life that the denial of sexuality in this life must be thought 'superior' to its practice? Is the denial of sexuality any closer to the asexuality of heaven, than is the embrace of sexuality in this life?

Post/modernity, as the culture of consumer capitalism, has claimed the family as its own; but it has done more than this. It has claimed the heavenly family also. Indeed post/modernity is the family of heaven now, a realized eschatology. The family of heaven is radically egalitarian, for everyone has the same father and mother, and each is the brother or sister of all. In the same way post/modernity imagines a radical equality of relationships, an ideology which is perhaps nowhere more evident than in the discourse of the computer internet, of cyberspace and virtual reality. And just as the heavenly family dissolves all earthly hierarchies and familial bonds, so post/modernity renders everything and everyone an equal consumer and consumable, such that sexual and family ties are infinitely variable: if you can think of a new way to connect then connect. Promiscuity, which is the logic of post/modernity, is one realization of the heavenly family. If everyone is a family member, then all sexual relations are incestuous, and either no one or everyone may have sex with anyone else.[73] Both options have been tried in Christian history. The fraternal and sororal congregations represent the first option, and sexual congress between such spiritual brothers and sisters was once clearly understood as incestuous, as when Thomas More denounced Martin Luther's marriage to Catherine von Bora as 'shameful inceste and abominable lychrye'. On the other hand there were those Christians who took to heart St Paul's teaching that 'all things are lawful', and practised sibling incest, free in the Spirit from guilt. As Marc Shell notes, the difference between the celibate brothers and sisters and those Brethren of the Free Spirit that are said to have flourished between the thirteenth and seventeenth centuries, is but a polar opposition or inversion of the same logic.

> A celibate in the normative orders gracefully overcomes sexual desire and loves everyone (the same) as universal siblings; a libertine in the Brethren of the Free Spirit gracefully overcomes sexual desire or conscience and loves everyone (as the same). For both groups, sexual intercourse with a sibling is no worse or better than sexual intercourse with any other person. The religious celibate seeks liberty from physical desire; the libertine seeks liberty from rules that restrict physical intercourse. But for both, in the words of Saint Paul, 'Where the Spirit of the Lord is, there is liberty' (2 Corinthians 3.17).[74]

Post/modernity simply follows through on the libertine's interpretation of familial love. Post/modern promiscuity is in its root Christian eschatology, an understanding of present society as now already the heavenly family in which all siblings may love all other siblings, freed from the taboo of incest through the spirit of infinite consumption. Post/modernity does not wait for the coming of the heavenly household but instantiates it now already, perversely as we may think.

But where does the perversity lie? Is it in opting for promiscuity rather than celibacy, or rather is it in thinking sexuality the 'wholly singular thing' about the heavenly household? Might it not be that what matters about the heavenly family are forms of relationship other than the merely sexual, so that the presumed absence of the latter cannot be made the mark, the defining characteristic, of the blessed state? Might it not be that the heavenly family arrives through those relationships of fidelity and dispossession that render sexuality a means rather than an end in itself? This distinction would then mark the difference between post/modernity and churchly practice, for when the post/modern heaven has arrived there is no longer an end in view, a point beyond. The end is the means.

The church, on the other hand, still prays for an end that has not yet arrived, knowing that neither asceticism nor libertinism can be ends in themselves. Moreover, the church knows that it cannot finally imagine the heavenly family, but must await its arrival, discerning the signs of God that are its anticipation. The church seeks to promote the family insofar as the family seeks to repeat in its own circumstances the family of heaven. There is thus no one sort of earthly family that repeats the heavenly; but all families that listen for the command of God in faithful trust, already, in some measure, participate in the household of heaven.

Notes

1 See further Nina Auerbach, *Our Vampires, Ourselves* (Chicago: University of Chicago Press, 1995), pp. 119–47.

2 We also see clips from F.W. Murnau's *Nosferatu* (Germany 1922), Victor Fleming's *Gone with the Wind* (USA 1939) and Richard Donner's *Superman* (UK 1978) – with Christopher Reeves circling the globe, from behind which the sun is rising.

3 See above chapter 2 (Seeing in the Dark).

4 The forward slash in 'post/modern' reminds us that the postmodern condition is really only an intensification of certain modern interests and practices. Only theology can imagine a genuinely postmodern state, a life lived ahead of its arrival, the *future now*. See Gerard Loughlin, *Telling God's Story: Bible, Church and Narrative Theology* (Cambridge: Cambridge University Press, 1999), ch. 1.

5 This and other lines in the scene are taken directly from Anne Rice's novel, on which the film is based. Rice wrote the screenplay for the film. See Anne Rice, *Interview with the Vampire* (London: Warner Books, [1976] 2001), p. 310. The novel is the first of the 'vampire chronicles', of which the third, *The Queen of the Damned* (1989), has also been filmed by Michael Rymer (USA 2002). The film incorporates material from the second chronicle, *The Vampire Lestat* (1985). Rymer's film has not received the same acclaim as Jordan's.

6 Rice, *Interview*, p. 306.

7 Rice, *Interview*, pp. 309–10.

8 Rice, *Interview*, p. 310. This conversation is followed closely in the film.

9 For something of this see Stephen Toulmin, *Cosmopolis: The Hidden Agenda of Modernity* (Chicago: University of Chicago Press, 1990).

10 On the heroism of modernity see Michel Foucault's discussion of Charles Baudelaire's modern dandy, who makes 'his behaviour, his feelings and passions, his very existence, a work of art'. Michel Foucault, 'What Is Enlightenment?' in *The Foucault Reader*, edited by Paul Rabinow (Harmondsworth: Penguin

Books, [1984] 1991), pp. 32–50 (pp. 41–2). It is just such an 'ironic heroization of the present, this transfiguring play of freedom with reality, this ascetic elaboration of the self' (p. 42), that Foucault seeks to carry forward in his own work and practice. We make ourselves through study of how we have been made, viewing the present as if it were already past, in order to determine the 'limits that we may go beyond' (p. 47). In this way the post/modern hero seeks to live ahead of where he is. But since he is always looking backward, while craning forward, he is always within modernity (post/modernity).

11 On the invention of the 'invert' see Gert Hekma, '"A Female Soul in a Male Body": Sexual Inversion as Gender Inversion in Nineteenth-Century Sexology', in *Third Sex, Third Gender: Beyond Sexual Dimorphism in Culture and History*, edited by Gilbert Herdt (New York: Zone Books, 1994), pp. 213–39.

12 Bram Stoker, *Dracula*, edited by Maurice Hindle (Harmondsworth: Penguin Books, [1897] 1993), ch. 3 (p. 53).

13 Stoker, *Dracula*, ch. 3 (pp. 53–4).

14 Stoker, *Dracula*, ch. 3 (p. 55).

15 See further Christopher Craft, '"Kiss Me with Those Red Lips": Gender and Inversion in Bram Stoker's *Dracula*', *Representations*, 8 (1984): 107–33.

16 Stoker, *Dracula*, ch. 3 (p. 56).

17 Stoker, *Dracula*, ch. 21 (pp. 370–1). The allusions are to Genesis 2.23 and Isaiah 63.3 – 'I have trodden the winepress alone, and from the peoples no one was with me' – which verse provided the popular medieval image of Christ in the winepress, his blood mixing with the juice of the grapes that he is trampling underfoot. Vampire blood is the inversion of Christian blood, that Dracula must first drink. For more on Christianity in *Dracula* see Christopher Herbert, 'Vampire Religion', *Representations*, 79 (2002): 100–21. Herbert argues that the novel presents Van Hesling and the Crew of Light as Christians ostensibly battling superstition, that spreads from the East like an infection. But closer inspection suggests that they may be battling within or even against Christianity, since they are as superstitious as their enemy, viewing moral purity as a physical attribute and wielding sacred wafers as magical talismen. In the Count they confront the return of Christianity's repressed blood lust. Herbert makes much play with Wesleyan hymns, and their blood imagery. But one might go back to the popularity of blood imagery in medieval piety, and thus see in Dracula the return of a repressed Catholicism. Perhaps Mina cries out because she has been made to partake in the Catholic Mass, the repugnant transubstantiation. 'Oh my God! My God! What have I done? What have I done to deserve such a fate, I who have tried to walk in meekness and righteousness all my days. God pity me!' Stoker, *Dracula*, ch. 21 (p. 371).

18 On the 'postmodern condition' see Fredric Jameson, *Postmodernism or the Cultural Logic of Late Capitalism* (London: Verso, 1991) and Graham Ward, *Cities of God* (London: Routledge, 2000).

19 See Andrew Ross, 'Cowboys, Cadillacs, and Cosmonauts: Families, Film Genres, and Technocultures', in *Engendering Men*, edited by James A. Boone and Michael Cadden (New York, 1990), pp. 87–101.

20 On why the family as 'haven' is deeply unchristian see Rodney Clapp, *Families at the Crossroads: Beyond Traditional and Modern Options* (Downers Grove: Intervarsity Press, 1993), pp. 149–69.

21 On Schwarzenegger's roles in the two films see J. Hoberman, 'Nietzsche's Boy', *Sight and Sound*, 1/5 (1991): 22–5. See also Tony Rayns' review of *Terminator 2* in the same issue (p. 51). Schwarzenegger returned to the role in *Terminator 3: Rise of the Machines* (USA 2003).

22 Joris-Karl Huysmans, *Là-Bas*, edited by Yves Hersant (Paris: Gallimard, 1985); ET *The Damned*, translated by Terry Hale (Harmondsworth: Penguin Books, 2001).

23 See further Kim Newman's review of the film in *Sight and Sound*, 5/2 (1995): 46–7.

24 Oscar Wilde, *The Picture of Dorian Gray* (London: Ward, Lock and Company, 1891).

25 Rice, *Interview*, p. 113. In the film, the relationship between Louis and Claudia is largely drained of the sexuality that is present in the book. 'At dawn she lay with me, her heart beating against my heart, and many times when I looked at her – when she was at her music or painting and didn't know I stood in the room – I thought of that singular experience I'd had with her and no other, that I had killed her, and taken her life from her, had drunk all of her life's blood in that fatal embrace I'd lavished on so many others, others who now lay moldering in the damp earth. But she lived, she lived to put her arms around my neck and press her tiny cupid's bow to my lips and put her gleaming eye to my eye until our lashes touched, and, laughing, we reeled about the room as if to the wildest waltz. Father and Daughter. Lover and Lover.' (Rice, *Interview*, p. 112.) This passage is imaged in the film, but more fraternally, less erotically.

26 Here there may be a question of how much Rice and Jordan are in danger of promoting 'homophobia', but the sexual politics are complicated because the film, at the time of its release, boasted some of Hollywood's hottest male properties – Tom Cruise, Brad Pitt, Christian Slater and Antonio Banderas. Many in the audience will have swooned with Pitt when he is bitten by Cruise, or willed the kiss that teasingly doesn't quite happen between Antonio and Brad. And yet however seductive the vampires – the reporter Molloy wants to become one after hearing Louis' story – Louis remains disturbed by his vampirism/homosexuality, though repeatedly enjoined to accept his 'nature' by Lestat and Armand.

27 On homosexuality in *Dracula* see Talia Schaffer, '"A Wilde Desire Took Me": The Homoerotic History of *Dracula*', *English Literary History*, 61 (1994): 381–425.

28 Rice, *Interview*, p. 275.

29 Rice, *Interview*, p. 248.
30 For the corresponding passage in the novel see Rice, *Interview*, p. 98.
31 L. Hoffman, 'Holy Family, Sons of the', in *The New Catholic Encyclopedia*, 15 volumes (New York: McGraw-Hill Book Company, 1967), vol. 7, p. 67.
32 The Sisters of the Holy Family of Villefranche in 1816, the Congregation of the Sisters of the Holy Family in 1842, the Sisters of the Holy Family in 1872, the Sisters of the Holy Family of Nazareth in 1875, and the Congregation of Missionaries of the Holy Family in 1895. See *The New Catholic Encyclopedia*, vol. 7, pp. 66–9.
33 On the ubiquity of the nineteenth-century bourgeois family – and its perpetuation in Christian evangelicalism – see Clapp, *Families at the Crossroads*, pp. 30–4 and 54–7.
34 G.W.F. Hegel, *Aesthetics: Lectures on Fine Art*, 2 volumes, translated by T.M. Knox (Oxford: Clarendon Press, 1975), vol. 2, p. 819.
35 Hegel, *Aesthetics*, vol. 1, p. 542.
36 G.W.F. Hegel, *Philosophy of Right*, translated by T.M. Knox (Oxford: Clarendon Press, 1952), p. 110.
37 Hegel, *Philosophy of Right*, p. 112.
38 Hegel, *Philosophy of Right*, p. 113. Hegel notes that the denial of the body in relation to divinity or spirituality is 'in keeping with the monastic doctrine which characterizes the moment of physical life as purely negative and which, precisely by thus separating the physical from the mental, endows the former by itself with infinite importance' (pp. 112–13).
39 Hegel, *Philosophy of Right*, p. 111.
40 Hegel, *Philosophy of Right*, p. 114.
41 Hegel, *Philosophy of Right*, p. 114.
42 Hegel, *Philosophy of Right*, p. 115.
43 Hegel, *Philosophy of Right*, p. 115.
44 Hegel, *Philosophy of Right*, p. 117.
45 Hegel, *Philosophy of Right*, p. 114.
46 Laura Gellott, 'The Family, Liberalism, and Catholic Social Teaching', in *Catholicism and Liberalism: Contributions to American Public Philosophy*, edited by R. Bruce Douglass and David Hollenbach (Cambridge: Cambridge University Press, 1994), pp. 269–95 (p. 272).
47 Gellott, 'The Family', p. 273. On this theme see further Rowan Williams, *Lost Icons: Reflections on Cultural Bereavement* (London: T. & T. Clark, 2000), ch. 1.
48 John Paul II, *Familiaris Consortio* (London: Catholic Truth Society, 1981), section 11 (pp. 20–1).
49 John Paul II, *Familiaris Consortio*, section 13 (pp. 25–6).
50 John Paul II, *Familiaris Consortio*, section 19 (p. 36).
51 John Paul II, *Familiaris Consortio*, section 13 (p. 24).
52 This is to broach a large question concerning John Paul II's attempt to understand 'woman' (which abstraction is part of the difficulty). It is addressed in

Mary C. Segers, 'Feminism, Liberalism, and Catholicism', in *Catholicism and Liberalism: Contributions to American Public Philosophy*, edited by R. Bruce Douglass and David Hollenbach (Cambridge: Cambridge University Press, 1994), pp. 242–68. See more recently the *Letter of Pope John Paul II to Women* (London: Catholic Truth Society, 1995), and 'Women Respond to the Pope', *The Tablet* (15 July 1995): 920–1. The difficulties attendant on the Pauline analogy of ecclesial and spousal covenants is considerably eased by understanding the relation of 'Christ/husband' to 'Church/wife' in (Johannine) terms of 'service', and in freeing-up the mapping of this gendered relation on to male and female bodies, so that *both* men and women may be 'Christ/husband' *and* 'Church/wife' – in the same way that all Christians are called to be both 'sheep' and 'shepherd', followers of Christ and Christ for others. See further Gerard Loughlin, 'Baptismal Fluid', *Scottish Journal of Theology*, 51 (1998): 261–70.

53 John Paul II, *Familiaris Consortio*, section 27 (p. 27). The church is the primary family of Christian existence, into which all members are 'born' at baptism. The Holy Family (Jesus, Mary and Joseph) of the gospel narratives – as opposed to that of a later piety – is, in the course of the gospel story, dissolved and reconstructed as the family of the church. See further Clapp, *Families at the Crossroads*, pp. 67–88.

54 On the family as 'household' see David Matzko McCarthy, *Sex and Love in the Home: A Theology of the Household* (London: SCM Press, 2001).

55 John Paul II, *Familiaris Consortio*, section 21 (p. 39).

56 John Paul II, *Familiaris Consortio*, section 21 (p. 40). But here it is important to remember that the nuclear family of modernity is not the only form of *domus* or household within the larger domesticity of the church.

57 Gellott, 'The Family', pp. 285–6.

58 John Paul II, *Familiaris Consortio*, section 11 (p. 20).

59 Joseph Ratzinger, *Letter to the Bishops of the Catholic Church on the Pastoral Care of Homosexual Persons* (London: Catholic Truth Society, 1986); reprinted in *Theology and Sexuality: Classic and Contemporary Readings*, edited by Eugene F. Rogers Jr (Oxford: Blackwell, 2002), pp. 249–58, section 12 (p. 254). Ratzinger rightly notes that this teaching will invite 'bitter ridicule', but appears to be unaware that if the suffering of homosexuals is akin to that of Christ on the cross, then those who nailed Christ to the cross are akin to those who, like Ratzinger, inflict suffering on homosexuals. God's love has the power to bring life out of death, but Ratzinger's argument is in danger of perverting this into the teaching that one can secure life through willing death.

60 Ratzinger, *On the Pastoral Care of Homosexual Persons*, section 9 (p. 254). Having maligned homosexuals in this way, Ratzinger goes on to deplore those who make homosexuals the 'object of violent malice in speech or action', but not without offering a tacit justification for such violence by noting that when a society legislates to protect homosexuals, 'neither the Church nor society at large should be surprised when other distorted notions and practices gain ground,

and irrational and violent reactions increase'. For a critique of this preposterous argument and other aspects of the Catholic Church's teaching and practice of homosexuality see Mark D. Jordan, *The Silence of Sodom: Homosexuality in Modern Catholicism* (Chicago: University of Chicago Press, 2000), pp. 31–40. See also Gerard Loughlin, *Homosexuality and Christian Ethics* (Cambridge: Cambridge University Press, forthcoming).

61 'The Homosexual Movement: A Response by the Ramsey Colloquium', published, unsurprisingly, in *First Things*, 41 (March 1994): 15–20, and, bewilderingly, in *The Month* (July 1994): 260–65. As so often, many of those who bewail the demise of the family celebrate the consumer capitalism that is its true enemy, because the enemy of all authentic human relationships. In so far as they succeed in promoting the one they fail in protecting the other, since capitalism has already made the family a commodified simulacrum of that of which we are in want. It should be understood that sexual libertinism, gay or straight, is but one aspect of that more generalized promiscuity which is the 'market'. See further Clapp, *Families at the Crossroads*, pp. 48–66.

62 John 14.2.

63 Caroline Walker Bynum, *The Resurrection of the Body in Western Christianity, 200–1336* (New York: Columbia University Press, 1995), pp. 97–8.

64 Bynum, *Resurrection of the Body*, pp. 99–100; Augustine, *The City of God*, bk 22, chs 17–18.

65 Bynum, *Resurrection of the Body*, p. 37.

66 Bynum, *Resurrection of the Body*, p. 67.

67 John Paul II, *Mulieris Dignitatem: On the Dignity and Vocation of Women* (London: Catholic Truth Society, 1988), section 6 (p. 21).

68 Karl Barth, *Church Dogmatics*, vol. III/4: *The Doctrine of Creation*, edited by G.W. Bromiley and T.F. Torrance (Edinburgh: T. & T. Clark, 1961), p. 183.

69 Barth, *Church Dogmatics*, III/4, p. 266. That this is little understood in the churches, let alone outside them, is illustrated by the remark of the Rt Revd Mark Santer (at the time Anglican Bishop of Birmingham), that married couples need a good reason for not having children. See *The Tablet* (1 July 1995): 851. On the contrary, Christian couples need a good reason *for* having children, since faith in the resurrected Christ frees them from the necessity to reproduce; or rather, there are no Christian reasons for having children outside the *ratio* of God, which comes to us as grace and gift. Here, as elsewhere, I am indebted to Stanley Hauerwas and Samuel Wells. See the latter's *Transforming Fate into Destiny: The Theological Ethics of Stanley Hauerwas* (Carlisle: Paternoster Press, 1998), pp. 172–8; and Clapp, *Families at the Crossroads*, pp. 100–1 and 133–48. For Clapp, God gives children so that we 'can become the kind of people who welcome strangers' (p. 138).

70 Barth, *Church Dogmatics*, III/4, pp. 241–2.

71 John Paul II, *Familiaris Consortio*, section 16 (p. 29).

72 John Paul II, *Familiaris Consortio*, section 16 (p. 30).

73 See Marc Shell, 'The Want of Incest in the Human Family or, Kin, and Kind in Christian Thought', *Journal of the American Academy of Religion*, 62/3 (1994): 625–50.

74 Shell, 'The Want of Incest', p. 636. See further Robert E. Lerner, *The Heresy of the Free Spirit in the Later Middle Ages* (Berkeley: University of California Press, 1972); and, for a highly ideological, somewhat silly but free-spirited account – a 1960s Nietzschianism – see the book by the one-time 'Situationist', Raoul Vaneigem, *The Movement of the Free Spirit* (New York: Zone Books, [1986] 1998).

Part IV

CONSOLATIONS

Eat, friends, drink, and be drunk with love. (Song of Songs 5.1)

Figure 8 Angelic Singing

Newton (David Bowie) and Mary Lou (Candy Clark) in *The Man Who Fell to Earth* (Nicholas Roeg, USA 1976). Photo: British Film Institute.

Chapter 8

THE MAN WHO FELL TO EARTH

From the beginning, heavenly visitors have walked the earth, such as the 'sons of God', who seeing the fairness of men's daughters took them as wives.[1] Indeed, once upon a time, even the Lord God would walk the earth 'at the time of the evening breeze'.[2] And though God and his 'sons' ceased to visit, the world having grown more historical, other divine beings still came to earth, angelic ambassadors such as the three men who appeared to Abraham 'by the oaks of Mamre', as he sat at the door of his tent in the 'heat of the day';[3] or the two 'angels' who came to Lot as he was 'sitting in the gateway of Sodom'.[4]

Heavenly visitations have not ceased in the long history of human storytelling, though the names of the visitors have changed, as also the places from whence they come. In modern times their homes are more closely mapped among the stars, the trajectory of their flight more carefully calculated, but their arrival on earth is still uncanny. They still appear in the time it takes to raise your eyes or turn your head. They appear suddenly on empty roads, as when a caped man appears to two pilgrims on their way to Santiago de Compostela, at the beginning of Luis Buñuel's *La Voie Lactée* (*The Milky Way*, France 1969). He strides along the road toward them, as once angels strode out of the day's heat, or walked up to the city gate, but now he appears in the blink of a shutter, out of the unseen darkness between two frames of a film. And such a visitor still fascinates and frightens, seduces and repulses, occasioning the embrace of blows.

Coming to Town

Thomas Jerome Newton, the visitor in Walter Tevis's 1963 novel *The Man Who Fell to Earth*, arrives in the morning, when it is still cool, having walked for two miles, from where we are not told, but arriving in the small town of Haneyville, population 1,400. In Nicolas Roeg's masterful 1976 film of Tevis's book, which tells the story as a tragicomedy, the visitor is first seen in silhouette, on the ridge of a shale escarpment, taking exaggerated, awkward steps, as small stones and shards of rock roll from beneath his feet on the steep incline. He is descending toward a disused mine, the rusting remnants of a redundant industry, including the incongruous hulk of a steam engine.[5] He wears a short dark greenish-brown duffle coat, and even with its hood up we can tell that he is a gaunt, spindly figure. This visitor arrives alone, without companions, a stranger come among strangers.

Nicolas Roeg (b. 1928) is a reticent storyteller, interested in visual rather than verbal narrative, and narrative under strain. His films require active rather than passive viewing. They are examples of what Roland Barthes called writerly (*scriptible*) texts, as opposed to readerly (*lisible*) ones. The latter are texts – novels or films – that we already know, or think we know, how to read. They gratify instantly because they repeat forms we have already learned and that have become conventional. They exemplify familiar genres. Writerly texts, on the other hand, are produced ahead of the conventions that will allow us to comprehend their meaning. As such, they may cause dyspepsia, for they have to be well chewed. The reader has to write the text; the viewer has to script the film.[6]

> The writerly text is a perpetual present, upon which no *consequent* language (which would inevitably make it past) can be superimposed; the writerly text is *ourselves writing*, before the infinite play of the world (the world as function) is traversed, intersected, stopped, plasticized by some singular system (Ideology, Genus, Criticism) which reduces the plurality of entrances, the opening of networks, the infinity of languages.[7]

For Barthes the writerly is an ideal that exists, if it exists at all, before or in the writing, but not afterward, when at least in part the text will become readable, interpretable. The ideal writerly text is a 'galaxy of signifiers, not a structure of signifieds; it has no beginning; it is reversible; we gain access to it by several entrances, none of which can be authoritatively declared to be the main one; the codes it mobilizes extend *as far as the eye can reach*, they are indeterminable'.[8] Roeg's films do not attain to this pitch of indeterminacy, which is hardly realizable, but are what Barthes calls 'incompletely plural texts, texts whose plural is more or less parsimonious'.[9] The films are neither univocal nor equivocal, but in Barthes' terminology, polysemous, connotative. They are suggestive of multiple allusions, which attend a story that while it can be told, can never be fully determined, that escapes total comprehension, differing each time it is recollected. Roeg's films do not so much unfold stories, as baroquely complicate them, folding them upon themselves, intricately.

Roeg refuses a straightforward narrative structure, a zero degree of dissonance between the story and its telling.[10] The narrative is often elliptical, and uses analepses that may be either recollections or premonitions, or even pure fantasies, scenes from another story, another film. The viewer is forced to construct and reconstruct his or her own account of the story being told. In this, Roeg's cinema relocates a biblical narrativity that already refuses the simply sequential and consistent. Abraham, sitting at the door of his tent, sees three men, but addresses them as one Lord. Sarah makes three cakes and having eaten them, they ask after her, but he – the one Lord – promises her a son, and asks why she laughs, and then rises to go on his/their way.[11] The text is undecided and undecidable as to there being one man or three.[12] It is as if two similar but slightly different scenes had been intercut, producing an unsettling effect; a tremor of uncertainty in the narrative. Yet even if we suppose that the text in Genesis is the result of confusing two or more sources,[13] the final form of the narrative is entirely fitting for its purpose, the disclosure of the divine in the mundane. As Karl Barth remarked of this and other visitations, the 'contradiction in the statements is the appropriate form for indicating at least what has to be said. The apparent obscurity of these presentations is the real clarity with which the matter has to be presented'.[14] The presentation of Roeg's story is similarly appropriate, producing a sense of the uncanny in the everyday, of something out of joint.

Matters are more straightforward in Tevis's novel, in which we learn from the first that Newton is an alien visitor, who only seems to be human.

> He was not a man; yet he was very much like a man. He was six and a half feet tall, and some men are even taller than that; his hair was as white as that of an albino, yet his face was a light tan color; and his eyes a pale blue. His frame was improbably slight, his features delicate, his fingers long, thin, and the skin almost translucent, hairless. There was an elfin quality to his face, a fine boyish look to the wide, intelligent eyes . . . There were other differences, too: his fingernails, for example, were artificial, for he had none by nature. There were only four toes on each of his feet; he had no vermiform appendix and no wisdom teeth . . . Yet he did have eyelashes, eyebrows, opposed thumbs, binocular vision, and a thousand of the physiological features of a normal human. He was incapable of warts; but stomach ulcers, measles and dental caries could affect him. He was human; but not, properly, a *man*. Also, man-like, he was susceptible to love, to fear, to intense physical pain and to self-pity.[15]

Newton is not properly a man, but nor is he an angel or a divine being. He is already too human to be anything other than a fallen creature, fallen into our world and away from a biblical ideal of the heavenly visitor. Though in some sense a warning angel, who has come to earth to save humanity from destroying itself and thereby securing a new home for his own species, the Antheans,[16] he succumbs to the terrors and beauties of our world. He is defeated by the loss of home and family, and by fear and desire of our alien environment. 'This world is doomed as certainly as Sodom', he tells Nathan Bryce, 'and I can do nothing whatever about it'.[17] He is an angel who stays in the city, while 'brimstone and fire' rain down upon it.[18]

Looking beneath the Skin

Roeg's film is not really interested in why Newton has come to earth, but it is interested in the earth to which he has come, the advanced capitalist society of North America in which he seeks salvation. It is also interested in the fears and desires that Newton's seeking provokes in others. In the film, Newton has come from a desert planet, dying for lack of water. 'Where I come from', Newton tells Bryce, 'there's a terrible drought. We saw pictures of your planet on television. In fact our word for your planet means "planet of water"'. The fortune that Newton amasses through the exploitation of his alien technologies, is to fund the building of a spaceship that will allow him to return home, but in the film it is never explained how this might help his family. Will the ship somehow transport water to his planet,[19] or bring his people back to earth, as explained in the novel?[20] Roeg and his scriptwriter, Paul Mayersberg, are not really interested in the mechanics of the story, but in the alien visitor's experience of our dissociated world, a world that has already become alien to itself.[21]

We see a society in which images proliferate, but none of which pictures the society as it is, except in and through their proliferation. It is a society that looks but does not see. 'Television!' Newton exclaims to Bryce, 'Strange thing about television is that it doesn't tell you everything. It shows you everything about life on earth, but the true mysteries remain. Perhaps it is in the nature of television. Just waves in space'. The same might be said of Roeg's films, which seem to show us more than we need to know about the simple stories they narrate, but at the same time, do not tell us enough, since we are never quite sure what we have seen, can never quite determine the lineaments of the story we have watched. For Roeg, simplicity is unobtainable, identity forever uncertain. 'Perhaps it's naiveté on my part, but I don't think a story of any kind can be simple. If you were to ask me to summarize my own life, I'd never be sure if I described it accurately. The past changes all the time for me. Finally, I come to the conclusion of never talking about it. Even if I described it exactly, I'd finally have to say it was not exactly that way'.[22] The irony, of course, is that photography in general, and film in particular, is taken to be a guarantor of identity. As if the photograph, still and moving, were a reproduction rather than a representation of the things and people it images. This is why we have photographs in our passports. When we look like our photographs, we can traverse boundaries without loss of identity.

The most prominent of all Newton's products, by which he makes his fortune, is a photographic system, camera and self-developing film, that in Roeg's movie also seems to have the ability of taking pictures from a point of view at some distance from the camera. Newton's invention thus produces a seemingly objective image that is freed from the partial eye of the photographer. Bryce, the scientist who comes to work for Newton and later betrays him, first becomes aware of Newton's company when he notices one of his cameras, that the student with whom Bryce is having sex uses to take pictures of their cavorting in bed. But for Bryce, these photographs do not proffer an excitement or truth of the body, but a mystery to be solved.

Prior to his arrival on earth, Newton has learned about our world through the study of television transmissions. He knows us by our own constructed self-images, and when he comes to earth, he surrounds himself with television sets, which grow in number as the film proceeds. It is as if these simulations of earthly life are more comforting than the lives of those around him. He also seeks to communicate with his family on Anthea by appearing on television commercials for his products, in the hope that the pictures may reach his wife and children. But even if they reach his family they will communicate only the distance between them, the distance that is opening within Newton himself, as his alien and human identities diverge.

The commercial starts with a recurring Roeg conceit: Newton standing with his back to the camera, unable to see his observer. When he turns around he is holding one of his cameras, that might actually have taken the picture from behind him, creating a loop between camera and image, observer and observed: photographic mediation is lodged within the sight of oneself. The commercial which both shows Newton while refusing his identity (through denying us sight of his face) is watched by Bryce and Newton together. Bryce wants to know Newton's identity, but cannot see it in his face. He has arranged to secretly take an X-ray photograph of Newton, that will reveal his alien form. It is only by photography that he can see the alien in the human. But the photograph will constitute only another loop, displaying only another photographic skin, and not what is beneath the skin. By the end of *The Man Who Fell to Earth*, the attempt to remove Newton's skin, in order to see the alien beneath, will have been literalized, as surgeons attempt to detach his nipples. But flesh is all they find, for identity is only skin deep.

As already indicated, Newton is a heavenly messenger who succumbs to that which he foretells, the doom of Sodom. Like the angels who come to Lot, he is at first welcomed and entertained by people who are happy to profit from the commercial exploitation of his science. But after he has revealed the reason for his visit, which is in part, or so he says, to save humankind from self-destruction, the 'men of the city', the shadowy overseers of American society, seek him out in order to 'know' and destroy him.[23] In the novel Newton is arrested by FBI agents for being an 'unregistered alien',[24] and interrogated by them and by members of the CIA. In the film their provenance is more vague, an undefined alliance of state and corporate interest. The chief agent is Mr Peters (Bernie Casey), who is reminded by his superior that he is not working for the Mafia, but for people determining the nation's 'social ecology'. The unprecedented success of Newton's corporation – World Enterprises – is 'technologically overstimulating', destabilizing the nation's economy, and Peters must take 'flexible', 'elastic' measures to put things right. 'This is modern America and we're going to keep it that way'.

Unlike Lot's visitors, Newton does not escape through smiting his enemies with blindness.[25] Instead, he loses his own sight. Newton is then more like one of the servants sent to the vineyard, who are variously beaten, stoned and killed by the wicked 'husbandmen'.[26] Newton's loss of sight is actual in the novel, but metaphorical in the film. In the novel he is blinded when some FBI agents, seemingly ignorant of his alien physiology, insist on taking an X-ray picture of his eyes. 'Haven't you been informed about me? Haven't you been told about my eyes? Certainly they know about my eyes . . . They are sensitive to X-rays'.[27] But Newton's alien eyes are unseen behind his contact lenses, and when he offers to remove them, he finds that he cannot, and the doctors cannot see them. So, like Alex in Stanley Kubrick's *A Clockwork Orange* (1971), Newton is restrained, his head held in place and he is made to look into the binocular lenses of the X-ray camera that will permanently change the way he sees the world. As the camera is fired, Newton screams: 'Don't you know I'm not human? I'm not a human being! . . . I'm not a human being at all'.[28]

In the novel Newton's blinding seems to confirm his claimed identity. In the film, however, the X-ray camera does not blind Newton but fuses the contact lenses onto his eyes, or so he claims, so that he can no longer establish his alien identity, even to himself. Thus neither he, nor any of the other characters in the film, nor we the viewers of his story, can be sure of his identity. Perhaps his recollections of his home world are fantasies, delusions. *The Man Who Fell to Earth* is replete with shots of people looking in mirrors and at reflections, and through windows and lenses, whether worn as eye glasses or used in laboratories. Sight is always mediated; knowledge always imagined. Everything is as it *appears*.

Indifferent Suffering

Roeg is not only uninterested in the mechanics of his science fiction story, he also seems less concerned than Tevis with its religious resonance, and more concerned with its sexual aspects. But in fact it is rather that the religious is subsumed in the sexual, as will be discussed below. Furthermore, the film does explicitly, if fleetingly, connect alien visitations with religious concerns. When Newton, alone in the desert with Bryce, admits his alien identity, he also insists that the earth has always been visited. 'On my own planet we found evidence of "visitors". You must have seen them here . . . I've seen them. I've seen their footsteps and their places'. Bryce denies such knowledge, arguing that the supposed traces of visitors are speculations, not facts, to which Newton gnomically responds: 'I know all things begin and end in eternity'.

In Tevis's novel, Newton is explicitly associated with Christ. In the country home of Newton's lawyer, Oliver Farnsworth, there is a 'large painting of a religious figure', whom Newton recognizes as 'Jesus, nailed to a wooden cross'. He is startled by the face of the crucified man, because its 'thinness and large piercing eyes' remind him of his own face, 'the face of an Anthean'.[29] During a drunken conversation between Bryce and Newton, Bryce suggests that the 'big war' will begin in five years, and that only Christ's Second Coming might stop humankind from destroying itself. Newton, who needs ten years to complete his space ferry and bring the rest of the Antheans to earth, laughs, 'soft and pleasantly'.

> 'Maybe it will be the second Coming indeed. Maybe it will be Jesus Christ himself. In ten years.'
>
> 'If he comes', Bryce said, 'he'd better watch his step.'
>
> 'I imagine he'll remember what happened to him the last time,' Newton said.[30]

These words stay with Bryce, who increasingly entertains the idea that Newton is an extraterrestrial, possibly a Martian, but a drunken Martian? 'But why not a drunken Martian? Christ himself drank wine, and he came down from heaven – a wine-bibber, the Pharisees said. A wine-bibber from outer space'.[31]

If the novel's religious references seem lacking in the film, it is only because they are not verbally expressed, and the film visually develops the novel's other figure of alien descent, the fall of Icarus. The first and last of the novel's three unequal parts are respectively entitled '1985: Icarus Descending' and '1990: Icarus Drowning'.[32] *The Fall of Icarus*, attributed to Pieter Bruegel (c. 1525–69),[33] pictures the end of the story of Daedalus and Icarus as told in Ovid's *Metamorphoses*. It shows Icarus in the bottom right-hand corner, having fallen headlong into the sea, his legs thrashing above the waves, while in the foreground a ploughman concentrates on cutting his furrow, while in the middle-distance a shepherd rests on his staff, looking up into an empty sky, with his back to the disaster at sea. The painting not only combines in one image the various elements that are set forth sequentially in the poem, but it turns the rural labourers from amazed witnesses of human flight, as they are in the poem, into indifferent bystanders of the disaster. Ovid's story was newly translated into English by Bruegel's contemporary, Arthur Golding (1536–1606).

He fastened to his shoulders twaine a paire of uncoth wings.
And as he was in doing it and warning him of things,
His aged cheekes were wet, his handes did quake, in fine he gave
His sonne a kisse the last that he alive should ever have.
And then he mounting up aloft before him tooke his way
Right fearfull for his followers sake: as is the Bird the day
That first she tolleth from her nest among the braunches hie
Hir tender yong ones in the Aire to teach them for to flie.
So heartens he his little sonne to follow teaching him
A hurtfull Art. His owne two wings he waveth verie trim,
And looketh backward still upon his sonnes. The fishermen
Then standing angling by the Sea, and shepherdes leaning then
On sheepehookes, and the Ploughmen on the handles of their Plough,
Beholding them, amazed were: and thought that they that through
The Aire could flie were Gods. And now did on their left side stand
The Iles of *Paros* and of *Dele*, and *Samos*, *Junos* land:
And on the right, *Lebinthos*, and the faire *Calydna* fraught
With store of honie: when the Boy a frolicke courage caught
To flie at randon. Whereupon forsaking quight his guide,

Of fond desire to flie to Heaven, above his boundes he stide.
And there the nerenesse of the Sunne which more hote aloft,
Did make the Wax (with which his wings were glewed) lithe and soft.
As soone as that the Wax was molt, his naked armes he shakes,
And wanting wherewithall to wave, no helpe of Aire he takes.
But calling on his father loud he drowned on the wave:
And by this chaunce of his, those Seas his name for ever have.
His wretched Father (but as then no Father) cride on feare
O *Icarus* O *Icarus* where art thou? tell me where
That I may find thee *Icarus*. He saw the feathers swim
Upon the waves, and curst his Art that so had spighted him.[34]

Bruegel's strange, dream-like vision of Ovid's tale, combining mythic drama with bucolic serenity, is differently rendered in what is arguably the first proper scene of Roeg's film, showing the impact made by Newton's spacecraft as it crashes into the still waters of a Kentucky/New Mexico lake,[35] sending huge sprays of foamed white water into the air. This shot comes immediately after a sequence constructed from stock footage of rockets and spacecraft, which is perhaps meant to indicate the arrival of Newton's spaceship, or humankind's first steps into space at the same time as a starman steps onto earth. As in the painting, which shows Icarus just after he has entered the water, so the film cuts to the crash of Newton's ship just after it has entered the lake. We see the effect of its arrival but not the arrival itself, a fume of water without apparent cause, seemingly inexplicable, its violence contained by the indifferent silence of the forested hills surrounding the lake.

In the novel, a print of Bruegel's painting hangs in Bryce's university office; in the film it appears in a book published by Newton's corporation – *Masterpieces in Paint and Poetry* – that Bryce receives from his daughter. The picture is printed facing the last verse of W.H. Auden's 1938 poem, 'Musée des Beaux Arts', on which the camera lingers, for the audience to read, and which Bryce partly quotes in the novel, 'in a soft, ritualistic voice, without any particular expression or feeling'.

In Bruegel's *Icarus*, for instance: how everything turns away
Quite leisurely from the disaster; the ploughman may
Have heard the splash, the forsaken cry,
But for him it was not an important failure; the sun shone
As it had to on the white legs disappearing into the green
Water; and the expensive delicate ship that must have seen
Something amazing, a boy falling out of the sky,
Had somewhere to get to and sailed calmly on.[36]

The painting, which Bryce takes with him when he goes to work for Newton, provides him with a clue to Newton's alien identity, and he reflects that 'Icarus had failed, had burned and drowned, while Daedalus, who had not gone so high, had escaped from his lonely island'.[37] Later, when Newton proposes to Bryce that they fly to Chicago, Bryce quips, 'Like Icarus?' and Newton replies, 'More like Daedalus, I hope. I wouldn't relish drowning'.[38] Newton sees the picture in Bryce's house and remarks how its landscape, the 'mountains, snow, and the water', resembles that of Kentucky.[39] He draws Bryce's attention to the fact that the sun is setting in the picture, but that it was noon when Icarus fell.[40] 'He must have fallen a long way. In the picture, the sun was half-way below the horizon, and Icarus, leg and knee flailing above the water – the water in which he was about to drown, unnoticed, for his foolhardiness – was shown at the moment after impact. He must have been falling since noon'.[41] Newton has been falling for a long time, and falling fast, and soon he will be drowning. It is during the same conversation in which they discuss the picture that Bryce secretly takes the X-ray photograph of Newton that will confirm his alien identity.

The figure of Icarus, who pervades both book and film, is also a clue to Newton's Christic identity, since the concern of Auden's poem is not so much the 'foolhardiness' of Icarus as the indifference of the world to 'the disaster', to the miracle and the martyr, to the 'important failure'; in short, to human suffering, and in particular the suffering of Christ. We eat while torturers practise their trade.

> About suffering they were never wrong,
> The Old Masters: how well they understood
> Its human position: how it takes place
> While someone else is eating or opening a window or just walking
> dully along;
> How, when the aged are reverently, passionately waiting
> For the miraculous birth, there always must be
> Children who did not especially want it to happen, skating
> On a pond at the edge of the wood:
> They never forgot
> That even the dreadful martyrdom must run its course
> Anyhow in a corner, some untidy spot
> Where the dogs go on with their doggy life and the torturer's horse
> Scratches its innocent behind on a tree.

Auden's poem may also be read as alluding to Bruegel's *The Census at Bethlehem* (1566) and *The Adoration of the Kings in the Snow* (1567), in both of which their putative subjects – the arrival of Mary and Joseph in Bethlehem and the visitation of the magi – are almost lost amidst the Netherlandish townsfolk, going about their business, unaware of the birth that is imminent in one picture and celebrated in the other. In both, children play upon the ice, though skating on 'a pond at the edge of the wood' is more accurate of some of Bruegel's other paintings. The poem also alludes to Bruegel's *The Massacre of the Innocents* (1566), in which 'dogs go on with their doggy life', while soldiers, horsed and on foot, snatch children from their mothers and slay them in the snow, while others look on – though no horse 'scratches its innocent behind on a tree'. Dogs also pursue their own interests in *The Procession to Calvary* (1564), in which the figure of Christ drags his cross almost unnoted by the crowds of people who are making their way to the site of execution, far distant in the top right-hand corner of the painting. Like the dogs, few of the people are concerned with what is happening to Christ, most attending to their own business, while some are walking out of the picture. Even the figures of John and the three Marys, foregrounded in the bottom right of the painting, have their backs to the scene, consumed by grief.

Bruegel's paintings display a profoundly incarnational theology. His divine subjects are not signalled with golden halos or other penumbra, but are simply men and women among other men and women. Only our looking will show a difference. *The Man Who Fell to Earth* displays a similar sense of the extraordinary in the ordinary, of epiphany in the mundane. Taken up with the daily round, most people fail to notice what is passing before their eyes, and those who notice something, think it less trouble to turn and look the other way. Just as the ship sails on, having 'somewhere to get to', after seeing 'a boy falling out of the sky', so in Roeg's film the powers of this world refuse to be turned from their course by the arrival of an alien being, as once they refused to be stirred by the advent of God's Messiah. The potentially disturbing is ignored or dispatched.

From the first, Newton's arrival has been noted by government agents. In the opening scenes of the film, as Newton makes his way down the stony hillside, the camera zooms out to reveal the figure of a watcher, standing on a higher promontory. He will turn out to be an agent of the state, just as Newton's hired driver and bodyguard – named Brinnarde in the book – will prove to be an FBI agent.[42] Newton's arrival has not gone unnoticed, but nor has it astounded. It is merely another fact to be scrutinized, catalogued and controlled. Newton disturbs not because he is an alien, but because his hugely successful business threatens to destabilize the world market. As with Christ, what matters about Newton is not his offer of a new world order, but his threat to the existing one. Consequently he has to be neutralized.

The latter part of Roeg's film plays out a passion narrative. Newton is the forlorn Messiah, Nathan Bryce and Mary Lou his erstwhile disciples. More than the novel, the film portrays Bryce as Judas. In the novel his betrayal of Newton is inadvertent, taking the X-ray photograph for his own interest, and unwittingly conversing with Newton in rooms that are bugged by the CIA. But in the film, Bryce is complicit in Newton's downfall. Newton, having twice before asked for Bryce's trust, declares his own trust in Bryce, having spent the day with him, alone in the desert, explaining who he is and why he has come to earth. Bryce cannot look him in the face, but traces a pattern in the sand with a stick. Later, after Newton's arrest, we see Bryce in Peters' company, reassuring him that he can persuade Newton to see things their way. 'I'll talk to him. I know he'll be alright.' Bryce becomes a watcher, like the man on the hill at the beginning of the film, the camera pulling back to reveal him in the operating theatre, when surgeons unsuccessfully try to remove Newton's skin in order to reveal the alien beneath. As they cut into him, Newton sees Bryce and cries out for help, but Bryce runs away.

The scene in which Bryce dissembles his betrayal to Mary Lou, denying that he has seen Newton, is counterpoised with the confession of another cinematic traitor: Holly Martins (Joseph Cotton) in Carol Reed's *The Third Man* (UK 1949). Martins is himself a kind of alien, an American in post-war Vienna, who betrays his old friend, Harry Lime (Orson Welles). The scene of Bryce and Mary Lou, dining in a restaurant, is cross cut with that of Newton, in his hotel prison, undergoing a further medical examination while watching Reed's film on a large projected television screen. 'Well, they asked me to help take him, and I'm helping', Martins tells Anna Schmidt (Alida Valli), referring to her lover Harry Lime, but through Roeg's cross cut it is also what Bryce doesn't say to Mary Lou about her lover. The effect is typical of Roeg's metonymic cinema, his cutting between two discrete scenes producing a third, a coagulation in the viewer's imagination as the different scenes from the two films bleed into one another. Like the illusion of cinematic motion itself, produced between the still frames of the film in the mind of the viewer, so Roeg produces significance from the intercut, in the space between scenes. Moreover, Bryce's betrayal of Newton gains its biblical resonance from the intercut of film and scripture. The same is true of Mary Lou, whose name, changed from that of Betty Jo in the novel, suggests her figuration of Mary of Nazareth, Christ's mother, and Mary Magdalene, Christ's disciple and, in some Gnostic stories, Christ's lover.[43]

When Mary Lou first encounters Newton, she is working as a chambermaid in the hotel where he is staying. She operates the elevator, but it moves too fast for Newton, who haemorrhages and collapses on the floor. Mary Lou picks him up, and, cradling him in her arms, carries him, pietà-like, to his room, where she continues to look after him. It is in his vulnerability that Newton is perhaps most Christ-like. Apart from the later scenes where he becomes frustrated with Mary Lou, because frustrated with himself, he is remarkably passive throughout the film. He offers little resistance when he is finally arrested and imprisoned. Like Christ, his actions provoke violence in others, but he does not instigate or return it. Roeg admits to admiring people who are 'fragile and receptive'.[44]

Queer Bodies

Where Roeg's film most departs from Tevis's book is with regard to Newton's body and its sexuality. Tevis's alien is albino, but Roeg's alien has flame-red hair, revealed near the beginning of the film, when having almost walked into an oncoming car, Newton removes the hood from his head and walks away from the camera. It is the second of three little shocks, the third being a large inflated plastic clown, partly unmoored and buffeted by the wind, seemingly jeering at Newton as he enters Haneyville. The red hair is worn by David Bowie, in whom Roeg had found the perfect actor to play his alien.

David Bowie (b. David Jones 1947) was already a hugely successful popstar, who had, with other singers like Marc Bolan (T. Rex) and Bryan Ferry (Roxy Music), reinvented British rock 'n' roll music at the start of the 1970s, producing a fusion of rock and pop idioms that became known as 'glam' or 'glitter rock'. He did so, moreover, through the creation of his most famous persona, Ziggy Stardust, a parody of pop-star pretensions, in whose habitation Bowie had become an influential and successful performer, twice removed from the originary David Jones. Ziggy and his band – the Spiders – first appeared on stage in January 1972, and on vinyl in the same year, to be followed in 1973 with a third character, Aladdin Sane.[45]

> Bowie was attaining rock-mythological status by becoming one huge aggregation of real and imagined personalities. As if releasing an alien virus, Bowie had set in train the *idea* of David Bowie – a one-man collective of media personae – changing form and content rapidly, shedding personalities like unwanted shards of skin and inhabiting different terrains of pop music and culture in the process.[46]

By the time Bowie came to film *The Man Who Fell to Earth* in 1975, he had already left Ziggy and Aladdin behind, metamorphosing into what his biographer, David Buckley, calls the 'gouster' – a 'streetwise, sharp-talking, coolly dressed all-American dude'[47] – and then into the character of the Thin White Duke, who first appears in Roeg's film. According to Buckley, Newton's sartorial appearance in the film – 'crimson and blond center-parted hair, jacket and fedora' – was devised by Bowie,[48] and Newton's famished, insomnious look, was the result of Bowie's 'astronomic' consumption of cocaine.[49] All rock stars are supposed to live the emotions they perform, their music a heart-felt expression of their inner state, and so – even for Buckley – Bowie is the alien, having 'spent his first forty years on the planet acting like a man from the Andromeda galaxy'.[50] Certainly, he had performed the alien from the earliest days of his career, when, against the background of the American moon landing (20 July 1969) and Stanley Kubrick's *2001: A Space Odyssey* (1968), he released what was to become his first major hit, 'Space Oddity' (1969). As Ziggy Stardust, the 'space invader' ('Moonage Daydream'), Bowie sang of the 'starman waiting in the sky' who would 'like to come and meet us' but 'thinks he'd blow our minds' ('Starman'); and the reason for that was not his celestial origin or music, but his body; his sexuality and gender.[51]

In January 1970, the British gay magazine *Jeremy* published an interview with David Bowie, and in January 1972 he came out as gay in an interview with Michael Watts for *Melody Maker*.[52] Already in 1971 he had appeared on the cover of his third album, *The Man Who Sold the World*, with long hair and wearing a silk dress and reclining on a chaise-longue. As Ziggy Stardust and Aladdin Sane, his hair would be cropped, but dyed red, and he would wear lipstick and mascara, in a provocative refusal of normative gender behaviour for British men. Same-sex relations between men (aged 21 and over) had only become legal in 1967, in the long wake of the Wolfenden Committee on Homosexual Offences and Prostitution.[53] Bowie's 'coming out' was commercially risky, but gained attention and proved to be astute publicity.

As a self-declared gay man, Bowie nevertheless slept with women. At the time of the interview he was still married to Angie Barnett, whom he had married in 1970, and who had given birth to their son in the following year, and from whom he would not divorce until 1980.[54] Yet even if Bowie was a heterosexual posing as a homosexual,[55] as John Gill insists, the adoption of a queer persona not only enhanced the allure of Bowie's androgyny for would-be rebellious teenagers, but it helped to create a space in popular culture where even heterosexual men could, for a time, be relieved from the burden of normative heterosexuality. In Bowie's performance of himself as alien it became possible to see that what was supposed natural for the body might at the same time be alien to it.

It may have been because Bowie's body was already marked as queer, the site of an ambiguous, ambidextrous sexuality, that Mayersberg and Roeg dropped the suggestions in Tevis's novel of a homosexual sheen to Newton's character. When, in the novel, Newton remains unmoved by Betty Jo's (Mary Lou's) attempt to seduce him, she momentarily wonders if he is 'queer' – 'anybody who sat around reading all the time and looked like he did' – but then reflects that 'he didn't talk like a queer'.[56] But then again, and though married, 'maybe he was queer – being married didn't prove anything that way'.[57] Almost the first thing that Nathan Bryce notices about Newton is the way that he walks.

> He walked slowly, his tall body erect, but with a light gracefulness to the movement. There was an indefinable strangeness about his way of walking, a quality that reminded Bryce of the first homosexual he had ever seen, back when he had been too young to know what a homosexual was. Newton did not walk like that; but then he walked like no one else: light and heavy at the same time.[58]

How do queers walk? Like Ziggy Stardust? Like an alien, unused to earth's gravity? Like an angel, 'light and heavy at the same time'? How do they talk? Like Tommy Newton? Like an Englishman in a world of Americans? Not quite, for while there are no homosexual characters in the novel, there are in the film. Mayersberg and Roeg not only make Newton's lawyer, Oliver Farnsworth (Buck Henry), gay, but they provide him with a lover, Trevor (Rick Riccardo).[59] We see Oliver and Trevor eating breakfast together, we see them getting ready for bed, Oliver undoing his bow tie, while Trevor, still in his dinner jacket, is laying out his tarot cards; and, briefly, we see Oliver embracing Trevor. The bedroom scene is ominous, for though Trevor claims to see nothing in the cards, he might have espied that he and Oliver will be the only two characters to die in the film. The short scene of their embrace comes after that of their deaths.[60]

When the 'men of the city' decide to rein in Newton's World Enterprises, kidnapping him while he is making his way to his now completed spaceship, they also decide to eliminate his lawyer, the man who oversees the running of World Enterprises. Farnsworth is thrown through the window of his high rise apartment. The window doesn't break on the first throw. Farnsworth apologizes to his assailants, and they tell him not to worry, and with a second swing he smashes through the glass and falls to his death, the camera following his descent, with his breathing and quickened heartbeat amplified on the sound track. He is shortly followed by Trevor, and Trevor by his dumb-bells.

Oliver and Trevor's weights fall in silhouette against a dark blue sky, and are followed almost immediately by another silhouetted figure, falling through the air against the glare of the sun, and which at first we take to be a continuation of the previous scene, which has been briefly interrupted by the short scene of Oliver and Trevor embracing. But in fact, the silhouetted figure is the instigator of their murder, Mr Peters, who is not falling but diving into his swimming pool. The camera, in one of the film's most arresting shots, smoothly follows Peters' lithe and naked body as he enters the water, swims beneath its surface to where his wife, also naked, is standing in the water. As the shot continues in slow motion, he lifts her out of the water and places her on the pool side, where he joins her. They embrace, in bright sunlight and with precise focus, as drops of water glisten on their skin, and the diamonds on her rings catch the light. The immediately following scene shows Peters and his wife putting their children to bed, and he muses if they always say and do the right thing. 'To the children?' his wife asks. 'No, everything', he replies. This entire sequence is open to a number of readings. Is it an affirmation of familial heterosexuality, the city having been cleansed of deviations? Is it but a brief interlude, an aside, showing how white corporate America – symbolized in pool, diamonds and wife – has come to embrace the once disenfranchised black man? At another level, Peters' dive into the pool and his emergence from it into the arms of his wife is a counterpart to Newton's own fall into the lake at the start of the film, from which he too emerges into the arms of Mary Lou. Perhaps Peters is another Icarus, and his marriage and family another way of drowning.

The scenes of murder and familial domesticity, linked by those of bodies in air and water and sexual embrace, are original to Mayersberg and Roeg, having no basis in Tevis's novel, and would seem gratuitous. But they can be seen as part of the film's complex consideration of alien sex, the intercut of bodies. *The Man Who Fell to Earth* suggests that it is above all in sexual congress, in the relationship that promises loving union, that we are both most alone and at the same time most liable to lose or find our identity. Just as Roeg's scenes bleed into one another, as if they simultaneously occupied the same space, so also the bodies of his characters are seeking but rarely achieving a single occupancy of space, an interpenetration of flesh.

The film presents a series of couplings, all of which are fraught with social anxiety. Professor Bryce has sex with his female students, to whom he stands *in loco parentis,* as each compares her father's penis with his; Farnsworth has sex with another man, and Peters, who arranges Farnsworth's death, is a black man who has sex with his white wife. Finally, Newton, the alien Anthean, has sex with the human, Mary Lou. Each relationship crosses a divide, whether of age, gender, race or species. Each can be named as a perversion: incest, homosexuality, miscegenation, bestiality. They comprise an almost levitical list of abominations; variations on the theme of crossing the border between the same and the other.

Sleeping with Angels

In Genesis, God's sons are lured to earth by the beauty of women; they come to have sex with the daughters of men. (If some were also lured by the beauty of men's sons, we are not told, nor of their attraction for the women they took.) This archaic coupling of divine and human is exemplary of all relationships that seek to cross frontiers, and its results are monstrous, issuing in the Nephilim or giants.[61] Thus St Paul warned the Christian women of Corinth to veil their heads, lest their beauty attract the angels.[62] Mary Lou, who attends church, might have known of this injunction, but if so is unheeding, and wantonly seeks to seduce her angel (see figure 8).[63] In the novel, Newton disdains Betty Jo's advances, but in Roeg's film, the sexual relationship between alien and earth woman is central.

The first scene of Newton and Mary Lou's sexual intercourse is tender and romantic; a mutual caressing of bodies by candlelight. It contrasts with the earlier scenes of Bryce frolicking with his students, shots of him with different girls alternating in quick succession so as to suggest his interest in them as young flesh rather than as individuals. Moreover the first of these scenes is intercut with one of Newton eating in a Japanese restaurant, where a kabuki-style sword-play is being performed.[64] The ritualized thrusts of the sword fighters enact the mounting excitement of Bryce and his partner, whose ecstatic moans are heard but not seen. Disturbed, Newton leaves the restaurant as the off-screen lovers climax. Newton's own lovemaking with Mary Lou has no such violent connotations. They gently explore one another's bodies, each having licensed the other's hands to venture upon a 'new found land'.[65] The scene is intercut with shots of Mary Lou exploring other new worlds: amoebal life on a microscope slide, and, through a telescope and impossibly, the sun, which in its excitement appears to be giving off coronal spermatozoa.[66] It is almost as if Roeg had replaced scopic metaphors (cosmic and microcosmic) for John Donne's geographic metaphor of America as the body of his mistress; and for Donne, union with his mistress was union with an angel.[67] In the film, Newton is the angel and Mary Lou his lover, whose new found land is not America, but England. Yet at the same time she is a bodily synecdoche of his new found land, America.[68] Each is the other's alien, a strange body in which they may either find or lose themselves.

The scene of Newton and Mary Lou's lovemaking ends with them curled in one another's arms, asleep, almost indistinguishable from one another. Moreover, immediately prior to these concluding shots we are shown two iconic portrait images, framed by burn outs to white. In the first Newton and Mary Lou are in profile, facing one another, their faces filling the cinemascope screen. In the second, they are still side by side, but now facing the camera, looking directly at the audience. Both shots are bleached white, so as to flatten the image and enhance the similarity of their faces. The second, in particular, recalls Ingmar Bergman's *Persona* (Sweden 1966), and the striking composite image of Liv Ullmann and Bibi Andersson, their faces fused in order to suggest their psychological merger. Roeg's faces do not merge, but they are rendered almost identical: the same face, but different.[69] It is at one and the same time a picture of the proximity and distance between Newton and Mary Lou, and of the distance within themselves. Framed by white light, this double portrait is the still central image of the film, to which the first half moves and from which the second departs. It is the image of a possible union that the film will find to be impossible, a conjunction attempted but failing. And because of the angelic and Christic identity of Newton as alien, this impossible possibility resonates with the attempted union of divine and human that is the possible impossibility ventured in religious, and, more specifically, Christian faith.

The growing distance within Newton leads to a distance growing between himself and Mary Lou, which she doesn't understand and cannot accept. Finally he attempts to show her how far they are from one another, while at the same time still attempting to traverse the distance between them. After their most acrimonious exchange, when Mary Lou in her desperation has both entreated and jeered at Newton, he locks himself in the bathroom, and stands naked in front of two mirrors. The scene is shot from behind, accentuating Newton's vulnerability, and the viewer's sense of watching something private. Moreover, the viewer is now like Newton, unable to see his face, only its reflection in the mirrors, one of which magnifies and distorts. Newton feels his false nipples, and then, just out of shot, below the level of the picture frame, his false penis. In a close-up, but again shot from behind, we see him raise a pair of tweezers to his eyes in order to remove his human contact lenses. He then unlocks the bathroom door, and with staring yellow snake eyes, shows himself to Mary Lou: hairless and without nails, nippleless and unsexed, castrated. Touching her on the neck, he passes by her on his way to the bedroom, and she stands immobile with terror and urinates on the floor.[70] Newton lies on the bed, on his back, his naked body clearly ungenitalled. This contrasts with the earlier scenes in the film, where Nathan Bryce's penis is inspected by the college girls, as he too lies on his back. Mary Lou fights her fear and approaches Newton, and after first removing her pants and skimpy chemise, climbs on to the bed beside him and with a terrified touch begins to caress his now alien flesh.

While Mary Lou can see only Newton's transfigured body, he recollects or fantasizes making love to his wife on Anthea, shots of which are interposed with those of him and Mary Lou. Anthean sex appears to be like an aerial ballet, a gymnastic engagement of almost weightless bodies in mid-air. More startlingly, both of them are entirely covered in a viscous white liquid, which appears to emanate from their skin, and occasionally splashes across the entire screen: a non-specific all-over ejaculate.[71]

In response to Mary Lou's caresses, Newton places a hand on her body, and as he takes it away, leaves behind his bodily secretion. This proves too uncanny for Mary Lou, and with a scream she flees the bedroom. The sequence ends with a shot of her crouched and whimpering in the kitchen, still naked, as if seen through Newton's alien eyes, the image horizontally distorted. Then he is again standing in front of the mirror in the bathroom, one human contact lens already in place, while he inserts the other with a pair of tweezers.[72]

Though Newton returns to his human form, and in the final part of the film briefly resumes his sexual relationship with Mary Lou, they never regain their former intimacy, and eventually they admit that they no longer love one another. Their final sexual encounter is very different from their first, shots from which are intercut with the later scene, as also of alien sex between Newton and his Anthean wife. In their last meeting, Newton and Mary Lou are clearly having sex, as opposed to making love. He postures aggressively, threatening her with a gun, which turns out to fire blanks, an obvious symbol of his now all too human impotence. Newton and Mary Lou have become like Bryce and his students, making bodily contact but no emotional connection.

The Man Who Fell to Earth offers two paradigms of sexual union, the one phallic and violent, the other asexual and pacific. The sexual antics of Bryce and his students, and later of Newton and Mary Lou, exemplify the first, encounters that are truly deadly, emotionally and spiritually sterile. The other kind of sexual union is only ever partly realized, and presented as a past or future possibility, as a dream or fantasy. A joyful, tender reciprocation of bodies is presented as alien sex; as something almost beyond corporal possibility. It is also presented as sex outside the law of the phallus.

In his alien form, Newton ceases to be identifiably male. One might read this unmanning of his body as its feminization, revealing the woman beneath the skin, so that his encounter with Mary Lou becomes a scene of lesbian, same-sex intercourse. However, this would be to over-determine the scene, and would require thinking woman's sex as lack, as the absence of the phallus, as in the traditional Freudian gesture; so that what terrifies Mary Lou about Newton's alien form is seeing in it the truth of her own, emasculated body. Instead, however, we can see Newton's alien body as beyond the sexual polarity of male and female, as a third androgynous sex.

Newton's unmanning destabilizes the web of gender relations in which he is placed, most notably with regard to his 'wife' on Anthea. For if Newton is not humanly male, the designation of 'husband' and 'wife' are clearly borrowed terms, translating a relationship we can only imagine. Perhaps he is the 'woman' to her 'man'; or perhaps, like the Gethenians on the planet Winter, in Ursula Le Guin's novel *The Left Hand of Darkness*, they are asexual except when in a state of 'kemmer' or sexual potency, when they develop masculine or feminine features for the period of their kemmering, their particular sexualization being temporary and unknown beforehand.[73] These speculations go beyond anything presented in the film, which merely offers the union of alien and human as an impossible ideal, suggesting, perhaps, that it is the impossible ideal of all human relationships.

I earlier suggested that in Roeg's film, the religious is not so much displaced in favour of the sexual, as that the latter subsumes the former. This is most evident in the scene where Mary Lou makes love to Newton as an alien, when he has shed his human skin. Their intimacy bespeaks the intimacy of human and divine lovers, the latter folded upon the former. To love God and be loved by God, is, on the face of it, the love of aliens; a love that is most to be desired and feared. *The Man Who Fell to Earth* invests the attempted lovemaking of Anthean and human with religious dread and yearning, and, at the same time, nostalgic regret at its failure.

When Mary Lou screams at the sight of Newton in his alien form, it is the scream of any terrified girl in countless horror films; the scream of the girl who has desired to see, or to see too much.[74] But it is also the terror of one who has seen the face of God, since no one can see God's face and live. Moses once survived God's presence, because God, as he passed by, covered Moses with his hand, so that Moses saw only God's backside, not his face.[75] Mary Lou, however, sees the face of her divinity, who is more fully incarnate, figured as a lonely, melancholic Christ. The scene of her terror is also a scene of his desolation, of his loss and yearning. As Newton lies prostrate and naked on the bed, in a room suddenly grown dark, he has become the deposed Christ, lying in the tomb, awaiting his anointing for burial. As Mary Lou climbs on to the bed with him, raising and kissing his hand, we are reminded of Christ cradled in the arms of mourning women, and of Newton, similarly cradled by Mary Lou at the beginning of the film, when she picked him up from the hotel floor and carried him to his room. 'I lifted you up once', she reminds him as she kisses him, and he replies: 'You must believe Mary Lou'.

Notes

1 Genesis 6.2.
2 Genesis 3.8. See also Genesis 7.16, 8.21 and 11.7.
3 Genesis 18.1.
4 Genesis 19.1.
5 Trains recur throughout the film, symbols of promise and possibility. The rusting engine we see at the film's beginning, however, is an ominous sign of how the visitor's journey will end.
6 As Roeg has said, the 'film belongs as much to the spectator as the director . . . if not more so'. Roeg quoted in Gordon Gow, 'Identity: An Interview with Nicolas Roeg', *Films and Filming* (January 1972): 18–25 (p. 21).
7 Roland Barthes, *S/Z*, translated by Richard Miller (London: Jonathan Cape, [1970] 1975), p. 5.
8 Barthes, *S/Z*, pp. 5–6.
9 Barthes, *S/Z*, p. 6.
10 For the nature and importance of the distinction between *narrative* and *story* see Gerard Loughlin, *Telling God's Story: Bible, Church and Narrative Theology* (Cambridge: Cambridge University Press, [1996] 1999), pp. 52–63.

11 Genesis 18.1–16.

12 One man in verses 3, 10, 13–15; three men in verses 2, 4, 5, 8, 9 and 16. Like Abraham's visitor(s), Buñuel's stranger (Alain Cuny) in *La Voie Lactée* is both one and three: a magician who, as he walks away from the two pilgrims, is suddenly accompanied by a dwarf who throws a dove over his shoulder, becoming a vaudeville Trinity.

13 See Claus Westermann, *Genesis 12–36: A Commentary*, translated by John J. Scullion SJ (Minneapolis: Augsburg Publishing House/London: SPCK, [1981] 1985), pp. 272–82. Westermann supposes that Abraham addresses the leader of the three men, but recognizes that this does not explain the textual vacillation between them and the one who speaks and is addressed, which he ascribes to the combination of two variant stories (p. 278).

14 Karl Barth, *Church Dogmatics*, vol. III/3, translated by G.W. Bromiley and R.J. Ehrlich (Edinburgh: T. & T. Clark, 1960), p. 491.

15 Walter Tevis, *The Man Who Fell to Earth* (London: Bloomsbury, [1963] 1999), pp. 6–7. Two other Tevis novels were made into major films, *The Hustler* (filmed by Robert Rossen, US 1961) and *The Color of Money* (filmed by Martin Scorsese, US 1986), both starring Paul Newman as Fast Eddie Felson.

16 Tevis, *The Man Who Fell to Earth*, pp. 127–8.

17 Tevis, *The Man Who Fell to Earth*, p. 182.

18 Genesis 19.24. Richard Dyer sees a similar affinity between the angel – 'an archetypal "sad young man", beautiful but melancholy' – and the people whose destruction he has come to announce, in the film *Lot in Sodom*, made in 1930 by Melville Webber and James Sibley Watson. See Richard Dyer, *Now You See It: Studies on Lesbian and Gay Film* (London: Routledge, 1990), p. 110.

19 This is supposed in John Izod, *The Films of Nicolas Roeg: Myth and Mind* (London: Macmillan, 1992), p. 88.

20 When the film was released in America, audiences were provided with explanatory notes. Neil Sinyard, *The Films of Nicolas Roeg*, Letts Film Makers (London: Charles Letts, 1991), p. 58.

21 For Mayersberg's account of working on the screenplay with Roeg see Paul Mayersberg, 'The Story So Far . . . *The Man Who Fell to Earth*', *Sight and Sound* (Autumn 1975): 225–31. The sense of a 'dissociated' society is partly the result of Mayersberg and Roeg's attempt to make a film in the form of a 'circus'. 'It has dozens of scenes that go together, not just in terms of plot, but also like circus acts following one another; the funny, the violent, the frightening, the sad, the horrific, the spectacular, the romantic and so on' (p. 231).

22 Roeg quoted in Joseph Lanza, *Fragile Geometry: The Films, Philosophy, and Misadventures of Nicolas Roeg* (New York: PAJ Publications, 1989), p. 16. Lanza's book is by far the best of those on Roeg's cinema, being lively, appreciative and imaginative.

23 Genesis 19.4–5.
24 Tevis, *The Man Who Fell to Earth*, p. 138.
25 Genesis 19.11.
26 Matthew 21.33–41; Mark 12.1–12; Luke 20.9–19.
27 Tevis, *The Man Who Fell to Earth*, p. 167.
28 Tevis, *The Man Who Fell to Earth*, p. 168.
29 Tevis, *The Man Who Fell to Earth*, p. 15.
30 Tevis, *The Man Who Fell to Earth*, p. 85.
31 Tevis, *The Man Who Fell to Earth*, p. 88.
32 The second part of the novel is entitled '1988: Rumpelstiltskin'.
33 The attribution of the painting is questioned. See, for example, John White, *Pieter Bruegel and the Fall of the Art Historian*, Charlton Memorial Lecture (Newcastle upon Tyne: University of Newcastle upon Tyne, 1980).
34 Ovid, *Metamorphoses*, translated by Arthur Golding (1567); reprinted as *Shakespeare's Ovid*, edited by W.H.D. Rouse (London: Centaur Press, [1904] 1961), bk 8, ll. 282–311 (pp. 165–6). See also Ovid, *Metamorphoses*, translated by Mary M. Innes (Harmondsworth: Penguin Books, 1955), bk 8, ll. 183–235 (pp. 184–5).
35 The film relocates the novel's Kentucky scenes to New Mexico.
36 W.H. Auden, *Collected Poems*, edited by Edward Mendelson (London: Faber & Faber, 1976), pp. 146–7. Only the last three lines are quoted in Tevis's novel (p. 21).
37 Tevis, *The Man Who Fell to Earth*, pp. 87–8.
38 Tevis, *The Man Who Fell to Earth*, p. 111.
39 Tevis, *The Man Who Fell to Earth*, p. 108.
40 This identifies the painting as the one which hangs in the Musées Royaux des Beaux Arts in Brussels. A second version of the painting belongs to the D.M. van Buuren Collection (Brussels). It shows the sun at its proper place in the sky, consistent with its reflection in the sea, and the shepherd looks up at Daedalus, as he successfully flies away from the sun. But the former painting is the more uncanny of the two. 'Nothing is real in this reality. All is a dream. There is no straining at the harness for this horse; no jerking at the reins or heaving at a juddering handle for this tip-toeing ploughman as the blunt board of his wooden plough turns easy furrows, neat as ribboned felt. There is no wind to catch the ploughman's coat. There is no whisper in the air to stir a single leaf, and still the ship sweeps on, its great sail billowing, its rigging creaking, in a ghostly, silent gale of its own making'. White, *Pieter Bruegel*, p. 27.
41 Tevis, *The Man Who Fell to Earth*, p. 109.
42 While the 'watcher' has a function in the plot, he also represents the viewer of the film, seeking to understand the characters and their story. For Roeg the 'watcher' also serves as a reminder that we are always observed by others, including ourselves. 'We *are* being watched, if not by other people,

then by ourselves, which can be even worse . . . No matter what you do, you are always accountable to another person. Someone is formulating your life from an angle you may know little about'. Roeg quoted in Lanza, *Fragile Geometry*, p. 113. The 'angels' who consort with men's daughters in Genesis (6.4) are also known as 'watchers' in later renditions of the story, in the Genesis Apocryphon and the Testament of Reuben (5.4–6).

43 The blurring of boundaries between characters is common to both Roeg's cinema and Christian reading of scripture. For example, St Ephrem (306–73), and other Syrian writers, confused or elided Christ's mother with Mary Magdalene in her meeting with the risen Christ in the garden. See Robert Murray, *Symbols of Church and Kingdom: A Study in Early Syriac Tradition* (Cambridge: Cambridge University Press, 1975), pp. 146–8.

44 Lanza, *Fragile Geometry*, p. 23.

45 *The Rise and Fall of Ziggy Stardust and the Spiders from Mars* (RCA 1972); *Aladdin Sane* (RCA 1973).

46 David Buckley, *Strange Fascination: David Bowie: The Definitive Story* (London: Virgin Books, 1999), pp. 143–4.

47 Buckley, *Strange Fascination*, p. 212. Bowie performs as the 'gouster' on his tenth album, *Young Americans* (RCA 1975).

48 Buckley, *Strange Fascination*, p. 232.

49 Buckley, *Strange Fascination*, p. 229.

50 Buckley, *Strange Fascination*, p. 14.

51 Another allusion to Bowie's character and song would appear in John Carpenter's 1984 film, *Starman*, in which Jeff Bridges plays an alien, returning the calling card dispatched to the galaxy on Voyager II (1977). The conceit of an alien response to human missives (to the gods) had been used earlier by Robert Wise in *Star Trek: The Motion Picture* (1979).

52 Michael Watts, 'Oh You Pretty Thing', *Melody Maker*, 22 January 1971, pp. 19 and 42.

53 See Jeffrey Weeks, *Sex, Politics and Society: The Regulation of Sexuality Since 1800*, second edition (London: Longman, [1981] 1989), pp. 239–44; Richard Davenport-Hines, *Sex, Death and Punishment: Attitudes to Sex and Sexuality in Britain since the Renaissance* (London: Collins, 1990), pp. 314–29.

54 Bowie married Iman Abdulmajid in 1992.

55 John Gill, *Queer Noises: Male and Female Homosexuality in Twentieth-Century Music* (London: Cassell, 1995), pp. 106–13.

56 Tevis, *The Man Who Fell to Earth*, p. 57.

57 Tevis, *The Man Who Fell to Earth*, p. 58. The alien visitor in Carpenter's *Starman* (1984) also walks oddly, being unused to the human body he has appropriated. He is also taken for queer, when, ignorant of the etiquette of human urination, he stands smiling at a urinating man in a gas station rest room: 'Every God damn place you go'.

58 Tevis, *The Man Who Fell to Earth*, p. 79.

59 Scott Salwolke espies a third gay character in Newton's servant-jailer. *Nicolas Roeg Film by Film* (Jefferson, NC: McFarland & Company, Inc., 1993), p. 68.

60 Vito Russo identifies *The Man Who Fell to Earth* as one of the few American films to present homosexuality as incidental rather than constitutive of its gay characters. (Vito Russo, *The Celluloid Closet: Homosexuality in the Movies* (New York: Harper & Row, 1981), p. 187.) Nevertheless, Oliver and Trevor's relationship is not thematically incidental, since, along with all the other relationships in the film, it counts as 'alien' (queer) to normative heterosexual (white) marriage.

61 Genesis 6.4; Numbers 13.33. The primeval story of the coupling of angels with humans and their offspring also features in the *Book of Enoch* (*1 Enoch* or *Ethiopic Enoch*), which, written before the third century BC, was influential in the early church, though later rejected and lost. See Margaret Barker, *The Lost Prophet: The Book of Enoch and its Influence on Christianity* (London: SPCK, 1988). See also the *Book of Jubilees* (second century BC).

62 'For this reason a woman ought to have [a symbol of] authority [*exousia*] on her head, because of the angels' (1 Corinthians 11.10). In Greco-Roman culture, the veil that a woman placed upon her head symbolized her authority to avert a shaming male gaze (human or angelic), and yet also her subordination to the gazer(s) thus denied. Tertullian understood Paul's curious remark about the angels as referring to such as the lustful angels in Genesis 6 ('On the Veiling of Virgins', 1.7), as did other ancient authorities (Clement of Alexandria, Paulinus of Nola), and as also several modern scholars. See, for example, Gail Patterson Corrington, 'The "Headless Woman": Paul and the Language of the Body in I Corinthians 11.2–16', *Perspectives in Religious Studies*, 18 (1991): 223–31; Dale B. Martin, *The Corinthian Body* (New Haven: Yale University Press, 1995), pp. 244–7.

63 Mary Lou takes Newton to church, where, in his honour as a visiting Englishman, the congregation sing an old English hymn, William Blake's 'Jerusalem' (from the Preface to 'Milton', 1804–8): 'And did those feet in ancient time/Walk upon England's mountains green? And was the holy Lamb of God/On England's pleasant pastures seen?' Candy Clark (Mary Lou) has good reason to grin throughout the scene, for not only do the lines have multiple significance within the film, but it is the only scene in which Bowie sings, or tries to sing. See figure 8.

64 The stylized violence of Japanese theatre is associated with Bryce, while the serenity of other aspects of Japanese culture attract Newton, who adorns his house with Japanese artefacts. See Mayersberg quoted in Lanza, *Fragile Geometry*, p. 89.

65 The allusion is of course to John Donne's Nineteenth Elegy, 'To his Mistress Going to Bed': 'Licence my roving hands, and let them go/Before, behind, between, above, below./O my America, my new found land' (ll. 25–27).

66 One has to suppose that the telescope is one of Newton's strange inventions.

67 'Now off with those shoes, and then safely tread/In this love's hallowed temple, this soft bed./In such white robes heaven's angels used to be/Received by men; thou angel bring'st with thee/A heaven like Mahomet's paradise; and though/Ill spirits walk in white, we easily know/By this these angels from an evil sprite,/Those set our hairs, but these our flesh upright' ('To his Mistress Going to Bed', ll. 17–24).

68 In the film, David Bowie not only plays an Englishman in America, but is an Englishman surrounded by American actors. *The Man Who Fell to Earth* was heralded as the first entirely British financed film to be shot in America. It was made by British Lion.

69 Roeg had explored the merging of faces and characters in his first film, made with Donald Cammell, *Performance* (completed 1968; released 1970), in which Chas Devlin (James Fox) fuses with the ex-rock star Turner (Mick Jagger).

70 This shot, along with several others, adding up to some 20 minutes, was cut from the film for its initial release in America. A complete version was eventually released in 1980. See Lanza, *Fragile Geometry*, pp. 53–4.

71 Roeg's visualization of Newton's wet dream clearly proved too much for Neil Feineman, who nevertheless missed the point or was being coy when he described it as 'a process that can best be described as the mutual splashing of mud on each other's bodies'. See Neil Feinemann, *Nicolas Roeg* (Boston: Twayne Publishers, 1978), p. 115. The scene is so rarely remarked in commentary on the film, that it would seem to have embarrassed most critics.

72 The framing of the alien sex sequence between shots of Newton in the bathroom, looking at himself in the mirror, allows for the possibility that it has only taken place in his imagination. The dialogue between him and Mary Lou after their aborted encounter could as well refer to what they said before it, as during it.

73 Ursula Le Guin, *The Left Hand of Darkness* (London: Virago Books, [1969] 1997). The Gethenians consider people of a fixed, determinate sex, male or female, as 'perverts'. I am grateful to Rowan Williams for bringing this novel to my attention.

74 Lanza (*Fragile Geometry*, p. 145) suggests that Mary Lou's 'Grade B scream' on seeing 'David Bowie's Grade B alien suit' is a tribute to directors like Herschell Gordon Lewis, who was notorious for such gory 'meat-movies' as *Blood Feast* (1963) and *Color Me Blood Red* (1964). Roeg, at an earlier stage in his career, had worked with the master of horror B movies, Roger Corman, as lighting cameraman on *The Masque of the Red Death* (1964). Its famous tracking shot of Jane Asher walking through a series of coloured rooms, is reprised in *The Man Who Fell to Earth*, when a waiter pushes a trolley through a series of garishly decorated rooms on his way to the bedroom where Newton is imprisoned.

75 Exodus 33.20–23. Moses, while denied sight of God's face, was also, of course, privileged to see God's face, and live. This contradiction in the narratives renders the story indeterminate, so that we can have little idea of what it would be to 'see' the 'face' of God. See further Daniel Boyarin, 'The Eye in the Torah: Ocular Desire in Midrashic Hermeneutic', *Critical Inquiry*, 16/3 (1990): 532–50.

Figure 9 Affinity

The lovers (Johnny Mills and Keith Collins) in *The Garden* (Derek Jarman, UK 1990). Photo: British Film Institute.

Chapter 9

THE GARDEN

Mary is alone in the garden when she comes upon a man whom she takes to be the gardener. She doesn't pay him much attention, because she is looking for someone else, even though he is dead. Weeping, she is looking for a corpse, which is not where it was left, in its tomb. 'Sir, if you have carried him away, tell me where you have laid him, and I will take him away'. She hardly expects an answer, because she has already turned to go when the man speaks to her, and says her name. At once she recognizes him. Impossibly, it is the man for whom she is looking: her dead teacher, her rabbi, her lost lover. Turning, she embraces him, clings to him; but he breaks away from her, from her grip. 'Do not hold on to me', he says. 'I am ascending to my Father and your Father, to my God and your God'.[1]

Intensely poignant, this strange story of the meeting of Mary and Jesus in the garden of the tomb contains the entire gospel of the Christian church: hope in a memory of the future, the promise that one day we will walk again with Christ in the garden.[2] As imagined in the tradition of the Church, this scene is charged with sexual yearning; nowhere better seen than in Titian's *Noli me Tangere* (c. 1515). Mary is shown on her knees, reaching out to an all too fleshy Christ, and he, almost naked, and supporting his weight on his hoe, leans towards her, while seeking to further cover his loins with his shroud, which he draws away from her reaching hand. The painting is remarkable on many counts, not least for its depiction of a north Italian landscape, bathed in early morning light; a serene setting for the drama of the two lovers, caught in the stilled moment of their reunion and parting. On her knees, Mary's weight is supported with her left hand, placed on the jar of ointment with which she had come to anoint Jesus' cold, drained body.[3] But now his flesh is anything but deathly. It is warm, soft, enlivened. Christ is standing before Mary, leaning towards her, but drawing away at the same time. They look at each other intently, and the line of their gaze and the curve of Christ's body, forms a triangle that, just off centre, is the focus of the picture. Christ's face is at the apex and the other two points are marked by Mary's face on the right, and, at the same level, the swirling knot of cloth that covers Christ's genitals on the left. At the same time, the line of their mutual look and the curve formed by their right arms – hers reaching out, his pulling back – forms an ellipse that, laid on the triangle, draws the viewer into the dynamic of their relationship, the desiring of their bodies.[4]

Desiring Christ

The strangely overt but concealed sexual coding of the relationship between Jesus and Mary in Titian's painting, follows in the long tradition that has identified Mary Magdalene with the woman taken in adultery, with the woman who bathed Jesus' feet with oil and with her tears and who dried them with her hair.[5] That Jesus knew such a woman – such women – and befriended her/them, and she/they him, has always invested this most chaste of men with a sexual potency, that has, from the earliest days of telling his story, excited curiosity about his intimate companions. Was he aroused when Mary kissed and caressed his feet, and washed them with her tears and dried them with her hair, as if she were anointing him with herself as well as with the ointment that she would later bring to him in an 'alabaster jar'?[6] The question is less perverse when we recall that in Hebrew tradition the feet could stand in for the genitals, as when Ruth crept up on the sleeping Boaz and 'uncovered his feet'.[7] Perhaps Mary asked Jesus, as Ruth asked Boaz, to be covered with his cloak.

Many berated Martin Scorsese's *The Last Temptation of Christ* (USA 1988) for showing Mary Magdalene as a prostitute, already known to Jesus before he rescued her from stoning. But Scorsese was only being faithful to Christian tradition; more faithful than some earlier, ostensibly more pious film-makers. Cecil B. DeMille's *The King of Kings* (USA 1927) opens with a lavish banquet, hosted by the courtesan Mary Magdalene, who is bewailing her desertion by Judas, her lover. He has left her for a 'band of beggars, led by the Carpenter from Nazareth'. Jumping into her chariot, Magdalene goes in pursuit, only herself to fall under the allure of the carpenter, who frees her of seven demons.[8] Lauded for its reverent portrayal of the gospel story,[9] DeMille's opening scenes are entirely invented, and far more titillating than the somewhat demure scene in Scorsese's film, that has Jesus waiting his turn in the brothel where Mary Magdalene is plying her body.

The Last Temptation of Christ is of course a reimagining of the Easter meeting of Jesus and Mary in the garden, when Jesus does not depart but stays, and becomes Mary's actual spouse. Based on Nikos Kazantzakis's novel, *The Last Temptation* (1961), Scorsese's film seeks to explore that supposedly most Byzantine of themes, the struggle between flesh and spirit in pursuit of union with God.[10] The novel pitches profanity and sanctity together, as sibling possibilities within everyone. Jesus is not only a carpenter, but also a maker of crosses, who is beset by God as if by a demon.[11] By betraying his people he hopes to frighten God away. Mary Magdalene, who is the daughter of a rabbi, has left home for a life of prostitution, having been rebuffed by Jesus; and he is tormented both by his desire for her and by God's incessant calling.

This is Christ's last temptation, to desert his destiny for the pleasures of domesticity and familiality, to channel his desire toward carnal pleasure and paternity; the 'primal route of all striving after vanities'.[12] Perhaps it was because the film associated hearth and home – the 'nuclear family' – with the demonic, that so many Christian groups railed against its showing, and yet how strange that they should have been revolted by that in Christ which in themselves they found so admirable, namely homely heterosexuality. But their outrage was not entirely misplaced, for the portrayal of Christ as family man is inconsistent with the Christian tradition. Though many gnostic writers, both ancient and modern, have sought to marry Christ off to someone like Mary Magdalene, the early orthodox tradition always resisted such sexual and familial ties, insisting on Christ's spiritual polygamy with his brethren.[13] Yet the outrage of 'fundamentalist' Christians at Scorsese's depiction of Christ's last temptation was finally misplaced, because in book and film Jesus resists the allure of hearth and home, refusing patriarchal domesticity for death on the cross. Scorsese's Jesus is not only faithful to the gospels, but to that line of underground resistance that everywhere subverts, if only symbolically, an authorized straightness. Christ will not stay and marry his Mary. It was only later that people would come to think marriage an appropriate ending for a story.[14]

However intimate the relationship between Jesus and Mary, orthodox tradition never supposed that it was physically consummated, though such a calumny was not unknown to the orthodox. Martin Luther (1483–1546) could jest that 'Christ was an adulterer for the first time with the woman at the well, for it was said, "Nobody knows what he's doing with her" [John 4.27]. Again [he was an adulterer] with Magdalene, and still again with the adulterous woman in John 8[.2–11], whom he let off so easily'.[15]

The canonical gospels suggest that Jesus was not married, and that he had male and female disciples and male and female friends, four of whom he particularly loved, and who loved him. 'Now Jesus loved Martha, and her sister [Mary], and Lazarus',[16] who perhaps was the beloved disciple, the young man who laid his head against Jesus, resting on his bosom, and to whom Jesus disclosed the identity of the betrayer, though that disciple is traditionally identified as John.[17] Jesus' affection for these people, and theirs for him, is quickly but tellingly told in the gospels. It is Mary, Martha's sister, who washes his feet with perfume and dries them with her hair. When he is faced with the death of Lazarus, and the weeping of the sisters, he too weeps and inwardly groans.[18] However fleetingly, Jesus is shown within a web of relationships, of endearments and affective bonds, of expectations and consolations. He is bound to others as they to him with ties of trust and affection, and some, no doubt were ties of particular friendship.[19] The image of Jesus with John, the disciple whom Jesus loved, lying on his breast, is redolent of true friendship, the companionship of intimates. 'David had his Jonathan, Christ his John'.[20]

That the relationship of Jesus and Mary Magdalene was more than merely affectionate has been a common enough speculation, made by both early Christian gnostics and modern secular novelists. Both the Gospel of Mary and the Gospel of Philip present Mary Magdalene as Jesus' beloved disciple, who was at one and the same time his mother, sister and companion. But while the gospels give grounds for this heterosexual speculation, they also provide evidence for a homosexual one, of a more than friendly relationship between Jesus and John. Again this idea lived as a calumny in the Western tradition. A little later than Luther, the English playwright Christopher Marlowe (1564–93) was reported by Richard Baines to have declared that 'St John the Evangelist was bedfellow to Christ and leaned alwaies in his bosom . . . he used him as the sinners of Sodama.'[21]

It remains the case, however, that while the scriptures allow for Christ's sexual orientation in any one of several directions, the majority interest has been to suppose Jesus unmarried and celibate, though this also is a purely speculative claim, an induction from silence. However, it has not been a Christian interest to suppose Jesus asexual, lacking in ardour. On the contrary, Christian thought has supposed that Christ loves passionately, unconditionally and without exhaustion, and elicits the same kind of response in his lovers. The classic sites for such passion are the spiritual discourses of the medieval 'mystics', male and female; and the trope of Christ as lover was made possible by the much earlier acceptance of the Song of Songs into the canon of scripture. 'Let him kiss me with the kisses of his mouth.'[22]

Desire and Displacement

As already indicated, the question of Jesus' possible sexual relationships is not itself a modern one, but the question of his *sexuality* most certainly is. It is a modern question because the concept of sexuality is itself a modern idea, a defining characteristic of the modern self and its desires. The ancient world had no discourse of sexuality by which to constitute an experience of sexual orientation. This is not to say that ancient people did not experience the greed and hunger we associate with the libidinal body, or that their desires were not driven by their flesh. But it is to say that they were not characterized by sexuality, when that is understood as an inner drive that is ordered toward certain practices, by which alone it is known. This desire constitutes identity, knowledge of which provides the truth of human being. Furthermore, it is to say that modern discourses on sexuality are not sacrosanct, as if defining the truth of the sexed body for all time, so that other discourses, of past ages and other cultures, are always secondary, at best belated. Rather we must understand that what our discourse names is established by that discourse, as its imaginary ground, so that its stability over time and across cultures is always the venture of a judgement. Thus the truth of Jesus' body, of his sexuality, can only come into view in our discourses and not in his. As Graham Ward reminds us, in his nice rewriting of Derrida, bodily '[t]issue is *not* text, but there is tissue only because there *is* text'.[23]

Given the textuality of flesh, the informing of bodily tissue by cultural mediation, the question of Jesus' sexuality seems to repeat the error of the nineteenth-century quest for the historical Jesus.[24] That quest supposed it possible to somehow see through the texts of scripture to a preceding, non-textual reality, that could be grasped and given without the mediation of cultural formations. Nevertheless, despite the danger of being lured into positivist speculation, and the alien nature of sexuality for the ancient world, there is some necessity to stay a little longer with the question of Jesus' sexuality.

We should ask about Jesus' sexuality, not in order to determine the past but in order to interrogate the present. Would it matter to us if Jesus was a man who desired men, instead of women, or a man who desired only women, or who desired both women and men, and was alike desired by them? The historical question is not whether Jesus was hetero, homo or bisexual, but whether it now matters if he were, or if those who follow him are? It certainly matters to some people.

In the same year as Nicolas Roeg's film *The Man Who Fell to Earth* (UK 1976) appeared, the British weekly newspaper *Gay News*, published a poem by James Kirkup (1918–), 'The Love that Dares to Speak its Name'. In the poem, a centurion – perhaps the centurion of the gospels who is so awed at Christ's death[25] – declares his love for Jesus, and Jesus' love for him and other men. While the women are away fetching the grave clothes, the centurion makes passionate love to the dead Christ. Admittedly pornographic and necrophilic, and later disowned by its author,[26] the poem would have been but of momentary interest, if the moral campaigner Mary Whitehouse had not brought a private prosecution against *Gay News* on the grounds of blasphemy. The case was taken up by the Crown prosecution service, and in 1977 an Old Bailey jury found against the journal and its editor, Denis Lemon (1945–94). He was fined and given a suspended prison sentence, though this was later rescinded on appeal.[27]

An irony of the case is that for the most part the poem's expression of devotion to Christ through sexual intercourse is entirely traditional. Only the suggestion that Jesus had sex with numerous men goes beyond the limits of canonical devotion. The Song of Songs licensed the use of sexual metaphors for describing the soul's relationship to Christ, and both women and men availed themselves of this licence. The defence council for *Gay News* was not allowed to call on expert testimony as to the literary worth of the poem, let alone its theological merits. Thus the jury that was so affronted by Kirkup's centurion penetrating the wounds of Christ, could not have been informed that the sexualization of Christ's wounds was at one time an established trope of spiritual communion. The Spanish artist Francisco Ribalta (1565–1628) painted St Francis embracing Christ (c. 1620) hanging on the cross. Francis, his eyes closed in ecstasy, puts his lips to the wound in Christ's side from which the blood is flowing, while Christ reaches down to crown Francis with the thorns from his own head. Ribalta's Francis bears the stigmata, the very wounds by which he enters into Christ's flesh, and by which Christ enters into his.[28] The English poet Richard Crashaw (1612/13–49) likened Christ's wounds to eyes and mouths, which could repay the Magdalene for her tears and kisses.

> This foot hath got a Mouth and lippes,
> To pay the sweet summe of thy kisses:
> To pay thy Teares, an Eye that weeps
> In stead of Tears such Gems as this is.
>
> The difference onely this appears,
> (Nor can the change offend)
> The debt is paid in *Ruby*-Teares,
> Which thou in Pearles did'st lend.[29]

No doubt those for whom Ribalta and Crashaw produced their works would have been as horrified by Kirkup's poem as the jury that judged its publication a blasphemous libel. Nevertheless, Ribalta's painting and Crashaw's poetry, and the tradition of 'sacred eroticism' to which they belong, challenges the godly twentieth-century readers of Kirkup's poem. Their horror reminds us that sexuality is at one and the same time most intimate to, and estranged from, Christ's body. For such readers sex is utterly alien to Christ, so that they cannot find a place for sexual desire in his body; and yet Christ came so that he could know us intimately, feeling the joys and terrors of our flesh.

Given the centrality of sexuality for the modern self, it is impossible not to ask about the sexuality of Jesus if we follow the Cappadocian dictum that the unassumed is the unredeemed. For God to redeem the world he must become all manner of flesh, black and white, male and female, straight and gay. The Greek Fathers supposed that in Christ, God took on human flesh as such, becoming, as it were, humanity and not merely a man. But the *human* as such can seem too abstract, too removed from any one body, let alone all bodies, to be human at all. Someone like Gregory of Nyssa could hold that God took on both male and female flesh, because, though a man, Christ's flesh was entirely of his mother, in whom he had dwelled.[30] Moreover, since Eve's flesh came from Adam's, scripture textualizes male and female flesh as a single tissue, a differentiated but continuous body. It is this idea of an extended, expanded body – as of Eve from Adam, Jesus from Mary, Church from Christ – that Graham Ward has developed in his Christology of the displaced body of Jesus Christ.[31]

Starting with the body of the Jewish Jesus, the man from Nazareth, Ward traces its continuous displacement into the ever-growing body of the Gentile church. Ward works through the gospel narratives, showing the successive transformations, stretchings and displacements of Jesus' body, from its birth and circumcision (which affirms its sexed nature), via its transfiguration and eucharistic transposition (transubstantiation), to its crucifixion, resurrection and ascension. Jesus' body has a mercurial materiality that becomes less particular and more generalized as the story proceeds.[32] Moreover, with each displacement the body becomes more desirable. The beauty that attracts in Jesus is increasingly that of the divine glory that shines in and through him, drawing us toward and beyond him. He becomes luminous. 'His corporeality becomes iconic.'[33] Jesus' body is gradually lost to sight with its crucifixion, resurrection and ascension. But it leaves only in order to return, infinitely transposed in the eucharistic body that feeds the body of the church, which becomes Christ's body, not metaphorically, but actually, as its non-identical, analogical repetition. It is in this way that the body of Jesus, whether hetero, homo or bisexual, becomes the 'multigendered', sexually polymorphous body of Christ, the body in which 'all other bodies are situated and given their significance'.[34]

While the idea of 'displacement' captures the differentiated nature of the Christic body, it runs the risk of suggesting that at each stage of extension one body is replaced by another, so that Christ's body replaces the body of Jesus, obliterating the specifics of his life and teaching. Thus Christ becomes more word than flesh, more of an idea than an historical undertaking.[35] But against this, Ward insists that 'displacement is not the erasure but the expansion of the body'.[36] Therefore we should not imagine a series of disappearing bodies, as rather an increasingly disseminated, mutating body, that, in all its parts, is 'continuous' with the body of Jesus.

Leo Bersani and Ulysse Dutoit suggest that Christ was 'exalted and martyred' by centuries of art; made to disappear through his repeated, non-identical representation. 'His appearance, once conventionalized, became recognizable in art, but it is never repeated in exactly the same manner, with the result that his multiple presences are identical to an unending disappearance.' Uniquely, according to Bersani and Dutoit, the artist Caravaggio (1573–1610) painted Christ's disappearance through his rendering of the models who stood in for Christ in his paintings. Their bodies resist the symbolization they are made to bear. 'The models, standing in for figures nowhere else to be found, enact the brute suppression of icons whose glory they have been ordered, and paid, to serve, and whom they replace by their very service.' Thus, for Bersani and Dutoit, Christ disappears into his artistic resurrection, where he appears only as a ghost. It is a process of disincarnation.[37]

Bersani and Dutoit's analysis is close to Ward's account of displacement. Yet it misses the difference that Christ's resurrection makes to the fate of his body. For when the tomb is found empty, Jesus' body is not so much disappeared or displaced, as deterritorialized. It has passed beyond the confines of mortal flesh, the lineaments of a single frame. Jesus is transfigured, but not just as Moses or Elijah.[38] He has become the flesh of every foreign body, the touch of every stranger; the glory of an alien encounter.[39] If Jesus' body is deterritorialized, and so no longer located in any one place, then every other body is set free, since Christ has become for us a common humanity, the difference in the same. Thus what Bersani and Dutoit read as Christ's disappearance into the flesh of Caravaggio's models, is in fact the appearing of Christ in the bodies of those models, in their carnal substantiality.[40] We see Christ most clearly when we see only their bodies, luminous with the density of Christ's flesh in theirs.

On this understanding of the-body-of-Jesus-become-the-body-of-Christ, the question of Jesus' sexuality is not a question about his desire for John or Mary or whoever, but about the place of such desire, such a flight of yearning, within the body of Christ, the communion of the church. Are hetero and homosexuals within the body? Are they analogously related, not to the body of Jesus who was, but to Christ's body that is coming and even now arriving? The question about the sexuality of Jesus is thus entirely legitimate, indeed vital, for a Cappadocian theology that understands salvation as incorporation into the story of Christ, the tissue of his flesh, the text of his body.[41] And the question about the sexuality of Jesus is the question that he answers when he tells Mary not to hold on to him, but to return to the disciples. To have waited on this question is to have waited with Jesus and Mary in the garden of the tomb.

Touching the Gardener

Mary is not allowed to hold her risen Lord. In Titian's painting, Jesus' withdrawal of his flesh, just out of reach of Mary's outstretched hand, is almost coy, teasing. Mary wants to feel what she can see but cannot quite believe, as if only touch will validate sight. Thomas also requires to see and feel the Lord, to put his finger in the mark of the nails, and, unlike Mary, he is invited to touch as well as see, to put his hand into Jesus' side.[42] But it is a mute point as to whether he does, since Thomas's extravagant expression of faith – 'My Lord and my God!' – immediately follows the injunction to handle Jesus' flesh. While several artists have portrayed Thomas touching Jesus, as Bernardo Strozzi in *The Incredulity of St Thomas* (c. 1620), Thomas perhaps believed without touching, as Mary believed as soon as she heard Jesus call her name. She desires to touch and hold Jesus, not out of incredulity, but out of joy at his being there. Again, John's narrative is unclear as to whether Mary actually embraces Jesus. Perhaps, in Titian's painting, she has put her arms around him, but he has pulled away from her, causing her to fall to her knees; or perhaps she first fell and then reached out, only to have Jesus step back, and yet move towards her, leaning as he does, as if to embrace her without touching.[43]

It is sometimes said that Jesus refuses Mary's actual or attempted embrace because she is being taught to love him in a different way, spiritually rather than carnally, in the way that all must learn to love him, now that he is ascended.[44] According to the allegory of Maximus the Confessor (c. 580–662), Mary Magdalene mistakes Jesus for the gardener because she has not realized that the Creator of all changeable things is beyond the senses, beyond change and corruption, and carnal embrace.[45] As with the story of Thomas, whose doubt is contrasted with the belief of those who neither see nor touch the Lord, so Mary, who has seen and touched, must now believe *in memoria*, on the basis of the story that she herself will tell to others. In the future – that is in the present, when the story is told and heard – sight and touch of the Lord will not be the basis, but the reward, the fulfilment of faith. Thus Christ comes to those who, knowingly or unknowingly, love him already, yearn for him the most.

While Mary's future love for Jesus may be more spiritual, however, it is not necessarily less carnal, less bodily. Jesus tells Mary not to cling on to him because he has not yet ascended to his Father, *as if she might hold him once he has ascended.*[46] She is told to go to the disciples, to announce his departure, and we hear no more about her in John's gospel. Instead, we have the stories of Jesus appearing to his (male) disciples in the locked room when Thomas is absent and when he is present, and to seven of the disciples, including Thomas, when they are fishing on the Sea of Tiberias. In these meetings, their departing Lord gives them the Holy Spirit, the gift of forgiveness, and enjoins them to follow him.[47] Jesus never seems more present than when he is breakfasting with his friends on the sea shore, as the sun begins to rise, and he passes around the bread and fish that has been cooking on a charcoal fire. If their relationship is now to be more spiritual, less material, it could hardly seem more corporeal; and if he is going to their Father, how are they to follow him?

Jesus never tells the disciples he meets in the locked room or by the seashore that he is going to their Father. They have already been told that by Mary. When Jesus comes to the disciples – when they are still fearful after his death, and when, more emboldened, they have returned to their fishing – he does not do so in order to take his leave, for he has already left. Dead and buried and risen, he comes to them as the ascended Lord, who is already one with the Father. He is present with them *because* he is ascended, and his ascended state is corporeal, feeding them as they feed his sheep. Thus it is that Mary can touch him once he is ascended, once he is with his disciples in their following of him, in their forgiving and feeding of others. It is in their caring for one another, and for others, that they touch the Lord, and he embraces them, holding them in his arms; his touch being their embrace.[48]

In Matthew's gospel, Mary Magdalene has a companion, 'the other Mary', with whom she meets Jesus, after she and the other Mary have first met with an angel, burning with the brightness of snow. Both the angel and

Jesus tell the women not to be afraid, but to go and tell the disciples that Jesus is raised and going ahead of them to Galilee.[49] This is much the same as in John, except that Mary and Jesus have been doubled, making the story less private and more social. And like John, when Jesus meets his brothers in Galilee, he does so as the ascended Lord, the one to whom all authority in heaven and on earth has been given. As such, he remains with his disciples, working 'with them'[50] until 'the end of the age'.[51]

Much the same can be said of the gospels of Mark and Luke, except that in Mark, Mary is joined by Salome and Mary the mother of James, and in Luke she becomes a small group of women, that includes Mary the mother of James and Joanna.[52] While originally Mark may not have ended with the women fleeing in 'terror and amazement', the young man whom they meet at the tomb tells them to go to Galilee, where they and the other disciples will see Jesus.[53] In the appended longer ending of Mark, as in Luke, the Jesus with whom the disciples meet in Galilee has passed into glory, so that even though both gospels end with Jesus' departure, he yet remains with his disciples, working with them, and filling them with 'great joy', so that they are 'continually in the temple blessing God'.[54]

When Jesus withdraws from his disciples,[55] he is not other than still with them, for they are in the only place that he could be, the world itself being 'place'. The 'men of Galilee' who 'stand looking up toward heaven'[56] are looking in the wrong direction. Rather they must turn their step to Jerusalem – the city on the hill – where their risen and ascended Lord will be with them, in the toil of the city's streets. Though it is only in John's gospel that we find a fully 'realized ascension', whereby the departed Christ is wholly present with and in his disciples, it is yet nascent in the other gospels, where even though Jesus departs, he does not abandon his followers. In the same way, though it is only in John that the story of Jesus and Mary in the garden fully articulates the need to let go in order to pass from the desolation of the empty tomb to the presence of Jesus with and in his disciples, it is yet already broached in the other gospels, in the command to meet with Jesus, not in the garden, but in Galilee, and then in Jerusalem, where the Spirit arrives.[57]

It is possible to meet Jesus in the garden, but only Mary does so, or Mary and the other women. It is they who meet the departing, ascending Jesus; and the Jesus whom they and the other disciples meet later in Galilee is the departed and ascended Jesus, the Jesus who is with them because he has departed. This is why Mary must not cling to Jesus, not because she must learn to love him differently, after the spirit rather than the flesh, but because she must learn to love him more truly, more corporeally. She must not hold on to a discarnate, phantom Jesus, a mere ghost.[58] Her lover is departed and returned, present with her in her companions, in her fellow disciples, who are not spirits but bodies. She will love Jesus differently, but more not less carnally.

Mary will learn this more bodily love of Christ through learning to love other bodies, that are the extended body of Jesus, and she will learn this love outside the garden.[59] But the garden is where the learning begins, and to which the learning will lead, since love of the body-in-Christ – Christ's body – is the love of bodies in paradise, the garden of which we have hope of return. It will appear at the heart of the city,[60] and be lit by the lamp of the Lamb.[61]

Eden in England

'Paradise haunts gardens, and some gardens are paradises. Mine is one'.[62] But the garden of Derek Jarman (1942–94) was not as some might imagine paradise, not the green park of the word's Persian origin. In 1986, Jarman bought a small fisherman's lodging – Prospect Cottage – overlooking the shingle beach at Dungeness, a bare windswept expanse on the south coast of England, bereft of trees and dominated by the Dungeness nuclear power station – though even its bulk is dwarfed by the expanse of the sky.[63] A forest of pylons spreads northward from the power station, carrying electricity to the Home Counties. 'The nuclear power station is a wonderment. At night it looks like a great liner or a small Manhattan ablaze with a thousand lights of different colours. A mysterious shadow surrounds it that makes it possible for the stars still to glow in a clear summer sky.'[64] Jarman was attracted by the bleakness of the place, and the adversity of making a garden that was as much a matter of flint and driftwood, as it was of dog rose, gorse and sea kale, resisting the elements.

> The easterlies are worst; they bring salt spray which burns everything. The westerlies only give a battering. We have the strongest sunlight, the lowest rainfall, and two less weeks of frost than the rest of the UK. Dungeness is set apart, at 'the fifth quarter', the end of the globe; it is the largest shingle formation, with Cape Canaveral, in the world.[65]

Jarman's love of gardens had started at a young age. 'I was always a passionate gardener – flowers sparkled in my childhood as they do in a medieval manuscript.'

> I remember daisies – white and red – daisy chains on the lawn, fortresses of grass clippings, and of course the exquisite garden of Villa Zuassa, by Lake Maggiore, where in April 1946 my parents gave me my first grown-up book: *Beautiful Flowers and How to Grow Them*. The garden cascaded down to the lake, its paths banked by huge camellias. The beds were full of fiery scarlet pelargoniums – the scent of red.[66]

Associated with childhood, and with his first love, Davide, the garden would constitute not only a haven, but a mythic space in which the artist encounters both his anguish and its comforting. In the garden, time is touched by eternity, and beatitude is momentarily embraced, promising infinite succor for life's inchoate yearning. 'The gardener digs in another time, without past or future, beginning or end. A time that does not cleave the day with rush hours, lunch breaks, the last bus home. As you walk in the garden you pass into this time – the moment of entering can never be remembered. Around you the landscape lies transfigured. Here is the Amen beyond the prayer.'[67]

It amused Jarman that having settled in Dungeness and begun to nurture his shingle garden, he acquired a new reputation as a serious gardener, among people who knew little, and cared less, for his avant-garde films and gay activism. Gardens recur throughout Jarman's films as they do throughout the Bible – the garden of Eden; the garden that is my sister, my spouse; the garden of Gethsemane; and the tomb garden. As with other biblical sites and characters these gardens are both different and the same; different places but the same space, an imaginative locale for the staging of human lives. Walking in any one garden, you sense the presence of the others; foreboding of death in paradise, regret for what is lost but still promised in the vicinity of the tomb. Death is presaged in every new bud, and Spring in every fallen leaf and scattered seed. Michael O'Pray suggests that Jarman's gardens are both Gethsemane and Eden, places of 'pain and pleasure'.[68] Viewed one way, they yet must always threaten or promise the other. For O'Pray, this duality of suffering and delight is characteristic of Jarman's life and work, his own homosexuality causing him 'pain and joy',[69] and his films identifying repressive authority with homosexual sado-masochism, while yet evoking the possibility of ideal, gay relationships, elegically rendered (figure 9).[70]

> Here at the sea's edge
> I have planted my dragon-toothed garden
> To defend the porch,
> Steadfast warriors
> Against those who protest their impropriety

Even to the end of the world.
A fathomless lethargy has swallowed me,
Great waves of doubt broken me,
All my thoughts washed away.
The storms have blown salt tears,
Burning my garden,
Gethsemane and Eden.[71]

Jarman presented himself not only as a gardener, but also as a sort of Christ figure, combining in himself the roles of horticulturist and suffering visionary. Like the alien in Tevis's *The Man Who Fell to Earth*, Jarman saw himself and other gay men as abandoned angels, wandering the earth, prey to the hostility of the benighted, stubbornly ignorant middle-classes. 'Surely we were the angels denied hospitality by the Sodomites. Was not Sodom a tight little suburban dormitory mortgaged out to the hardhearted somewhere beyond Epsom?'[72] In 1989, when Jarman wrote these words, he had already been diagnosed with HIV, and felt personally affected by the reluctance of the British Government to fund AIDS research while it was willing to pass homophobic legislation. Two years previously, in 1987, the Conservative government had added the now infamous Clause 28 to the Local Government Bill, forbidding local authorities from intentionally promoting homosexuality, or from promoting 'the teaching in any maintained school of the acceptability of homosexuality as a pretended family relationship'. It was at this time that 'homosexuals' began to identify themselves with the once abusive term of 'queer', and Jarman did likewise.[73] His anger was also drawn by the churches, which he felt had forgotten how to love. 'We are dealing with people who are actually morally reprobate.'[74] In September 1991, in the garden at Prospect Cottage, the Sisters of Perpetual Indulgence – 'men who dressed as nuns in order to expiate homosexual guilt and promulgate universal joy' – canonized Jarman as St Derek of Dungeness, 'the first Kentish saint since Queer Thomas of Canterbury'.[75] Jarman died on the evening of 21 February 1994, when the British Parliament voted on whether to lower the age of consent for gay men to 16, and settled on 18.

Gay Gardening

Jesus the gardener was a common Renaissance image, adorning all manner of devotional objects, from altar cloths to book covers. These images of Christ, equipped with hoe, spade or watering can, reminded people that gardening was a godly activity, since the deity himself had planted paradise.[76] So it is entirely fitting that Derek Jarman, a student of the English Renaissance, should have staged his Christ movie in the mythic space of paradise, filmed in his own Eden at Dungeness, and named *The Garden* (UK 1990).[77]

One of Jarman's early ideas for *The Garden* was to have a spaceman come to earth at Dungeness. There he would discover a desolate land, destroyed by pestilence. Digging in the shingle, he would find a capsule that contains the only remaining images of 'our vanished world', and these images would constitute the main part of the film. Jarman had used a similar conceit in his earlier film, *Jubilee* (UK 1978), where the alien visitor was Elizabeth I, who, with the help of her necromancer John Dee, pays a visionary visit to England's future, a dystopian vision in which Buckingham Palace has become a recording studio and Westminster Cathedral has become a nightclub, and marauding punks do battle with the police.[78]

As finished, *The Garden* is still presented as a vision, but not as disclosed to an alien visitor. It is dreamed by Jarman himself, who is first seen fallen asleep at his desk, with water splashing onto various objects around him, including a small crucifix.[79] Here he dreams of Adam and Eve being expelled from paradise, with a satan-serpent in bondage gear, slithering on his belly, in chains and black leather;[80] and all staged beneath the glaring arc lamps in Jarman's garden, outside his cottage. A suited young man holds aloft a burning flare and looks in at the window. But all he sees is his own reflection. Perhaps he is the cherubim who bars the way back to Eden with a flaming sword;[81] a doubled gatekeeper. Jarman continues to sleep.

Later in *The Garden* we see Jarman on a hospital bed, sleeping fitfully, and attended by guardian spirits, who circle the bed with flares held aloft, walking in the sea as it comes to shore beneath the sleeping film director. Here Jarman dreams himself dying, directing from betwixt life and death; and he was increasingly ill throughout the making of the film. 'Something terrible has overtaken my nights – shaken about like a limp rag doll.'[82] Indeed, Jarman is a kind of alien, who has fallen into a world where he is not at home, or only at home in his garden – we see shots of him watering, digging and potting his plants – at the edge of the world, 'at the threshold of the other'.[83] But the film has another, more disquieting alien visitor; not a spaceman or a monarch, but Jesus Christ, who returns to earth to show the wounds of his torture and death.

As played by Roger Cook, Jarman's Christ is also a visitor from earlier, more straightforward Christ films. Dressed in white sheets, with one covering his head, he looks like Max von Sydow's Jesus in George Steven's *The Greatest Story Ever Told* (USA 1965), moving with the same slowness. While there was once a world in which such a figure was relevant, a time when Hollywood could make money from devotion, Jarman's Christ is confronted with disbelief and indifference. In one scene – that returns throughout the film – he meets with a runner on a road at Dungeness, that seemingly goes from nowhere to nowhere, following the line of electricity pylons that loom overhead. Christ raises his hand as if in greeting, showing the wounds made by the nail in his palm and the spear in his side, the marks of his agony for a world that couldn't care less. The runner blows his whistle and runs on. Jarman's Jesus is silent and lost.

It might almost be said of *The Garden*, as Colin McCabe remarked of Jarman's early super-8 films, that it is 'irredeemably private', to be fully enjoyed only by those who made it.[84] In his diary Jarman remarked that 'the film must show the quaint illusion of narrative cinema threadbare'.[85] *The Garden* also shows Jarman's interest in the esoteric and arcane, as earlier displayed in the films he made in the 1970s.[86] Much influenced by Jung's alchemical theories, and fascinated by John Dee, Jarman's films have always affected a certain obscurity, a delight in symbols and hermetic signs.[87] For Jarman, such an interest is congruent with homosexuality, as the hidden secret of heteronormativity. And with such films the point is not to try and discover the code, but to relax into the 'ambient tapestry' of their 'random images'.[88]

Yet nothing that makes use of common signs can be wholly devoid of meaning for others. *The Garden*, at least in part, alludes to the story of Jesus, and this allows the viewer to map its disjointed scenes and tableaux against a familiar narrative. Thus, for example, we see the 'Madonna of the photo opportunity': a nativity scene in which the three wise men are transformed into balaclavaed paparazzi, who then turn into something like Herod's soldiers, as they pursue Mary (Tilda Swinton) – her baby abandoned – across the beach at Dungeness.[89] Or later in the film we see a tableau of Pentecost, in which twelve old men sit at a table with lighted tea-lights on their heads. Such scenes, despite their transpositions and varying film styles, give *The Garden* what Leo Bersani and Ulysse Dutoit describe as a 'powerful narrative directionality', preserving a basic comprehensibility.[90] Though this directionality is more a result of the story that the scenes invoke than the scenes themselves, which are fragmented throughout the film, and so never at just one place in the narrative.

On first viewing, one might think *The Garden* an anti-Christ film, and certainly an anti-Christian one, since it seems to mock the church and deliberately affront Christian sensibilities. It identifies Christ's passion with the persecution of a young gay couple, who are mocked, tarred (treacled) and feathered by police, scourged by monks, and forced to carry the cross of their humiliation. Indeed they are Christ, taking on the single role that Jarman had wanted Sean Bean to play,[91] and undergoing the torture that Christ's devotions attracted.[92] In another satirical tableau, Roman cardinals laboriously drag a huge golden boulder behind them, straining with the effort of their greed. Jarman was certainly affronted by the Christian churches, despising the 'muscular Christianity' that shadowed his school days, and seeing in the Church of England the continuation of a 'murderous tradition that still manage[s] to legislate against us'.[93] Something of this antipathy to the established order is seen in the otherwise mystifying tableau in which the young Jarman/Christ stands on a table, spinning a black globe, while old schoolmasters beat their sticks on the table, and open and shut dusty tomes.

While Jarman rejected the churches that seemingly rejected his experience of passion and love, he could not leave behind the Christian faith of Renaissance England by which he was enchanted. The Garden is both an attack on the state church which crucifies gay love, and an incorporation of that love into the mythic space of Jarman's garden, which, with its necromancers, devils and angels, is not without theological resonance. With George Herbert, Jarman looks to see his 'God and King' in all things, not to 'stay his eye' upon the glass, but 'through it pass, And then the heav'n espy'. Like the alchemists of old, Jarman is searching for the stone, the elixir, that will turn base metal into gold, remaking the world. If for Herbert that stone was Christ, for Jarman it is *The Garden*, the poetic work, the cinematic myth, in which the Christ of the churches is also transformed. Jarman's work is a search for the touch of God, but *The Garden* is also an affirmation of that 'which God doth touch and own'.[94]

In many ways the film, while highly esoteric, is a more faithful, if idiosyncratic, reflection on the gospel story than many mainstream Christ films.[95] Jarman likened his film to Pier Paolo Pasolini's *The Gospel According to St Matthew* (Italy 1966), which was dedicated to Pope John XXIII (1881–1963), and whose Jesus, like Jarman's, displays an unflinching passivity in response to the violence attracted by his affections for the maimed and outcast. Like Pasolini, Jarman worked with non-actors and coaxed non-actorly performances from his professional actors.[96] Moreover, Jarman's telling of Christ's passion is not just about something that has happened, but is happening; in the same way that the church reads its scriptures as contemporary texts, needing present performance.[97] Michael O'Pray thinks that the film's rendering of the 'Christian myth' is undermined by Jarman's identification of himself with Christ.[98] But it is this very identification that saves the film from being simply anti-Christian polemic; indeed, it allows the film to perform the story of Christ now, seeing contemporary lives in the life of Christ, and Christ in those lives. The gospels were not written to show how things were, but how they might be.

Jarman's film does not retrieve a gay Christ, who can be invoked against the churches' disparagement of homosexual people. Rather he shows us certain refractions of Jesus' body within the body of Christ. Jarman suggests that the gay lovers, like Christ, are persecuted for loving too much. Certain scenes suggest that the white-sheeted Jesus – Roger Cook – stands by these lovers, but that his support for them is ignored in both secular and ecclesial cultures; that, indeed, it scandalizes the prurient purveyors of tabloid morality. In Jarman's film, Cook's Christ is betrayed with a homosexual kiss, caught on camera by the press photographers who had hounded Mary, and who then, dressed as Santa Clauses, come upon the gay lovers sleeping in their bed. In the face of such interests – populist, ecclesial and political – Jarman's Jesuses are ineffectual and helpless. And yet it is precisely in the way that Jarman calls upon the church's story of Jesus in order to narrate what is happening to his gay lovers in twentieth-century Britain, that we find him enacting a Christology of displacement and dissemination. Their story is transfigured into the mercurial space of Jarman's garden, and there into the story of Jesus, where they become analogical repetitions of his body, broken for loving. It is in this way that Jesus gains his homo/sexuality.

Angelic Gardeners

Jarman's gardens – at Prospect Cottage, on Hampstead Heath, in his films, in *The Garden* and *The Angelic Conversation* (UK 1985) – are populated by angels, young men who, like the occupants of Gregory of Nyssa's paradise, are 'strangers to marriage'.[99] Resurrection life, according to Gregory, will be like that of the angels, who 'neither marry nor are given in marriage',[100] and paradisal life – to which we are to return, restored to our 'ancient state' – will be an unmarried, angelic life. In Gregory's account of paradise, marriage or the lack of it would seem to stand in for sex or its absence, and Gregory, intrigued by the heavenly population, speculates on how angels might reproduce without marriage/sex. From the fact that there are 'countless myriads' of angels in heaven it follows that marriage/sex is not necessary for reproduction, and that if Adam and Eve had not fallen, 'neither should we have needed marriage that we might multiply'. There is thus some 'unspeakable and inconceivable' mode by which angels increase in number, and this would have been available to Adam and Eve if they had not fallen.[101] Gregory imagines an asexual, amoebic form of reproduction; a paradise of clones.

Jarman's angels, on the other hand, have sex without multiplying. They copulate as gay men, as lesbian women, as straight couples contraceptively, in a manner that is both modern and ancient, *traditional*.[102] They copulate as Christ with the soul, the divine bridegroom with his bride, pasturing his flock among the lilies.[103] But Jarman's angels are not so much the opposite of Gregory's, as their fleshly embodiment, since for Gregory sexual desire is not incompatible with heavenly yearning. For him, one form of desire leads to the other, and the second is a dispossessive form of the first. As argued by Mark Hart, Gregory wrote as an ironist, in the tradition of Plato.[104] He wrote for different audiences who were yet reading the same work, in which they were addressed together and separately, simultaneously. Just as the words of scripture bear more than one sense – a bodily and a spiritual sense, at least one spiritual sense – so Gregory's texts require a double reading if we are to catch the sense of his words, the drift of his discourse.[105]

There would seem to be no copulating or eating in Gregory's paradise, since Adam and Eve were given metaphors for food, the fruit of the trees in paradise being the words of the Lord, the true 'tree of life'.[106]

> I, . . . when I hear the Holy Scripture, do not understand only bodily meat, or the pleasure of the flesh; but I recognize another kind of food also, having a certain analogy to that of the body, the enjoyment of which extends to the soul alone: 'Eat of my bread',[107] is the bidding of Wisdom to the hungry; and the Lord declares those blessed who hunger for such food as this, and says, 'If any man thirst, let him come unto Me, and drink': and 'drink ye joy', is the great Isaiah's charge to those who are able to bear his sublimity.[108]

If we read Gregory in the same way as Gregory reads scripture, attending to the spiritual in the bodily sense, we will find that Gregory's texts are neither as straightforward nor as contradictory as they might otherwise appear. For in his treatise *On Virginity*, Gregory, who was himself married,[109] can both execrate matrimony and laud virginity,[110] and yet insist that virginity is for the weak, for those who cannot control their 'sexual passion',[111] unlike the sober and moderate who may pursue 'heavenly things' through marriage. The 'diviner love' may be sought in the embrace of wedlock. In

Gregory's favourite simile, desire flows like water in an irrigation channel, and the wise man can divert desire through the bedroom, and still aim at heaven.[112] Thus 'marriage' and 'virginity' are not just matters of sexual practice and abstinence, but of *attachment* and *detachment*.[113]

Gregory often uses 'marriage' as a metaphor for possessive relationships, when the subject becomes obsessed with the object of devotion. Gregory contrasts this with 'virginity', which figures dispossessive desire, flying towards the beautiful on the wings of the Spirit, not in order to have, but in order to partake of beauty, and thereby become beautiful in return. Thus we can have a sort of virginal marriage, not in the sense of abstaining from sex – though such marriages were practised[114] – but in the sense of abstaining from possessive attachment, from a hungry consumption of the beloved. Marriage figures attachment, or over-attachment, to that which, no matter how beautiful, is not the most beautiful to which desire would bring us; it figures those attachments which detach us from the source of all desire. And the renunciation of marriage figures the abasement of such attachments – through dispossessive conjugality – for a yet greater adherence to the divine; a yet greater participation in the divine desiring.

The virginal life of paradise should not be understood as necessarily lacking the joy of bodily encounters, of graced embraces, but only those forms of congress that are not at the same time a form of detachment in which we learn a greater attachment, which is one that includes the beloved, since all are consummated in the divine union. Just as marriage should be practised virginally, chastely, so virginity should be practised amorously, desirously, out of love for the Other in the other.[115] Gregory's virginity is a 'passionlessness' form of sexuality,[116] in the manner of St Paul's prostitutional sex, in which – in Christ – husband and wife give their bodies over to one another's use.[117] But such passionless, virginal sex is not outside the economy of (divine) desire, outside the language of passion that Gregory repeatedly employs in order to describe dispossessive, non-attached 'virginity'.

> Seeing, then, that virginity means so much as this, that while it remains in Heaven with the Father of spirits, and moves in the dance of the celestial powers, it nevertheless stretches out hands for man's salvation; that while it is the channel which draws down the Deity to share man's estate, it keeps wings for man's desires to rise to heavenly things, and is a bond of union between the Divine and human, by its mediation bringing into harmony these existences so widely divided – what words could be discovered powerful enough to reach this wondrous height?[118]

As Gregory's question indicates, he is having to stretch words and domains of discourse in order to speak of matters – 'the mysteries of paradise' – that only St Paul was given to see.[119] Reading Gregory *On Virginity* and *On the Making of Man*, one might think that he was against desire and passion, so negative are his comments on marriage. But in fact his is a theology of passionate desire, which passion is given by God so that we might find God in God's desiring.[120] The virginal soul is not without desire, but consumed with a 'lofty passion'.[121] And virginity is itself desirable since it is beautiful, being desire that flows to the supreme beauty, without wasted diversion. Desire never ceases to flow, since it is the movement of an eternal source that knows no cessation. The only question is where it flows, and whether it is diverted into other channels that do not meet up again with the main course, but exhaust it in their diversions.[122]

Toward the end of his treatise in praise of virginity, Gregory sets before us two kinds of marriage, the carnal and the spiritual, and bids us choose between them.[123] He makes the point that virginity defeats death, since it produces no offspring, who are always destined to die, and whose passing brings grief for those of whom they are beloved.[124] Gregory imagines two kinds of intercourse. '[T]he propagation of mortal frames is the work which the intercourse of the sexes has to do; whereas for those who are joined to the Spirit, life and immortality instead of children are produced by this latter intercourse'.[125] But the latter offspring cannot be the opposite of the former, since immortality is given to those who are first framed in flesh. One can be 'joined to the Spirit' in joining with another, and produce 'life and immortality' through propagating mortal frames.

Gregory imagines a paradise without marriage but with reproduction. But this 'reproduction' is beyond the domain of death; it is reproduction not as replacement but as intensification, as the enhancement of life that is ever more lively. And the marriage missing from heavenly life is not the absence of bodily desire – for we are never more bodily than when we are in paradise – but the absence of attachments that detach us from desire, from the ecstatic dance of God's desiring. It is this angelic life that is figured in Jarman's garden, in the imagining of a place where the practices of dispossessive desire are nurtured, as one nurtures the flowers growing among the stones of the seashore, in a garden that has to be continually wrested from the elements, from the bitter easterlies and the scorching sun.

Leo Bersani and Ulysse Dutoit are highly critical of Jarman's portrayal of gay relationships, suggesting that they are often associated with violence and destructive power, and that when they are positive – as in *The Garden* – they are presented with a 'sappy sentimentality', in 'sequences worthy of soft-porn cinema'.[126] Of such scenes they cite those of the gay lovers in *The Garden*, when they embrace and caress one another in a bathtub, and pour water over one another, as in a baptism. But later in their critique, Bersani and Dutoit note that there 'are moments in Jarman's work when a sort of non-desiring connectedness is shown even in homosexual love.' The scene of the boys in the bathtub is cited, along with other scenes in *The Angelic Conversation*. In these scenes the embrace of the lovers is de-eroticized and treated with a certain tenderness, as a movement of bodies in space, without subjectivity; 'the particular "line" of one body reaching toward another'.[127] For Bersani and Dutoit this tenderness is non-desiring, a break with human desire which is always violent because always the satisfaction of a hunger, the incorporation of wrested objects. But better, is it not a picture of that dispossessive desire which, in different ways, Paul and Gregory have figured for us in the practices of mutual sex slavery and detached attachment? Paul's nuptial prostitution and Gregory's virginal marriage are alike practices of 'tenderness', of reaching out toward one another in space. And how strange that Bersani and Dutoit should find in Jarman's films that most traditional of images for this tenderness: the lover leaning over to kiss his beloved. 'Let him kiss me with the kisses of his mouth!'[128]

Same Difference

Bersani and Dutoit also find for us other strange conjunctions between Jarman's garden and Gregory's paradise. Jarman's choice of actors for his gay lovers, and his directing, dressing and photographing of them, in both *The Garden* and *The Angelic Conversation*, accentuates their similarity, as they caress one another, and gaze into each other's eyes. In the other they see something of themselves, a sameness in their difference. For Bersani and Dutoit, this 'narcissism' is not the assertion of an essential solipsism in gay relationships, but rather the recognition that in the other we must be able to recognize something of ourselves if the other is not to be absolutely alien, totally monstrous. A 'non-antagonistic relation to difference' depends upon the recognition 'that *we are already out there*'.[129] We are already the alien, and the alien is already ourselves. But we should find ourselves in the other, who is yet other; and the other in ourselves, who are yet ourselves, but other. Sameness and difference are not opposed, but implicated in one another. (Things that are not the same in some regard are beyond difference; which really only appertains to the different 'difference' of God.[130])

But the doubling of Christ as two men is more than just a happy accident of casting difficulties, or a gesture to the necessity of non-identical similarity for peaceful difference, mutuality in otherness. It is also, in a film on the gospel story, a figure for the profound difference in sameness that the Christian tradition locates in Christ and in the Trinity. For the rule of the triune God is that each divine 'person' is the same as the other two, but *differently*.[131] The mutual gaze of gay lovers perfectly repeats the Augustinian image of the loving Trinity: the lover and the beloved united through the love that passes between them.[132] And this is repeated in the nuptial relationship between Christ and the soul, which, though female, is played by both women and men. And this is repeated – acted out – in Jarman's garden, with his doubled Christ parodying both the mutual regard of Father and Son and, as Chris Perriam notes, the bride and bridegroom.[133] This is the same difference, the difference-in-the-same, for which every saint yearns.

Gregory's ascending soul becomes a non-identical double of the divine mystery, a reflection of the most beautiful, 'a mirror of the purity of God'. The soul rises on the wings of the descending dove – the Spirit's allegory – to become 'bright and luminous', shining in the communion of the 'real Light'.[134] Thus real virginity, 'real zeal for chastity', finds its end in 'seeing God'.[135] Participating in Christ, the soul participates in the mutual gaze of Son and Father. And again this is finely figured in Jarman's same-sex lovers – his gay Christ(s) – since the same difference that is Father and Son, Christ and soul, is – for Gregory – beyond heterosexual difference. For in God there is no (hetero)sexual difference,[136] and neither is there in paradise for souls returned to their angelic state, when their now 'buried beauty' shines forth again. For in the first paradise, Adam 'found in the Lord alone all that was sweet', and Eve merely helped him to delight in his sweetheart. He had no eyes for her until they were 'driven forth from the garden'.[137] When restored to paradise we are returned to our original 'homosexuality'.

Virginia Burrus contends that Gregory's fluid thought produces not a 'gendered plurality' but a 'singular – and singularly graceful – masculine subjectivity that derives its position of transcendent dominance "from its power to *eradicate the difference between the sexes*".'[138] The same might be said of Jarman's *The Garden*, at least to the extent that we find in it a parody for Gregory's paradise. Jarman's economy of interacting bodies is for the most part single-sexed, whether between the lovers and their oppressors, or between the lovers themselves. Admittedly, women appear throughout *The Garden*, not least in one of the film's most enigmatic scenes, when a mute chorus of twelve women, seated at a long table and facing the camera, produce celestial notes by circling their fingers around the rims of water-filled wine glasses. These women appear again at what might be the wedding of the two Christs, as Maribel la Manchega dances flamenco on the table: Jarman's reworking of the wedding at Cana.[139] There is only one identifiable female character that is played by a woman, Mary by Tilda Swinton, while a man in drag – Spencer Leigh – plays the other identifiable woman, Mary Magdalene.[140] However, the presence of Swinton's Madonna is felt throughout the film. She appears as the weeping, howling mother, the *mater dolorosa*; as a presiding priestess; and as a figure that moves between the men, between the scenes of their story, as the love that moved between Adam and his Lord, that moves between the Son and the Father. Moreover, though Jarman's film promotes gay love in the face of homophobia, and promotes it as a pretended family relationship,[141] his gay lovers – as interpreted by Bersani and Dutoit – represent all those whose relationships recognize the same in the other and the other in the same; a common humanity in those who are different and the differences in our common humanity. They figure not so much male bonding as same-sex union, and not so much same-sex union as the possibility of non-antagonistic relationships, in which the other is not irreducibly alien, but the same difference that we are from ourselves, and in which we encounter the different 'difference' by which we are given.

Moreover, Gregory himself does not so much eradicate the difference between the sexes, as the stability of this difference, which remains, but in a more uncertain, uncanny manner. For Eve was still helpmeet to Adam before their sexual differentiation, with each the other's non-identical double, so that though 'male' and 'female' it is impossible to say how they differed other than as one body from another.[142] It is only with their fall into history, into social orders and cultural hierarchies, that it becomes possible to demarcate Adam and Eve as 'man' and 'woman'. Gregory imagines a paradise in which there are neither male nor female bodies, so bodies without sex, and yet it is a space where bodies are also 'virginal' – like God – and so sexed in a way that is 'unspeakable and inconceivable', ineffable. They are bodies untouched by those attachments that detach us from God's desire, and so fully participate in that divine eros which we yet only know, can only speak, in the amorous language of carnal copulation, of sexual delight.

There is no escape from this uncanny sexuality by saying that in paradise there is eros but no sex. This, for example, is the view of Sergii Bulgakov (1871–1944), who, writing in the Orthodox tradition, and so heir to the Gregorian, Cappadocian theology of paradise, seeks to free desire from its fleshly embodiment.[143] But we can only think this prelapsarian eros in terms derived from our fallen nature, our sexual yearning, and so the very intelligibility of Bulgakov's edenic eros depends upon what it would deny, namely our hunger for carnal reciprocations. We can only think paradise from our knowledge of earthly gardens.[144]

There are no male or female bodies in Gregory's paradise, yet a kind of sexual difference remains as the difference between bodies that are sometimes 'male' and sometimes 'female', that in their ascending have surpassed the unstable orders of heteropatriarchy.[145] Gregory's bodies are always on the move toward the divine light, and so forever transfiguring, transgendering; purely transsexual, male and female, and moving between.[146] Thus Gregory does not really envision a fundamental homosexuality, let alone a gay male paradise. The most we can say is that same-sex love best figures the paradisal state, since it shows us that the final point of carnal yearning is not the pleasures of married life – sexual satisfaction, companionship and the birth of children – but the encounter with the divine lover who loves us in our loving, homosexual and heterosexual. That same-sex love can figure this for us, in our cultural moment, does not mean that homosexuality is somehow 'superior' to heterosexuality, as the latter's inner truth. Rather homosexuality is itself but a passing figure for a possibility that opens in both homosexual and heterosexual encounters: those bodily encounters in which we learn to seek that which withdraws even as we draw near, and so draws us on, infinitely. For this is the mystery of the difference-in-the-same, which is above all a figure for the incarnate God, the doubled lover. It is the ineffable 'affinity' of divine and human, and so of human and human.[147] It is the kiss of Christ. Yet the fruit of this encounter is heterosexually figured, since the birth of a child – however anticipated – is the figure for that spiritual birth which is the fruit of consorting with the divine bridegroom, as when St Paul begets 'the largest family of any' through the preaching of the gospel, 'bringing to birth whole cities and nations'.[148] So we cannot really privilege same-sex unions as traces or anticipations of paradisal bliss, since the latter returns us to the fecundity of female flesh, in order to find there the birth of Wisdom in the birthing of a child. Yet this is no straightforward heterosexuality, since the birth of Wisdom in the soul is a possibility for both women and men,[149] and Gregory's privileged example of such union and birth is the Virgin Mother, whose affinity with the Spirit issues in the birth of the bridegroom himself, that most inestimable of lovers.[150]

Gregory's paradise can be seen only from the midpoint of the story, in our present. And so for us, who can think paradise only after our own gardens, paradise is always also Gethsemane and the garden of the tomb. No matter how blissful, our gardens are also places of loss and foreboding; of falling leaves and the chill winds of approaching winter. Yet if we find the tomb empty, as did Mary on Easter morning, we can also find there the consolation for our sorrow, a renewed hope for our yearning. We can catch the scent of approaching Spring. It is the promise that back in the city, in the midst of our lives with others, we will find the uncanny in the mundane, the difference in the same. There, in the midst of things, with our lovers, friends and families, we will find the love that draws us on in the touch of another.

Eat, Friends, Drink, and Be Drunk with Love

The Garden does not have a crucifixion scene. We see the lovers dragging their cross, and we see the empty crosses of Golgotha, once the bodies of the doubled Christ and the doubled thief have been removed. A lone woman stands in front of the crosses and slowly, ritualistically, proffers a sponge to the corners of the screen – the sponge doused in sour wine that was offered to Jesus on a hyssop branch,[151] the sponge with which the lovers played in their baptismal bath. Now the woman puts it to her face, as if to wipe away or to collect her tears. Then Mary comes upon the dead lovers, lying together as if asleep, one resting on the other's chest, and wrapped in a common shroud. Jarman forgoes the scene of lost and regained paradise, when Mary meets with the gardener, close by the tomb. And yet there is a scene, the last of the film, which is perhaps that of Mary returning to the other disciples in the city, and learning there how she might once again touch and be touched by the Lord. This is the scene that Michael O'Pray describes as a utopian coda of 'communality'.[152]

The scene is set in an unidentifiable place, merely a darkened film studio, perhaps after the actors have finished playing their parts, but when still in costume. Coming at the end of the film it is reminiscent of the meals that the risen/ascended Jesus ate with his disciples, at the closing of the gospels. The two lovers are seated at a table with an old man and a young boy, when Mary, Madonna and Magdalene, approaches in the one person of Tilda Swinton, and from her basket produces *biscotti*, which they all proceed to eat.[153] Then they roll the biscuit papers into tubes and light them, which, turning to ash, fly up in the current of hot air produced by their own burning. The ashen papers dance between the friends like so many cinder angels.

Jarman stages a very quiet, peaceful meal, a symbolic exchange as at a very English Eucharist. But scripture is less reticent when it comes to imagining paradisal joy. On the day of Pentecost, when the Spirit has illumined the dark, Peter and Mary Magdalene and the other disciples are so enlivened that people think they are drunk, 'filled with new wine', though it is only nine o'clock in the morning.[154] But the revelry of the disciples, as they come out into the day, is not a utopian dream. Their newfound 'communality' is the embodiment of the promise, the prayer and the hope, of that which even now is arriving in their festivity. They are learning the practice of detached attachment, a bodily language that like all languages cannot be private. They have come out into the world together because the language of dispossessive affinity, its grammar and vocabulary, can be learned only through the response of others. Within, they have learned to see what they must look for without; and without they must look for Christ in the touch of others, in the caress of alien flesh.

Notes

1 John 20.11–18.

2 On the recollection of the future see the discussion of *Memento* above in chapter 1 (Desiring Bodies, 'Amorous memory').

3 Titian borrows the pot of ointment from the other gospels (Luke 23.55–24.1). In John's Gospel it is Joseph of Arimathea and Nicodemus who are to anoint Jesus, Nicodemus having brought a 'mixture of myrrh and aloes, weighing about a hundred pounds' (John 19.39).

4 This triangular dynamic is lodged within the lower section of a cross, formed by two curving lines of energy. The first curve reaches from Jesus' right foot, up along the line of his body to his head and on, in an arc that, within its ambit, encompasses the city on the hill. 'The other curve starts at the tip of Mary's trailing crimson robe. It follows the line of her body under the robe to her head. Then it shoots heavenward up the tree-trunk. So, unlike the first curve, it starts shallow but ends steep.' John Drury, *Painting the Word: Christian Pictures and their Meanings* (New Haven and London: Yale University Press, 1999), p. 119. See also Katherine Ludwig Jansen, *The Making of the Magdalene: Preaching and Popular Devotion in the Later Middle Ages* (Princeton, NJ: Princeton University Press, 2001), pp. 32–5.

5 Luke 7.36–50; Matthew 6.6–13; Mark 14.3–9; John 12.1–8 On the tradition of the composite figure of Mary Magdalene see David Brown, *Discipleship and Imagination: Christian Tradition and Truth* (Cambridge: Cambridge University Press, 2000), pp. 31–61.

6 The question is raised in John A.T. Robinson, *The Human Face of God* (London: SCM Press, 1973), p. 64.

7 Ruth 3.7. See further Howard Eilberg-Schwartz, *God's Phallus and Other Problems for Men and Monotheism* (Boston: Beacon Press, 1994), p. 111; and Calum Carmichael, '"Treading" in the Book of Ruth', *Zeitschrift für Alttestamentliche Wissenschaft*, 92 (1980): 48–66.

8 Mark 16.9; Luke 8.2. For medieval speculation on Mary's preconversion life see Jansen, *The Making of the Magdalene*, pp. 147–67.

9 W. Barnes Tatum, *Jesus at the Movies: A Guide to the First Hundred Years* (Santa Rosa, CA: Polebridge Press, 1997), pp. 75–85.

10 Nikos Kazantzakis, *The Last Temptation*, translated by P.A. Bien (London: Faber & Faber, [1961] 1975), p. 8.

11 '*The Last Temptation* is . . . really a psychological film about the inner torments of the spiritual life; it's not trying to create a holy feeling . . . It's a tortured human struggle about a common man possessed by God and fighting it. God is a demon in that way.' Paul Schrader interviewed by Kevin Jackson in *Schrader on Schrader and Other Writings*, edited by Kevin Jackson (London: Faber & Faber, 1990), p. 136.

12 Gregory of Nyssa, *On Virginity*, in *The Nicene and Post-Nicene Fathers*, vol. 5: *Gregory of Nyssa*, edited by Philip Schaff and Henry Wace (Edinburgh: T. & T. Clark, 1994), VII (p. 352).

13 The growing intimacy of Christ and the Magdalene can be traced from the Gospel of Mary, through the Pistis Sophia to the Gospel of Philip, where the relationship is most explicitly sexual (the other disciples are jealous for the kiss of grace that Christ gives Mary on the lips). See Jansen, *The Making of the Magdalene*, pp. 25–7. On one modern attempt to marry Christ to Mary Magdalene see Gerard Loughlin, 'Holy Texts of Deception: Christian Gnosticism and the Writings of Michael Baigent and Richard Leigh', *New Blackfriars*, 76 (1995): 293–305.

14 For Gregory of Nyssa, in the fourth century, horror stories began with marriage. 'They are regarded as myths on account of their shocking extravagance; there are in them murders and eating of children, husband-murderers, murders of mothers and brothers, incestuous unions, and every sort of disturbance of nature; and yet the old chronicler begins the story which ends in such horrors with marriage.' Gregory, *On Virginity*, III (p. 348).

15 Martin Luther, *Works*, vol. 54: *Table Talk*, edited and translated by Theodore G. Tappert (Philadelphia: Fortress Press, 1967), p. 154. These remarks were recorded (between 7 April and 1 May 1532) by John Schlaginhaufen, who failed to provide the context of their delivery.

16 John 11.5.

17 John 13.23–6.

18 John 11.33–8.

19 For a non-canonical account see Tina Beattie, *The Last Supper According to Martha and Mary* (London: Burns & Oates, 2001).

20 George Herbert, 'The Church Porch', l. 276; in *The Complete English Poems*, edited by John Tobin (Harmondsworth: Penguin Books, 1991), pp. 5–21 (p. 15).

21 Richard Baines, 'A Note Containing the Opinion on Christopher Marly Concerning his Damnable Judgement of Religion, and Scorn of God's Word', in *Marlowe: The Critical Heritage, 1588–1896*, edited by Millar Maclure (London: Routledge, 1979), p. 37; quoted in Richard Rambuss, *Closet Devotions* (Durham, NC: Duke University Press, 1998), p. 64. On Baines's account, Marlowe's Christ was bisexual, since 'the woman of Samaria & her sister were whores & that Christ knew them dishonestly'.

22 Song of Songs 1.2. See above chapter 1 (Desiring Bodies, 'Renunciation and Return').

23 Graham Ward, *Cities of God* (London: Routledge, 2000), p. 115. Compare Jacques Derrida: 'il n'y a pas de hors-texte' [there is no outside-text]. See *Of Grammatology*, translated by Gayatri Chakravorty Spivak (Baltimore and London: The Johns Hopkins University Press, [1967] 1976), p. 158.

24 Ward, *Cities of God*, p. 113. For the studies Ward criticizes, see Tom Driver, 'Sexuality and Jesus', *Union Seminary Quarterly Review*, 20 (1965): 235–46; Stephen Sapp, *Sexuality, the Bible and Science* (Philadelphia: Fortress Press, 1976); and Rosemary Radford Ruether, 'The Sexuality of Jesus', *Christianity and Crisis*, 38 (1978): 134–7.

25 Mark 15.39; Matthew 27.54; Luke 23.47. The centurion was famously played by John Wayne in George Stevens' *The Greatest Story Ever Told* (USA 1965).

26 See James Kirkup's obituary of Denis Lemon in *The Independent* (23 July 1994): 45.

27 Twenty-five years later a group of prominent writers and performers gave a public reading of the poem at St Martin-in-the-Fields, London, on 11 July 2002, and were not arrested, and *The Guardian* printed the poem's most offensive verses. See Blake Morrison, 'Rude Awakenings', *The Guardian G2* (11 July 2002): 6–7.

28 For a reproduction of Ribalta's painting see *The Image of Christ* (London: National Gallery Company Limited/Yale University Press, 2000), p. 123.

29 From 'On the Wounds of our Crucified Lord', ll. 13–20; in *The Complete Poetry of Richard Crashaw*, edited by George Walton Williams (New York: New York University Press, 1972), pp. 24–5. Crashaw returned to Christ's weeping mouth-wounds on a number of occasions, as in his Latin poem 'In Vulnera Pendentis Domini' (*The Complete Poetry*, p. 391). On Crashaw see further Rambuss, *Closet Devotions*, pp. 26–39.

30 See Verna E.F. Harrison, 'Gender, Generation, and Virginity in Cappadocian Theology', *Journal of Theological Studies*, 47/1 (1996): 38–68 (p. 42).

31 Ward, *Cities of God*, ch. 4 (pp. 97–116).

32 Ward, *Cities of God*, p. 100.

33 Ward, *Cities of God*, p. 102.

34 Ward, *Cities of God*, p. 113.

35 See Ross Thompson, 'Postmodernism and the "Trinity": How to Be Postmodern and Post-Barthian Too', *New Blackfriars*, 83 (2002): 173–88 (p. 175). John Macquarrie also wonders if Ward has 'cut us off too quickly from history and left us with a somewhat docetic Christ?' He worries that there might be nothing beyond the texts. See John Macquarrie, *Twentieth-Century Religious Thought*, 5th edn (London: SCM Press, [1963] 2001), pp. 472–3.

36 Ward, *Cities of God*, p. 112.

37 Leo Bersani and Ulysse Dutoit, *Caravaggio* (London: British Film Institute, 1999), p. 48.

38 Matthew 17.1–8; Mark 9.2–8; Luke 9.28–36.

39 Matthew 25.31–46.

40 Those who are without Christ are without substance. They are mere wraiths, no matter how tangible their blows or insidious their canker.

41 For a narrativist construal of such soteriology see Gerard Loughlin, *Telling God's Story: Bible, Church and Narrative Theology* (Cambridge: Cambridge University Press, [1996] 1999), pp. 211–20.

42 John 20.24–9.

43 A fourteenth-century legend relates how the Magdalene appeared to Charles Martel in 1279, informing him where he might find her bones still lying in Provence, and not in Burgundy (Vézelay) as many supposed. Among the several proofs of their authenticity, Charles found clinging to Mary's skull the flesh touched by Jesus when he had met her in the garden. See Jansen, *The Making of the Magdalene*, p. 44.

44 'Mary's gesture concedes that what she loves is now unattainable in the terms familiar to her, that the fulfillment of her love will not be physical, but spiritual.' Neil MacGregor quoted in Drury, *Painting the Word*, p. 118.

45 Maximus the Confessor, *Ambigua* (Books of Difficulties) 10.18 (*Patrologia Graeca*, 1132C–D); translated in Andrew Louth, *Maximus the Confessor* (London: Routledge, 1996), p. 112. See also Maximus the Confessor, *Chapters on Knowledge*, II.45; in *Maximus Confessor: Selected Writings*, trans. George C. Berthold (New York: Paulist Press, 1985), p. 157.

46 John 20.17.

47 John 20.19–21.23.

48 Gregory of Nyssa makes the same point that Christ no longer comes in his own flesh, but in ours; or rather, in our flesh-become-his. 'No longer indeed does the Master come with bodily presence; 'we know Christ no longer according to the flesh' [2 Corinthians 5.16]; but, spiritually, *he dwells in us and brings his Father with him*, as the gospel somewhere tells [John 14.23].' Gregory, *On Virginity*, II (pp. 344–5); emphasis added. See also Jean-Luc Nancy, *Noli me tangere: essai sur la levée du corps* (Paris: Bayard Éditions, 2003). This pertinent book only came to my attention at proof stage, but in it Nancy recognizes that the glory of the risen body cannot be seen in apparitions but only in the flesh of those who remain. Mary Magdalene is the apostle to

the apostles because it is she who first brings them Christ's risen body: 'Marie-Madeleine devient le corps véritable du disparu' (p. 79).

49 Matthew 28.1–10.

50 Mark 16.19.

51 Matthew 28.16–20.

52 Mark 16.1; Luke 24.10.

53 Mark 16.5–8.

54 Mark 16.20; Luke 24.52–3.

55 Luke 24.51.

56 Acts 1.11.

57 Acts 2.1–4.

58 This is what Juliet Stevenson has to learn in Anthony Minghella's *Truly, Madly, Deeply* (UK 1990).

59 From the first ninth-century *vita* of the Magdalene, we learn that after Jesus' ascension she lived as a hermit in the desert for 30 years. But a later, eleventh-century *vita apostolica*, informs us that she and some other disciples eventually arrived in Marseilles, from where they proceeded to convert the Gauls. Mary eventually retired to a cave, where she died. She was buried at Saint-Maximin in Provence. In the eighth century her remains were found by the monk Badilus, and he took them to Vézelay in Burgundy, where, in 1050, she became the patron saint of the Romanesque basilica, previously dedicated to the Virgin, but now possessing the bones of the Magdalene. Vézelay became an apostolic church, the home of the saint whose life-story gave hope to all sinners. As a result, Vézelay became one of the great churches on the pilgrimage route from Germany to Santiago de Compostela in Spain. But unfortunately for the Benedictines of Vézelay, Charles Martel of Salerno discovered in 1279 that the deceased Magdalene was still residing in his own Provence. She was duly disinterred, and with her head placed in a jewelled casket she became the protectress of the house of Anjou. The Dominicans became the wardens of the saint's second body at Saint-Maximin, and in 1315 produced the *Book of Miracles of Saint Mary Magdalene*, to which further refinements regarding her rediscovery by Charles were later added. See Jansen, *The Making of the Magdalene*, pp. 36–46.

60 Revelation 22.1–2.

61 Revelation 21.23.

62 Derek Jarman, *Derek Jarman's Garden*, with photographs by Howard Sooley (London: Thames and Hudson, 1995), p. 40.

63 Derek Jarman, *Kicking the Pricks* (London: Vintage, [1987] 1996), pp. 239–45. Jarman was always less likely to mention the Romney, Hythe and Dymchurch miniature railway that snakes behind Prospect Cottage, taking tourists out to the power station and lighthouse. It is a little too cute for the mythic space of Jarman's garden, cultivated between the sea and the monstrous machine; a landscape in crisis, as Tilda Swinton remarked (p. 242).

64 Jarman, *Derek Jarman's Garden*, p. 67.
65 Jarman, *Derek Jarman's Garden*, p. 14.
66 Jarman, *Derek Jarman's Garden*, p. 11. See further Jarman, *Modern Nature: The Journals of Derek Jarman* (London: Vintage Books, [1991] 1992), (6 February 1989) pp. 10–11.
67 Jarman, *Modern Nature*, (7 March 1989) p. 30.
68 Michael O'Pray, *Derek Jarman Dreams of England* (London: British Film Institute, 1996), p. 38.
69 O'Pray, *Derek Jarman*, p. 12.
70 The most obvious example of this is Jarman's Latin language film *Sebastiane* (UK 1976). 'In the early *Sebastiane* – except for the idyllic scene of two of the soldiers rather chastely making love in the water – desire seems synonymous with the exercise of power. The camera lingers on the captain's torture of Sebastian [Ken Hicks], and the final sequence treats us to the lovely Sebastian's body being martyred on the cross, repeatedly pierced by arrows.' Bersani and Dutoit, *Caravaggio*, p. 55.
71 Jarman, *Derek Jarman's Garden*, p. 82.
72 Jarman, *Modern Nature*, (13 April 1989), pp. 53–4.
73 Tony Peake, *Derek Jarman* (London: Little, Brown and Company, 1999), p. 419.
74 Jarman quoted in Peake, *Derek Jarman*, p. 445.
75 Derek Jarman, *Smiling in Slow Motion*, edited by Keith Collins (London: Century, 2000), (22 September 1991) p. 52.
76 See Philip C. Almond, *Adam and Eve in Seventeenth-Century Thought* (Cambridge: Cambridge University Press, 1999). p. 92; and Charlotte F. Otten, *Environ'd with Eternity: God, Poems, and Plants in Sixteenth and Seventeenth-Century England* (Laurence, KS: Coronado Press, 1985), p. 14. For the Renaissance paradise see James Grantham Turner, *One Flesh: Paradisal Marriage and Sexual Relations in the Age of Milton* (Oxford: Clarendon Press, 1987).
77 Earlier titles for the project that became *The Garden*, were *Borrowed Time*, *The Wanderer*, *The Dream of the Rood* and *The Garden of England*. Peake, *Derek Jarman*, p. 443.
78 On *Jubilee* see O'Pray, *Derek Jarman*, pp. 94–110.
79 Jarman's 'dream allegory', *The Last of England* (UK 1987), also opened with Jarman writing at his desk. See Jarman, *Kicking the Pricks*, p. 188.
80 Genesis 3.14.
81 Genesis 3.24.
82 Jarman, *Modern Nature*, (30 December 1989), p. 212.
83 Chris Perriam, 'Queer Borders: Derek Jarman, *The Garden*', in *'New' Exoticisms: Changing Patterns in the Construction of Otherness*, edited by Isabel Santaolalla (Amsterdam: Rodopi, 2000), pp. 115–25 (p. 117).
84 Colin McCabe, 'Edward II: Throne of Blood', *Sight and Sound*, 1/6 (October 1991): 14.

85 Jarman, *Modern Nature*, (4 September 1989), p. 143.
86 See Derek Jarman, *Dancing Ledge*, edited by Shaun Allen (London: Quartet Books, 1984), ch. 5; and on the early Super-8 films. O'Pray, *Derek Jarman*, ch. 3.
87 See Jarman, *Dancing Ledge*, ch. 8.
88 Jarman, *Dancing Ledge*, p. 129.
89 Jarman, *Modern Nature*, (1 September 1989), p. 141.
90 Bersani and Dutoit, *Caravaggio*, p. 49.
91 Jarman, *Modern Nature*, (28 November 1989), p. 188. 'Sean unable to play Christ, his parents are Jehovah's Witnesses. This has left me with a gap at the centre – we'll have to develop the two lovers, make it *their* passion.' On Peake's account, Jarman had wanted Sean Bean and Rupert Graves to play the two lovers (*Derek Jarman*, p. 450).
92 The persecution of the gay lovers in *The Garden* repeats that of the gay couple in *Jubilee*, Angel and Sphynx (Ian Charleson and Karl Johnson), who the police murder at the end of the film.
93 Jarman, *Modern Nature*, p. 126.
94 George Herbert, 'The Elixir', in *The Complete English Poems*, p. 174.
95 The film earned a Special Mention at the International Catholic Organization for Cinema and Audiovisual Media at the 1991 Berlin Film Festival. O'Pray, *Derek Jarman*, p. 183; Peake, *Derek Jarman*, p. 467.
96 For a discussion of Pasolini as Jarman's predecessor see William Pencak, *The Films of Derek Jarman* (Jefferson, North Carolina: McFarland & Company, 2002), pp. 171–84. This is an ambitious study, which seeks to read Jarman's films as providing a history of gay people, but its discussion of the films, and in particular *The Garden* (pp. 29–43), is by turns wayward and pedestrian.
97 See Loughlin, *Telling God's Story*, chs. 4 and 5.
98 O'Pray, *Derek Jarman*, p. 180. In *Caravaggio* (UK 1986), Jarman identifies with the artist who is identified with Christ. See Bersani and Dutoit, *Caravaggio*, pp. 30–49.
99 Gregory, *On Virginity*, XIII (p. 360).
100 Luke 20.35–6.
101 Gregory of Nyssa, *On the Making of Man*, in *The Nicene and Post-Nicene Fathers*, vol. 5: *Gregory of Nyssa* edited by Philip Schaff and Henry Wace (Edinburgh: T. & T. Clark, 1994), XVII.2 (p. 407). Sex is a remedy for the fall, since God, foreseeing that humanity would fail 'to keep a direct course to what is good' (*On the Making of Man*, XVII.4, p. 407), and so lose the mode of angelic reproduction, gave us sex instead. 'He formed for our nature that contrivance for increase which befits those who had fallen into sin, implanting in mankind, instead of the angelic majesty of nature, that animal and irrational mode by which they now succeed one another.' (*On the Making of Man*, XVIII.1, p. 407) Moreover, sex was taken over from the nature of the brute animals. '[S]o man seems . . . to bear a double likeness to opposite things –

being moulded in the Divine element of his mind to the Divine beauty, but bearing, in the passionate impulses that arise in him, a likeness to the brute nature.' (*On the Making of Man*, XVIII.3, p. 407) The brutish may drag down the divine element, but the latter may elevate the former; though the divine element is most often subject to gravity, to the 'heavy and earthy element' (*On the Making of Man*, XVIII.6, p. 408).

102 It may be noted in passing that the modern divorce of sexual pleasure from reproduction may intensify, but does not constitute, the commodification of children, which was never more prevalent than when Paul inveigled the Corinthians to conjugality for the sake of propriety rather than reproduction. Paul may have disapproved of contraception, but he – or the Pauline inheritance – was happy enough with human slavery. See Colossians 3.22–4.1; Titus 2.9–19; Philemon; 1 Timothy 6.1.

103 Song of Songs 2.16, 6.3.

104 Mark D. Hart, 'Gregory of Nyssa's Ironic Praise of the Celibate Life', *Heythrop Journal*, 33 (1992): 1–19 (pp. 12–19). See also Virginia Burrus, *'Begotten Not Made': Conceiving Manhood in Late Antiquity* (Stanford, CA: Stanford University Press, 2000), pp. 84–97. Burrus offers a more undecided reading, a more indeterminate Gregory. For a yet more confused, inconsistent Gregory, on the nature of the paradisal body, see Caroline Walker Bynum, *The Resurrection of the Body in Western Christianity, 200–1336* (New York: Columbia University Press, 1995), pp. 81–6.

105 Hart, 'Gregory of Nyssa's Ironic Praise', p. 11.

106 Genesis 2.16; Gregory, *On the Making of Man*, XIX.5 (p. 409).

107 Proverbs 9.5.

108 Gregory, *On the Making of Man*, XIX.1 (p. 409).

109 But see Burrus, *'Begotten Not Made'*, p. 97.

110 'What other gift of the soul can be found so great and precious as not to suffer by comparison with this perfection?' Gregory, *On Virginity*, XIII (p. 360).

111 Gregory, *On Virginity*, VIII (p. 353). 'It would be well . . . for the weaker brethren to fly to virginity as into an impregnable fortress, rather than to descend into the career of life's consequences and invite temptations to do their worst upon them'. Gregory, *On Virginity*, IX (p. 354). This is the opposite of the Pauline teaching, for which marriage is the bastion of the weak.

112 Gregory, *On Virginity*, VIII (p. 353).

113 Hart, 'Gregory of Nyssa's Ironic Praise', p. 10.

114 See Dyan Elliot, *Spiritual Marriage: Sexual Abstinence in Medieval Wedlock* (Princeton: Princeton University Press, 1993).

115 Burrus allows for the reading proffered here – that physical virginity figures real virginity, which may also be found in non-virginal life – but resists the certainty of this reading because Gregory's 'poetic art resists the sharp distinction between literal and figurative language'. The figurative means something *more*, but not always something *else* (*'Begotten Not Made'*, p. 94). But that

which is figured always returns upon the figure, such that the location of the 'literal' becomes uncertain. Thus Burrus's more undecided reading is itself a determination of the text; one that is possible, but not pursued here.

116 Gregory, *On Virginity*, p. 344.

117 1 Corinthians 7.3–4. See above chapter 6 (Sex Slaves, 'Undecidable Bodies').

118 Gregory, *On Virginity*, II (p. 345). Elsewhere, Gregory imagines the virgin as one who cleaves to Christ 'so as to become with Him one spirit, and by the compact of a wedded life has staked the love of all her heart and all her strength on Him alone'. Gregory, *On Virginity*, XIV (p. 361).

119 Gregory, *On the Making of Man*, p. 407.

120 Gregory, *On Virginity*, Introduction (p. 343).

121 Gregory, *On Virginity*, V (p. 351).

122 'Whenever the husbandman, in order to irrigate a particular spot, is bringing the stream thither, but there is need before it gets there of a small outlet, he will allow only so much to escape into that outlet as is adequate to supply the demand, and can then easily be blended again with the main stream. If, as an inexperienced and easy-going steward, he opens too wide a channel, there will be danger of the whole stream quitting its direct bed and pouring itself sideways.' Gregory, *On Virginity*, VIII (p. 353).

123 Gregory, *On Virginity*, XX (pp. 365–6).

124 Gregory, *On Virginity*, (p. 360).

125 Gregory, *On Virginity*, (p. 359).

126 Bersani and Dutoit, *Caravaggio*, p. 56. 'The sentimental images are weak; Jarman's most powerful representations of homosexuality are representations of extreme aggression, of getting beaten or forcibly fucked or tortured.'

127 Bersani and Dutoit, *Caravaggio*, p. 71.

128 Song of Songs 1.2.

129 Bersani and Dutoit, *Caravaggio*, p. 72. See chapter 4 above (Alien Sex).

130 'We cannot . . . know God's distinction from and transcendence of creatures through our knowledge of how oneness differs from multiplicity, because, if God transcends *all* differences, then God transcends also that difference between oneness and differentiation. To put it more plainly, it is not . . . that before the absolute oneness of God differentiation falls away; it is rather that, before the absolute transcendence of God, *both* oneness *and* differentiation fall away . . . All our terms of contrast state differentiations between creatures. There are none in which to state the difference between God and creatures.' Denys Turner, *Eros and Allegory: Medieval Exegesis of the Song of Songs* (Kalamazoo, MA: Cistercian Publications, 1995), pp. 63–4. Turner is expounding the Pseudo-Dionysius, *The Mystical Theology*, ch. 5 (1.1045D–1048B) in *Pseudo-Dionysius: The Complete Works*, translated by Colm Luibheid and Paul Rorem (New York: Paulist Press, 1987), p. 141.

131 Gregory of Nazianzus (c. 330–90) makes the point as nicely as anyone. '"He was the true light that enlightens every man coming into the world" [John 1.9] – yes, the Father. "He was the true light that enlightens every man

coming into the world" – yes, the Son. "He was the true light that enlightens every man coming into the world" – yes, the Comforter [John 14.16 and 26]. These are three subjects and three verbs – he was and he was and he was. But a single reality *was*. There are three predicates – light and light and light. But the light is one, God is one. This is the meaning of David's prophetic vision: "In your light we shall see light" [Psalm 36.9]. We receive the Son's light from the Father's light in the light of the Spirit: that is what we ourselves have seen and what we now proclaim – it is the plain and simple explanation of the Trinity.' Gregory of Nazianzus, Oration 31.3, in *On God and Christ: The Five Theological Orations and Two Letters to Cledonius*, translated by Frederick Williams and Lionel Wickham (Crestwood, NY: St Vladimir's Seminary Press, 2002), p. 118.

132 See Augustine, *The Trinity*, translated by Edmund Hill OP (Brooklyn, NY: New City Press, 1991), bk IX.

133 Perriam, 'Queer Borders', p. 121.

134 Gregory, *On Virginity*, XI (p. 356).

135 Gregory, *On Virginity*, XI (p. 357).

136 Gregory, *On the Making of Man*, XVI.7 and 8 (p. 405). See Verna E.F. Harrison, 'Gender, Generation, and Virginity in Cappadocian Theology', p. 66. 'This transcendence is not a disguised form of maleness hierarchically related to femaleness, but rather escapes all hierarchical categories, defined as they are by temporal or spatial extension.' Indeed, if the Father were to have a sex it would be more nearly female than male, since Mary's virginal motherhood is most akin to the Father's generation of the Son. But in her maternity, Mary is already passing over to paradisal virginity.

137 Gregory, *On Virginity*, XII (p. 358).

138 Burrus, *'Begotten Not Made'*, p. 97; quoting Luce Irigaray, *This Sex which Is Not One*, translated by Catherine Porter with Carolyn Burke (Ithaca, NY: Cornell University Press, [1977] 1985), p. 74.

139 John 2.1–11.

140 While this leads Chris Perriam to ponder the political correctness of drag ('Queer Borders', pp. 122–3), one may also be reminded that for Gregory of Nyssa, the soul, male or female, is always being transposed, since it is male when wooing Christ as Sophia and female when welcoming Christ as bridegroom. The soul is always in transition; a transsexual movement.

141 In one scene the two men appear in pink suits, with one cradling a baby, while Jessica Martin mimes to 'Think Pink', and gay pride marchers pass on the screen behind them.

142 For a similar destabilizing of sexual dimorphism see above chapter 8 (*The Man Who Fell to Earth*, 'Sleeping with Angels').

143 See Sergii Bulgakov, *Kupina neopalimaia* [*The Burning Bush*] (Paris: YMCA Press, 1927), pp. 164–5; cited in Paul Valliere, *Modern Russian Theology: Bukharev, Soloview, Bulgakov: Orthodox Theology in a New Key* (Edinburgh:

T. & T. Clark, 2000), p. 369. On the Cappadocian paradise, in Basil and the two Gregorys, see Verna E.F. Harrison, 'Male and Female in Cappadocian Theology', *Journal of Theological Studies*, 41/2 (1990): 441–71.

144 But it is because Bulgakov does not banish eros from agape that his Gregorian theology may, as Paul Valliere suggests, 'be used to sanction untraditional forms of love'; except that these forms may be less untraditional than they at first appear, when the tradition is read against its perceived grain. See Valliere, *Modern Russian Theology*, p. 371.

145 See Verna E.F. Harrison, 'A Gender Reversal in Gregory of Nyssa's First Homily on the Song of Songs', *Studia Patristica*, 27 (1993): 34–8; and Sarah Coakley, *Powers and Submissions: Spirituality, Philosophy and Gender* (Oxford: Blackwell, 2002), ch. 7 (pp. 109–29) and ch. 9 (pp. 153–67). 'Gregory's eschatological body is an ever-changing one; . . . the body is labile and changing in this life and is on its way to continuing change into incorruptibility in the next' (pp. 162–3).

146 On the unchanging dynamism of desire see above chapter 1 (Desiring Bodies).

147 For 'affinity' as the name of the ineffable unity-in-difference of Jesus and God, and of friends and lovers, see John Milbank, 'The Gospel of Affinity', in *The Strange New Word of the Gospel: Re-Evangelising in the Postmodern World*, edited by Carl E. Braaten and Robert W. Jenson (Grand Rapids, MI: William B. Eerdmans, 2002), pp. 1–20. Milbank, in Schleiermacherian fashion, states that 'Jesus was God because his *affinity* with God was so extreme as to constitute his identity – although an identity not of substantial nature, but of character, *hypostasis, persona.* And Jesus communicated to his disciples not simply teaching, but precisely this character, which they were to repeat differently, so constituting a community of affinity with Jesus . . . Affinity is the absolutely non-theorizable; it is the ineffable. Affinity is the sacred' (p. 15). Unlike Milbank, however, I do not find 'heterosexuality' to be a privileged name for this 'affinity'. Unity-in-difference occurs between bodies (*hypostases, personae*), and not between abstract 'genera' ('male' and 'female') – an odd usage (similar to that of Luce Irigaray), since the members of different genera, let alone species, rarely if ever copulate with one another. But if we had to choose between 'heterosexual' and 'homosexual' models for 'affinity', then the tradition would point us to the same-sex image of Father and Son. But it is precisely because the Trinitarian unity-in-difference surpasses our sexed bodies that our bodies and their relationships are reduced to passing figurations of what is yet their possibility: the transfiguring touch of the Other in the other. Milbank's essay reappears – expanded, more nuanced but still uncorrected – as the last chapter of his powerful and passionate book, *Being Reconciled: Ontology and Pardon* (London: Routledge, 2003), where, however, his fertile but fleeting remarks on the divine Sophia should be noted (p. 208).

148 Gregory, *On Virginity*, IXX (p. 365); 1 Corinthians 4.15; Philemon 10.

149 Gregory, *On Virginity*, XX (p. 366).

150 Gregory, *On Virginity*, II (p. 344). 'What happened in the stainless Mary when the fullness of the Godhead which was in Christ shone out through her, that happens in every soul that leads by rule the virgin life.'

151 John 19.28–30.

152 O'Pray, *Derek Jarman*, p. 183.

153 We may recall that in both the Eastern church of the third century and in later western medievalism there was a tendency to merge the multiple Marys of the gospels into the one figure of the Virgin Mother, who was thus disseminated into all the other Marys; the maternity in their Marianism. See Jansen, *The Making of the Magdalene*, pp. 28–32.

154 Acts 2.1–15; taking Mary Magdalene to be included with the women gathered with Mary the mother of Jesus and the other disciples as mentioned in Acts 1.12–13, an inclusion that was established in the medieval period.

INDEX

Note: '*n.*' after a page number indicates the number of a note on that page; '*ill.*' after a page number indicates an illustration on that page.